Hildegard of Bingen's
Book of
Divine Works
with Letters and Songs

Hildegard of Bingen's
Book of
Divine Works

with Letters and Songs

edited and introduced

by

Matthew Fox

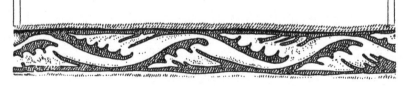

Bear & Company
Rochester, Vermont

Bear & Company, Inc.
One Park Street
Rochester, VT 05767
www.bearandcompanybooks.com

Permission to translate sections of Heinrich Schipperges's *Welt and Mensch: Das Buch "De operatione Dei"* (1965) and a selection of songs from Pudentiana Barth's *Hildegard von Bingen: Lieder* (1965) was granted by the publisher, Otto Muller Verlag, Salzburg.

Library of Congress Cataloging-in-Publication Data

Hildegard, Saint, 1098-1179.
    Hildegard of Bingen's book of divine works.

    Translation of: De operatione Dei.
    Contents: De Operatione Dei—Letters and sermons—
Songs.
        1. Mysticism—Catholic Church—Collected works.
2. Catholic Church—Doctrines—Collected works. I. Fox,
Matthew, 1940-   . II. Title. III. Title: Book of
divine works.
BV5080.H5213   1987   248.2'2   87-1451
ISBN 978-0-939680-35-1

Printed and bound in the United States

20 19 18

Designer: Janis Campaniello
Illustrations: Angela Werneke
Cover Art: William Field, Santa Fe
Typesetting: Solaris Press, Rochester, MI / Copygraphics, Inc., Santa Fe

To four persons who, like Hildegard, fought the good fight to awaken church and society in their lifetimes:

Sr. Marjorie Tuite, O.P.
Bob Fox
Ken Feit
Tony Joseph

And to Jose Hobday, who is still doing so.

Contents

Introduction   ix

THE BOOK OF DIVINE WORKS

FIRST PART: THE WORLD OF HUMANITY

Translator's Note   2
Foreword   5
First Vision: On the Origin of Life   8
Second Vision: On the Construction of the World   22
Third Vision: On Human Nature   56
Fourth Vision: On the Articulation of the Body   80

SECOND PART: THE KINGDOM OF THE HEREAFTER

Fifth Vision: The Places of Purification   152

THIRD PART: THE HISTORY OF SALVATION

Sixth Vision: On the Meaning of History   178
Seventh Vision: Preparation for Christ   186
Eighth Vision: On the Effect of Love   204
Ninth Vision: Completion of the Cosmos   210
Tenth Vision: On the End of Time   222

LETTERS

Translator's Note   270
Letter One, Hildegard to Bernard of Clairvaux   271
Letter Two, Hildegard to Pope Anastasius IV   272
Letter Three, Hildegard to Bishop Eberhard II of Bamberg   276
Letter Four, Hildegard to Archbishop Eberhard of Salzburg   283
Letter Five, Hildegard to Archbishop Philip of Cologne   285
Letter Six, Hildegard to King Konrad III   287
Letter Seven, Hildegard to Frederick   289
Letter Eight, Hildegard to Frederick   290
Letter Nine, Hildegard to Bertha   292
Letter Ten, Hildegard to King Henry II of England   292
Letter Eleven, Hildegard to Her Spiritual Daughters   293
Letter Twelve, Hildegard to Her Spiritual Daughters   294
Letter Thirteen, Hildegard to Abbot Kuno   297
Letter Fourteen, Hildegard to Prior Albert   299
Letter Fifteen, Hildegard to Abbot Helenger   302
Letter Sixteen, Hildegard to the Monks of Zwiefalten   304
Letter Seventeen, Hildegard to Abbot Helmrich   306

Letter Eighteen, Hildegard to Abbot Adam of Ebrach   307
Letter Nineteen, Hildegard to Abbot Withelo   311
Letter Twenty, Hildegard to the Five Burgundian Abbots   311
Letter Twenty-One, Hildegard to Monks St. Eucharius   314
Letter Twenty-Two, Hildegard to Abbot Philip   320
Letter Twenty-Three, Hildegard to Abbot Philip   321
Letter Twenty-Four, Hildegard to Philip and the Clergy   322
Letter Twenty-Five, Hildegard to Werner of Kirchheim   328
Letter Twenty-Six, Hildegard to a Religious Superior   331
Letter Twenty-Seven, Hildegard to an Abbot   332
Letter Twenty-Eight, Hildegard to a Priest   333
Letter Twenty-Nine, Hildegard to an Abbot   334
Lettery Thirty, Hildegard to a Priest   335
Letters Thirty-One & Thirty-Two, Hildegard to Gertrude   336
Letter Thirty-Three, Hildegard to Bishop Eberhard   337
Letter Thirty-Four, Hildegard to Elisabeth of Schongua   338
Letter Thirty-Five, Hildegard to Elisabeth   340
Letter Thirty-Six, Hildegard to Christian Lay People   342
Lettery Thirty-Seven, Hildegard to an Excommunicant   344
Letter Thirty-Eight, Hildegard to an Unknown Lay Person   346
Letter Thirty-Nine, Hildegard to Wibert of Gembloux   347
Letter Forty, Hildegard to Wibert and the Monks of Villers   351
Letter Forty-One, Hildegard to the Prelates of Mainz   354
Letter Forty-Two, Hildegard to Archbishop Christian   360

SONGS
Introduction   364
  1. Kyrie   366
  2. O Virtus Sapientiae, O Moving Force of Wisdom   367
  3. De Sancta Maria, In Praise of Mary   369
  4. De Spiritu Sancto, To the Holy Spirit   372
  5. Item De Virginibus, Praising Virgins   374
  6. De Sancta Maria, To Mary   376
  7. O Felix Anima, O Happy Soul   380
  8. O Vis Aeternitatis, O Eternal Vigor   382
  9. De Martyribus, In Praise of Martyrs   385
  10. De Innocentibus, To the Innocents   387
  11. De Sancto Disibodo, In Honor of St. Disibode   389
  12. O Coruscans Lux, O Burning Light   392

Appendices   394

INTRODUCTION

Hildegard of Bingen has been called an "ideal model of the liberated woman" who "was a Renaissance woman several centuries before the Renaissance."[1] There is much truth to these statements, for Hildegard was indeed a woman of tremendous stature and power who used her gifts to the utmost. Her interests and accomplishments include science: her books explore cosmology—stones, rocks, trees, plants, birds, fishes, animals, stars and winds. They include music: her opera, *Ordo Virtutum*, is on record and has been playing live by a European group called Sequentia in both Europe and North America, and she wrote about seventy other extant songs. They include theology: her book *Scivias* is a study of biblical texts and ecclesial practice combined with personal insight and criticism. They include painting: *Scivias*, for example, contains thirty-six renditions of her images or visions. They include healing at the personal level: she writes of the appropriate herbs and remedies for psychic and physical ailments—and at the social level: many of her sermons and letters, in particular, take on issues of social disease and injustice. Hildegard was painter and poet, musician and healer, theologian and prophet, mystic and abbess, playwright and social critic. Her life (1098-1179) spanned four-fifths of the twelfth century—a century of amazing creative and intellectual achievement in the West. She contributed substantially to the awakening to a living cosmology and to the influx of women's experience into the mystical literature of the West.

Hildegard's Life Briefly Summarized

At the confluence of the Nahe and Glan rivers, very near their outlets into the Rhine River, is found a pre-Christian spiritual site that became known as Disibodenberg in the time of Hildegard. It derives its name from Saint Disibode, one of the Celtic monks and missionaries from Scotland or Ireland who lived as a hermit at this mountain in the seventh century.[2] By the ninth century, he was already honored as a saint in the diocese of Mainz. The first monastic foundation in the area can be dated to about the year 1000, when the site was home for a religious foundation of twelve priests who served the people of the surrounding areas. Archbishop Ruthard (1089-1109) brought the Benedictines of the Cluny reform to the site and managed to wrestle the monastery from the dominance of the nobility to the direct control of the bishop. While the first generation of monks did not succeed in their efforts to establish a community (1098), the second group was successful eight years later. The Archbishop appointed the Abbot of St. John's in Mainz to head the new community and the first monastic buildings were begun in 1108. A women's cloister was part of this monastery from the first (1106), and in 1112 Jutta of Spanheim was given leadership of this community of noble women.

It was in 1106 that Hildegard's parents, having offered her to God as a gift and maybe even a tithe—for she was the tenth of ten children—put her into the hands of Jutta, who was then living an eremetical life adjacent to the monastery. Under Jutta's tutelage, Hildegard studied and matured into the amazing woman she was to become. On Jutta's death in 1136, Hildegard was chosen to lead her community. Hildegard's most controversial decision—in addition, of course, to her vast writing and preaching—was to leave the famous Disibode monastery with all of her sisters and with all of their dowries. What drove her to this decision, a decision that she had to defend for the next twenty-seven years? There was friction between the local nobility—to whom she owed a certain allegiance—and the bishop, but also the monks were returning to pre-Cluny privileged practices, such as the use of stewards as administrators and bailiffs to handle their vast properties. In addition, Hildegard's fame from her first and very successful book, *Scivias*, drew more and more women to study and live with her and the male community members seemed reluctant to move over and give the women's community the space it needed. Hildegard left Disibodenberg in 1147, and in 1151 she and her sisters moved into a new cloister built for them in Rupertsberg near today's town of Bingen. There, Hildegard lived as abbess and wrote poems and hymns and even a modest-sized biography of St. Disibode, praising him for his love of monasticism and subtly critiquing the Archbishop of Mainz and the Emperor Frederich Barbarossa by implication. Hildegard's warnings to the monks of Disibodenberg about their privileges and wealth did not, alas, go heeded. Armed battles were fought between monastic and episcopal supporters there in the thirteenth century, and the monastery was actually converted into a fortress. By the mid-thirteenth century, the monastic buildings were in ruins and the Benedictine morale was in an equally sad state. Disibodenberg was never resurrected.

Unfortunately, Hildegard has been far less celebrated since her lifetime than during it. The letters in the present volume give ample evidence of her immense influence with all strata of society from

monks and popes to emperors and kings and queens, from lay persons and religious sisters to bishops and social changers. Until Bear
& Company published their first book of Hidegard's writings in 1982,
Meditations with Hildegard of Bingen, she was never translated into English except for a few pages in a book printed in 1915. Bear has
since brought out my book on *Illuminations of Hildegard of Bingen*
and the text of her first book, *Scivias*. Now this present volume
allows us once again to cease our learned ignorance of one of the
greatest intellectuals and mystics of the West. For in this book, we
have brought together the most significant portions of her greatest
cosmological work, *De operatione Dei*, and the most significant of
her letters and sermons, and twelve representative poems and songs.

Why would the work of a twelfth-century abbess be of interest or
concern for those of us preparing—hopefully—to usher in a twenty-
first century and a third millenium? In many respects, the work of
Hildegard in the texts presented in this book answers that question
directly.

De operatione Dei

In the first text of this volume, that of *De operatione Dei* ("'The
Book of Divine Works"), Hildegard offers western civilization a deep
and healing medicine for what may well be its number-one disease
of the past few centuries: *anthropocentrism*. The West's preoccupa-
tion with the human, its terrible and expensive ignoring of other
creatures and nature's cycles, its reduction of the mystery of the
universe to a machine, has brought us to the point of Earth-murder.
And this even without a nuclear holocaust taking place. Hildegard is
a prophet to our day because she lays out the possibility of, and
therefore hope for, a living cosmology. According to the twentieth-
century psychologist Otto Rank, the most basic neurosis of our
species in this century has been the divorce of religion from a
cosmology. "When religion lost the cosmos in the West," he remarks,
"society became neurotic and we had to invent psychology to deal
with the neurosis."[3] The post-Newtonian worldview in physics and
in religion is awakening the West to a living cosmology once again.
But Hildegard shows us how this awakening will come about and
take shape. Her great gift is a cosmological gift in a time of excessive
attention rendered to human affairs alone.

In *De operatione Dei*, Hildegard brings together the three essential
elements of a living cosmology. The first element is science; she was

never, as so many well-heeled preachers of human guilt and salvation are today—anti-intellectual or anti-science. In fact, she declares that "all science comes from God," and that the greatest gift God has given us is our intellects. The second element essential for a living cosmology is a healthy mysticism. In this regard, Hildegard urges *heart* knowledge, not just *head* knowledge. "Search out the house of your heart," she advises. She trusts her experience of the powerful interconnectivity of all things—psyche *and* cosmos, divinity *and* humanity, humanity *and* nature. Her cosmology is not a scientific head-trip but a way of seeing and affirming and trusting in the entire universe. Included in this yielding to creation's splendor is a living out of an ethics based on the wisdom of the universe itself. Essentially, this ethic for Hildegard is one of "awakening to justice," doing justice, paying attention to the "moral household of the human soul" and to health, which is the "proper equilibrium" or "symmetry" that is found therein. "We can do wonderful things," she declares, for the human species is "completely the image of God." Humanity is a mirror of divinity called to walk on the path of justice and to "sing justice into the hearts of men and women." Justice for Hildegard is the balance lived out between the human and the Earth. Hildegard's mysticism is an Earth mysticism but a prophetic one as well; she insists, as do the prophets of ancient Israel to whom Hildegard frequently compared herself, that justice toward the Earth means living out our divine calling. She is a realist about the work of peace-making when she says: "Peace has to be fought for with difficulty in a changeable world and can be preserved only with difficulty."

 The third element of a living cosmology is art. Neither science nor theology is enough to awaken a people. It is the artist's gift to do the awakening but to do it not out of a kind of patriarchal pessimism or an ego-inflated or ego-deflated stance. Rather, the artist takes the living cosmology as it begins to bubble up—Hildegard calls God a "bubbling source" in this text—from science's rediscovery of a new creation story about the essential mystery and benevolence of the universe. This living cosmology also bubbles up from religion's rediscovery of its oldest roots, namely those of the non-dualistic creation- centered tradition of mystics, prophets, and biblical writers. The artist takes this powerful scientific / spiritual energy and re-creates it, weaves it, sings it, dances it, dramatizes it, ritualizes it—i.e. gets it into the minds and hearts and imagination and bodies of the people. From there, it moves into the institutions and into forming ones that are needed. Hildegard was deeply aware of this pressing need of the artist carrying the new paradigm; this is why she was driven not just to write a book but to include in it thirty-six paintings, an opera, numerous poems and songs. Hildegard is a first-class artist— painter, musician, imager, and poet. She points out in the text below that we experience so much brilliance in our lives that we need allegory to approach it. She urges creativity on all people, declaring that we are indeed "co-creators with God." We are a microcosm of the universe, which is the macrocosm; and just as God fills the universe, so God fills us and urges us to participate in the birthing and the completing of the universe's task. She compares herself to a "living well that speaks" and urges that we all "cooperate in the task of creation." She urges all people to fly since "we all have wings to fly" and to shout with joy simply because we are created.

Hildegard, in her *De operatione Dei*, does not so much admonish us to live out a cosmological vision as present us with a model, a way, a hint of hope that it is possible. That model and way and hint of hope is none less than herself. For she lived what a cosmology is: science, mysticism / prophecy, art. It would be the height of folly— one of her most pressing concerns is the difference between folly and wisdom—for western civilization to ignore her in our times as we did for the past 800 years. For to ignore this cosmic and Earth wisdom would, in today's situation, guarantee the obliteration of Mother Earth and with it all the other creatures, humanity included. Hildegard's vision is not petty, trivial, or essentially moralistic. It is cosmic, intellectual, scientific, and artistic or aesthetic. She urges humankind to wake up, to embrace wisdom, to re-establish its social relationships and institutions on justice, and to celebrate. For we are "powerful in holiness," she believes, and we are called to complete God's glory.

In her lifetime, Hildegard wrote three major works, which were her visionary books. *Scivias*, "Know the Ways," was her first and was written from 1141 to 1151. *Liber vitae meritorum*, "The Book of Life's Merits," was a moral treatise written from 1158-1163. And *De operatione Dei*, "The Book of Divine Works," was the last, and in many respects the most mature, of her visionary trilogy. Written from 1163-1173, it is her most cosmic work. There is far less moralizing in this work than in many of her others. The pictures that accompany the text are described in detail by Hildegard but were not executed by her. The ones we possess were painted twenty-one years after her death. Her other works include a handbook on nature, *Physica* or

Liber simplicis medicinae, and a handbook on holistic health, *Causae et curae* or *Liber compositae medicinae.* She also wrote brief lives of St. Disibode and St. Rupert and a brief commentary on the *Rule of St. Benedict.* The book presented in this volume, *De operatione Dei,* thus constitutes the final work in her trilogy, which was the major intellectual achievement of her amazing life.

Her Letters and Sermons

The second part of this volume contains Hildegard's letters. Approximately 145 of Hildegard's letters are extant today. The reader will notice that some of the letters translated herein are sermons which Hildegard was requested to put down in written form. That is no surprise, since her sermons—which were preached to monks and priests, to lay persons and bishops, to abbots and abbesses, all over Germany and Switzerland—very often struck to the quick of the personal, social, and church struggles people were involved in during her lifetime. In her letters and sermons, we find the *practical* application of Hildegard's cosmology which she had so beautifully laid out in *De operatione Dei.* The letters gathered here span her entire lifetime as a mover and shaker on the German ecclesial scene—and, given the spiritual/temporal interaction of the Middle Ages, on the German social scene as well. The first one, as will be noted, is written to St. Bernard in 1147; and the final one is written to the Archbishop of Mainz concerning her and her sisters' excommunication or interdiction. This letter, written in 1179, is the last we possess; her death occurred six months after the writing of this letter. One might understand the first text in this volume, her *De operatione Dei,* as her mystical work and the second text, her letters and sermons, as her prophetic work. While there are elements of mysticism and prophecy interwoven into both texts, the mystical cosmology clearly dominates in the first, and her outrage and cajoling and criticizing and denouncing in her efforts at church reform dominate in the second. Her letters give us a deep glimpse of the mystic-in- action, i.e. her prophetic struggles to affect her culture and church.

There is a promise made through the prophet Joel that at the time of a great spiritual awakening, the Spirit of God "will pour out my spirit on all humankind. Their sons and daughters shall prophesy, your young ones shall see visions, your old folks will dream dreams." The earliest Christians, Peter in particular, appropriated this promise in their original Pentecost experience (see Acts 2:14-25). Hildegard

was busy appropriating this message to the spiritual awakening and
pentecost event of her lifetime as well. I believe she calls us to do the
same. Pope John XXIII called for a "new pentecost" in our time, and
his was just one of many prophetic voices in this century calling for
a spiritual awakening that could move mountains and change the
dead-end ways of militarism and racism, sexism and classism,
injustice and unemployment. The biblical promise that the spirit's
times will be marked by visions and dreams suggests that rationality
is not the answer to our ills. Otto Rank says something similar when
he declares that too much rationality is what is killing the planet and
our species, our psyches, and our very souls.

> People, though they may think and talk rationally—and even
> behave so—yet live irrationally. . .Man [sic] is born beyond
> psychology and he dies beyond it but he can *live* beyond it only
> through vital experience of his own—in religious terms,
> through revelation, conversion or re-birth. . . .Our age was up to
> recently so highly rationalized that the irrational had only the
> ·neurotic form of expression. But to attempt to cure this result of
> rationalism by more rationality is just as contradictory as a war
> to end wars.
> The only remedy is an acceptance of the fundamental irra-
> tionality of the human being and life in general. . .a real
> allowance for its dynamic functioning in human behavior,
> which would not be lifelike without it. When such a construc-
> tive and dynamic expression of the irrational together with the
> rational life is not permitted, it breaks through in violent distor-
> tions which manifest themselves individually as neurosis and
> culturally as various forms of revolutionary movement which
> succeed *because* they are irrational and not in spite of it[4]

Mother earth will not be saved and mother church will not be
reborn by the rational mode alone. In Hildegard, we find a healthy
balance of the rational and irrational. Hildegard never sacrifices the
rational to the irrational or the irrational to the rational. She dances
the dialectical dance of both/and, of science *and* intuition, of feeling *and* cognition. She is neither anti-intellectual nor impractical,
but is bent on "what is useful," to use her own words. Much of her advice offered in these letters is of a deeply practical and useful kind.
Yet her images and symbols, born of a passionate visionary irra-
tionality, touch and move us at depths that are frequently ineffable.
"From the heart comes healing," she advises. Depression comes

from dualism, she teaches in these letters. We are urged to "be saturated at the fountain of wisdom" and to do justice and not bury justice. Angry at "bungling abbots" and clergy who grumble "like bears and asses," she urges a "new order of justice for the church." God is "the purest spring" and all are to celebrate the fact that "you are divine." She images herself as a "small tent" and as a "small feather." She urges the clergy "whose tongues are dumb" to start trumpeting justice and become prophetic again. She laments how the clergy have separated themselves from the people and have rendered their hearts lukewarm instead of loud on behalf of the oppressed. "Our age is full of pain," she comments—an observation not at all unapt for our times. She herself proves in these letters how true it is that women are called to be prophets to church and society alike. She herself consciously states that she is chosen as a prophet, and she struggles with the ineffable depths of her own insight when she declares that "I can't fully understand the things which I see." She urges a spiritual awakening that will be marked by an "outpouring of the prophetic spirit" when art and spirituality will awaken people from their slumber.

Her Poetry and Songs

Seventy-five of Hildegard's songs, for which she wrote the lyrics as well, are extant today. Toward the end of her life, she gathered them together in a collection entitled, "The Symphony of the Harmony of Heavenly Revelations." In addition, she wrote an opera, the earliest morality play we know of in the West put entirely to music, which she called *Ordo Virtutum* or the *Play of the Virtues*. It is appropriate that we reproduce not only Hildegard's great cosmological study and her letters, but also a representative number of her song-poems. Hildegard insisted on bringing art or symbolic expression into all that she did and wrote; like John of the Cross and most mystics, she was aware that words cannot bear the weight of the treasure of her deep experience. Thus she turns to symbols—music, paintings, poetry—to express her truest self. This is one of her gifts to us—a gift of holistic education. She lives what she preaches and is creative from the depths of her being. Thus both right and left brain, body and mind, are incorporated by her in the pursuit of expressing her truth and her wisdom. Her songs reproduced here have been chosen by Brendan Doyle, who has been teaching persons to sing her music in the Institute in Culture and Creation Spirituality for four years. Persons who sing her music will no doubt encounter experiences that

ICCS students have encountered: there is a getting high, a light-
headedness, a quasi-hyperventilation that occurs on singing Hildegard's music. She demands so much of the lungs and diaphragm
that I have observed that everyone who sings her music either gets
high, faints, or leaves the class. Hildegard is not just talking *about*
body and spirit; in her music, she brings spirit *out* of body. It is a kind
of yoga, a demanding but deep discipline that refreshes and sustains
and offers vision and opens up chakras and imagination.

Her music explicates the poetry which is also rich and indeed *dripping* (she constantly uses this imagery of our human existence on
this "sweaty" Earth) with passion and earthiness. I would characterize
her poetry as sensual and earthy, and yet soaring and cosmic. Her poetry
is not unlike the "wings of wisdom" she writes about in her song,
"Virtus Sapientiae," wherein one of wisdom's wings soars in the sky,
another dips to the dripping and sweaty Earth, and the third moves
through and through all things. In another poem reproduced here, she
calls Earth a "womb" and sings to its erotic, green lushness. She invites
all humans to participate in this lushness. She praises the Spirit who
"makes life alive" and "wakens and reawakens all that is," and she
makes homage to Dabhar, the "vigor of Eternity" that keeps all things
in order "in the heart" of the Godhead. And she honors and celebrates
human strength —a favorite theme of hers in all of her works. She
extolls the strength of the martyrs, the virgins, and St. Disibode whom
"no armed power is strong enough to attack." And she names her
passionate outrage at the killing of the innocents. Her anger and her
cosmological worldview save her from all sentimentalism in her poem
to the Innocents, where she repeats several times that "the clouds cry
out in pain over the Innocents' blood." She names the heart of the
mystery that humanity is—humanity the "very mirror of Divinity"
wherein the Spirit finds a dwelling place. Humanity is thus the image
of God, a royal person "crowned with divine imagination and
intelligence." And Mary is extolled as Dame Nature, as the goddess
and divine force of the maternity of all things who has made all things
wet and green, refreshed and rejoicing, once again.

Hildegard's music puts this deep and earthy theology, this spiritual
and grounded cosmology, this living message of creation spirituality-
in-action, into the playfulness and unforgettable power that only art
can accomplish. Her music makes her poetry, her theology, her faith,
her God all incarnate. And those of us who particpate in it, whether
as singers or listeners, are also rendered into living images of the living
God. We, too, are made incarnate once again, provided we have the ears

to hear and the heart to listen openly. Hildegard's art—her mandalas and her music and her poetry—has the power to open our hearts up and to make them grow larger. She gives us *courage* therefore (from the French for "large heart") as only the artist can give it, by eliciting it from *inside-out*. "It was already there," she would say. But it needed to be awakened. Hildegard is a great awakener. No one could encounter her music or her message and nod off.

The text on which we rely for Hildegard's songs in this volume is the critical edition from Otto Müller Verlag in Salzburg (1969), *Lieder*, edited by Pudentiana Barth, OSB, M. Immaculata Ritscher, OSB and Joseph Schmidt-Gorg. It is reproduced by permission of the publishers.

Some Advice on Reading Hildegard

We need to bring our whole selves into an encounter with our deepest mystics and prophets. This means we need to bring our right brains—our hearts—as well as our left brains—our intellects—into this encounter. Reading Hildegard with the right brain, or open heart, means that we place ourselves in her presence and, in a non-judgmental fashion, simply allow her images and words to wash over us. When such an image or word alerts you or strikes you or surprises you, do not hesitate to linger on it, to be with it, to make connections from it. Feel free to respond with poetry or dance or clay or drawing when Hildegard's words have so moved you. In this way, you can be sure that Hildegard is awakening the mystic in you and drawing it out. This is a primary reason for reading such mystics and prophets as Hildegard in our time—not to do them honor but to awaken the mystic/prophet in us.

Reading with the left brain ought to, as a rule, follow on reading with the heart or right brain. But how does one read the mystics with the left brain or with intellectual understanding, analysis, and criticism? I have found that the most suitable way is to do so out of the rich theological tradition from which Hildegard operates, sometimes consciously and sometimes unconsciously. That is, out of the creation-centered spiritual tradition and the four paths that constitute its essence and the twenty-six themes that this tradition celebrates. These four paths and the twenty-six themes they contain constitute a very practical and usable grid by which to grasp much of the depth of Hildegard's thought. In fact, I found that in writing my book *Illuminations of Hildegard of Bingen*, wherein I drew on her poetic, scientific, theological, and pastoral works, Hildegard came leaping off the page and wrapped herself around my neck whenever I applied this grid. Our spiritual giants deserve an intellectual structure by which to understand their deep contribution. The grid of creation theology's four paths and twenty-six themes offers such a structure. While I delineate them in detail in my book, *Original Blessing: A Primer in Creation Spirituality*, I offer them here in list form. By reading Hildegard and other creation mystics with this grid in the forefront of one's mind, much can happen between the reader and the mystic. The alert reader will find Hildegard treating all four paths and most of these themes, deepening them and offering her own unique nuance to them. This should come as no great surprise, since Hildegard is so rich a part of that spiritual tradition. She deserves to be called the "grandmother of the Rhineland mystic movement," that was as prophetic as it was mystical and culminated in the tragic story of Meister Eckhart and his condemnation in the year 1329. It was a movement that deserves our attention today, in our age "so full of pain," for its rich commingling of the cosmological and the prophetic, of art, mysticism, science, and social transformation.

THE CREATION-CENTERED GRID FOR READING THE CREATION MYSTICS

Path I   Befriending Creation: The Via Positiva

Theme 1   Dabhar: The Creative Energy (Word) of God

Theme 2   Creation as Blessing and the Recovery of the Art of Savoring Pleasure

Theme 3   Humility as Earthiness: Our Earthiness as a Blessing along with Passion and Simplicity

Theme 4   Cosmic, Universalist: Harmony, Beauty, Justice as Cosmic Energies

Theme 5   Trust: A Psychology of Trust and Expansion

Theme 6   Panentheism: Experiencing the Diaphanous and Transparent God

Theme 7   Our Royal Personhood: Our Dignity and Responsibility for Building the Kingdom/Queendom of God. Creation Theology as a Kingdom/Queendom Theology

Theme 8   Realized Eschatology: A New Sense of Time

Theme 9   Holiness as Cosmic Hospitality: Creation Ecstasies Shared Constitute the Holy Prayer of Thanksgiving and Praise

Theme 10   Sin, Salvation, Christ from the Perspective of the Via Positiva: A Theology of Creation and Incarnation

Path II   Befriending Darkness, Letting Go and Letting Be: The Via Negativa

Theme 11   Emptying: Letting Go of Images and Letting Silence be Silence

Theme 12   Being Emptied: Letting Pain be Pain: Kenosis

Theme 13   Sinking into Nothingness and Letting Nothingness be Nothingness

Theme 14   Sin, Salvation, Christ from the Perspective of the Via Negativa: A Theology of the Cross

Path III   Befriending Creativity, Befriending Our Divinity: The Via Creativa

Theme 15   From Cosmos to Cosmogenesis: Our Divinization as Images of God Who Are Also Co-Creators

Theme 16   Art as Meditation: Creativity and Birthing as Meditation, Centering, a Return to the Source

Theme 17   Faith as Trust of Images: Discipline—Yes! Asceticism—No!

Theme 18   Dialectical, Trinitarian: How Our Lives as Works of Art Spiral Beauty Back into the World

Theme 19   God as Mother, God as Child: Ourselves as Mothers of God and Birthers of God's Son

Theme 20   Sin, Salvation, Christ from the Perspective of the Via Creativa: A Theology of Resurrection

Path IV   Befriending New Creation: Compassion, Celebration, Erotic Justice, The Via Transformativa

Theme 21   The New Creation: Images of God in Motion Creating a Global Civilization

Theme 22   Faith as Trusting the Prophetic Call of the Holy Spirit

Theme 23   A Spirituality of the *Anawim*: Feminists, Third World, Lay, and other Oppressed Peoples

Theme 24   Compassion: Interdependence, Celebration, and the Recovery of Eros

Theme 25   Compassion: Interdependence and Erotic Justice
Theme 26   Sin, Salvation, Christ from the Perspective of the Via
           Transformativa: A Theology of the Holy Spirit[5]

My deep thanks are rendered to the translators of the texts below,
Robert Cunningham (*De operatione Dei*) and Reverend Jerry Dybdal
(*Songs*) and Ron Miller (*Letters*). Each did a superb job, I believe, in
capturing both the sense and the spirit of Hildegard's passionate
visions and personality. Thanks also to Barbara Clow of Bear &
Company for her patient advice and counsel on the form this book
has taken. And Brendan Doyle for his heartfelt appreciation of
Hildegard's music as expressed in his choice of songs and in his
introduction to them.

I also wish to thank Father Dybdal for his footwork around Austria
securing permissions for these translations as well as for his advice
on editing *De operatione Dei*. The reader may want to know the
history of the text we are translating and why we are reproducing only
some of Hildegard's great work. The appendix makes it clear what
sections have been omitted by us. We are working from the critical
German text by Heinrich Schipperges, *Welt und Mensch* (Salzburg,
Austria, 1965). In that text, Schipperges wisely returns to the University of Ghent manuscript of *De operatione Dei*, Codex 241. This
manuscript has been accurately dated to 1170-1173. It was completed
at Rupertsberg under the supervision of Hildegard herself. Thus the
source of the present translation is the oldest and surest of the Hildegard manuscripts. In addition, another copy which dates to the
Rupertsberg scriptorium and is included in the Wiesbaden Codex of
Scivias was also consulted by Schipperges for the translations from
which we are translating this English text. Additional manuscripts
consulted from the thirteenth century include Codex 681, which
originated in Clairvaux and now resides in the Bibliothèque
Municipale de Troyes; and the Lucca Manuscripts, Codex 1942,
which contains the pictures which are skillfully redrawn in our
volume by artist Angela Werneke. The Archbishop of Lucca, Johan-
nes Dominicus Mansi (1692-1769), was deeply affected by Hildegard's
De operatione Dei and actually published the text of a codex by
Stephanus Daluzius (Lucca, 1761). This was the text used by Migne
in his *Patrologia Latina* (volume 197, col. 739-1038). However, it is
not reliable and has not been the source of Schipperges' translation
or of the one in this volume. Its advantage is, however, that it does

contain the entire work of Hildegard and is worthy of being consulted for what we are not translating here. Since this volume was designed to be a "Hildegard Reader," we did not want to expend the cost or the time necessary to reproduce Hildegard's entire text. Even Schipperges, in his critical text, chose not to translate Hildegard's entire book, since it is so long and is sometimes repetitious. To publish the whole work will take several more years and, of course, it is our fondest wish that scholars and scholarly publishing houses will undertake such an exercise. For getting Hildegard known, however, the publishers, Bear & Company, and I felt that the present volume is appropriate in size and cost to the reader.

The Migne edition states the complete title to this work to be: "The Book of the Divine Works as Written Down by a Simple Human Being." The older version, that of the twelfth century, simply calls it *De operatione Dei*. We are following this title, calling the book simply: "The Book of Divine Works."

Lastly, I need to thank Hildegard herself for her active harmonizing at this time of great pain to mother earth. I hope that her voice coming from the communion of saints to the many hearts opening up to pain and promise today might have the kind of effect Hildegard would be pleased with: justice and celebration. For these two elements, she teaches, are what constitute a *truly human life*.

MATTHEW FOX
INSTITUTE IN CULTURE AND CREATION SPIRITUALITY
HOLY NAMES COLLEGE, OAKLAND

References

1. Joseph McLellan, "Recordings: Hildegard in the Spotlight," *The Washington Post*, March 30, 1986, page H4.
2. Much of my recounting of this history is from Wolfgang Seibrich, "Zur Geschichte des Disibodenbergs," in *Der Disibodenberg* (1979), pp. 7-13. Additional background to Hildegard and her story can be found in Matthew Fox, *Illuminations of Hildegard of Bingen* (Santa Fe: 1985), pp. 6-20; and Bruce Hozeski, trans., *Scivias* (Santa Fe: 1986), pp. ix-xxxii.
3. See Otto Rank, *Beyond Psychology* (New York, 1941).
4. *Ibid.*, pp. 11, 16, 289.
5. For a filling out of this outline of a creation-centered "grid," see Matthew Fox, *Original Blessing: A Primer in Creation Spirituality* (Santa Fe: 1983). The grid presented here actually constitutes the Table of Contents for *Original Blessing*.

The Book of Divine Works
Ten Visions of God's
Deeds in the World and Humanity

Translated by
Robert Cunningham

TRANSLATOR'S NOTE

This English version of Hildegard of Bingen's account of her ten great visions is based on Heinrich Schipperges's German translation from Hildegard's medievel Latin text. Schipperges's version, which is entitled *Welt und Mensch: Das Buch "De operatione Dei,"* was published in 1965 by the Otto Muller Verlag of Salzburg. Matthew Fox, O.P.—the man whose enthusiasm for Hildegard of Bingen's mystical thought has made her writings known to many English-speaking persons—chose Schipperges's version as the basis of this translation because of its accurate interpretation of the difficult original text.

Schipperges's version is based primarily on Codex 241, a manuscript in the library of the University of Ghent entitled *De operatione Dei* (On God's Work). This codex, it is believed, was prepared under Hildegard's supervision at her establishment on Mount St. Rupert (Rupertsberg) in the Rhineland between 1170 and 1173. Scholars have detected the handwriting of two copyists on the manuscript, which was for a time in the possession of St. Eucharius's Monastery (now St. Matthew's) in Trier prior to reaching the University of Ghent.

In addition, Schipperges made use of the following other versions of the work: a thirteenth-century copy of Codex 241 found in the Wiesbadener Riesencodex (giant codex at Wiesbaden); (2) Codex 683 of the Bibliothèque Municipale at Troyes, which was once at the Abbey of Clairvaux; and (3) Codex 1942 of the Biblioteca Governativa at Lucca, which contains the beautiful illustrations on which those in this book are based. All these versions are entitled *Liber divinorum operum* (The Book of Divine Works).

The first printed version of the work was brought out in Lucca in 1761 by that city's archbishop, Giovanni Domenico Mansi (1692-1769). Mansi's version appeared in a publication entitled *Miscellanea* by Stephanus Baluzius. In the nineteenth century, Jacques-Paul Migne used Mansi's edition in volume 197 of *Patrologiae Latina,* which is entirely devoted to the works of Hildegard of Bingen.

Sections in the text marked with brackets are not translations of Hildegard's text; they are summaries by Schipperges of original passages that he judged to be either redundant or repetitious. I, too, summarized certain passages, and these are designated with ** marks at the beginning and end. In both cases, such summaries are offered in this translation because they add to the understanding of the text.

Finally, concerning the use of italics in this translation. The sections of quotations, when Hildegard is writing down the "voice" she hears, were not set in italic in the German translation. However, Bear & Company followed this style with their earlier Hildegard translation of *Scivias,* and felt that this design element helps improve the readability of the present volume.

R. C.

First Part
The World of Humanity

5

Foreword

And it occurred in the sixth year, after I had been troubled for five years with marvelous and true visions. In these visions a true view of the everlasting light had shown me—a totally uneducated human being—the diversity of many ways of life [in the *Liber vitae meritorum*].

It was the beginning of the first year of the present visions that this took place; and I was in my fifty-sixth year. Then I had a vision so deep and overpowering that I trembled over my whole body and began to fall ill because of my bodily weakness. For seven years I wrote about this vision but could scarcely complete the task.

It was in the year 1163 of the Incarnation of our Lord, when the oppression of the See of Rome under Henry, the Roman emperor, was not yet ended.* A voice from heaven resounded, saying to me:

> O wretched creature and daughter of much toil, even though you have been thoroughly seared, so to speak, by countless grave sufferings of the body, the depth of the mysteries of God has completely permeated you. Transmit for the benefit of humanity an accurate account of what you see with your inner eye and what you hear with the inner ear of your soul. As a result, human beings should learn how to know their Creator and should no longer refuse to adore God worthily and reverently. Therefore, write this down—not as your heart is inclined but rather as my testimony wishes. For I am without any beginning or end of life. This vision has not been contrived by you, nor has it been conceived by any other

*In 1163 Pope Alexander III (r. 1159-81) was engaged in a bitter struggle with the Holy Roman Emperor Frederick Barbarossa (r. 1155-90). Alexander was one of the great medieval popes. During his pontificate Thomas â Becket was canonized and the Third Lateran Council was held.—TRANS.

human being. Instead, I have established all of it from before the beginning of the world. And just as I knew the human species even before its creation, I also saw in advance everything that humanity would need.

I—wretched and fragile creature that I am—began then to write with a trembling hand, even though I was shaken by countless illnesses. In this connection I had confidence in the testimony of that man [Volmar] whom—as I mentioned in my earlier visions—I had sought out and visited in secret. And I also had confidence in that girl [Richardis] whom I have already named in my earlier visions. While I set about my task of writing, I looked up again to the true and living light as to what I should write down. For everything I had written in my earlier visions and came to know later I saw under [the influence of] heavenly mysteries while my body was fully awake and while I was in my right mind. I saw it with the inner eye of my spirit and grasped it with my inner ear. In this connection I was never in a condition similar to sleep, nor was I ever in a state of spiritual rapture, as I have already emphasized in connection with my earlier visions. In addition, I did not explain anything in testimony of the truth that I might have derived from the realm of human sentiments, but rather only what I have received from the heavenly mysteries.

And once again I heard a voice from heaven instructing me. And it said, *"Write down what I tell you!"*

First Vision: On the Origin of Life

VISION ONE: 1

And I saw within the mystery of God, in the midst of the southern breezes, a wondrously beautiful image. It had a human form, and its countenance was of such beauty and radiance that I could have more easily gazed at the sun than at that face. A broad golden ring circled its head. In this ring above the head there appeared a second countenance, like that of an elderly man, its chin and beard resting on the crown of the first head. On both sides of the figure a wing grew out of the shoulders. The wings rose above the above-mentioned ring and were joined there. At the topmost part of the right wing's curve appeared an eagle's head. Its eyes were like fire, and in them the brilliance of angels streamed forth as in a mirror. On the topmost part of the left wing's curve was a human head, which shone like the gleaming of the stars. Both faces were turned toward the East. From the shoulders of the figure a wing extended to its knees. The figure was wrapped in a garment that shone like the sun. Its hands carried a lamb, which shone like a brilliant day. The figure's feet trod upon a monster of dreadful appearance, poisonous and black, and a serpent which had fastened its teeth onto the monster's right ear. Its body was wound obliquely across the monster's head; its tail extended on the left side as far as the feet.

VISION ONE: 2

I, the highest and fiery power, have kindled every spark of life, and I emit nothing that is deadly. I decide on all reality. With my lofty wings I fly above the globe: With wisdom I have rightly put the universe in order. I, the fiery life of divine essence, am aflame beyond the beauty of the meadows, I gleam in the waters, and I burn in the sun, moon, and stars. With every breeze, as with invisible life

that contains everything, I awaken everything to life. The air lives by turning green and being in bloom. The waters flow as if they were alive. The sun lives in its light, and the moon is enkindled, after its disappearance, once again by the light of the sun so that the moon is again revived. The stars, too, give a clear light with their beaming. I have established pillars that bear the entire globe as well as the power of the winds which, once again, have subordinate wings—so to speak, weaker winds—which through their gentle power resist the mighty winds so that they do not become dangerous. In the same way, too, the body envelops the soul and maintains it so that the soul does not blow away. For just as the breath of the soul strengthens and fortifies the body so that it does not disappear, the more powerful winds, too, revive the surrounding winds so that they can provide their appropriate service.

And thus I remain hidden in every kind of reality as a fiery power. Everything burns because of me in such a way as our breath constantly moves us, like the wind-tossed flame in a fire. All of this lives in its essence, and there is no death in it. For I am life. I am also Reason, which bears within itself the breath of the resounding Word, through which the whole of creation is made. I breathe life into everything so that nothing is mortal in respect to its species. For I am life.

I am life, whole and entire (vita integra)—not struck from stones, not blooming out of twigs, not rooted in a man's power to beget children. Rather all life has its roots in me. Reason is the root, the resounding Word blooms out of it.

Since God is Reason, how could it be that God, who causes all divine actions to come to fruition through human beings, is not active? God created men and women in the divine image and likeness, and marked each of these creatures according to a fixed standard in human beings. From eternity it was in the mind of God to wish to create humanity, God's own handiwork. And when God completed this action, God gave over to act with it just as God had formed the divine handiwork, humanity.

And thus I serve by helping. For all life lights up out of me. I am life that remains ever the same, without beginning and without end. For this life is God, who is always in motion and constantly in action, and yet this life is manifest in a threefold power. For eternity is called the "Father," the Word is called the "Son," and the breath that binds both of them together is called the "Holy Spirit." And God has likewise marked humanity; in human beings there are body, soul, and reason. The fact that I am aglow above the beauty of earthly realms has the following meaning: The Earth is the material out of which God forms human beings. The fact that I am illuminated in the water signifies the soul, which permeates the entire body just as water flows through the entire Earth. The fact that I am afire in the sun and moon signifies reason; for the stars are countless words of reason. And the fact that I awaken the universe with a breath of air as with the invisible life that contains everything, has the following significance: Through air and wind whatever is growing toward maturity is enlivened and supported, and in no way does it diverge from its inner being.

VISION ONE: 3

And again I heard a voice from heaven saying to me:

God, who created everything, has formed humanity according to the divine image and likeness, and marked in human beings both the higher and the lower creatures. God loved humanity so much that God designated for it the place from which the fallen angel was ejected, intending for human beings all the splendor and honor which that angel lost along with his bliss. The countenance you are gazing at is an indication of this fact.

For what you see as a marvelously beautiful figure in God's mystery and in the midst of southern breezes—a figure similar to a human being—signifies the Love of our heavenly Father. It is Love—in the power of the everlasting Godhead, full of exquisite beauty, marvelous in its mysterious gifts.

Love appears in a human form because God's Son, when he put on flesh, redeemed our lost humanity in the service of Love. On this account the countenance is of such beauty and splendor that you can more easily gaze at the sun than at it. For the abundance of Love gleams and shines in the sublime lightning flash of its gifts in such a way that it surpasses every insight of human understanding by which we can otherwise know in our soul the most varied things. As a result, none of us can grasp this abundance with our minds. But this fact will be shown here in an allegory so that we can know in faith what we cannot see with our outward eyes.

VISION ONE: 4

Another golden ring surrounds the head of this appearance, for the Catholic faith, which has spread throughout the entire globe, began out of the most brilliant glow of the first dawn.

Only faith grasps in deepest reverence the abundance of this love, which exceeds all understanding: the fact that God through the Incarnation of the divine Son redeemed humanity and strengthened it through the inspiration of the Holy Spirit. Thus the one God is known in the Trinity— God who was God in the godhead eternally and without any beginning. In this circular image you see above the head also another head, which is like that of an elderly man. This signifies that the overpowering loving-kindness of the Godhead, which is without beginning and end, hastens to the aid of believers. Its chin and beard rest on the crown of the first countenance. In God's total design and providence the climax of the highest love was that God's Son in his humanity led the lost human race back to the heavenly kingdom.

VISION ONE: 5

A wing emerges from each side of the figure's neck. Both wings rise above the ring and are joined there because the love of God and the love of our neighbor—if they proceed through the divine power of love in the unity of faith and embrace this faith with the greatest longing—cannot be separated as long as the holy Godhead conceals the immeasurable splendor of its glory from human beings and as long as human beings abide in the shadow of death. For they are bereft of the heavenly garment they lost through Adam.

VISION ONE: 6

On the topmost part of the right wing's curve you can see the head of an eagle with fiery eyes. In those eyes a choir of angels shines as in a mirror: When people subject themselves to God on the height of triumphant subservience and overcome Satan, they will advance and enjoy the bliss of divine protection. And if they are inflamed by the Holy Spirit and lift up their hearts and turn their eyes to God, the blessed spirits will appear within them in total brightness and carry up to God the surrender of those individuals' hearts. For spiritual people, who in the devotion of their hearts often gaze at God like the angels, are marked with an eagle. Therefore, the blessed spirits who constantly gaze at God rejoice in the good deeds of the just. They display these deeds to God by their own being. And thus they persist in praising God and never cease to do so, for they can never exhaust the divine fullness. For who could ever count the immeasurable works God accomplishes in the power of divine omnipotence? No one! The brilliance of many reflections in a mirror is characteristic of the angels. Within this brilliance the angels gaze at God. For no one acts and has such power as God, and no one is like the Deity. For God is not subject to such a thing as time.

VISION ONE: 7

Everything God has done was done by the Deity before the beginning of time in the divine present. In the pure and holy Godhead all visible and invisible things shine before all eternity without a temporal moment and without the elapse of time, just as trees and other bodily things are reflected in adjacent waters without being within them in a bodily fashion, even though their outlines may appear in this mirror. When God said, "Let it be done!" things were enclosed at once within their forms, just as the divine providence had seen them in an incorporeal way before time was. Just as everything in front of a mirror shines within that mirror, all the works of the holy Godhead shine within it in a timeless way. For how should God exist without having prior knowledge of the divine works? And each divine work, once it has been enclosed within its body, is complete in the function that is appropriate for it. For the holy Godhead knew in advance how it would assist that work, serving it with knowledge and comprehension. As a ray of light lets us distinguish the form of a creature, God's pure providence sees the forms of creation even before they are enclosed within their bodies. This is because everything God wished to create, even before this work had a body, shone in the divine foreknowledge and according to the divine likeness, just as we can see the rays of the sun before we see the sun itself. And just as the sun's rays indicate the sun, the angels reveal God by their hymns of praise. And just as the sun cannot exist without its light, the Godhead could not be if it were not for the angels' praise. God's providence went before while the divine work came afterward. If this providence had not gone before, the work would not have appeared. In the same way, we cannot recognize someone from his or her bodily appearance unless we can see that person's face. But if we see the face, we will praise also the whole form of that individual. This is the way that God's providence and work are within us human beings.

VISION ONE: 8

At that time an immeasurably large choir of angels sought to make something of themselves. For when they beheld their remarkable glory and their beauty shining in all its dazzling fullness, they forgot about their Maker. They had not even begun to praise God when they thought that all by themselves the splendor of their glory was so great that no one could resist them. Thus they wanted to overshadow God's splendor. But when they saw that they could never exhaust God's wondrous mysteries, they turned away from the Deity, full of disgust. Those who were supposed to celebrate God's praise said in their self-deception that because of their dazzling splendor they should select another God. On this account they plunged downward into darkness, reduced to such a state of impotence that they can only affect a creature when the Creator lets them do so. For God adorned the first of all the angels, Lucifer, with so much of the beauty granted to all creation that the whole heavenly host of angels was illuminated by Lucifer. But now that he has turned toward contradiction, Lucifer has become uglier than ugliness itself. For by the might of anger the holy Godhead flung Lucifer down to the place deprived of all light.

VISION ONE: 9

Shining like the starry light, a human face appears above the top of the curve of the left wing. This means that those among us who take up the defense of our Creator are at the pinnacle of victorious humility since we humbly suppress the earthly things that, so to speak, attack us from the left. Such persons have a human face. For they have begun to live according to the dignity human nature has taught them and not like animals. Therefore, they make known their good intentions through the just deeds of their hearts, and they shine in the brightest splendor.

VISION ONE: 10

When God said, "Let there be light," the light of the spirit arose. This refers to the angels. Intended are both the angels who remained true to God and those who fell into the outermost regions of darkness without light. This happened because the fallen angels chose not to realize that the true light that shone forth in eternity before the origin of everything was

God, since they wanted to bring about something similar to God, even though the existence of such a being was an impossibility. At that time God caused another form of life to arise — a form the Deity clothed with a body.

This refers to humanity. God gave to us human beings the place and honor of the fallen angels so that we might complete God's glory, which is something those angels had refused to do. By this "human face" are marked those who are devoted to the world according to the deeds of the body. Yet according to their spiritual attitude they constantly serve God and do not forget, in the midst of all their worldly obligations, what belongs to the spirit in their service of God. Their faces are turned to the east because both the clergy and the laity in their longing to serve God and to preserve their souls for life should return toward the place where the holy conversion arises and the fountain of bliss is found.

VISION ONE: 11

From each shoulder of this figure a wing extends down to the knees, because the Son of God has attracted and kept, through the power of his love, the just and sinners. Since the just have lived correctly, he carries them on his shoulders, while he carries sinners on his knees because he has called them back from the path of error. He makes all of them partners in a higher community. In the same way someone wishing to carry a burden holds it partly on his knees and partly on his shoulder. In knowledgeable love we are led, soul and body, to the fullness of salvation, even though we often fail to maintain the proper attitude of constancy. Thus we are instructed to an incomparable extent in heavenly and spiritual things as the gifts of the Holy Spirit flow through us from above with a wealth of purity and holiness. In earthly affairs, too, these gifts educate us to the advantage of our bodily needs, yet in quite a different way. Nevertheless, we know ourselves to be weak and frail and mortal in these matters, even though we have been strengthened by so many gifts of grace.

VISION ONE: 12

The figure wears a garment that shines with the brilliance of the sun. This is a sign of the Son of God who in his love has assumed a human body unstained by sin and beautiful as the sun. Just as the sun shines sublimely over all creation at such a height that no one can encroach upon it, so no one can grasp the Incarnation of the Son of God in its essence— except through faith. In its hand the figure carries a lamb as brilliant as the light of day. For love has revealed in the deeds of the Son of God the gentleness of a true faith that outshines everything else—as this love chose martyrs, confessors, and penitents from the ranks of publicans and sinners, as it converted atheists into righteous believers, and turned Saul into Paul, so that all of them could fly into the harmony of heaven. Thus love has perfected its achievement, bit by bit yet clearly and definitely, so that no weakness may remain, and so that all fullness may be attained. We human beings cannot create anything like it. For when we are active with our limited possibilities, we can scarcely bear to end what we are doing so that it can be inspected by others. For we are aware that the little bird that emerges from the egg and as yet has no wings does not try to fly right away. After its wings have grown, the bird will fly because it sees that flying is appropriate for it.

VISION ONE: 13

The figure treads upon both a frightful monster of a poisonously dark hue and a serpent. For true love, which follows in the footsteps of the Son of God, tramples upon all injustice that is convoluted by the countless vices of dissention. Injustice is also dreadful in its very nature, poisonous in its temptations, and black in its abandonment. In addition, love destroys thus the old serpent lying in wait for believers. For the Son of God has destroyed this serpent by the cross. Indeed, the serpent has fastened its jaws to the monster's ear and coiled itself about the monster's head and body in such a way as to reach its feet. This symbolizes Satan who at times conceals his deceptions as a kind of kindness. He fastens his jaws in strife and, after this beginning, briskly trots out a whole family of vices. Finally, he openly displays the perversity of open conflict that he has previously concealed. For the serpent is more cunning than all the other reptiles and destroys as much as it can by acting with the utmost speed. This is what is indicated by the various hues of the serpent's hide. Satan acted in this same fashion. Realizing his own beauty, he aimed at being like his Creator. This is the very same advice he whispered into Adam's ear, so to speak, through the serpent's mouth. And Satan will not cease to do so until the Day of Judgment, as is shown by his tail.

But love is at work in the circles of eternity, without reference to time, like heat within a fire. In the divine providence God foresaw all creatures that were created in the fullness of divine love in such a way that humanity did not lack among them for refreshment or service. For God bound them to humanity the way a flame is bound to fire. Yet God created the first angel along with the fullness of beauty, as described above. When that angel looked at himself, he felt hatred for his lord and sought to rule all by himself. But God cast him down into the bog of the abyss. From this time onwards, that mutineer has gone about insinuating his evil counsel. And we human beings are in agreement with him.

VISION ONE: 14

When God created humanity, the Deity clothed us with a heavenly garment so that we would shine in great splendor. But Satan saw the woman and realized that she would be the mother who would bear in her womb a world of great possibilities. By the same cunning through which he had fallen away from God, Satan managed to get the better of God, so to speak, by bringing about an agreement between himself and this divine work, that is, between himself and the human species (*opus Dei quod homo est*). Since the woman felt that she had become different through her enjoyment of the apple, she gave it also to her husband. Thus both of them lost their heavenly garment.

VISION ONE: 15

Since God quickly asked, "Adam, where are you?" this indicated that the One who had created humanity in the
divine image and likeness wished to draw us back to God.
When Adam was sent into exile, God covered the man's
nakedness by an act of gracious cooperation. In place of his
luminous garment, Adam was given a sheepskin, and God
substituted for Paradise a place of exile. God bound the
woman to the man by an oath of loyalty that should never
be broken. Indeed, they were in agreement with each other,
like the body and soul God has joined together in unity.
Hence, anyone who destroys this bond of fealty and persists
in doing so without repentance will be expelled to Babylon,
a place full of chaos and drought. That land lies fallow,
deprived of both the green beauty of life and God's blessing.
The divine vengeance will befall such an individual up to
the last generation of blood relationship that may result
from his or her hot blood. For a sin of this nature will affect
the very last human being.

VISION ONE: 16

Just as Adam is the begetter of the entire human race,
spiritual people lead the way by means of the Son of God,
who was made flesh in the body of a virgin. Such people will
be fecund, just as by means of an angel God promised
Abraham that his seed would be as numerous as the stars of
heaven. For Scripture states: "'Look up to heaven and count
the stars if you can. Such will be your descendants,' he told
him. Abram put a faith in Yahweh, who counted this as
making him justified" (Genesis 15:5-6). This is to be
understood as addressed to you who pray to God, and
sincerely honor God, look at God's mysteries, and see the
reward of those who can shine before God day and night—to
the extent that this is possible for those encumbered with the
burden of their bodies. For as long as we enjoy the things of
the flesh, we can never fully grasp the things of the spirit.
But by means of true signs, a message will be given to anyone

who makes an effort to honor God with an exceedingly ardent heart. In this way the seed of your heart will be multiplied and placed in a clear light because you have sown on good soil that which has been watered with the grace of the Holy Spirit. Before the highest God this seed will ascend and shine in the blissful power of its virtue, just as a multitude of stars gleams in heaven. Therefore, whoever shows devout faith in the divine promise by clinging to the height of a true faith in God, by scorning earthly things, and by revering heavenly things, will be counted as righteous among the children of God. He or she has loved truth, and nothing false has been found in that person's heart.

VISION ONE: 17

For God knew that Abraham's mind was free of the serpent's deception because Abraham's actions did not harm anyone else. Therefore, God chose from Abraham's stock the dormant Earth that had within itself not a jot of the taste whereby the old serpent had deceived the first woman. And the Earth, which was foreshadowed by Aaron's staff, was the Virgin Mary. In her great humility she was the king's enclosed bridal chamber. For when she received the message from the throne that the king wished to dwell within her secret womb, she looked at the Earth of which she was made and spoke of herself as God's handmaiden. The woman who had been deceived [Eve] did not do so, and she was the one who desired something that she should not have possessed. Abraham's obedience—the obedience through which God tested Abraham by showing him the ram caught in the thornbush—was a prefigurement of the Blessed Virgin's obedience. She, too, believed the messenger of God and wished matters to be as he had stated. On this account God's Son took on the garment of flesh within her, as was prefigured by the ram in the thornbush. When God promised Abraham offspring as numerous as the stars of heaven, God foresaw that in the offspring the fullness of the heavenly community would be completed. Since Abraham was full of confidence in God and believed all these things, Abraham will be called the father of all who inherit the kingdom of heaven.

Let all who fear and love God open up their hearts, in complete devotion, to these words. Let them understand that such words are being proclaimed for the salvation of our body and soul—not by a human voice but rather by myself, the One who am.

Second Vision: On the Construction of the World

VISION TWO: 1

Then a wheel of marvelous appearance became visible right in the center of the breast of the above-mentioned figure which I had seen in the midst of the southern air. On the wheel there were symbols that made it look like the image I had seen twenty-eight years ago — then it took the form of an egg, as described in the third vision of my book *Scivias*. At the top of the wheel, along the curve of the egg, there appeared a circle of *luminous fire*, and under it there was another circle of *black fire*. The luminous circle was twice as large as the black one. And these two circles were so joined as to form but a single circle. Under the black circle appeared another circle as of *pure ether*, which was as large as the two other circles put together. Under this ether circle was seen a circle of *watery air*, which in size was the same as the circle of lumious fire. Beneath this circle of watery air appeared another circle of *sheer white clear air*, which looked to be as tough as a sinew of the human body. This circle was the same size as the circle of black fire. Both circles, too, were so joined as to appear to be but a single circle. Under this sheer white clear air, finally, there appeared still another *thin stratum of air*, which at times seemed to raise up high, light clouds and then again deep-hanging dark clouds. At times the stratum of air seemed to extend over this entire circle. All six circles were joined together without a wide space between them. While the topmost circle exceeded the other spheres in light, the circle of watery air moistened all the other circles with dampness.

From the edge of the wheel's eastern side a line separating the northern zone from the other areas extended in a northerly direction as far as the edge of the western side. In addition, in the middle of the sphere of thin air was seen a sphere, which was equally distant all around from the sheer

white and luminous air. The radius of the sphere had the same depth as the space extending from the top of the first circle to the outermost clouds, or we might say that this space extended from the distant clouds as far as the top of this sphere.

In the middle of the giant wheel appeared a human figure. The crown of its head projected upward, while the soles of its feet extended downward as far as the sphere of sheer white and luminous air. The fingertips of the right hand were stretched to the right, and those of the left hand were stretched to the left, forming a cross extending to the circumference of the circle. This is the way in which the figure had extended its arms.

At the four sides appeared four heads: those of a leopard, a wolf, a lion, and a bear. Above the crown of the figure's head, in the sphere of pure ether, I saw from the leopard's head that the animal was exhaling through its mouth. Its breath curved somewhat backward to the right of the mouth, became extended, and assumed the shape of a crab's head with a pair of pincers that formed its two feet. At the left side of the mouth the leopard's breath assumed the shape of a stag's head. Out of the crab's mouth there emerged another breath that extended to the middle of the space between the heads of the leopard and the lion. The breath from the stag's head extended as far as the middle of the space remaining between the leopard and the bear. All of these exhalations had the same length: the breath extending from the right side of the leopard's head to the crab's head; the breath stretching from the left side of the same mouth as far as the stag's head; the breath reaching from the stag's head to the middle of the space between the heads of the leopard and lion; and finally, the breath emerging from the mouth of the stag's head to the midst of the space between the heads of the leopard and lion.

All these heads breathed toward the above-mentioned wheel and the human figure.

[In like manner the exhalations of the other animals are described. After the leopard come the wolf, and lion, and the bear; after the stag and the crab, the serpent and the lamb. And all of them breathe concentrically toward the human figure in the center.]

Above the head of this human figure the seven planets were sharply delineated from each other. Three were in the circle of luminous fire, one was in the sphere of black fire beneath it, while another three were farther below in the circle of pure ether . . . [All the planets shone their rays at the animal heads as well as at the human figure] . . . Within the circumference of the circle that looked like luminous fire, there now appeared sixteen major stars: four between the heads of the leopard and the lion, four between the heads of the lion and the wolf, four between the heads of the wolf and the bear, and four between the heads of the bear and the leopard. Eight of them, which as medium-sized stars helped one another, were between the heads in such a way that two of them between two of the heads shone their rays toward one another at the image of the thin layer of air. But the other eight stars, which were neighbors of the other animal heads, directed their radiance at the circle of black fire.

The circle of pure ether and the circle of sheer white luminous air were completely full of stars which shone their rays at the opposite clouds. From this point one could see at the right of the above-described image, as it were, two separate tongues flowing like streams toward the above-mentioned wheel and the human figure. Also to the left of the previously mentioned clouds similar tongues emerged from time to time and were turned toward the wheel and the human figure as if to give rise to small streams. Thus the figure was entwined and surrounded by these symbols. I saw also that from the breath of the figure in whose breast the wheel appeared, there emerged a light with many rays that was brighter than the brightest day. In these rays were measured to an accurate and most precise standard the symbols of the circles and the symbols of all the other figures that were seen on this wheel as well as the individual marks of articulation of the human figure—I am speaking here of the image in the midst of the cosmic wheel. How this is to be interpreted is clarified by the preceding explanation, and it will be clarified even more by the explanation that follows.

VISION TWO: 2

Again I heard a voice from the sky which made this statement to me:

> God has composed the world out of its elements for the glory of God's name. God has strengthened it with the winds, bound and illuminated it with the stars, and filled it with the other creatures. On this world God has surrounded and strengthened human beings with all these things and steeped them in very great power so that all creation supports the human race in all things. All nature ought to be at the service of human beings so that they can work with nature since, in fact, human beings can neither live nor survive without it. This will be shown to you in this vision.
>
> For in the breast of the above-mentioned appearance there appears a wheel, marvelous to behold in all its symbols and much like the image you gazed at twenty-eight years ago in the form of an egg, just as it was shown to you in your earlier visions. For the shape of the world exists everlastingly in the knowledge of the true Love which is God: constantly circling, wonderful for human nature, and such that it is not consumed by age and cannot be increased by anything new. It rather remains just as God has created it, everlasting until the end of time. In its foreknowledge and in its workings the Godhead is like a wheel, a whole. In no way is it to be divided because the Godhead has neither beginning nor end. No one can grasp it, for it is timeless. And just as a wheel encloses within itself what lies hidden within it, so also does the Holy Godhead enclose everything within itself without limitation, and it exceeds everything. For no one could disperse its might or overpower it or complete it.

VISION TWO: 3

The above-mentioned figure was shown to you in your earlier

visions in the form of an egg. This was because the characteristics of the world-matter can best be shown by this
likeness. For while there is a similarity between the multi-
layered structure of the world-egg and the layers of structure
in which at one time or another its various materials are
distinguished, we should understand by this wheel the circumference and correct measurement of the world-ele-
ments. For none of these images incorporates the form of
the world because this world is indeed intact on all sides,
round and rotating. But such a ball, which is round and
rotating, most of all resembles that form of the world in all
its details.

VISION TWO: 4

The circle of luminous fire at the top of the curve indicates that fire, as the first element, is at the top because it
is light. It contains all the other elements and illuminates
them. It penetrates all creatures and endows them with the
joy of light. In this connection it is a symbol of God's
power, which dominates everything and gives light to all
living things. Under the circle of luminous fire is found
another circle of black fire. This indicates that the second
fire is under the power of the first fire. The second fire is a
judgment fire—almost a fire of hell—and is produced for the
punishment of evildoers. Sparing nothing on which it falls
as a just verdict, it is a sign that everyone who opposes God
will fall down into black darkness and all kinds of disaster.
When the sun climbs high in the sky in summer, this fire
carries out God's vengeance by the fire-causing lightning;
when the sun descends in winter, the judgment fire indicates condemnation and punishment by ice, cold, and
hail. For every sin will be punished according to its nature by
fire, cold, and other afflictions. The circle of luminous fire is
twice as strong as the dark circle of fire because the black
fire has such a strong and vigorous effect that, if it were not
half so thick, it would dissipate and darken the upper circle
of light. Equally dangerous is the punishment of human

sins so that we humans could not bear such punishment if
grace and God's loving-kindness did not cooperate with us.
Both these circles unite to form a single circle because they
glow in the burning of the fire. And thus God's might and
judgment have blended to form a single justice and cannot
be separated from each other.

VISION TWO: 5

Beneath this circle of black fire is another circle of pure
ether, which has the same density as the other zones of light
mentioned above. Under these light and black layers of fire
lies pure ether, which encompasses the whole world in its
curvature. The circle of pure ether emerges from the other
circles like lightning out of a flaming fire when the fire
belches forth its flames. This circle gives an indication of
the pure atonement of sinners—an atonement awakened
either by God's grace as from the luminous fire or by fear of
God from the black fire. This layer also has the same
dimension as the two fiery circles mentioned above because
it shines again from both these fires and has their same density. Thus it is neither gentler than the luminous fire in its
lightning nor is it harder than the black fire in its impact. In
this way God's just judgment comes to a decision. For day
and night signify nothing by themselves but only whatever
God's will decrees.

This zone of ether restrains both the upper and lower
zones so that they should not exceed their proper dimensions. It does not fall upon one of the creatures like a verdict. Instead, it simply offers resistance to creatures
through its purity and uniformity, just as repentance limits
the punishment of sinners. The zone of pure ether has the
same dimension as both of the layers of fire mentioned
above. Since the zone of ether has the same density as the
two layers of fire, this means that human beings ready for
repentance should contemplate within the light the case of
the first angel, who was a bearer of light. They should also
ponder, along with the density of the black fire, the case of

those who sin by disbelief and thoughtfulness. Inasmuch as we consider in this way God's just judgment, we should feel remorse in all sincerity.

VISION TWO: 6

Beneath the circle of pure ether another circle is seen— the circle of watery air that has the same dimension as the zone of luminous fire mentioned above. The circle of watery air is meant to show that waters are found under the zone of ether and within the circumference of the firmament; we know that such waters flow above the firmament. Their layer has the same density as that of the circle of luminous fire. The watery air indicates the holy works of exemplary and just individuals. Their works are as pure as water and cause every impure work to become pure, just as water washes away filth. Because of this condition such a work can achieve in its perfection whatever God's grace enkindles in this way by the fire of the Holy Spirit.

VISION TWO: 7

Under this circle of watery air is seen another circle of sheer white clear air, which has the same tensile strength as a sinew in the human body. In opposition to the dangerous waters up above, this circle prevents flooding by the watery circle through its force and tension. For such flooding might otherwise submerge the Earth in a sudden and overwhelming precipitation. With respect to our spiritual life, this should be an indication that discretion strengthens holy works by every kind of moderation. Similarly, we should restrain our body in such a way as not to fall down to our damnation, which might happen if we were to punish ourselves to excess.

The fact that this circle is the same size as the zone of black fire mentioned above indicates that the circle of sheer white clear air has been inserted as a benefit to humanity, like the discretion used in punishing sinners. But often the watery layers down below are drawn upward through the clouds in order to punish evil deeds in accord with God's just decree. Then out of the watery zone of air a certain moisture mounts up through this sheer white clear air. Similarly, something we humans have drunk may overflow into our bladder without causing damage to the bladder. Thus it happens that, in the case of flooding, such waters may rush down in such a dangerous way. Similarly, a power of discrimination decides about all human deeds on behalf of our salvation and in proper moderation. Indeed, God's judgment does not exceed the measure of human sins in fixing the punishment due for such sins. Instead, sins are judged correctly because our Protector and Guide holds equitably the scale of judgment. Both these zones are so closely tied to each other that they seem, so to speak, but a single layer. For they are soaked in moisture and pour out wetness upon other zones in the same way as the power of judgment (*discretio*) holds together the good deeds [of human beings] so that we should not go down to damnation.

VISION TWO: 8
Under this circle of sheer white clear air, there is still another one, which is known as the circle of the thin stratum of air. This circle indicates that air is exhaled from the upper layers and elements without being separated from the powers of the elements. In the same way the air of breath emerges from a human being without being separated from that person. Just as clouds often ascend and appear to be luminous and then descend and appear to be overshadowed, this zone of air seems to maintain everything above it that the watery air mentioned previously spews forth. This zone of air gathers all of this back again, just as a blacksmith's bellows exhales air and then sucks it back up again. And so it happens that certain stars roaming about in the upper layer of fire ascend in their orbit, and that the clouds draw them down again, appearing luminous as they do so. But if those stars descend in their orbit, they leave the clouds again, which in this case appear overshadowed

and emit drops of rain.

The above-mentioned thin layer of air is seen to extend along the entire circumference of the wheel because, in fact, everything in creation obtains vital power and stability from this air. Thus the just longing of believers who are in need of justice emerges under the protective layer of discretion from the higher powers of virtue and the Holy Spirit's invigorating influence. For this longing does not avoid virtue and the Holy Spirit but rather remains always closely tied to them in just subordination and reverence. And so the longing of believers causes their steadfastness to shine in confidence at times and at other times to tremble humbly and to ascribe to God whatever may arise from deeds of holiness and from their good example. Their steadfastness then knows how to gather all these things together again, just as a worker is rewarded by his or her work alone. A good conscience resulting from the fervor of the Holy Spirit should raise human beings up to heavenly things in justification. This same conscience carries along their whole attitude and purifies it. If then this conscience is reduced to the needs of a bodily existence, it has to turn its mind to such problems. These people then often appear upset, so to speak, amid the problems of everyday life and bear within themselves the moisture of tears. For they sigh because they have to cling to earthly things even though they have surrendered entirely to the omnipotence of God.

VISION TWO: 9

All these six circles are bound to each other without any interval. If the divine order had not strengthened them through such an association, the firmament would have to come apart and it would have not stability. This is an indication that the perfect powers of virtue in a believer are so bound to each other and strengthened by the infusion of the Holy Spirit that they can accomplish in harmony every good deed in their battle against the snares of the devil.

VISION TWO: 10

The top circle penetrates with its fire the other zones. But the watery circle moistens with its dampness all the other layers. Although the topmost element, fire, actually strengthens with its power and purity the other elements of the Earth, the watery circle distributes to all the other elements the freshness of life by means of its own moisture. Thus does God's almighty power, through the miracle of divine grace, sanctify believers and their achievements while the believers praise in the true reverence of holiness the loving kindness of their Creator.

VISION TWO: 11

From the beginning of the wheel's eastern region there extends, so to speak, as far as the border of the western zone a line that runs out into the universe in a northerly direction and cuts off this northern region from the other areas. From the sun's first rising in the east up to its farthest point of decline in the west, where the sun no longer shines, this line is bent this way and then backward, thus avoiding the northern region. For the sun does not shine over these areas. Instead, it neglects them since the old deceiver chose to make his dwelling there. Therefore, God keeps these zones free of the sunshine. In the same way believers put on the sincerity of justice, in contrast to injustice, from the beginning of the good deeds they initiate through the divine power. They distinguish strictly the diabolical crafts from good and holy deeds because they cling loyally and spontaneously to God and seek to avoid whatever might harm their soul. And so they pay attention to what has been put down in scripture.

VISION TWO: 12

"To those who prove victorious I will give the hidden manna and a white stone—a stone with *a new name* written on it, known only to the man who receives it" (Revelation 2:17).

This statement should be understood in the following way: Those who flee from the left side have taken upon themselves

a mighty battle against the serpent coiled about itself. For
that creature constantly seeks to attract people to itself in
the area on the left. But if people persist in this struggle by
fleeing from Satan and refusing to come to an agreement
with him, I shall endow them with the living bread that
comes down from heaven — the bread hidden from all the
baseness of male lust as well as from all the old serpent's
cunning. On this account I shall give to them communion
with the One who is the cornerstone and who in shining
splendor is both God and man. In him there lives the name
of the second birth, which is Christ because of whom we are
Christians. This, however, is a fact that none can fully comprehend as long as they remain in this fragile, time-bound
existence and until at last they achieve the life of eternal
bliss as their heavenly reward.

VISION TWO: 13

The ball in the midst of the circle of thin air is about as far
removed as possible from the circle of sheer white clear
light. Now this ball represents the Earth, which has its existence in the midst of the rest of the world-matter so that it
can receive proper guidance from all sides. It is maintained
on all sides by these circles, is tied to them, and receives
constantly from them the greening freshness of life and the
fertility needed for the Earth's support.

The active life symbolizes, so to speak, the Earth. This
life dwells, in fact, in the midst of correct efforts and rushes
first this way and then that way, striving in proper devotion
to help out the forces of moderation. Among believers this
kind of life submits at times to spiritual exercises and at
other times to bodily needs — but always to a correct degree.
For those who love discretion direct all their activity toward
what God wishes.

The radius of this ball is as extensive as the space from
the top of the uppermost zone down to the outermost
clouds, or the space from the edge of the clouds to the top of
this ball. This is because the Earth has been so compacted

by the highest Creator and so constructed that it cannot be dissolved by the uproar of the upper elements nor by the force of the winds nor even by the might of the falling waters. In this way believers measure in the depth of their hearts the extent of God's omnipotence and behold the changeable nature of their opinions and the weakness of their flesh. And thus they keep all their actions within the proper measure so as not to exceed moderation in the achievements necessarily associated with either the higher or the lower life and in this way to fall into guilt.

VISION TWO: 14

"Do all that has to be done without complaining or arguing and then you will be innocent and genuine, perfect children of God among a deceitful and underhanded brood, and you will shine in the world like bright stars because you are offering it the word of life" (Philippians 2:14–16).

This is to be understood in the following way: Humanity stands, as it were, at a crossroad. If human beings seek in the light for salvation from God, they will receive it. But if they choose evil, they will follow the Devil to the place of punishment. Human beings should fulfill their human nature and accomplish all their deeds as follows: without complaint and free from the ugliness of sin, without argument and like people living in the right faith. In their love of good and hatred of evil, they will have no doubt that they will be free at the Last Judgment, separated from all the lost ones who have turned from good to evil deeds. Those who do these good deeds and harm no one will live without any bitter lamentation as God's children in the simplicity of their just deeds. Far from the artfulness of deception, they will undoubtedly enjoy the esteem of those who prove themselves to be brave and glorious in an evil, perverted world. In the fullness of faith they will shine among such people like the stars that illuminate the universe in the order established by the Creator of the cosmos. Through their teaching, which is concerned for life, they will lead as

many as possible to God, just as God's sinless Son has given
light to everyone in the world. But God has placed two
lights in the firmament, the sun and the moon, which were
to be images of the knowledge of good and evil in human beings. For just as the universe is strengthened by the sun and
the moon, so, too, humanity is brought hither and thither
to the knowledge of good and evil. And just as the sun and
the moon complete their course without diminishing their
orbit, so, too, good conscience takes its course without feeling the lack of evil. Instead, it treads on bad conscience,
scolds it, and destroys it because there is no use for it. Good
conscience curses bad conscience into hell when it tries to
satisfy its desire. And as the moon wanes and waxes, so,
too, evil despises good and calls it foolish and vain, even
though it knows what is good. The Devil also knows God,
even though the Devil sets himself in opposition to God.

VISION TWO: 15

In the midst of this wheel there appears the figure of a
human being. The crown of the head extends upward, while
the feet extend downward against the previously mentioned
circle of the sheer white clear air. The fingertips of the right
hand are extended to the right while those of the left hand
are directed to the left, both of them toward this vision of
light as if the figure had stretched out its arms. This has the
following message:

*Humanity stands in the midst of the structure of the
world. For it is more important than all other creatures
which remain dependent on that world. Although small in
stature, humanity is powerful in the power of its soul. Its
head is turned upward and its feet to the solid ground, and it
can place into motion both the higher and the lower things.
Whatever it does with its deeds in the right or the left hand
permeates the universe, because in the power of its inner
humanity it has the potential to accomplish such things. Just
as, for example, the body of a human being exceeds in size*

*the heart, so also are the powers of the soul more powerful
than those of the body. Just as the heart of a human being
rests hidden within the body, so also is the body surrounded
by the powers of the soul since these powers extend over the
entire globe. Thus persons who are believers have their existence in the knowledge of God and strive for God in their
spiritual and worldly endeavors. Whether good progress is
made in these undertakings or whether they do not succeed,
those persons always direct their aspirations to God since in
both situations they constantly express their awe. For just
as human beings see with their physical eyes creatures on
all sides, so do they always look in faith at the Lord. It is
God whom human beings know in every creature. For they
know that he is the Creator of the whole world.*

VISION TWO: 16

Opposite the four regions there appeared the four
heads — those of a leopard, a wolf, a lion, and a bear — just as
on the four sides of the universe there are also the four
winds of the world. These four winds do not have at all the
form of these animals. Only in the powers of their nature do
they resemble these beasts.

To a certain degree human beings have their existence at
the crossroads (*quadruvium*) of worldly concerns. We are
driven there by countless temptations. The leopard's head
reminds us of the fear of the Lord, the wolf of the punishment of hell, the lion causes us to fear God's judgment, and
beneath the bear we are attacked and shaken through bodily
trials by a host of afflictions.

VISION TWO: 17

[From the heads of the animals there now emerge, in precisely described regularity, the exhalations that spin an
orderly cosmic network throughout the whole wheel of the
world and create a corresponding system of moral relationships.]

VISION TWO: 18

All these animal heads breathe toward the wheel described above and toward the human figure. It is these winds which keep the universe in balance with their raging and which keep human beings aware of salvation with their blowing. For the universe could not exist nor could humanity live if it were not kept alive through the blowing of the winds.

If we human beings rise up in spiritual tension and, mindful of our evil deeds, attain a state of repentance, at the same time the fear of God, which is like a leopard, arises above the crown of the head of the image in the symbol of pure ether—that is, the symbol of repentance. Out of our mouths flows the divine power of repentance which touches the human heart. This divine power gives us the opportunity to reach the head of the crab, which stands for trust. From the crab two sets of pincers emerge like two feet, hope and doubt. And thus this power—in contradiction to what one might think and with an increase in contrition—reaches the head of the stag, which stands for faith. Of course, as soon as we become mindful of the burden of our sins, there is an increase of the remorse in which we do not cease to fear God, even though we still keep the benefits of the world on the other side. We continue to do this until we have attained the trust out of which the two feet, hope and doubt, have sprung. Out of trust hope arises, although doubt is linked to hope. For in trusting God, we hope for forgiveness of our sins. Because we feel hope, we are able to make progress. But by thinking about our faults and the seriousness of our sins, we have doubts as to whether such defects could ever be forgiven. And so we fall behind, even though we still have trust in God. If we are bothered, on the other hand, by bodily suffering as a result of the ups and downs of life, we shall turn to the treasure of faith, which destroys in us our faithless doubt on the horns of true consolation. And so there emerges at the same time from the crab's mouth, that is, out of the mouth of trust, another breath, namely constancy, which advances to the fullness of perfection.

Constancy is in the middle, between fear of God and God's judgment. If, for example, we remain constant and perfect in our trust of God through our good deeds, we shall take hold of the fear of the Lord so as not to fail in a more serious way. In this way we shall look to God's judgment so as not to resign ourselves any more to our sins.

But out of the mouth of the stag, that is to say, out of the mouth of faith, there emerges another breath which is to be understood as holiness. It extends to the fullness of perfection that lies between fear of the Lord and bodily anguish. That means that believers, who are powerful in holiness, remain in that state of perfection so that they truly fear God and at the same time do not neglect to keep their bodies in check.

And although all these powers have various functions, they strive for the same bliss. For the same power of virtue emerges by force out of all of them and creates the proper way of life. But all these heads, that is, all these powers of virtue, exist in God's knowledge and are directed at God's knowledge. And thus they attend us, both in the necessities of life for our body and for our spirit.

If we allow ourselves to become spiritual through our awe of God, we shall also begin to revere our God by ourselves. We shall go through life in wisdom and accomplish good and just works. The confidence in which we trust our God touches us with constancy so that we are constantly loyal to God and direct all our thoughts to God. Thus the spirit of believers is strengthened through the power of constancy. But faith judges with holiness also whatever is to be condemned as unbelieving. Faith extends itself quickly and submerges believers by removing from their ears all confusion caused by perverse ideas and by ridding their hearts of indecent desires. If meanwhile, we give up the green vitality of these virtues and surrender to the drought of our indolence, so that we do not have the sap of life and the greening power of good deeds, then the power of our very soul will begin to fade and dry up. If we are submerged by lewd desires as by a flood, our soul will fade away on this slippery ground. But if we follow the right road, all our actions will give rise to good fruit.

VISION TWO: 19

"The King has brought me into his rooms; you will be our joy and our gladness. We shall praise your love above wine; how right it is to love you" (Song of Songs 1:4).

This is to be understood in the following way: I, the soul of a believer, have followed along on the path of truth the Son of God, who has redeemed human beings through his humanity. I was accompanied by the One who is the ruler of the universe into the fullness of the divine benefits, where I find all satisfaction in virtues and faithfully climb from virtue to virtue. Therefore, all of us who have been redeemed by the blood of the Son of God are happy with you. We rejoice with our whole soul in you, O Holy Godhead, through which we are here. We call to mind the sweetness of the heavenly reward which causes us to forget all the suffering and distress we have had to endure in conflict over the truth. All of that has become as nothing since we tasted what you have set before us as a sign of your commandments. And thus all who live justly in deeds of holiness love you with a true and perfect love; for you endow those who love you with all benefits and in the end you endow them with eternal life. Wisdom, however, pours into the chambers, that is, into the spirit of human beings, the justice of true faith through which alone God is known. There this faith presses out all the chill and dampness of vice in such a way that such things cannot germinate and grow again. At the same time faith presses out for itself all the powers of virtue in such a way that a noble wine can be poured into a goblet and offered to us as a beverage. On this account believers should rejoice and be glad in true faith in an eternal reward. They should bear before them the pennants of the good deeds they have accomplished. Thirsting for God's justice, they should now suckle the holy element from God's breast and never have enough of it, so that they will be forever refreshed by the vision of God. For the holy element outshines all human understanding. When we grasp justice in this way, we shall surrender to it, taste virtue, and drink. We shall be strengthened by it as the veins of someone who drinks become filled with wine. We shall never go to excess like persons drunk on wine who lose control of themselves and no longer know what they are doing. In this way the just love God of whom they can never have too much but from whom they have bliss forever and ever.

VISION TWO: 20

Under the feet of this human figure in the circle of watery air there appears, so to speak, a wolf's head, which sends an exhalation out of its mouth. This indicates that, under the power of the One who became a man for the sake of humanity, the west wind blows like a wolf out of the watery air in the western zone. It shows itself in the form of a wolf which has hidden in the woods and which grows ravenous whenever it looks for food. This means that when this wind bursts out of its hiding place, it quickly causes the plants to grow green. But then it causes them to dry up and wither away . . . [In the same way the other winds are discussed; all of them are not supposed to exceed their proper measure unless God permits this in the event of some catastrophe.]

VISION TWO: 21

These heads breathe toward the above-mentioned wheel and the human figure in the middle of the wheel in such a way that the winds maintain the world and humanity and everything in the universe in their powers and functions.

When, therefore, believers, by doing good, step on their feeble desires with exemplary justice, so to speak, the punishments of hell to a certain extent emerge as naked as a wolf from these holy achievements. If believers cease to sin and climb the path of justice, they show in this way how much they fear the punishments of hell that devour the soul . . . [At the same time human beings must sustain many kinds of bodily suffering before they become totally incandescent in their faith and free of doubts. For they are subject in their bodies to all these cosmic powers.] But inasmuch as all these powers are gazing at the vision of God which embraces everything, through the strength of their power they compel humanity to carry out God's will. For they create the punishments of hell only so that God may be feared. If we, in fact, really fear these punishments, we shall no longer sin. If we see also the good example of others, we shall endure better our own hardships and bear everything patiently and testify in all our actions to what is holy . . .

VISION TWO: 22

[Those who trust in God in this way will also honor the stability of the world: the orbits of the sun and the moon, winds and air, earth and water, everything God has created for the honor and protection of humanity. We have no other foothold. If we give up this world, we shall be destroyed by demons and deprived of the angels' protection.]

VISION TWO: 23

[To the right of the human figure there appears in the circle of luminous fire the head of a lion, which is the symbol of the south wind. Beside it are two auxiliary winds with the heads of a serpent and a lamb. Their powers are then described, both with respect to their close relationship and their differences.]

VISION TWO: 24

We become aware now of just how the winds are blowing toward the wheel and the human figure. For it is the winds —both the major winds and the ones subject to them—that by their power maintain the whole universe as well as humanity in which all creation is shared so that nothing becomes subject to destruction. The auxiliary winds are the wings of the major winds. Even when they are only gentle breezes, they are constantly blowing as breaths of air. But the major winds will not be summoned with their immense power until God's verdict is given in the judgment at the end of the world. The south and north winds, along with

their auxiliary winds, blow in accord with God's law because
this is God's will. The south wind blows with great heat and a
mighty surge while the north wind, by contrast, does so with
lightning and thunder, with hail and cold. But the major
winds from the east to west, along with their auxiliary winds,
are seen to be more restrained and slow—again in accord with
God's law. Similarly, in accord with the divine wish, they
give rise to the same conditions: great heat or cold and dryness
in winter. Then again they may cause a burning fire or rain or
similar problems. In this way they bring about damaging,
ruinous harm to the Earth and humanity.

Just as the winds sustain the universe by their power, they
also endow men and women with understanding through
their effects and cause us to realize what we ought to do. But
if these winds blow toward the Earth and spread out beneath
it, they can end up in subterranean caves, so to speak. They
will then stir up the Earth because they cannot find a way to
escape from the caves. But wherever they manage to do so,
they will be observed by human beings. And thus these
winds are spread out in the upper elements, as described
above, as well as under the Earth.

But human beings should understand that all these things
have a relationship to the salvation of their souls.

VISION TWO: 25-26
**The lion symbolizes God's role as judge of the world.
The serpent indicates cunning, the lamb patience, the crab
caution. All these symbols indicate that God is a just judge.
Human beings are bound to accept God's judgments, but if
they do not do so, they will be subject to punishments of
both a bodily and spiritual nature, as indicated by the
Psalmist.**

VISION TWO: 27
"Yahweh's right hand is winning, Yahweh's right hand is
wreaking havoc! No, I shall not die, I shall live to recite the
deeds of Yahweh" (Psalm 118:16-17).

This is to be understood in the following way: Out of fear of God and the punishments of hell, we first swerve to the left, and then out of love of God, we climb up to the right, that is to say, to a longing for the blessings of heaven. As we go along this path, we put on the strongest armor because we have separated a good conscience from a bad one. Therefore, the eye, which displays a watery ring lying within the white of the eye, is like a twofold conscience. Thus our vessel has a mirror because the knowledge of evil, which is grasped on the left side, is to a certain extent like a vessel of the knowledge of good, which is grasped on the right side. For the right eye of good conscience looks around on all sides and considers that the desires of the flesh are without value and do not gaze at the light of truth. And whatever frisks about wildly with indecent actions will afterward be submerged in sorrow beneath water and drowned. On this account the right side of good conscience rises up to God and steps on concupiscence and removes everything that is fiery.

And thus the right hand of the Lord achieves these great deeds by its power so that people can know God in faith and can also carry out their daily work in fear of God. This right hand raises me up in my repentance even though I was formerly sunk in the slough of my sins. This is the hand that, after I have atoned for my sins, creates the power of virtue so that I become inflamed with the love of God in such longing that I can never have too much of it. And thus I shall not die in my sins if I rise up in daily repentance. Instead, I shall live forever through the true, pure attitude of remorse I feel toward God. Snatched thus from death, I shall announce the wondrous deed of the Lord out of awe and love of God. For God has not abandoned me to death but has snatched me out of damnation in hell.

VISION TWO: 28

To the left of the image within the sign of the black fire there appears, so to speak, the head of a bear. It indicates that from the northern zone, which is often dangerous for humanity, a major wind emerges, like a bear from the black fire. That is the north wind, which often comes with dreadful periods of stormy weather, for this wind emerges from the black fire. And thus just as an angry bear growls and is bad-tempered, that wind often causes through its grumbling lots of disturbance and uproar and other dangers as a result of the storms it brings.

[The bear has various powers that affect humanity through its auxiliary winds and the subordinate powers of the lamb and the serpent. The main wind and its auxiliary winds express themselves in this way by their natural powers and remain in an orderly relationship to the nearby wind system.]

VISION TWO: 29

All these heads blow through the cosmic wheel and onto the human figure. For the above-mentioned powers of the winds keep the universe in motion by their blowing. They also constrain us human beings to realize that we need these powers so as not to go to our own destruction. When, therefore, one of the winds of the kind mentioned above blows, either through natural causes or a special decree of God, it penetrates without finding resistance into the human body. The soul receives the breeze in its inner chamber, and thus the wind reaches in a natural way the organs of the human body that correspond to its nature. And thus through the blowing of the winds we are either strengthened, as described previously, or we become feeble. For human beings, too, in the changing luck of earthly matters behave, in the sight of divine punishment, like a bear in bodily pain. The bear does not allow us to break out according to our desires. Instead, it forces us to inner meekness, causing us to walk along the right path by exercising patience like a lamb and to avoid evil by behaving as cleverly as a serpent. For through the distress of the body we often attain spiritual treasures through which we come into possession of a higher kingdom.

VISION TWO: 30–31

Everything in the world teaches us that we are bound both body and soul to God and called to salvation in God. Similarly, the seven planets have the task of moderating the power of the sun and the moon and of bridling the powers within the universe.

VISION TWO: 32

[Every cosmic power is directed and curbed by another power, just as a strong man may fall into the arms of an enemy to avoid killing himself or others.] Thus every creature is linked to another (*creatura per creaturam continentur*), and every essence is constrained by another. [In this way the planets are the special auxiliary powers of the sun. Without their power the sun could not exist. They give it its warmth just as the abilities to see, hear, and smell communicate to the brain their warmth and characteristic power.]

And now you have the following interpretation: The sign of the sun sends forth, to be sure, its rays. With some of them it reaches the leopard's head, with others the lion's head, and with still others the wolf's head. But none of the rays reaches the symbol of the bear. The sun is mightiest of the planets. It warms and strengthens the entire universe with its fire, illuminates the globe by offering to the east wind as well as to the south and the west a restraint with the powers of its power so that they do not exceed the limits imposed by God. But the sun does not affect the north wind since this wind is an enemy of the sun and scorns all the brilliance of its light. And thus the sun also scorns that wind, which sends forth no ray from itself. The sun is simply opposed to the north wind in the orbit in which the wind rages fearfully. But the sun itself does not go into those areas because the Devil displays his wickedness in the struggle against God.

The sun sends forth another ray over the symbol of the moon since the sun enkindles the moon with its warmth, just as through our senses and understanding our whole body is guided. The sun sends forth yet another ray over the brain and fastens it to both heels of the above-mentioned figure. For it is the sun which gives power and mass to the human organism from the highest to the lowest part by strengthening especially the brain. As a result, thanks to its insight, the brain directs the other functions of the body and, as the highest part of the human being, it penetrates all the inner organs with the power of its mind, just as the sun illuminates the Earth. If the elements under the sun should be shaken by disasters, the fire of the sun will be darkened, as happens during a solar eclipse. Then it becomes an indication of errors and a proof that our hearts and heads have turned to error. They are no longer able to walk along the right path of the law, but fight each other in many conflicts. The above-described ray touches also the heels of the human being since our heels, like the dominion of the brain over the body, bear up our entire body. In this way the sun moderates with its powers all our limbs, just as it keeps alive the rest of creation.

[In the same detail we are shown the paths of the rays emerging from the fifth planet and reaching the various animal heads. These different statutes are a symbol of the exact order of creation, which can nowhere break out of its appointed (mass). It is the moon that is especially important for the health of human beings.]

As you see, a ray falls from the symbol of the moon over both eyebrows and down to the two ankles of the figure because the moon holds the human body in balance through its natural power. Just as the eyebrows make it possible for the eye to see, and just as the ankle sustains a human being, our limbs are controlled from top to bottom through the power of the moon in accord with God's order. This does not occur with the same perfect power as the sun because the sun influences the human body more completely, while the moon only does so in a feebler and subservient way. And the moon accomplishes its course in heat and cold since it is warm as it waxes but cold as it wanes. By contrast, the sun is constantly

on its path from east to south in the same incandescence
and takes on coldness later when it is in the west. The
moon, too, receives its originally feeble light from the sun,
because the sun kindles with its scorching heat the extinguished circumference of the moon with a spark just as
happens with the light of a lamp. The moon is then at the
height of its orbit. After it has been kindled, it gives off light
and then descends again in its course. Just as the sun
enkindles the moon's circumference and causes it to shine,
the sun also strengthens all life in the firmament or beneath
it. The moon is only the sun's helper. It illuminates the
world below, just as the sun itself illuminates the upper as
well as the lower sphere. The moon, because of the dampness, the clouds beneath it, and the Earth's atmosphere, is
far colder than the sun. But the sun would scorch many
things if it were not opposed by the moon, which tempers
the sun's heat with dampness and chill.

But both of them—sun and moon—then serve humankind in accord with the divine order, bringing to us either
health or illness according to the mixture of atmosphere
and aura. By this is meant that when the sign of the sun
shines its rays toward the human figure from the brain to
the heel, the sign of the moon sends its rays from the
figure's eyebrows to its ankles.

If the moon is waxing, the brain and blood of human beings are also increased. If the moon is waning, the
substances of the brain and blood in human beings also
diminish. If, indeed, the human brain were to remain the
same, we should fall into madness and conduct ourselves
worse than wild beasts. And if the blood in an organism had
always the same substance and showed neither waxing nor
waning, we should waste away in an instant and not live.
When the moon is full, our brain is also full. We are then in
full possession of our senses. But when the moon is new, our
brain becomes emptier so that our sensory powers are injured. If the moon is hot and dry, the brain of some persons
becomes also hot and dry. They suffer from an inflammation

of the brain and a diminished mental capacity so that they no longer have their full mental ability to carry out sensible acts. But on the contrary, if the moon is damp, the brain of such persons becomes damper than usual. Then they feel head pains and are damaged in their minds. But when the moon is completely in balance, we enjoy full health of brain and head. We flourish in full possession of our minds. If there is harmony of external elements, the humors of the organism are at rest, but they are destroyed during a disturbance and disorder of the cosmic powers. For we human beings could not exist without the balance and support of these powers in the world . . . [In a similar way the sun influences all the regions of heaven except for the North, which the sun avoids because darkness and light cannot be in agreement with one another.]

In this manner and way the above-mentioned planets have their order in the universe from the Creator of the world. But you who behold the universe, understand that all external happenings need to be considered with respect to human spiritual processes.

VISION TWO: 33

[The seven planets, which are distributed among the spheres of the light and dark fire as well as in the sphere of the pure ether, signify the seven gifts of the Holy Spirit, which exceed all human reason and which have been effective three times in history: the period before the Law, the time under the Law, and the fullness of time in the gospel.]

VISION TWO: 34

[The individual gifts of the Spirit are associated with cosmic radiation between the planets and the animal heads, and they are explained with respect to the life of grace of human beings. Despite differences in these periods of history, the gifts point to the decisive act of human beings—their work—by which human beings should control their bodies by patience and prudence and direct their lives only toward God.]

VISION TWO: 35

You can see also that the sign of the sun emits rays by which it partly touches the sign of the leopard's head, the sign of the lion's head, and the sign of the wolf's head. But it does not touch at all the sign of the bear's head. This indicates that when the Spirit of Strength sends forth its breath, it touches upon fear of the Lord, God's judgeship, and certain punishments of hell. In this way we are told that we should be on guard against sin out of fear of God. Because of our dread of the judgment, we should refrain from sin, and in view of the most cruel punishments of hell, we ought to give up the habit of sinning.

On the other hand, the bear's head is not disturbed. This is because the Spirit of Strength avoids any anguish of body that does not occur for the sake of God alone. And yet at times the bear may display human habits while at other times it may display animal habits. For when we inflict upon our bodies injuries beyond measure (*sine discretione*), we bring them to a standstill. For our bodies have been so stimulated and at last exhausted by affliction and boredom that we are left in doubt as to our ability to endure this situation any longer. We then begin to roar like wild animals. Therefore, in the afflictions we have brought upon ourselves because of our lack of moderation, we cannot invoke the Spirit of Strength. Nor can we invoke that spirit in the injuries that may be inflicted upon us by others against our will. This is because the balance of discretion is missing from our afflictions. Since we are inconstant by nature, we may one day rise and then we may fall far down below on the next day and be buffetted excessively like creatures in flight. Thus by our own power we cannot attain stability, even though there is power in the same degree of constancy, and this does not vacillate in one way or another. Meanwhile, people who discipline their bodies either out of fear or out of love of God by observing discretion and justice will rejoice within their hearts as if they are at a banquet. For them all afflictions turn out to be less a punishment than a blessing. The Spirit of Strength accomplishes all these things so that those believers might persist in their deeds of justice. For such people are with God. . . .

VISION TWO: 36–38
[In a similar way the other gifts of the Holy Spirit are discussed with respect to their effect upon human beings.]

VISION TWO: 39
[In the circle of bright fire there appear the sixteen major stars described above. The stars extend their power of radiation as far as the district of thin air in much the same way as a person's blood vessels extend down from the head to the feet. And just as the blood vessels strengthen the whole body, these stars strengthen by their power the whole universe. Through the winds near them they control the universe in such a way that the world's fortress is not unduly disturbed. They keep the air in proper balance and in the end are like neighbors to one another, so that each of them helps the others to strengthen the universe.]

VISION TWO: 40–41
[The whole starry sky that warms and illuminates the firmament seeks to make the following statement to humanity: No one and no creature under the sun could exist without this concerned power in the world from on high. And thus that cosmic power is brought by the winds from the stars. From the winds it is carried to the signs in the clouds that look like tongues. And in this way that power is brought to us human beings for the sake of our salvation.]

VISION TWO: 42
This is the way in which that figure is marked and surrounded by the signs. We human beings exist by the power of the elements and the help of other creatures so securely and so steadily that no kind of hostile attack could ever eject us from our favored situation. Yet all of this might also be

understood in a different way.

When the sixteen major stars appear in the orbit of the circle that resembles the light area of fire, this indicates that within God's intact power are found the greatest teachers who have taught, and are still teaching, the perfection of God's ten commandments over the six periods of world history.

VISION TWO: 43–44

[Moreover, the stars and the clouds are an indication of the eight Beatitudes, of our willingness to do atonement, and of our love for God and our neighbors. Strengthened in this way, we human beings may appear before the eyes of the living God. God will heal all our wounds so that we need not blush as we appear up there in the light. People who do such things are already dwelling on the heights of heaven. They behold their king in blissful splendor and conduct their earthly affairs in wisdom by conscious decisions.]

VISION TWO: 45

In this way this figure is impressed and surrounded by those symbols. For believers who loyally follow the traces of the Son of God will be shielded and adorned by the splendor of the blissful powers of virtue. They will be surrounded by these powers in such a way that the powers can snatch them away from the Devil's snares and conduct them happily up to the bliss of heavenly joys, where the believers will rejoice forever.

This is what my servant Isaiah attests when he proclaims: "This man will dwell in the heights, he will find refuge in a citadel built on rock, bread will be given him, he shall not want for water. Your eyes are going to look on a king in his beauty, they will see an immense country" (Isaiah 33:16–17). This is to be understood in the following way: Whoever turns from the left side to the right side and heeds the fact that God dwells in a person who is modest and gentle of heart, will overcome the arrogant Devil by abrading his or her own "I" and saying: "God has illuminated me in both my eyes. By them I behold the splendor of light in the darkness. Through them I can choose the path I am to travel: whether I wish to be sighted or blind by recognizing what guide to call upon by day or by night. If I shroud myself in darkness, I can be a slave to the acts of lust, which I do not dare to do in the light since there I would be seen by all those around me. Accordingly, I shall attain no reward in the darkness, but the punishment of damnation. But I shall reduce the distress of my heart through which I took delight in sins. I shall call upon the living God to lead me on the paths of light and to heal my wound so that I will not have to blush in broad daylight because of these sins. As I do these things, the chains of my prison shall be loosened because I shall keep in bondage my enemy whose promptings I heeded in the darkness. For my enemy has been deceived with regard to me."

People who accomplish such deeds will dwell on the heights of heaven. And its bulwark—the rock that is Christ —will be their sublimity. There they will be given the bread of life whose refreshment no one can disdain because they will rejoice in the sweet savor of true love. And thus they themselves will become a fountain gushing from the water of life. Out of the gift of graces received from the Holy Spirit all their deeds will flow in such abundant holiness that the dove's eyes of the Holy Spirit could gaze at them. For these waters—that is, the believers—are a spring that can never be exhausted or run dry. No one will ever have too much of them. These waters flow out of the East, and none of us can see their height or plumb their depth so long as we are in our bodies, because the waters through which we are reborn to life have been sprinkled by the Holy Ghost. In this way believers will look upon the king or queen in the beauty of his or her bliss. In their consciences the believers will distinguish the land of the living because they will sharply separate themselves in their hearts and bodies from sin. And thus they can ponder on the choice they have to make.

VISION TWO: 46

Finally, do you see how out of the mouth of the above-
described figure (in whose breast the cosmic wheel appears),
a light brighter than the brightest day emerges like a
luminous cocoon? Out of the original source of the true love
in whose knowledge the cosmic wheel rests, there shines
forth an exceedingly precise order over all things. And this
order, which preserves and nourishes everything, comes to
light in a way that is ever new. Through these threads of
light one can measure the symbols of the above-mentioned
spheres, the symbols of the other figures sheltered in the
cosmic wheel as well as the individual symbols of the
human structure, including the figure appearing in the
midst of the wheel. They are measured by a correct and
balanced standard as stated in past and future descriptive
passages. It is love which here properly distinguishes and
moderately adapts the powers of the elements and of the
other lofty adornment associated with the strength and
beauty of the world as well as with the entire physical structure of humanity, which is the ruler of this world, as has
been explained to you in so many ways.

Out of this true love, which is totally divine, there arises
all goodness, which is to be desired above everything else.
Love draws to itself all who desire God, and with this impulse love goes to meet them. Love ponders all merits and
everything human beings do and accomplish for the sake of
God. Out of the mouth of my servant Jeremiah comes the
following statement:

VISION TWO: 47

"I, Yahweh, search to the heart, I probe the loins to give
each man what his conduct and his actions deserve" (Isaiah
17:10).

Here is how this statement is to be understood: Whoever is
in love should not seek through the narrow pass of a false
understanding anyone beside God. We should not tolerate
temptations of fleshly desires for other persons, even though

we may often carry out such desires, just as Adam tried to see how far he could go. Yet we cannot at the same time serve God and the Devil because whatever God loves, the Devil hates, and whatever the Devil is fond of, God does not desire. This is precisely our own situation: The flesh finds delight in what is sinful, and the soul thirsts after justice. Between these two—God and the Devil—the great dispute continues. All the same the deeds we human beings undertake are thus accomplished with great difficulty, just as a serf is forced to serve a master. For the flesh goes toward sin by acquiring mastery over the soul, while the soul accomplishes the work of goodness by overcoming the flesh.

When we live according to our soul's desire, we deny ourselves out of love of God, and become strangers to the lusts of the flesh. This is what the saints and the just have done. Abel acted in the same way when he beheld God. When Abel's blood was shed, the entire Earth sighed and at that moment was declared a widow: Just as a woman without the comfort of her husband remains fixed in her widowhood, the Earth was also robbed of its holy totality by the murder committed by Cain.

And so I, the Lord of the universe, am here to test contrite hearts if they deny their sins. And I put to the test their loins, which have refrained from the enjoyment of lust, and I give to all of them, according to their way of life and whatever is the result of the problems they have overcome, because I have written down for myself all the results of human actions. Those who overcome lust are just, but those who, in contrast, give way to every desire of their appetites, cannot be called just. Yet if such persons should be converted to goodness, their wounds will be washed in the blood of Abel, and the divine hosts of heaven then will look down at the wounds that have been healed and will burst into songs of praise in honor of God.

Let all those who fear and love God open up their hearts devoutly to these words and realize that these words are

proclaimed for the salvation of body and soul, not out of a
human mouth, but by myself, the one "I am."

Third Vision: On Human Nature

VISION THREE: 1

I looked—and behold!—the east wind and the south wind, together with their sidewinds set the firmament in motion with powerful gusts, causing the firmament to rotate around the Earth from east to west. Here in the West the firmament was snatched up by the west wind and the north wind, together with their side winds; it was driven by their blowing and thrown backward from west to east beneath the Earth.

I also saw that from the time the days grew longer, the above-mentioned south wind with its side winds to the south gradually ascended high up in a northerly direction, as if the winds were plunging the firmament downward until the days again grew longer. Then, as the days grew once more shorter, the north wind and its side winds, which hate the brightness of the sun, drove the sun backward. That wind pushed the firmament more and more downward until the south wind began once again to ascend at the beginning of the longer days.

I also saw how in the upper fire there appeared a circle that encircled the whole firmament from east to west. Out of this circle's west side a wind emerged which forced the seven planets to wander against the motion of the firmament. This wind and the other winds did not blow toward the Earth. As previously stated, they simply moderated the course of the planets.

Thereupon, I noticed how the humors in the human organism are distributed and altered by various qualities of the winds and air, as soon as such qualities come into conflict with one another, because the humors themselves take on these same qualities. To each of the upper elements there belongs an air portion corresponding to its quality, and the air portion is rotated by that element through the

strength of the winds. If this were not so, the element could not be moved. Through the help of the sun, moon, and stars, the air portion that correctly directs the world is ejected from each of the elements. But if just once—either as a result of the glow of the sun's orbit or at God's command—any one of these elements should be stirred toward one of the regions of the world, this element would then come into motion as a result of the peculiar movement of that very air. This element then emits from its layer of air a breath, which we call a wind, to the lower layer of air mentioned above. This wind at once mingles with that air because the wind arises in part out of this airy substance and is similar to it to a certain degree.

And thus the wind affects human beings. By such contact the humors of these persons are often altered, according to the kind of wind and air, which are both of the same nature. Sometimes the alteration may weaken the individuals, and at other times it may strengthen them.

And again I saw how one of the winds of the above-named qualities at some spot of the Earth—either because of irregular orbits of the sun and moon or because of God's command—was so stirred up as a result of a suitable mixture of its air portion that the wind sent out its breath to that spot. Thereupon, the wind sweeps across the world. And as the wind preserves with its moderating power all life in the world, this breath gives also to human beings a changing existence because of the state of our humors. If we human beings, whose natural disposition may correspond to that breath of the world, inhale this altered air and exhale it once again so that the soul can receive this breath and carry it even further into the body's interior, then the humors of our organism are altered. Often such humors may bring us, as mentioned previously, either illness or good health.

The humors behave just like a leopard that sometimes roars wildly within us and at other times more calmly. Inside us such humors often crawl forward or backward like a crab, signifying in this way our changeability. They can behave like a stag whose leaping thrusts are a sign of contradiction. They may also reveal themselves at other times to have the predatory nature of a wolf. Thus they can—as stated—sometimes plague us like a stag and at other times like a crab. They may behave like a lion that wishes to show off its unconquerable power or they may resemble a serpent, which can be either gentle or angry. They may pretend to be as mild as a lamb. Often they may growl within us like an angry bear. Frequently they may also display the behavior of a lamb or a serpent, as described above. Thus the system of humors of the human organism is changed in many different ways.

Changed in this way, the humors can often reach the human liver. In this organ there is tested our perception, which comes from the brain and which is held in balance by the powers of the soul. But the brain's moisture affects our liver in such a way that it can be fat and powerful and healthy. On the right side of our body, to be precise, the liver is situated as a great reservoir of heat, just as our right hand, too, is quick in making plans and taking action. On our left side are found the heart and lungs, which strengthen the liver for its task, and derive heat from the liver as if from an oven. Now if the blood vessels of the liver are affected by humors distributed in this way, they will impinge on the vessels of the ear and at times will cause a hearing disturbance because good health or illness in humans is often the result of our ability to hear. Similarly, happy circumstances often bring us joy while we are plunged into sorrow by misfortune.

I also saw how those humors at times try to reach our navel. This is also the site of our inner organs, which it keeps under mild restraint so that they do not disintegrate. The navel also protects the connecting links within these organs, warms them, and keeps a proper mixture in their blood vessels. Under the influence of humors, the navel lets the inner organs come into motion because otherwise human beings could not live. These humors also reach the sex organs, which can at times become playful and often both deceptive and dangerous, and which are held in check by sinews and blood vessels. In the humors there blooms also the gift of reason so that human beings know what they have to do and must not do. Therefore, people take pleasure in sexual activity if it is warmed and strengthened on the right side of the body by the breath of human respiration (*spiramen*) as well as by the liver. In this way we human beings preserve our sense of reverence and discipline by restraining the impulse of the other humors and bringing our actions under control.

At times these humors also affect the vessels of the kidneys and nearby organs leading to the vessels of the spleen, lungs, and heart. All of them are agitated by the inner organs on our left side because the lungs warm them while the liver inflames the right side of the body. The vessels of the brain, heart, lungs, and liver as well as those of our other organs endow our kidneys with strength, while the vessels of the kidneys at this point descend to the calves of the legs and give them power. If the humors then ascend through the vessels of the legs, they are united with the male sex organs or the female's womb, just as our stomach accepts food. These humors then endow those organs with the power to engender children, just as iron is strengthened by a stone. The powerful muscles of the arms and the calves of the leg—as well as the curves of the legs—are full of vessels and humors. And just as the belly contains both our inner organs and food, so also do the calves of the leg contain the vessels of the legs and their humors. These vessels and humors strengthen us with their power, and they sustain us, just as our belly nourishes us.

If we should run vigorously or undertake a rather long march, the tendons under our knees and the smaller vessels of the knees are strained to excess. This affects the blood vessels in the calves of the leg, which are all spread out in a vast network. Thereupon, they return as a result of fatigue to the vessels of the liver, affecting them through the vessels of the brain. And in this way they cause us to become exceedingly tired. In this connection the vessels of the kidneys affect the calf of the left leg more severely than the calf of the right leg because the right calf is strengthened by warmth from the liver. The vessels of the right calf ascend to those of the kidneys and nearby organs and then reach the vessels of the liver. In this connection the liver warms the kidneys in their bile, which is rich in humors. Thereupon the kidneys become dilated and bring quick relief, which they can then cease to do just as rapidly. Since, of course, the liver supplies us its warmth, we become merry and enjoy ourselves.

If, therefore, the humors within us are stirred up in an unnatural way, and if they then at times affect the vessels of the liver, as described above, their moisture is then diminished, the humidity of the breast is affected out of sympathy. Thereupon, the humors plunge into illness those persons who have been dried out in this way. If our phlegm then turns dry and poisonous and all of it rises to the brain, this gives rise to headaches and pain in the eyes. The bone marrow of persons ill in this way becomes parched so that at times epilepsy can affect us when the moon is on the wane.

The moisture of the area around the navel can be expelled by these humors and changed into dryness or toughness so that our flesh becomes ulcerous and bloated, as if we had leprosy (*lepra*), even though this is not the case. In addition, the vessels of the sex organs — abnormally excited by this moisture — affect the other vessels in such a way that the proper moisture in them dries out. Because of insufficient moisture, skin eruptions (*impetigines*) break out.

If the blood vessels of the kidneys are attacked in an abnormal way by the humors mentioned above, they will affect the vessels of the calves of the leg and the rest of the body, as described above. They will dry out the bone marrow and the vessels of the muscles. Thus we have to undergo a lengthy period of suffering and can drag out our lives for quite a while this way. At times the above-mentioned humors can flow excessively through our chest cavity and as a result flood the liver. Afterward, excessive and manifold fits of melancholy may occur so that we may think we are going mad. As soon as these humors ascend to the brain, they will attack it; they will then descend again to the stomach and cause a fever. And in this way people can be sick for a long time. In addition, these humors press against the small vessels of the ears with excessive phlegm and attack the vessels of the lung with the same mucus, so that people affected in this way experience an attack of coughing and are scarcely able to breathe. The same mass of mucus can extend from the vessels of the lung to those of the heart, causing a pain that may spread to the side regions and cause an inflammation of the lung (*pleurisis*). This can affect us just as if we have epilepsy when the moon is on the wane.

Through such flooding the humors stir up the inner organs around the navel as well. They ascend thus to the brain and can often cause it to go mad. If they disturb in this way the vessels in the region of the loins, they will affect the gall bladder so that we may be upset as a result and lapse into a senseless melancholy.

Sometimes these humors also affect through their unsuitable moisture the vessels of the kidneys and increasingly flood the vessels of the calves of the legs and other parts of the body. If, in addition, we should be overwhelmed by too much food and drink, the humors may often cause in us a case of oily form of leprosy, which will cause the muscles to swell. If, on the other hand, the above-mentioned humors are not too moist, but rather flow suitably and properly and moderately through all the articulations of the body, then we shall stay inwardly healthy. We shall thrive in our powers of perception, either for good or for evil.

VISION THREE: 2

And once again I heard a voice from heaven which made the following statement to me:

God has directed for humanity's benefit all of creation, which God has formed both on the heights and in the depths. If we abuse our position to commit evil deeds, God's

*judgment will permit other creatures to punish us. And just
as creatures have to serve our bodily needs, it is also easily
understood that they are intended for the welfare of our
souls.*

As you see, the east wind and the south wind, together
with their sidewinds, stir up the firmament with mighty
gusts and let themselves be blown across the Earth from
east to west. This has the following meaning: When the
breath of fear of the Lord and the breath of God's judgment
affect our inner mind through the other powers of virtue in
the might of holiness, they give rise to our mind in the fair
East and build it up to a fair completion as far as the fair
West. They allow us to remain victors over the things of the
flesh and in this way to persevere. Since, of course, we fear
God, we are afraid that the judgment of God might come
down upon us as a result of our debauchery. But if we begin
what is right and keep to it, we are concerned about an eternal reward. . . .

VISION THREE: 3

[And the same thing occurs with respect to the other
winds: Just as the wind stirs the humors, fear of God stirs
the human conscience — it is a warning to us to stride ahead
on the path of virtue. In this connection we often run into
bodily stress (*tribulatio corporis*) and become weary of good
works. But then, along with the south wind, God's grace
comes close to us in a gracious way and guides our spirit in
the earthly struggle.]

VISION THREE: 4

Now you see how in the upper fire there appears a circle
that encircles the whole firmament. From this circle
emerges a wind that forces the seven planets to take an orbit
contrary to the direction of the firmament. This signifies
that all of salvation (*integritas sanctitatis*) finds rest in the
divine might. It is this might that strengthens in every limb

the inner sense of those who bind themselves to God. And so there emerges from this might a breath (*exspiratio*), and the mysterious gifts of the Holy Spirit touch us human beings, who have begun to become dull as a result of our boredom. As a result, we shall awaken from our dullness and arise vigorously toward justice. Such conduct, of course, is not so simple for a human spirit because the body in which the spirit dwells according to divine decree will not always be obedient. Yet this spirit is often in agreement with the body, which is at the same time its dwelling place, with respect to the desires of the flesh. And so the exhalation of divine gifts frequently offers resistance to our human will.

This wind does not send forth its complaint into the universe like the previously mentioned winds. Rather, it moderates only the course of the planets, as previously described. The above-mentioned breath now emerges from the totality of the Holy One and does not reveal itself like the other powers of virtue which convert the abandoned human being of this world from evil to good. For even if we begin to do good with God's grace, we still do not live perfectly in the fullness of holiness. Only when we have truly attained this perfection, does holiness keep us in the full and perfect gifts of the Holy Spirit, and it no longer allows us to vacillate this way and that way. For just as the pillar of holiness is grounded below on Christ and reaches above up into heaven, so—if Christ preserves us—we in whom the seven gifts of the Holy Spirit have found their resting place can no longer be shaken or overcome by attacks of manifold temptations. This is written down in the book of Habakkuk, according to God's inspiration.

VISION THREE: 5

"Yahweh my Lord is my strength, he makes my feet as light as a doe's, he sets my steps on the heights. For the choirmaster; on stringed instruments" (Habakkuk 3:19). This is to be understood as follows: God, who has created

me, and who has power over me like a ruler, is also my own
power because without God I am unable to do any good
deed and because I have only through God the living spirit
through which I live and am moved, through which I learn
to know all my ways. Therefore, this God and ruler—if I
truly call upon God—guides my steps onto the flight of
divine commands, just as a shepherd is in a hurry when in
quest of a spring. And thus God leads me to that height
established for me in God's commandments. And God over-
throws my earthly desires in the victory of strength so that I
may sing God's praise when I shall attain the heavenly bliss.

For just as the sun is fixed in the firmament of heaven and
has power over the creatures of the Earth so that nothing
can overcome them, so also believers who have their hearts
and minds directed toward God cannot be forgotten by God.
And because the sun is firm in the universe, it truly looks
down on all that is on the Earth, and no one is annoyed at
the sun. The sun is not disturbed by any kind of problem of
this earthly life. Neither is the sun found in the robber's
cave, that is, in the house of craft and envy in which we
humans are so often deceived, nor does it walk in the confusion of inconstancy, after the manner of the fluctuating
lifestyle of those who do not mind their Creator. For they
behave according to their own free will. Therefore, such
persons resemble a crab walking backward and a whirlwind
drying up the plants.

VISION THREE: 6

Therefore, you see how—through different winds and air
as they encounter one another—the humors in human beings are stirred up and altered by taking on the manner of
those same winds. This shows that—through the different
kinds of breath found among the powers of virtue and
through the different longings of human beings—both these
developments are in agreement with one another. And if we
desire the things that are of God, then our reflections will
be moved by God and, skillful in doing good, we shall be

overcome by the dignity of the powers of virtue, which are like holy desires. Each of the upper elements is met by the air which is suitable for it and through which that element is forced by the strength of the wind to turn around. Otherwise, that element could not be moved. In a similar way, our desire shares in the higher virtues and powers because it is in harmony with them. And thus we are strengthened for the destruction of evil as a result of our desire. Otherwise we should never turn to what is good.

[To be sure, all goodness comes purely from God, but the Creator wanted us to decide freely for God in our concrete world. Finally, this is the meaning of the whole complicated association between winds and airs, as well as the meaning of the system of humors in human beings, which is only an indication and incentive for such decisions]. . . Of course, if we dominate the flesh in a reasonable way for God's sake, we are directing our inner spirit upward toward bliss, just as "Wisdom" itself asserts when it states:

VISION THREE: 7

"In the house of the virtuous there is no lack of treasure, the earnings of the wicked are fraught with anxiety" (Proverbs 15:16). This means that just as the sun at noon ascends to its apex and burns there in full heat, so also does the house stand like the mind of the just who carry out all their deeds in this way under the judgment of God. They turn out to be in fullness and wealth because they are progressing from virtue to virtue and are not hindered, just as the sun is not restrained in its ascent and suffers no loss of warmth in its orbit. For are we not all the more inflamed in our blissful effort because formerly we burned for what was good? We dwell already on those lofty places where we remain in full rapture and the greatest longing, where we cannot be satisfied with its sweetness. Our power exceeds the firmament and extends to the bottom of the abyss because humanity in the midst of creation (*homo cum creatura*) is exceedingly strong. And the whole world is at our service.

Moreover, the Earth is at times shaken by the motion of the

firmament and rent by quakes. And the firmament serves the Earth by flooding it and preserving it with the rain so that the Earth can splendidly produce its fruits as a result of the rain and dew. But blissful human beings are drawn to all that is earthly. Unshakable and without anxiety, we humans ascend the highest peak, and in this way we achieve good deeds in the joy of eternal life. But in the achievements of those who remain without awe in bad and perverse conduct there lies indeed a shock. For such people vacillate and stagger. They do not turn to the day, neither do they hope for the light of eternity. Instead, they will swallow the husks of swine. In this food they will not find life since such people will not renounce the desires of the flesh.

VISION THREE: 8

You also note how every one of the winds of the above-mentioned quality is stirred up, either through the different orbits of the sun and moon or through God's verdict. . . . [Here, too, the cosmic powers and the system of humors point out ways which grace uses in the moral household of the human soul as well as how human longing, conversely, examines all things on the basis of utility.]

In this way longing affects the human heart. If we humans, whose natural quality corresponds to that cosmic complaint, draw into ourselves and expel again air transformed in this way so that our soul can receive it in order to bring it farther within our body, the humors in our organism will also be changed and will bring to our body—as mentioned above—either illness or good health. This occurs when we, whose goodwill is in agreement with that breath, give up our longing for evil and oppose it. And because the soul carries this action out mysteriously within itself, the tumultuous thoughts cause a flooding and transformations within us so that they promise us at times happiness and at other times what is distasteful.

VISION THREE: 9

Humors arise savagely within us at times like a leopard. Then they become moderate again like a crab that sometimes crawls forward and at other times backward. And thus they indicate a multifold alteration. They also display their spirit of contradiction in the leaping and stamping of the stag. For even when we are permeated by the fear of God, there still arise within us thoughts that seek too much diversion in vain things. With the crab they warn us to stride forward carefully, and then they plunge us once again into doubt. With the stag they lull us into safety and then cause us once again to become vacillating. Such thoughts attack us sometimes like a ravenous wolf and at other times like a crab or a stag. Sometimes like a wolf, they depict to us the pains of hell. At other times, full of duplicity, they promise that we can be saved through the stag, that is, through faith as well as through the crab, that is, through trust, without need of other works of justice. And these thoughts plunge us at times once again into despair. Sometimes they pretend to us that our strength does not leave us any more than a lion can lose its strength. Like a serpent, they at times show themselves to be gentle and at other times to be angry in order to dissemble again with the mildness of a lamb when they depict to us God's judgment and cause us to believe that such a fate is not to be feared. Like the cunning, crawling serpent, our thoughts pretend that we can escape the judgment through cleverness, and they encourage us to fear nothing with the patience of a lamb, just as if we were not entangled in sins. Now we growl and grumble like an angry bear. Again our thoughts, as previously mentioned, may be like those of a lamb or a snake. With the bear our thoughts growl that we have to undergo bodily toil for God's sake; with a lamb's patience and the cleverness of a serpent such thoughts cause us to believe that we are punished and cleansed of our sins, where they still abandon us, full of contradiction, in our uncertainty.

In this way the humors often change within us because our thoughts, which are changing within themselves as a result of such attacks and also in other ways, at times lull us into confidence and then plunge us again into confusion, often guiding us upward into the proper spirit of reverence.

These changing thoughts take up their abode in the liver, the organ in which human perception is tested. Through the power of the soul, the right degree of perception emerges from the brain. The brain is refreshed by its own moisture so that it is fat, strong, and healthy. This means that our thoughts are often directed to the liver, that is, to the power of justice in which the just are active in a creative way with the power of perception. For the powers of the soul still point to the knowledge of good and evil, which because of this justice encloses life for believers, just as the Son of God enclosed within his heart the sinners and publicans to whom he later gave so much power by the inspiration of the Holy Spirit.

VISION THREE: 10

The liver dominates the right side of the human body, and for this reason there is great warmth there. Thus our right side is rapid and acts with speed. On the left side are found the heart and lungs, an arrangement that enables this side to endure burdens. Our heart and lungs are nourished by the liver with warmth as if by an oven.

This means that on the right side, that is, when the salvation of good and just people is progressing favorably, justice is active through the Holy Spirit so that such people rise up in victory to God and accomplish good deeds. But on the left side such people avoid evil, acknowledge God with upright hearts, and ardently wish the power of justice to establish what they have done. If the blood vessels of the liver are affected and moved by those humors, they will shatter also the small vessels of the ear and upset our hearing. This is perhaps because happiness over a joyful experience may excessively alter our hearing or because a disappointment may plunge our hearing into a deep sorrow. In this way it should be indicated that the self-reliant justice evoked by good thoughts guides us away from hearing evil things and points the way to what is good. We shall then be overcome both by what is holy and what is harmful, and we shall never find an equilibrium between good and evil. A good conscience is dumb unless it listens to what is good because a good sense of hearing accepts the things a good conscience knows. Much industry is needed in order to absorb and communicate what our hearing has received through a good conscience. Those who have managed to achieve all of this are happy to remain like someone who has placed a treasure in a chest. Just as they know both good and evil, they hide what is good in the secret chamber of their heart and keep evil away.

VISION THREE: 11

"Free your neck from its fetters, captive daughter of Zion. Yes, Yahweh says this: You were sold for nothing and you will be redeemed without money" (Isaiah 52:2-3). This statement has the following meaning: Because of your repentance you should consider as nothing the fetters of your earlier captivity and transgression, O human being, you who were scorned among the children of the highest peace in Paradise, you who after the loss of Paradise were subject to so many misfortunes. Therefore, the Ruler of the universe speaks to you who are now smothered in sins. Thus you have been redeemed without money, just as God promised pain to the first woman because she had to renounce Paradise for her transgression against God's commandment and for losing in this way her own name—the name of daughter of Zion. In addition, you have been redeemed without money and its earthly desire, just as the Redeemer rose from death in his virgin nature. Reborn in us through the spirit and water, he established life on a new basis and thus brought us back to the place of our heritage. He who will remain justified in his birth will not draw back from the height of Zion.

Believers, then, should on this account direct their thoughts to God. They should put aside their sins and leave behind them all that is evil. They should sigh in their longing for what is heavenly by requesting God's help for their good deeds. If they persist in such prayers, like the blind beggar on the highway, God's favor will look down on them. If God sees how they are striving for the light and rising up out of the darkness, God will help them in all things and inspire them to just and holy deeds. Such people have turned away from evil and rejoice in doing what is good and holy. They already taste the sweetness of such things because they will never turn away from their God, but will instead avoid the cunning of the serpent.

VISION THREE: 12

You also note how at times the humors aim at the human navel, which is in charge of our inner organs because it dominates them gently so that they do not disintegrate. The navel, in addition, preserves their alignment and warmth as well as our blood vessels in their proper blend. It is often subject to violent movements because without them we humans could not live.

This is also the way it is with believers. As soon as we exclude what is bad from our hearing, we shall keep close together the navel of many different kinds of desires through our good thoughts. In this way we shall progress on the path of true bliss because listening to what is evil often plunges us into the turmoil of evil.

Humors also often reach the human sex organs, which in their power (as if in some kind of game) are seductive and dangerous. These organs are held in place by sinews and the other veins. Nevertheless, reason comes into flower in these organs, too, so that we can know what to do and what to leave off. On this account we enjoy what we do. On the right side of our body we are warmed and strongly sustained by our breathing.

Thus we gather up our free will and all our discipline so that we can master the attacks of the other humors and complete our action in a disciplined way. We gird about our loins in which lust dwells. In this way we strengthen ourselves through the power of justice for the salvation of our souls, and thus we accomplish all things reverently and honorably.

At times those humors affect also the vessels of the kidneys and inner organs, which then extend to the veins of the spleen, lungs and heart. All these organs, along with the inner organs, are found on the left side of the body. For the lungs warm them while, of course, the liver inflames the right side. And so we sustain our kidneys by having correct thoughts, for the kidneys quite often affect the heart with their desire and incite us to evil. This is because the folly of the flesh affects the kidneys. And this is the conduct of those who enter upon the path of justice.

VISION THREE: 13

The veins of the brain, heart, lungs, and liver as well as the rest of our organs strengthen our kidneys. The vessels of the kidneys, in turn, flow down to strengthen them and ascend once more through the vessels of the legs in order to link up with the male sex organs or the woman's womb, just as the stomach brings together our foods. These vessels endow the sex organs with the power to beget children, just as a stone sharpens iron. When we, then, suppress carnal desires out of a sense of shame and have thus subdued the kidneys, we cleanse the kidneys through our inherent power of discernment, which is full of chastity. We gird ourselves about with constant justice and self-discipline, and we address ourselves to the mastery of what was formerly without restraint in us. We endow this mastery henceforth with a firm constancy so that we are no longer plunged into folly. As we strive toward God in self-mastery, we strengthen ourselves from that time forward as men or women. Relying on the many powers of virtue, we bring to the fore a heritage of holiness by walking along the just path of reverent discipline.

The muscles of the arms and legs as well as those of the thighs are full of vessels and moisture. Just as the abdomen contains the inner organs and food, the muscles of the arms

and legs contain vessels and humors, and they strengthen
us with their power and keep us upright, just as the belly
nourishes us. But self-mastery is an accumulation of the
strengths and preserving powers of justice. Surrounded by
the constant sighing of good thoughts, self-mastery nourishes the soul in holiness by gathering up the inner aspect of
the soul for its fulfillment and by holding onto the perfection of salvation. And thus our self-mastery nourishes our
whole person—body and soul—in holiness.

VISION THREE: 14

When we run swiftly or undertake a difficult hike, the
sinews beneath the knees and the small veins of the knees
are excessively enlarged. They then affect countless vessels
in the calves of the legs to which they are linked as if by a
network, and they return to the vessels of the liver in the
form of weariness. In addition, those sinews and veins affect the brain vessels and in this way cause the whole body
to become tired.

This is what happens when we try to alter in an ex-
travagant way the proper way of virtue. The excess of this
attitude misdirects us into an untenable situation and leads
our moderation into an exaggerated display of conscience.
As a result of excessive zeal, we shall deny ourselves even
things that are permitted. In the end we shall develop a feeling of disgust for other virtues. By fondly believing that we
are returning to justice and brimming over with scruples,
we shall prepare ourselves for the pitfall of weariness. This
is because we have abandoned our gentleness of spirit and
prudence. Finally, we may doubt whether we can ever exercise self-restraint and in this way we shall fall into the snare
of despair.

The vessels of the kidneys affect more of the left leg than the
right leg because the right leg derives its power from the warmth
of the liver. And thus the attitude of lust is all the more increased through excessive and immoderate abstemiousness. Indeed,
it is not decreased because such abstemiousness has occurred

neither in search of God nor for God's sake. For self-mastery, which proceeds with discretion, is strengthened through the virtuous power of a proper equilibrium . . . [The same thing occurs for the vessels of the right side of the body.] And since it is the liver which gives us warmth, we shall rejoice and be merry. Because we shall overcome the attitude of lust through self-mastery, which can only be authentic in God, we shall reflect whether we can ever go completely astray. But justice burns away in the fire of the Holy Spirit all lust, which wallows in filth, and justice will then lead our lust into nothingness. And thus all evil is dissipated and embittered, even if it formerly was a source of enjoyment, no matter how brief that enjoyment might have been. For as sinners, when we are justified, we can find our reward only in joy.

VISION THREE: 15

If the humors of the organism become unnaturally excited and if they then affect the vessels of the liver, the moistness of these vessels as well as those of the breast will be decreased. And human beings who become dried out in this way will undergo illness. Their phlegm will become parched and poisoned; it thus will ascend to the brain and cause headaches and eye pains; it will consume the bone marrow and give rise to occasional epileptic seizures when the moon is on the wane.

For if our thoughts grow opinionated and obdurate and enter in this way onto empty byways, we shall oppress justice as a result. It is justice which, when sprinkled by the dew of the Holy Spirit, ought to germinate good works through holiness. If our thoughts follow this course, then the other powers of virtue will be weakened and dessicated within us. Such thoughts will alter our conscience, which to some degree is both the beginning and the end of our striving as well as our power to do justice. This power, which formerly was so strong within us, is turned by our despair into a kind of dizziness. For the light of truth, which once illuminated us, has become feeble.

In addition, the moisture within the navel is dispersed and toughened by these humors. As a result, the muscular system becomes ulcerous and bloated. Such persons look like lepers, even though they do not have the disease. Therefore, the vessels of the sex organs become wrongly excited and stir up other organs in a similar manner so that the proper moistness within the human organism dries up. And thus pustules develop in the remaining humors. The *moistness* of self-mastery, which should have destroyed lust in the navel, is dissipated as a result of this obdurate, hard, and wrong way of thinking and is no longer sprinkled by the Holy Spirit. But when we abandon the Spirit, our sins will fester in evil habits and become obvious in all things — like leprosy with its foul odor. In addition, our loins will no longer be girt by chastity but excited by this way of thinking so that the vitality of honorable deeds will dry up within us. Bad example will be exalted in a foul manner, as Hosea foretold in the Holy Spirit in these words:

VISION THREE: 16

"I have seen horrors in Bethel, that is where Ephraim plays the whore" (Hosea 6:10). This is to be understood in the following way: In lewd places these people lie, placid and well-satisfied in their sins. And yet God must look down on them with his watchful heart: But I, who search through all the hidden places, have noted things that are unspeakably detestable — the degradation of impurity and lewdness in which they wallow, just as a pig is wont to do in its filth. Those who should have sought purity and should have gazed at it and embraced it, have now become contemptible and weak. For impurity both unnerves human beings and makes them go out of their minds. As a result, they regard neither the things of this world in perfect honorableness nor the things of God. This is because the fire of the flesh, in agreement with their will, suggests arrogance to them along with vainglory and all the evil we imbibe in this atmosphere.

VISION THREE: 17

The vessels of the kidneys of such persons become excessively excited and affected by the above-mentioned humors. They then disturb the other vessels belonging to the calves of the legs and the rest of the organism. They also dry up the bone marrow and the vessels in the attacked muscular system. And thus these people undergo a lengthy illness and can barely remain alive for a long time in a weakened condition.

And if such people forget to keep their navels and loins in check and if they at the same time let their thoughts wander in search of violence through idle fields, they will show scorn for the power of the virtues, which are a part of temperance. Similarly, the virtue of temperance itself should be preserved quietly and systematically (*discrete et ordinate*) because it contains chastity. As a result, the other attitudes of such individuals — since they lack an infusion of heavenly dew — will be turned into dryness and cause their souls to waste away until they once again find their way back to the vital source of the virtues (*ad vigorem virtutum*).

VISION THREE: 18

At times the above-mentioned humors in our chest overflow in excessive humidity and moisten our liver. For this reason countless and most varied thoughts arise within us so that we then behave either all too cleverly or all too foolishly. From this point the same humors ascend to our brain and infect it. They also descend into the stomach, where a fever arises. And in this way we undergo a rather lengthy illness.

The following point is thus illustrated: If the various kinds of thoughts we have are crudely suppressed by our self-indulgence, they will spread irresponsibility and indecent vanity. Then in their folly they will be inclined to smother justice within us. And thus it occurs that these thoughts, by rising up within us in this way, may now elevate us in wisdom, and again they may soon bring us

down in foolishness. These thoughts confuse our conscience and cause us to become greedy so that our soul is
ensnared by these evils as if by a constant sleepiness and it
may often undergo a dangerous depression. All the time the
humors affect the veins of the ears with an excess of
phlegm. With the same humor they also infect the vessels
of the lungs in such a way that we are overcome by
coughing fits and can scarcely breathe. The excess phlegm
moves from the lung vessels to those of the heart where it
causes pain. The pain there goes into our side and causes a
lung inflammation. As a result, we can be shaken to such an
extent that it seems as if we are experiencing epileptic fits
when the moon is on the wane.

All of this has the following meaning: Our contradictory
thoughts give rise to such an uproar that they will confuse
the ability of our soul to listen. As a result, we shall neither
be able to recognize what is good nor maintain it. Instead,
we may develop an aversion to goodness, as in a fit of
coughing. Such thoughts may confuse our heart to the point
of foolishness so that we shall have not a quiet moment of
productive activity left in our soul. Instead, we shall go
along—swaying now this way, now that way—like someone condemned to death. For the light of probity will be
darkened within us. Because of excess fluids, the inner
organs around the navel will be stirred up. And thus these
contradictory thoughts will ascend to our brain and often
cause us to go mad. They will, in addition, disturb the vessels
of the loins and stir up black bile there. And we shall be
perplexed by all these things. We shall become sad, that is, sad
beyond measure (*sine discretione*) because our thoughts,
which have been confused by an indecent infusion, will turn
our desires into lust. We shall also rend our conscience so that
we become besmirched by evil deeds. These thoughts will
leave our conscience in a poisoned state and completely
unstable in lewdness. But our melancholy will make us numb
and gloomy because we cannot accomplish the lust of the
flesh. At times these humors will affect also the vessels of the

kidneys with an unusual moisture. Irritated in this way, these vessels will infect our leg vessels and the other veins of the body to an unusual degree. Thereupon, we shall be flooded by any excess amounts of food and drink. As a result, we shall experience an outbreak of fatty eruption and our flesh will swell up immensely.

The significance of all these symptoms is as follows: If our thoughts at times excite in us any impure and obscene lust and induce us to commit disgraceful acts of weakness, they will drive out of us any power of the moderation which ought to restrain the flesh. And they will bring our self-indulgence to gluttony, which once again will enkindle the flames of passion. As a result, our thoughts will infect us with the idleness of sins, as if with leprosy. We shall then make hardly any resistance to the lusts of the flesh. For all who do not themselves restrain the flesh in proper moderation but rather nourish it through vice and desire will gather to themselves the obesity of sin and be puffed up with filth in God's eyes.

VISION THREE: 19

If the above-mentioned humors are neither excessively dry nor excessively wet but rather flow through our limbs in the correct amount and the proper way, we shall remain hale and hearty in our knowledge of good and evil. If our thoughts are neither too fickle and fleeting nor too obdurate and sluggish but rather harmonize well in the sight of humanity and God and in the honorableness of morality, these thoughts will cause us to assume peaceful habits in a physical sense and to become well-grounded in knowledge. Then we shall not care for the world's applause nor shall we be inclined to the right or the left. Instead, with the help of most of the virtues, we shall sigh for heavenly joys, as is written in the Song of Songs: "How beautiful are your feet in their sandals, O prince's daughter!" (Song of Songs 7:12). This is to be understood as follows: O you who rejoice in your heart and long for God in the good deeds through which you have hope of eternal life, this attitude is reflected in your joy, which is like the sunrise. You display to all other people a wondrously beautiful mode of life patterned after the way of the Son of God. You do so when you accept the mortification of the flesh. For by putting on your sandals you cover up to some degree the nakedness of your sins. This is because you love God with all your heart more than you do yourself. And at this point your soul is called a prince's daughter—the daughter of the One who is called "Prince of Peace." He, too, has overcome the ancient serpent and freed his people and washed away with his blood all enmity between God and humanity. The angels announced peace to humanity at the Incarnation of the Son of God. The Incarnation was the cause of sheer joy since God had bound God to Earth in such a way that human beings could behold God in human form, while the angels could gaze on God perfectly as both human and God.

Therefore, let those who fear and love God open up their hearts in all reverence to these words. Let them know that these words are announced for the salvation of their bodies and souls—not by a human voice but rather by myself, the One who am.

Fourth Vision: On the Articulation of the Body

VISION FOUR: 1

And I saw the firmament with its different images from its highest point to the summit of the Earth, and the firmament had a density similar to that of the Earth at its diameter. I also saw how the firmament's upper fire was convulsed from time to time and gave off scales, so to speak, like embers, which were directed at the Earth. These scales, in turn brought burns and wounds to humans and animals as well as to the fruits of the Earth. In addition, I saw a certain layer of fog falling out of the fiery area toward Earth. This fog shriveled the Earth's greening power and caused the moisture of the arable land to dry up. But the pure ether resisted those scales as well as the fog so that they did not cause excessive damage to the above-mentioned creatures.

I saw further how from the area of the sheer white clear air a layer of fog spread over the Earth, affecting humans and beasts with a dreadful plague so that many of them suffered a variety of illnesses while others died. The layer of watery air opposed this poisonous fog by holding it in check. As a result, the fog did not cause excessive harm to the creatures.

And, finally, I saw how moisture from the gentle layer of air flowed over the Earth. This air revived the Earth's greening power and caused all fruits to put forth seeds and become fertile. In the upper area, the moisture carried along certain layers of clouds that lent support to all the other layers. These layers, in turn, were strengthened by the previously mentioned layers. Right in the layer of air I also beheld a cloud of pure brightness, which was connected to it and was linked at both ends, so to speak, to the other clouds of the firmament. The cloud's center was curved like a bow and reached to the above-mentioned layer of air.

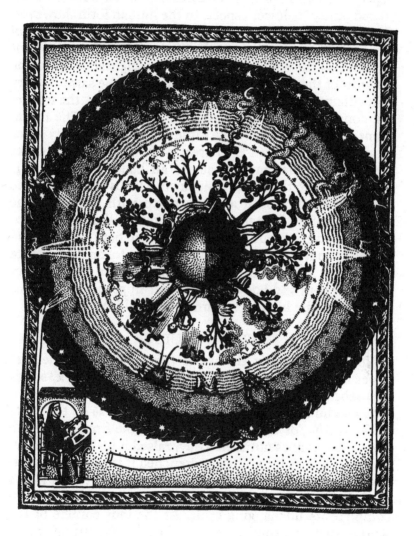

VISION FOUR: 2

God, who has created all things, has arranged the higher aspect of creation in such a way that God could not hold onto and purify its lower aspect. In the human form, however, God wanted also to relate all these signs to the salvation of the soul. Thus you see how the firmament with its different images has the same density from its highest point to the summit of the Earth, just as the Earth has the same density at its diameter. In this way, O men and women, the following concept is held up to you and announced: The firmament and the Earth have the same density. The empty space of air above the Earth is as great with respect to the upper resistance as the empty space of air beneath the Earth is with respect to the lower resistance. This is also true of the air space to the south and the north with respect to the resistance of the firmament. This should tell us that our inner spirit so announces our power in both earthly and heavenly matters that even our body can foster an intimate association in its creative power over these matters. For wherever soul and body live together in proper agreement, they attain the highest reward in mutual joy.

VISION FOUR: 3

Now you see how the upper fire on the firmament at times comes into motion and gives off, so to speak, scales like ashes toward the Earth. The scales inflict burns and injuries on human beings and animals as well as on the fruits of the Earth. For God has strengthened the firmament with fire so that it does not melt away; raised it up into the ether so that it comes into motion; drenched it in water so that it does not dry out; illuminated it with stars so that it glows brightly; and kept it in place with the winds so that it can complete its unchanging orbit. At the four corners of the world—east and south, west and north—the firmament is driven into orbit by the winds. But inasmuch as the luminous layer of fire is overcome by the moisture of the upper water and as a result turns away from its normal course, that same layer of fire sends forth those glowing scales as an angry judgment, as described above. This means that God's power holds the human mind under its dominion. When that power is challenged to a proper judgment, it avenges the misdeeds of men and women so that they become confused and scattered. For they no longer display human but bestial ways and cannot accomplish any fruits of good deeds.

VISION FOUR: 4

At times, out of the black fire a layer of fog sinks down toward the Earth, drying up everything green on the Earth and destroying the moisture of the farms. When, according to God's will, heat and cold are stirred up within this fiery layer, as stated above, a fog descends. Because of the dangerous heat it becomes smoky, but then because of the destructive cold it becomes damp. It is here for the punishment of sinners. Enkindled by the south wind, the black fire glows. From the north wind it receives hail because of the great cold. Both these phenomena are moderated by the east wind. The west wind swirls around within the watery air while the black fire is stirred up and causes a dangerous flooding. This is an indication that the black fire, when tested in a juridical way, directs other punishments at fleshly desires, plunges them contemptuously down into dryness, and totally consumes their fat fertility. Then God brings everything opposed to the divine will into the void.

VISION FOUR: 5-6

[Thus the other spheres also cause ruin to us earthlings and affect our spiritual existence insofar as we do not maintain a certain discretion. For discretion alone moderates everything needed for our bodily existence as well as for the life of the soul. And thus the watery layer of air opposes the deadly fog and moderates it so that disaster beyond measure is not visited upon us creatures.]

VISION FOUR: 7

From the gentle layer of air, moisture effervesces over the Earth. This awakens the Earth's greenness and causes all fruits to appear through germination, and it also bears aloft certain clouds containing all that is superior, just as they, in turn, are strengthened from on high. The whole process is based on the power by which this gentle air emits snow. The snow is, so to speak, scattered in flight over the Earth when it becomes cold as a result of the low position of the sun. This is because the drops of moisture from the upper cold are turned into snow. In the warmth of the rising sun, this air causes to descend upon the Earth a dew that the Earth exudes like honey in a comb. And this honey at times melts away in the east wind's gentleness to a rain that brings refreshment. This air also restrains dangers threatening from on high and acts like a defensive shield for the Earth. Indeed, it does so quite the way a shield protects a man from fierce blows. Out of the exceedingly mild and moderate glow of the sun this air sends down onto the Earth the dew of the blessing Jacob gave his son. At the same time, the air gives off smoke from the water's surge as well as the dampness of the dew—but this does not cause any damage. Instead, this air gently caresses all the Earth's fertility and purifies it of the dirty odor by which it has been defiled as a result of one of the violent storms.

VISION FOUR: 8

That layer bears up and sustains above itself the clouds described above, which at times are brightly luminous and at other times overshadowed. The clouds themselves have breasts, so to speak, from which they pour rain down upon the Earth, just as milk is suckled from a breast. From time to time the clouds stretch themselves upward and obtain power from the different elements. The clouds are strengthened by the fire, raised up by the ether, drenched by the waters, and contracted by the cold so as not to pour down from their breasts too much rainwater. These clouds signify that mirrorlike layer which people call the sky. For we behold the spaces set aside for the sun, moon, and stars through the clouds to some degree as in a mirror. As a result, we now think we have seen the very forms of the sun, moon, and stars. But this is not at all the case, since the clouds can perform this task only as a mirror image of the constellations and can only flow up to them in the same way as a mirror image is seen in reverse in water.

This comparison has the following meaning: Whenever we believers simply go about our work in life, our thoughts are turned in proper longing toward what is useful and fruitful. And so our thinking affects our greening power to bring forth many fruits of holiness. And our thinking lifts up our minds toward heavenly things so that we turn our desires upward, and in this way our thinking is strengthened. When we strive in proper longing for the fruits of good works, we despise earthly concerns and become so attached to things of a divine nature that we prove ourselves to be totally and utterly constant, just as if we were not human.

VISION FOUR: 9

In that layer of air you now perceive a certain cloud that has a bright power of illumination. Both edges of the cloud are as if attached at times to other clouds in the firmament. Its middle section is bent like a bow and extended upward toward this layer of air. For in these cloud formations that push that air upward and keep it there, yet another cloud is driven. This second cloud, which is milk-colored, sustains that air the way a pillar holds up a house. And thus the minds of certain people are so formed in the prescribed order of correct desire that those persons may expect a reward for what they do in both earthly and heavenly affairs in such a way as to please the highest Judge. And even though at times the perfection of their attitude may experience the ambiguity of the flesh by which they are twisted (so to speak), they still persist in their just desire, a situation described in the words of my servant Job:

VISION FOUR: 10

"Just men grow more settled in their ways, those whose hands are clean add strength to strength" (Job 17:9). This has the following meaning: Those who love justice keep to the right path under the threat of God's power. And those who keep themselves free of defilement will attain holiness through good works by keeping away from evil and turning toward everything pleasing to God. And thus they will attain life without end. The just embrace wisdom, and wisdom is in the midst of that form of reason that knows what is living and what is dead and thus learns the right path. But the blindness of heart that arises out of desire of the flesh overshadows pure knowledge. For, because of its willfulness in doing only what it pleases, this blindness of heart goes astray. Thus it will continue in its bewilderment until it perceives its own wounds and no longer has pleasure in what it is doing, and until it considers where it might be. For it has turned aside from God.

VISION FOUR: 11

Because of such considerations humanity should regard almighty God as a seal and recognize all the divine wonders and symbols. Like the firmament, we should strengthen our house so that we are not turned away from God because of any shocks due to fear or love. And thus God has established the firmament as the footstool of the divine throne. The firmament follows a circular orbit as a metaphor of God's might, which has neither beginning nor end, and no one can tell where the circular wheel begins or ends. God's throne is, indeed, the divine eternity in which God alone abides, and all living creatures are, so to speak, sparks from the radiation of God's brilliance, and these sparks emerge from God like the rays of the sun. And how would God be known as life if not through the fact that the realm of the living, which glorifies and praises God also emerges from God? On this account God has established the living, burning sparks as a sign of the brilliance of God's renown. All creatures should see that God has neither beginning nor end, and for this reason they will never have enough of looking at God. Thus they will behold God eagerly and without satiety, and their eagerness will never slacken. How would the One who alone is eternal be known if not so regarded by the angels? But if God did not give off those sparks, how would the divine glory become fully visible? And how would God be known as the Eternal One if brilliance did not emerge from God? For there is no creature without some kind of radiance —whether it be greenness, seeds, buds, or another kind of beauty. Otherwise, it would not be a creature at all. But if God did not have the power to make all things, where would God's creative power be?

VISION FOUR: 12

God delineated all the beauty in the works of divine omnipotence in the first angel. God adorned him like the starry heavens—with all the stars and with the beauty of the greening of every kind of sparkling rock. And God called him Lucifer because that angel bore the light from the One who alone is eternal.

For I, who am at my ease in all the corners of the world, have revealed my works in the east and south and west. But I left empty the fourth corner in the north; neither sun nor moon shed any radiance there. Therefore, hell is found in that region, which is outside the world's framework. Hell has neither a roof above nor a foundation below. It is in a place where much darkness reigns and which also serves all the lights of my fame. For how could what is light be known except through darkness? And how could we know about darkness except through the radiant brilliance of my bright servants? If this were not so, my might would not be perfect, and all my wondrous deeds could not be told.

But in this way my might is complete and fulfilled, and there is no lack of my wondrous deeds. Now if luminosity is without darkness, it is called pure light. The light is a living eye, but blindness is at work in the darkness. Through both these possibilities the eye is known as to whether it is good or bad. In the light we behold God's works, and in the darkness God's absence, which no longer affects the light — that is to say, among all those who out of arrogance do not wish to trust God's concern.

VISION FOUR: 13

The numberless cluster of sparks clinging to the first lost angel was reflected in the splendor of his total beauty in such a way as to fill the world with light. But that angel, who should have felt an obligation to serve with his great beauty, the Deity, turned away from God's love and toward the darkness as he rose up and said to himself: "How splendid would it be if I could act according to my own will and accomplish the works I see only God accomplishing." All of the angel's followers cried out in agreement: "Indeed, we wish to place our master's throne on the north side in opposition to the Most High!" And so they resolved to establish forever strife and conflict with the servants of God. Their master was to have the same power and majesty as the Most High of beings. At once, the eyes of the sole Eternal One were on fire. The Divinity flared up like a huge cloud of smoke and along with the angelic host swooped down upon the first transgressor and his followers. And God's angels cried out loudly in anger: "What kind of arrogance would make itself like God our creator, who rules all things in the divine power! You who owe your very existence to God's command are rushing to your own destruction out of an illusion that you can be like God!" And at once that angel fell, together with his followers, down into the place of darkness described above. Like a lump of lead he fell. Yet he still thought he could fight against God, whose works he could not behold shining in the darkness.

VISION FOUR: 14

Since then, God has fought an open battle against that angel. The Deity has placed upon the divine garment the expectation that has been with God from the very beginning through the divine providence. Here is where Satan, who fled from God, could not fully comprehend the Deity. And this is how things will remain until the conflict with Satan is fought to the very end. Then we shall behold Satan in the sorrowful despair of complete confusion. For he will be totally confused by the same just Judge at the end of time.

By the primeval decree that has been with God from all eternity, the Deity has ordained how the divine work is to be accomplished. God formed the human species out of the vile dirt. God accomplished this work, just as the Deity ordained the human form before there was time, and just as the human heart has reason within itself and sets in order every resounding word before it becomes audible. This is what God did in the divine Word, for God accomplished everything. The Word — that is to say, the Son — was within the Father, just as the heart remains hidden within a human being.

And God formed humanity according to the divine image and likeness. God already had it in mind that this very form should enclose the holy Godhead. For the same reason God delineated all of creation in the human species, just as the whole world emerged from the divine Word.

Like the curvature of a revolving wheel, the top of the human head is the brain against which there leans a ladder with various stages of ascent — the eyes for seeing, the ears for hearing, the nose for smelling, the mouth for speaking. Through these sense organs we humans gaze out at all the creatures. We know them for what they are, distinguish them, separate them, and give them names. For God has formed us and enlivened us with the living breath of the soul. The Divinity has provided us with flesh and blood, filled us out and strengthened us with bones, just as the Earth is strengthened with rock. For just as the Earth could not exist without rock, we humans could not exist without our bone structure.

The firmament could not have the sun, the moon, and the stars unless the places where they accomplish their orbits had been firmly established. For such heavenly bodies could not exist without their predetermined locations in space. Therefore, all these arrangements in space are ordained according to a definite standard, so that the curvature of the wheel of our world may assume its proper orbit in the firmament. And thus, all this order is indicated by our human form, even though we do not have that same power of order and perfection as the world above us.

VISION FOUR: 15

The crown of the human head indicates the beginning of the soul's action, which orders and plans all human deeds in accord with prudent reason. The soul itself is there like a summit which decides on everything in the human organism required and needed by the body. And the soul achieves this by four stages of ascent and descent—seeing, hearing, smelling, and tasting. Through these senses the soul understands creatures and has contact with them. Through them it keeps its fleshly vessel to a certain degree within creation and causes it to desire, along with the soul, what is proper for the soul. With all growing creatures the soul flies, so to speak, like air into all bodily needs in order to appease them; and in its awareness of the names of all creatures the soul rises up in accord with the body—whether in love or in hatred for those creatures.

This is because the human form has the same length and width, if we extend both our hands and arms out from the chest, just as the firmament is also as tall as it is wide. And thus the fact that we are as tall as we are wide gives us a way of measuring our knowledge of good and evil. For we recognize what is good by its advantage to us just as we recognize what is bad by its disadvantage to us. Through our fondness for flesh and blood the soul is involved in the human organism, just as wild game is caught by the hunter. As a result, the soul has scarcely begun to breathe before the body satisfies its own desires. But afterward the soul often causes the body to long for the soul.

VISION FOUR: 16

The sphere of the human head indicates the roundness of
the firmament, and the right and balanced measurements of
our head reflect the right and balanced measurement of the
firmament. Thus the head has its proper measurement on
every side, just as the firmament was established to the
same measurement so that on every side it can find its proper orbit, and so that no part will exceed the others in an unsuitable way.

God has formed humanity according to the model of the
firmament and strengthened human power with the might
of the elements. God has firmly adapted the powers of the
world to us so that we breathe, inhale, and exhale these
powers like the sun, which illuminates the Earth, sends
forth its rays, and draws them back again to itself. Thus the
roundness and symmetry of the human head indicate that
while the soul sins according to the desires of the flesh, it
will then renew itself contritely in justice. Thus the soul
displays symmetry because, even though it has delighted in
sinning, it has then become disturbed in sorrow. And so the
soul maintains a reverent attitude as well as firmness in its
reverence. It does not rejoice in sinning but rather acts only
through the enjoyment of our flesh with the flesh. Even if
we wished to wallow excessively in sin, we should always
be recalled from sinning because we are overcome by the
reverence within our soul. It is true that the soul can be van-
quished by our fleshly nature. Yet so long as body and soul
have to live with one another, they will be locked in a
powerful struggle. For the soul suffers whenever the flesh
rejoices in sinning. A powerful confusion arises in evil
spirits because they can never destroy in the soul of the just
an attitude of repentance, while the evil spirits themselves
can never experience sorrow over their actions because of
their strong hatred for God.

In these matters the soul displays in its essence both
roundness and symmetry because our perception of good

always fights against our perception of evil, and knowledge of evil resists knowledge of good. The one will be tested by the other. But knowledge of good is like a full moon because it overcomes the flesh through good deeds. On the other hand, if the soul is overcome, it is like a waning moon whose curve can only be seen when it is overshadowed.

VISION FOUR: 17

The three upper elements are indicated by the human head: The luminous fire with the upper black fire is indicated by the space from our skull to the forehead; the pure ether is indicated by the space from our forehead to the tip of the nose; the watery air and sheet white luminous air by the space from our nose to the throat. These regions are separated from one another by the same density as that of the upper fire; by the density of pure ether; and by the density of the sheer white luminous air.

Within the soul three powers exist: understanding (*comprehensio*) by which the soul grasps heavenly and earthly things through the power of God; insight (*intelligentia*) by which the soul has the greatest insight when it recognizes the evil of sin, which the soul then causes to become detestable as a result of repentance; and finally, execution (*motio*) by which the soul moves into itself as it accomplishes holy works according to the example of just persons in their bodily abode. Understanding and insight work together to promote an active execution on the part of the soul. For if the soul were to grasp more than it had insight for or could undertake, its standard would be incorrect. In this way, the powers of the soul agree with one another; none of them exceeds the other.

The understanding of the soul (*comprehensio animae*) surrounds the body and all its structures by moving everything in the body to the correct degree toward whatever the flesh demands with respect to our sense of touch and taste, just as a builder correctly measures out a house as the proper abode for human beings. Thus the body

is moved by the soul, and the soul cannot forget that it
needs to incite the body to its various actions. For the soul
has an understanding of what the body demands since the
body really derives its life from the soul.

And the soul, whose essence is life, lives as a living fire
within the body. But the body is a work that has been
shaped (*factum opus*). And thus the soul does not let itself
be kept from being effective in the two ways possible for it:
according to the desire of the flesh or according to the longing of the soul. In this connection, a good work of the soul is
like an exceedingly beautiful bulwark in the sight of God
and the angels, while a bad action resembles a house made
of dung and full of filth. And thus the soul, too, is praised
for its good deeds by God's angels. But if the soul should do
what is evil according to the desire of the flesh, all praise will
be denied.

The symmetry of the elements is related to the symmetry
extending from the top of our head forward to the eyebrows,
sideways to the ears, and backward to the beginning of the
neck. In this way, three basic powers are present in the soul
to the same degree: spiritualization (*expiratio*), knowledge
(*scientia*), and sensation (*sensus*). The soul fulfills its functions by means of these three powers. By spiritualization,
the soul undertakes whatever it can carry out, and this
points to the anterior part of the head. By knowledge, the
soul divides itself, so to speak, on two sides as far as the
ears. And by sensation, the soul turns backward to a certain
extent as far as the beginning of the neck. And these three
powers ought to be symmetrical throughout, since the soul
does not begin to achieve by spiritualization more than
knowledge can grasp or sensation carry out. And thus these
powers work in harmony since none of them exceeds
another, just as our head, too, has its proper symmetry.

VISION FOUR: 18

We find the same symmetry in our head. For example, our
lips distribute an equal amount of sluggishness from the head

and stomach to the areas above and below the lips. Thus the black fire of judgment brings about a process of purgation while the sheer white pure air moderates and restrains that fire. Both areas, however, have the same density. This can be seen by the distance from one of our ears straight across our head to the other ear, as well as by the distance from the openings of our ears down to the shoulders, or by the distance from our shoulders to the base of the throat.

In this way, it is shown that in higher (that is, heavenly) matters and in lower (that is, earthly) matters, we humans must reject evil as it affects our body and our soul. With our mouth we must praise God in the same zeal. For God sustains both souls and bodies.

It is the same distance from one of our ears to the other as the distance from our ears down to the shoulders or the distance from our shoulders to the base of the throat. This means that we take in God's commandments with our ears; we carry them loyally upon our shoulders; we swallow them down, as it were, with our throat; and as we do all these things, we ought to maintain the same, tactful moderation so that we may attain an evenness of disposition that admits of no misgivings. For, no matter how much our body has sinned, the soul attached to it will feel all the more confusion; and no matter how much our body has been disciplined in repentance through continence, the soul will rejoice all the more over its reward of eternal bliss. For just as we behold the beginning of a course of action, we will consider with equal joy its conclusion and its achievements.

The soul has been sunk so deeply within the human form that it seems as if our form were animated of its very self. For the soul knows that it has come from its creator, and we humans give names to our God—whether in a false faith or a true faith—because this characteristic is rooted within us out of the good powers of our soul. Therefore, in our search for God we rise up onto the heights and place upon ourselves a strict discipline so that we may show reverence to the One we are invoking.

The soul, too, knows about God's judgment, which will
befall it for transgressions of the law. Therefore, at times
the soul causes tears to gush forth from its garment [the
body] because of faults the soul has accumulated in sorrow
in the same way as phlegm is ejected through our lips. By
this sorrow, the soul awaits itself to such a degree of the
body, in which the soul lies hidden, that it can cause the
body to blush over its unlawful deeds. Similarly, the body
often gives in to its fleshly desires and keeps the soul from
following the path up onto the heights, where it can see
God. And so our body deceives our soul, but cannot oppress
it so much that we do not feel sorrow over our sinning, no
matter how much we delight in sinning. The evil spirits are
never able to experience this kind of repentance. Therefore,
they blush red with shame because they cannot rob us of
our repentance.

VISION FOUR: 19
The soul has two capacities by which it controls equally
well both the tension and the release of its passionate activity. Through its first capacity, the soul ascends to the
heights, where it experiences God. Through the other
capacity, it takes possession of the whole body in which it
exists, in order to achieve its own work by means of that
body. For the soul rejoices at being able to achieve things
with the body. That body has been formed by God, and thus
the soul is most anxious to perfect the body's work (opus
corporis).
The soul itself experiences the organic functions of the
entire body, and thus the soul can ascend into the brain, the
heart, and blood, or the marrow. In this connection, the
soul cannot achieve more than the limits of our bodily element allow. No matter how eager the soul may be to do as
much good as possible within the body, the soul cannot go
further than divine grace permits it to go. Often the soul
does things according to the desires of the flesh. It will continue to do so until the blood dries out more and more in

our veins as a result of exhaustion, and until sweat is ejected through our marrow. At this point, the soul will retreat into inactivity until it can again warm up the blood of the flesh and replenish the marrow. In this way, the soul urges the body to be vigilant and revives it to do its proper work. And if at times the body succumbs to the desires of the flesh, disgust will usually ensue. While from this time forward the body renews its powers, it will turn again totally to God's service. If the soul then acts according to its own wishes, it will rise up to God and heed the words of David who, under my inspiration, says: "Hide me under the shadow of your wings from the onslaughts of the wicked" (Psalm 17:8–9). This statement has the following meaning: You who defend all believers, hide me in the silence of your very great power. For I remain under the power of the wicked, even though I beseech you, revere you, and place no trust in any alien or false god. And free me from the evil and shameful desires of the evil spirits who disturb me by attacking my flesh. And thus the soul says after every victory: "O my flesh and you my limbs, in which I have my dwelling, how much do I rejoice that I have been sent to you who are in agreement with me and who send me out to my eternal reward." But when the soul is affected by evil deeds, it says anxiously: "O woe is me that I have found such a dwelling which leads me into the shadow of death. Its delight drives me onto a treadmill. I do the deeds of death."

VISION FOUR: 21

Our body as a whole is associated with the head, just as the Earth and all its structures are adapted to the firmament. And we humans as a whole are guided by the sensory organs of our head, just as earthly functions are fulfilled by the firmament. Therefore, an experience in heavenly as well as earthly matters adheres to the soul, and reason, which perceives heavenly and earthly matters, is infused into the soul. For just as the word of God has penetrated everything in creation, the soul penetrates the whole body in order to have an effect on it. The soul is the green life-force of the flesh. For, indeed, the body grows and progresses through the soul, just as the Earth becomes fruitful through moisture. And the soul is also the moisture of the body because the soul moistens it so that it does not dry out, just as rain flows down into the Earth. When the moisture of the rain falls down in a proper, orderly way and not to an excessive degree, it causes the Earth to germinate. But if the moisture overflows in a disorderly way, it destroys the Earth by smothering the seeds within it. Indeed, certain powers emerge from the soul to vivify the body, just as the moisture is vivified by water. On this account, the soul rejoices to act through the body.

When we humans work in accord with the strivings of our soul, all our deeds turn out well. But our deeds turn out ill if we follow the flesh. The flesh exudes its moisture through the soul because the breath of the soul stirs the flesh, just as its nature requires. And we acquire a desire for everything as a result of the breath of the soul. For the soul ascends to heavenly matters and knows them by way of perception. Thus the soul judges all deeds according to their merits. And just as the whole body is dominated by our sense of feeling, the reasonable soul gathers all the deeds of the human organism and considers what that organism might accomplish in accord with the soul's wishes. In this way, the soul causes our limbs to germinate the same way that moisture causes the Earth to germinate, because the soul is infused throughout the human organism, just as moisture is infused throughout the Earth. And just as the Earth causes both useful and useless things to grow, human beings have within themselves a longing for higher things as well as a fondness for sin.

VISION FOUR: 22

From the very top of our cranium to the outer edge of our forehead, seven points are found, separated from one another by equal intervals. This symbolizes the planets, which are also separated from one another in the firmament by like intervals. The highest planet is indicated by the top of the cranium. In the most remote part of the forehead, there is the moon, while the sun is found right in the midst of the space between the highest planet and the moon. On each side of this spot, the other planets—the two upper ones and the two lower ones—are seen; there is the same interval between them with respect to their distance from the sun and from other planets. For the features on our head are proportionately just as far apart from one another as the planets are from one another in the firmament.

The uppermost planet is symbolized by the cranium, because this planet has the widest orbit among the planets. The forehead is compared to the moon because, just as shame appears on our forehead, the tides and other characteristics of time are distinguished on the moon, which at its ascent looks like a forehead. But in the midst of all this is the sun, which is, so to speak, a prince among the heavenly bodies. The sun has above it again two planets for its defense as a protection against the upper fire. Also below the sun are two planets by which the sun keeps the moon in place. The moon, which has the lowest orbit, is separated from the uppermost planet by the same interval as that planet in its upper position is separated from the sun. This is because both the moon and the upper planet have the same intervals, as has been previously described.

The upper and lower parts of the firmament are as round as a mixing bowl on whose upper curve is located the sun, which penetrates the firmament above and below and pours forth its brilliance, just as wine is poured out of a pitcher. This signifies that the soul in our bodies, from the very beginning of its deeds until their completion, has to revere the seven gifts of the Holy Spirit with the same zeal. At the beginning of its activities, let the soul consult *Wisdom;* at the end, let it preserve *Fear of the Lord.* In their midst, may the soul be endowed with *Power;* with *Understanding* and *Counsel,* may it be strengthened toward heavenly things;

with *Knowledge* and *Piety*, may it surround itself in earthly affairs, which should be embraced reverently as helping powers. Thereupon, may this soul take care to extend itself first of all in Wisdom. But lastly it should maintain itself in fear with reverence. But, in the meantime, it should adorn itself in Power with the ornament of Understanding and Good Counsel and at last strengthen itself with Knowledge and Piety, as already mentioned. One of these gifts is connected with another so that a good deed may be completed in dignity: the spirit of Wisdom and the spirit of Power, as well as the spirit of Fear of the Lord. All of them saturate our soul in such a way that we appear in true strength. In all things, let Fear hold sway and thus, with the other gifts of the Holy Spirit, cling in equal courage to our highest creator.

The motion of the reasonable soul and the work of the body (*opus corporis*), with its five senses through which we have our total being, possess a similar dimension. For the soul cannot urge the body to do more than it can achieve, and the body cannot achieve more than the soul has set into motion while the various senses are never separated from one another. Instead, they strongly cling to one another and illuminate our entire person beneficially in both our upper and lower aspects.

VISION FOUR: 23

The human brain consists of no more than three small chambers. It is subject to moisture and gives the entire body its ability to feel as well as its greening power of life. In this way, it symbolizes the power of the sun, which illuminates the east, the south, and the west, but avoids the north. Through the helpful sweetness of dew and rain, the sun sends down its power to Earth again and again. Through this same power, the sun strengthens and moderates the creatures of the entire world.

Just as the brain is preserved by the strength of the skull, the sun's powers are increased by the heat of the upper fiery light. When the sun begins its orbit and the days grow longer, there is greater danger to the Earth from the sun's fire than when the sun is on the decline and hides, so to speak, its face. As the sun declines, the waters with their constellations come to meet it and sustain it with the air. The sun ascends thus, as if under the very footstool of the Lord, and remains in position there. So the sun dominates everything beneath the Earth the way a hen guards its chicks. Then the sun ascends with the cheerful daylight above the Earth and fortifies everything living upon it the way a hen coaxes its chicks out of the eggs.

Just as we humans work by day and sleep at night, the sun goes above and below the Earth in a dual pattern. It sends down its rays upon the Earth during the day and darkens the Earth's surface at night, when the sun disappears. Through the powers of our soul, the body is refreshed after it becomes exhausted. This is because the soul has the task of preserving our flesh and blood so that we may not waste away. Similarly, whenever the moon disappears, it is rekindled by the fire of the sun.

VISION FOUR: 24

In this way our soul, which is fully aware of its powers, directs the body. In matters pertaining to what is good, perfect, and holy, we understand, feel, and know the things that are God's. We revere the true God in the Trinity and do not look in false hope to another god, just as the powers of the soul are linked to one another by working together in unity.

If the soul is so affected by the Spirit of Power that it considers from every viewpoint the beginning and execution of its deeds as well as their conclusion, it will turn away from evil. Thus the soul will bring the sweetness of the higher gifts of grace to the body as their abode. With these gifts, the soul will direct all our limbs toward honorable deeds, because the capacities of the soul are kept united by God's power. If this strengthening gives power to the soul in such a way, the soul will cause these gifts to serve our entire body, so that we will often shed tears and utter sighs. The soul will preserve us in such quiet humility that we can control ourselves both in earthly and spiritual matters and be very well informed about all good things. Thus the soul, working, so to speak, in full zeal on a lucky day, rises up onto the heights. But if our soul should agree with the desires of the flesh, it will be oppressed, as if by torpid nightly slumbers. As a result, it will at times be strengthened and at other times it will surrender to sloth. Zeal for goodness is like a day when we can ponder everything in our mind, while laziness is like a night when we can no longer see anything at all. Just as the night is often moonlit and then later overshadowed if the moon goes under, our deeds are all mixed up. Sometimes they are luminous and at other times they are dark. If our soul, under the body's urging, does evil with the body, the power of our soul will be darkened, because the light of the truth is missing. But if later the soul feels humiliated by sin and rises up again in opposition to the desires of the flesh, it will henceforth harry that flesh and hinder its evil deeds. Thus the light of bliss will rise above the night of sin. The soul overcomes the flesh by conscience, and the body disciplines itself by repentance and the rejection of evil. If the flesh is subdued in this way, the soul will awaken in it a longing for heavenly things. Strengthened in the Spirit of Power, the flesh will quickly surrender to the Fear of the Lord.

Indeed, the soul sustains the flesh, just as the flesh sustains the soul. For, after all, every deed is accomplished by the soul and the flesh. And, therefore, the soul can achieve with the body good and holy things and be revived as a result. In this connection, it often happens that our flesh may feel bored when it cooperates with the soul. In such a case, therefore, the soul may give in to its fleshy partner and let the flesh take delight in earthly things. Similarly, a mother knows how to get her crying child to laugh again. Thus the soul accomplished good deeds with the body, even though there may be some evil mixed up with them. The soul lets this happen so as not to overburden the flesh too much. Just as the body lives through the soul, the soul also finds life again by achieving good through the body. For the soul is entrusted with the work of the Lord's hands. And as the sun overcomes the night and then rises up until midday, we humans avoid evil deeds and enter into a state of integrity. But when the sun declines in the afternoon, the soul enters into an agreement with the flesh. Finally, just as the sun rekindles the moon to keep it from disappearing, our flesh is preserved by the powers of the soul lest the flesh fall down into perdition.

VISION FOUR: 25

Since our brain is moist and soft, it is of itself cold. All the blood vessels and the whole organism bring warmth to the brain. Similarly, everything that shines upward in fire brings fire to the sun, which at times causes dew and rain to fall down upon the Earth, so that the Earth may not lose its warmth. And since the brain is moistened by wetness and strengthened by warmth, it preserves and directs the entire body, just as a combination of moisture and warmth causes the whole Earth to germinate. Moisture from our heart, lungs, and liver, and all our internal organs rises to the brain and fills it. As soon as the brain is filled with these bodily fluids, some of this moisture is distributed to the other organs and quickly fills them.

Similarly, our conscience sends to the soul the moisture of tears when sins grow cold within us and when integrity, along with other good deeds, instills into the soul the warmth of heavenly longing. In the same way, the other powers of virtue hasten to assist the strength that pours out the dew of holiness into believers. If the soul is flooded in this way with the dew and warmth of the Holy Spirit, it will overcome the flesh and force it to serve God together with the soul. From good thoughts and an honest profession of faith, the power of holiness extends through justice and spiritual longing into the conscience of the soul. It strengthens the soul to such an extent that by this power we are secured against all adversity with a generous addition of patience. As a result, we shall no longer be able to succumb to a multiplicity of vices. For just as the upper stars serve the sun with their fire, all our inner organs contribute to the soul the powers it needs to accomplish its task. And while the soul accomplishes what is right and despises what is sinful, it rises upward by means of its reason. When the soul feels that the body is in want, it comes to help the body so that our body should not suffer any kind of want.

The soul, indeed, is a living breath that moves our whole body, yet it often surrenders against its will to the desires of the flesh. If our soul wishes to persist in doing good, it is like the sun. If it remains with the lust of the flesh, it is like the moon. If it sins with the body, it disappears, just as the moon disappears at its waning. Yet that same soul will rise up again to do battle against the flesh, just as the sun continues to rise. Thus we rise up again against the soul's complaint, as the moon, also, is re-enkindled by the sun.

Through the power of moisture, the flesh finds pleasure in its sins, while, through the power of heat, the flesh mourns in repentance. Yet moisture comes from our body while heat comes from our soul. Through both these powers all works — both those of goodness and those of evil — are accomplished, just as through both these powers the earth causes both useful and harmful things to germinate.

Now the soul is a reasonable spirit. In the abode of the heart its wisdom is at home — the wisdom by which the soul thinks through and arranges everything, just as the father of a family has his affairs in order in his own home. Therefore, the soul possesses the cleverness to arrange for its vessel [the body] everything useful in a proper way. In the same way, the heart is concealed by the lungs. And, from this circumstance, the soul possesses that kind of discretion that separates off everything correctly, just as our inner organs are connected in a right and proper way to one another.

The soul has also a fiery nature. On this account, it warms up all the life processes it brings to the heart and rouses them to the point of unity. At the same time, the soul controls them so that not one of them is separated from another. The soul fills them up so that none of them lacks anything, and in this way it arranges in wisdom and care the total structure of the human organism. In a good and holy intent, the soul rises up in faith to God, because it knows that it has been sent by the Divinity. Then, just as dampness rises from the lower organs to the brain, the soul draws all the functions of our body upward through its holy efforts and its knowledge of God. And, just as this moisture descends again to saturate the lower organs, the soul descends again into the elements of the body, so that the body's functions are not judged to be in contradiction to God.

VISION FOUR: 26

The brain exudes a secretion when in a state of fullness, and the inner organs begin the process of digestion as soon as they are full. This happens quite often in the human organism. In exactly the same way, moisture and warmth descend upon the Earth and cause it to send forth shoots. But after the fruits attain their full ripeness, the moisture and warmth are recalled. On this account the air ascends when winter appears to approach at the beginning of the chilly season. In certain regions the air congeals under the sun's warmth, becomes elongated like a thread, and flies away. Then the Earth is weakened by the upper moisture and gives off a dirty kind of foam. In the same way the flesh perspires when it meets the needs of its bodily function. As a result, we receive pleasure and begin to create in our enjoyment of this pleasure. If the soul then feels in its conscience that it has acted according to the wishes and desires of the flesh, the soul will often instill into the flesh a feeling of anxiety about sin. This is because evil has been committed. Afterward, the soul will withdraw from the lusts of the flesh and will seek to have no further knowledge of sin. And the body, too, will also wish to withdraw from what is sinful.

The soul never forgets that it needs to put pressure on the body. Thus once sin has been committed, the soul will cause a feeling of bitterness in the body. Therefore, we are constantly in distress because the soul has to complain of the flesh while the flesh must nurture lust. And thus in sin just as in digestion, evil is recognized. The soul often participates in the desires of the flesh, even though the soul later detests what it has done. In the same way the Earth is both drenched in moisture and burnt up by heat so that it can bring forth both what is useful and what is useless. Even though the daily habit of sinning has implanted sin within us, our soul can still illuminate our body so that it often obtains repentance from God, just as moisture and heat are always withdrawn upward. And thus, in the midst of contradictions, we accomplish both good and evil. Although at times our flesh goes all out in search of desire, the soul strives passionately for reason despite the fact that the soul is often hindered in this effort by its earthly citizenship. If, for example, the body in its generative power repeats the process of its generation and sins, then the reasonable soul will begin to grow cold and to go along with the flesh. Nevertheless, the soul will ascend once again to reason; it will show us the evil we have done and disturb our heart, causing us to sigh and weep. In this way the flesh will be overcome so that the body, as a result of the soul's power, will no longer continue its sinful actions. Instead, flesh will lay aside its earlier obduracy through the merciful dew of the Holy Spirit. Our flesh will take a sober look at its sins and at once see them to be nothing but filth.

VISION FOUR: 29

As already mentioned, the whole body is held together by the power of the brain, just as the sun strengthens the upper and lower regions. The sun illuminates the upper as well as the lower region and, with the exception of the northern side, goes around the entire firmament. For when God strengthened the whole Earth with living creatures, God left empty a single place so that they could know God's splendor and their own individual nature. For light is honored by darkness, and the darker part serves the lighter part. Lucifer chose for himself this empty place when he wished to become like his master.

The sun rises in the east and becomes stronger and stronger in its incandescence in the south. But after the sun has reached its midday position, it begins to decline and thus completes its course until the next morning. And because the sun does not penetrate the north, it is cold on Earth toward morning and evening.

> But I, who am without beginning, am the fire by which all the stars are enkindled. I am the light that covers the dark places so that they cannot grasp the light. Therefore, light does not mingle with the dark places, and therefore the darkness does not come to the light.

Thus human beings, too, have been created by God to have a good conscience, which is the light of truth. And just as those who have an evil conscience, which is an empty space without enduring merit or reward, are inclined to evil, we see that heaven and Earth, that is, light and darkness, are indicated in human beings. . . . [And just as believers are guided by God while those who have gone astray are alienated from God, all elements in believers are established according to a definite order.]

The soul appears like fire, but reason is within the soul like the light, and the soul is penetrated by reason in its illuminating way just as the world is illuminated by the sun. For the soul foresees and knows by means of reason all things that reason achieves within us. We have within us both instincts and longings, and over these two powers the blood in our veins as well as the heat of our marrow are set into motion. We act on them like a wheel which has to complete its revolution once put into motion. For the body—through the force of its instincts and the impulse of its longings—drives the soul this way and that way. As a result, the soul must constantly adjust its actions.

VISION FOUR: 32

When joy or sadness touches our heart, the small vessels of the brain, breast, and lungs become disturbed. On this account the small arteries of the breast and lungs send their humors up to the small arteries of the brain, which receive them and flood the eyes. And thus they give us tears. When the moon waxes or wanes, the firmament is disturbed by storms and, in turn, it stirs up with its commotion the sea and the other waters of the Earth. In the same way the humors of the body produce a definite vapor and a characteristic humor. . . . [This also occurs among spiritual persons who break out into fits of weeping when they become upset by fear of the Lord. Such individuals are like clouds which obtain moisture from the upper regions and drop it down as rain.]

And thus out of sighs and tears the greening life-force of repentance arises. Awakened again by our good deeds, we consider the seriousness of our sins so earnestly and so contritely that our flesh and limbs often become dried out. So much bitterness awakens within our heart that we often say to ourselves: "Why was I placed in the world to do such crimes? With my soul I have committed an outrage against God and with my soul I now make amends by the sighs I send up to God—to the One who condescended to accept Adam's form from the Virgin. Thus I trust that God will not scorn me. Instead, God will free me from my sins and even accept me, a penitent sinner, in true faith before the countenance of his or her holy humanity." Instantly the body and soul become united in a mutual bond. Together they send up sighs to God, for sinning can never give joy to the soul. Instead, the soul is forced to give in to the stupidity of the body's fleshly desire. Of course, if the soul also takes pleasure in sin, we should constantly wallow in a state of filthy depravity. Thus the soul has no joy in sin, even though it may cooperate with the body in sinning. Similarly, the material components of humanity do not force us to sin. Instead, they direct us in accord with God's judgment even as we are sinning. But when we do good deeds, they extend to us all sweetness and gentleness.

Whenever forced to do evil along with the body, the soul will fill us with sorrow, for such conduct is displeasing to the soul. Yet if it, together with the body, carries out a good deed, the soul will bring joy to the body. Therefore, a person who has unwittingly done a good deed gains the love of others as a result of God's favor. Such a person may have progressed so far that he or she constantly wants to do only what is good, just as the angels can look at God's countenance and never become weary of doing so. And thus the soul of such a person feels joy over good deeds even as it goes down to the body, purifies it from sin, and infuses into it the sighs and tears of humble repentance. As a result, the body will gain strength for the powers of virtue. And all this occurs in the same way the clouds draw up the waters of the Earth and then rain them down again.

VISION FOUR: 33

Just as no visible form is without a name, none is without a dimension of its own. And thus our two eyes have the same dimension, and their reflecting lenses have the same range. For God has separated virtues from vices and holy works from sins, just as the Divinity has distinguished the creatures known to us by their shapes and names. And so we can see with our eyes what is good. We can judge the good, and we have the pure gift of decision making. If we exceed our proper dimension in what is good, we may fall down into the abyss. And if we strive too hard after what is evil, we will be completely ruined in despair.

VISION FOUR: 34

The soul shows by the power of reason what sin is and how it takes place. It also knows the extent of sin and repentance. Out of the soul's wealth, we humans are steeped in repentance if we attack our sins through atonement, just as rain puts out fire. Yet in view of the eternal bliss attained through indescribable reparation, we can scarcely imagine how it is possible for us to be redeemed. Even if our repentance were to rise up over all the deserts and all the waters of the sea, we could hardly realize what salvation means with all its joys of eternal life and indescribable rapture.

And where would one find people who could refuse to carry out the desires of the flesh—even if they wished to avoid sin! The soul endowed with reason through its understanding knows of two possibilities: It knows about good and experiences evil, and so it rewards good and punishes evil. These are the tasks of the soul—the tasks by which it lives in the body and achieves much within it in accord with the requirements of the body. And therefore we humans are, so to speak, steeped in goodness by day and evil by night.

VISION FOUR: 35

We see with our eyes, smell with our nose, and taste with our mouth. Similarly, the sun, the moon, and the highest stars emit onto the starry world certain rays, which have to serve these heavenly bodies. And thus one light is awakened by another light.

If the soul beholds mean and evil actions, it sinks down in sorrow. Since such conduct has been learned through evil repute—so to speak through the sense of smell—the soul sends up sighs. And since such actions are done to some extent through the sense of taste, they cause us to weep. The soul then sends us repentance as a result of our conscience; it sends us sighs as a result of the evil reputation due to sin; and it sends us tears once the evil actions are carried out.

In this way, repentance acts as the light of the soul. In repentance, there are sighs and tears. Guilt is quickly dissolved among people in whom such sighs and tears arise. Similarly, once the other powers are awakened, they illuminate believers through the Spirit of Power and Fear of the Lord.

VISION FOUR: 36

Just as everything in the human head is maintained by the chin, all the above-described cosmic forces, each in its own place, are maintained by the clouds. This means that the attitudes of believers are so strongly drawn to the stability of good works that these believers can abide in the good and attain the heavenly sphere. Heat indicates bones in the human organism, and cold indicates the marrow. This is because the soul cooks the bones by means of fire while it causes the marrow to freeze by means of the cold that the soul draws into its vessel. In summer and in winter the whole Earth is so tested that its fruits lie frozen in winter beneath the Earth by means of the firmament's cold, while they become free again in summer as a result of the heat. The sun's heat and moisture from the waters are so united and mingled in the clouds that all the Earth's fruits receive guidance and strength. This is because the sun's heat and the moisture of the waters cultivate the whole Earth, make it fruitful, and complete it, just as a potter completes his vessels by turning his wheel. Then the heat and moisture are united so solidly in the clouds that nothing can penetrate or upset this union before the Last Judgment nor can any part of it melt away or be separated from it.

The soul, too, is strengthened to all manner of good by the fire of the Holy Spirit, but it is weakened by the coldness of indifference and neglect. The powerful fire and its attitude of contrition mingle in us and produce good fruit. They so strengthen and adorn us in all usefulness that we can no longer be separated from God's service and love. If we fall victim to the burden and excess of our sins, these sins will bunch up within us like a fire that becomes so smothered by dense smoke that it can no longer burn freely. But if carnal desires are driven from the mind by the power of the spirit, we shall burst into sighs of longing for our Father's heavenly home. In a similar way does the bee construct its honeycomb out of its own honey. And thus our new deed and old action are so mingled that they will not burn out or dry up because they are carried out in true humility.

The power of human virtue is fulfilled in the fire of the Holy Spirit and the moisture of humility within the vessel of the Holy Spirit, where Wisdom has made her abode. And thus we bring together our powers, so to speak, in the aroma of all fragrance. And these powers, which are full of good cheer before God and his angels, are where they shall never cease.

VISION FOUR: 58

Certain birds of immense strength, which we see flying about in the air, are sustained by this same air, which at times descends into the rivers to fortify the big fish there so that the fish can live for a while without food.

Similarly, the soul, by reaching an agreement with the body, flies up into the heavens like a bird in the air. Just as a bird cannot fly without atmosphere, our body, too, is kept in motion by the soul and not by itself. If at times we agree with the longings of the soul, we are totally consumed by the love of God. Thus day by day we fly up into the brightness of eternal joy when we take delight in contemplative faith and the wisdom of holy scripture. Through the sweetness of these writings, we are invisibly nourished and fortified, just as a fish that has been fortified by air and rushing water can live for a time in water without nourishment.

VISION FOUR: 59

In union with the watery air, the atmosphere stirs up the sea, out of which the different rivers flow separately to moisten and fortify the whole body with blood.

The soul, which is of an airy nature, is the agency by which all human works are accomplished, just as all the Earth's fruits are produced by the air. Now the soul presents all actions to us humans through the grace of the Holy Spirit so that we can distinguish what is useful from what is harmful by our thinking process, which surges like the sea.

In this way, we often undergo shipwreck if we are plunged by our sins down into great confusion because we have not reached an agreement with our soul's good thoughts. Only by great effort can we still row the ship of our thoughts unless—under the Holy Spirit's inspiration—we ground our thoughts on the rock called Christ. For when human attitudes are enlarged by the powers of virtue and turn to the praises of God, they build on that rock a solid foundation that storms—such as the various temptations of the Devil—cannot shatter. And just as our blood system holds the body together by means of sinews so that the body cannot fall apart, the virtuous power of humility binds and preserves good works lest they be scattered by pride.

The rivers give rise to smaller streams that sustain the Earth by their greening power. All the rivers and streams are stirred up by the air, as mentioned above, and cause everything to germinate by their warmth and moisture. This is how it is when the soul overcomes the desire of the flesh and founds its longing within us humans. The soul itself and the body complete their work in harmony, and as a result fly up in the pure joy they feel over holy actions and the sweet perfume of virtue. And just as the larger rivers pour out of themselves the smaller streams that cause the Earth to germinate, the soul—if it dominates the body—awakens in that body love, obedience, and humility as well as the other mighty powers of virtue by which the soul causes us to praise God and practice good works.

VISION FOUR: 60

The Earth is always muddy because of the summer's warmth and the winter's chill, and it is this mud that causes the Earth to become fruitful. In this way, the body should be subject to the soul, just as a maid is subject to her mistress, even though at times the soul may be overpowered by the body or the mistress by the maid. The soul causes all goodness within us, just as summer causes all fruits to ripen. But if the body should oppose the soul through the rottenness of sin, we may say to ourselves: "I will not live in such rigor that I have to deny my flesh constantly and against the wishes of the flesh. Instead, whatever

I do will be right for me." Even though we tell such lies
because of the rottenness of our sins, we may still recall the
good we previously did and turn away from our filthy sins
toward the works of justice and holy virtue—a situation we
once enjoyed. And just as the muddy Earth preserves within
itself all fruits in winter so as to produce them in summer
for our enjoyment, we shall adorn our earlier virtues with
previous jewels and return them even lovelier than they
were in the past.

VISION FOUR: 78

In the youthful, ripening period of life, we come into
complete flower. In old age, we are brought back to the
period of fading, just as Earth in summer is adorned with
flowers by its greening power and later transformed by the
chill of winter's pallor.

When the soul overcomes the body in such a way that the
body is in agreement with the soul in goodwill and simplicity of heart, and refreshed by good treatment as if by
nourishing food, we cry out in our longing for heaven: "How
sweet are the words of justice to my throat—even sweeter
than honey to my mouth." And so we live in childish
simplicity and a state of innocence without feeling the
desires of the flesh. The soul floods us with its longing until, as we climb from virtue to virtue, we begin to feel a
greening power. We start to bloom in the good works and
examples left us by the Son of God. This is because we have
not been stained by sin. And so we find joy and let ourselves
be adorned. And just as the greening power and the flowering as well as the ripening of all fruits come to an end in
winter, we also fade away at death along with all our good
and evil works. Those of us, however, who have performed
good works in our childhood, maturity, and old age will
mount up with our soul to God, radiant in our good deeds
and as if adorned with jewels. And the body by which the
soul has done all these things will scarcely be able to wait
until both body and soul are together again in the abode of
joy.

VISION FOUR: 79

The fertile Earth is symbolized by the sex organs, which display the power of generation as well as an indecent boldness. Just as unruly forces at times rise from these organs, the recurring fertility of the Earth brings about a luxuriant growth and an immense overabundance of fruits. Of course, everything we do under the sun and moon over the course of the months is achieved by our soul's power of wisdom, knowledge, and diligence. Through the soul, which is of a fiery and airy nature, we accomplish both good and evil like the moon, which waxes and wanes. Through this power in the soul, we are of a heavenly nature in our recognition of goodness. And thus we think about and achieve all our deeds. We distinguish the course of the seasons as well as the elements of our actions through the decision-making power of the mind. We provide names for all the things we identify. And just as the power of correct procreation and infirmity, of happiness and misfortune, lie hidden within the sex organs, and just as the Earth causes both useful and useless things as well as everything needed for human existence to germinate through the sun, moon, and air, there exists a mighty power within the soul. By this capacity we are able to bring to fulfillment both good and evil, both useful and useless things.

VISION FOUR: 80

The Earth lies in the midst of the atmosphere like a honeycomb in the midst of honey. The Earth rises up to various levels of elevation so that one of its parts has hills with excessively great heat, while other parts have hills with excessively great cold. As a result, these are uninhabitable regions. Yet still another part of the Earth has heights with moderate heat and cold. The Earth is strengthened by its hills like a city by its towers and for-tifications. Thus hills cover the valleys while mountains defend the Earth against all kinds of storms. And thus the Earth is surrounded and strengthened by mountains and hills as if by a wall.

For the soul, which at God's command is completely tied to the body, all this means is that the soul knows itself to be at work within the body, along with the rest of creation. The soul also realizes that God, who judges all our evil actions as well as our good deeds, is praised by all the angels and saints. For God is the sovereign and ruler of all things in heaven and the liberator of all earthly matters. God accepted and freed humanity in the mortality of the flesh. And thus the soul realizes that this wonderful God has accomplished many miracles through the saints. Even though we may sin according to the lusts of the flesh, we are often recalled to repentance by the soul. But if we do not renounce sin and subdue the soul in this way, the soul within us will complain in a voice wracked by sobs. For the hunger of the soul's nature cannot be stilled so long as the soul can scarcely gather hope of salvation with God. The grace of God, however, causes us to recognize our guilt in bitter repentance. It encourages us to abandon the worldly things that have so often injured the soul. And thus our deeds resemble the Earth, which is surrounded by the atmosphere above, below, and on all sides. For the soul exists with the body like the Earth with the air and the honeycomb in the midst of honey. For just as the Earth has some elevations of moderate heat and cold, where people can live, as well as other elevations with excessive climates that are uninhabitable, we are able to practice the good works that will bring us to our heavenly home. At the same time, we are also led to practice evil works that will lead us to a place of punishment.

If the soul overcomes the desires of the flesh and remains victorious, it will rejoice in accord with its nature. For the soul is a spirit that serves God in the love of faith, like the angels who gaze upon God's countenance. But the soul compels a body that finds the desires of the flesh distasteful to undertake good and holy things. The soul that overcomes the body in this stubborn struggle over good works will be adorned by its good deeds and strengthened like a city by its towers and fortifications.

The soul is humble. Because of the infirmity of the flesh, which oppresses the soul, our soul raises up its voice in complaint. In this way, it never permits the fullness of joy to those people who ascend onto the hill of pride. Such people cannot find joy in a mood of atonement for the burden of their sins. And thus the soul harries us by its increased humility lest we wander about on the idle path of pride. The soul ascends on the ladder of humility to a high mountain, which is the abode of the heavenly Jerusalem. The soul constantly admonishes us to renounce pride and to embrace humility lest we be overcome by the old serpent's cunning. Just as hills protect the valleys from excessive rainfall, humility protects us from evil. And just as the Earth is protected from all sorts of storms by mountains, which defend and strengthen it like a wall, our soul—when far removed from Satan's wiles—can attain its heavenly home through holy works that have been strengthened by humility as if by a wall.

VISION FOUR: 81

The Earth is located with respect to the sun's orbit in such a way that the sun can moderate the Earth on every side. Thus the soul, which is moderated by wisdom, saturates human beings with the waters of a gushing stream, which is God. We should walk on the paths of discretion and holy longing in order to know God. Out of love for God we should give up sinful desires. But those among us who act according to the soul's longing are illuminated by good deeds through our soul, just as the Earth is illuminated by the sun as it performs all its tasks.

VISION FOUR: 82

The Earth is strengthened by rocks and trees. Like it, we humans are created because our flesh is like the Earth; our bones without marrow are like rocks; our marrow-containing bones are like trees. Therefore, we construct our houses —in accord with our own architect's drawing—out of earth, rocks, and blocks of wood.

The soul, which is in opposition to the wishes of the flesh, is the firmament of the whole organism. By saturating the body with its power, the soul achieves and carries out all its dealings with us. We become, in this way, gardens in bloom which the Lord beholds with pleasure so long as we continue to act in accord with the soul's plumbline. But if we act according to the desires of the flesh, we will not shine in God's eyes; instead, we shall be like the sun on the day of an eclipse. Those of us who do good are like an orchard full of the fruit of good works. Such persons are like the Earth, which is strengthened and adorned by rocks and trees. But if we do evil works in the stubbornness of sin, we shall remain sterile in God's eyes, like the stubborn Earth that bears no fruit. Human flesh indicates the good conscience that displays a fruitful kind of softness. Our bones indicate the bad conscience that is hardened against God. Bones without marrow indicate the evil works themselves.

The soul acts within us to point the way to God. Just as God has established heaven in the full joy of heavenly things, and just as God has given us the Earth as our abode, the soul accomplishes in joy its good deeds of a heavenly nature; in sadness and sorrow it accomplishes evil deeds of an earthly nature. The knowledge of good and evil represents, so to speak, the innermost part of the soul—the part that teaches us humility, which is the mother of all the virtues. When we sin, the soul harasses us with all its might so that we can never find true joy in sinning. And just as we consider in advance, according to our builder's plan, all the parts of a house we plan to erect, the soul orders all deeds within us in accord with its own capacity.

VISION FOUR: 83

The Earth has been placed in the midst of space in such a way that there is as much atmosphere above the Earth as beneath it. This is also true on both sides of the Earth. The soul, which has been sent into the body as the living breath of God's Spirit, tells us how to observe patiently God's commandments in this troublesome life of ours. It dwells within us at the same spacial distance from us as we find between the Earth and heaven. And the soul still remains within us so that we, who cannot fully grasp by our understanding our own being, might aspire to reach our Creator despite the hard struggle between patience and obedience. Just as the air, which sustains and strengthens the Earth, exists in the midst of the Earth, the soul dwells in the midst of the body and sustains it. And, within the body, the soul acts in accord with the requirements that it makes of the body.

VISION FOUR: 95

In its control of the body, the soul is like the wind. We cannot see it blow; we can only hear it. Like a current of air, the soul may deploy, as a result of its airy substance, a fit of anger, sighs of contrition, or all kinds of thoughts. The soul is like the dew in the moisture of that wisdom by which it aims its good intentions at God. Just as the sun's brilliance illuminates the whole world without any loss of power, the soul exists as a totality within our small human form. And just as the soul can be everywhere on the wings of thought, it can ascend to the stars by its good deeds for God's glory, and it can topple down into the realm of darkness by its evil works. For such relationships let the sun serve as a model— the sun which shines in its power upon the Earth by day and sinks beneath the horizon by night. [The knees, shins, and ankles symbolize the northern winds and our bad intentions, which are mightily opposed by our reason in the power of the mind (*vis rationalis*).] For we accomplish all our works—both those that are good and those that are bad —by the power of the intellect. In this same way are the fruits of the Earth produced in summer. Now God has created the soul with four capacities—fire, air, water, and earth—so that our soul can guide with wisdom its vessel, the body. Through these basic powers, the soul accomplishes all its tasks in the organism in harmonious cooperation with the body. Before the soul was sent into the body, it had no special functions. And it will again have no functions when it has left the body.

God indicated the four winds along with their eight aux-iliary winds by the joints of the body—that is, the arms, elbows, hands, groin, knees, and feet. One of these winds, the west wind, is tied to the power of the dawn, which removes dew from the throat of the night and drops it down upon the Earth. For the early light shines upward in the morning. At the first hour, the sun illuminates the day as it begins to send its burning rays down upon the Earth. At the sixth hour, the sun takes on its full glow. This means that, at first, we can breathe freely as a result of our good intentions, but later we will weep. After this dew of tears, our good intentions begin to germinate in holy concern for goodness like the south wind, which begins by sighing in order to blow reverently in good will, as if it were in the east. Then, in the west, the restless conflicts by which the soul has controlled the body grow mellow. Thus the sun's glow, which arises in the east and reaches its climax in the south, grows mellow as it goes westward. In the same way as east and south are joined by the heat of the day, the soul links one power to another power. The soul does its good deeds in the same way as the hand acts as a tool for the arm. After the day is done, the sun sinks in the west in the same way as our knees, together with our feet, rush over the Earth. At evening the merriment of the day changes into vexation and dismay. No longer do we rejoice in the daylight, but dismay and sleepiness overcome us. If we long for the desires of the flesh, if we are completely captivated by them and neglect the heavenly power of goodness, we ourselves will take on the nature of the night. But if we practice virtue within our soul through the fire of the Holy Spirit, we shall be restored by the love of Christ and removed from the concupiscence of the flesh.

For the soul, out of its spiritual nature, produces words by making sounds; it adds to these words in the same way as a tree puts out shoots. In this way—as if from a tree—all human powers arise. Whatsoever we accomplish should be perceived as the fruit of a tree. The soul has a fourfold capacity to take flight: the senses (*sensus*), knowledge (*scientia*), will (*voluntas*), and understanding (*intellectus*). Through the wings of the senses, the soul realizes its own fragility, but is still inclined to whatever the flesh loves. For the soul is forever a most changeable sort of breath. Through the wings of knowledge, the body hungers after activity. For it knows the extent to which it lives through the soul. Through the wings of will, the soul has an impulse to work within the body. Indeed, the soul perceives the body as its most characteristic work. Through the wings of understanding, the soul at last knows the fruitfulness of all kinds of activity — whether it be activity of a valuable nature or activity of little value. For the soul knows that it abides in a limited form of life. Through these four wings, the soul has eyes. In the knowledge of goodness, it flies forward like a bird toward good deeds; in the knowledge of evil, it flies backward to do evil.

VISION FOUR: 96

[The strong power of the winds restrains the roaring north wind. This wind has been dark ever since the fall of Lucifer, that is, ever since God exiled that spirit into a place of darkness. Along with Lucifer, other evil spirits, too, were scattered about the world. Yet God did not give them permission to make themselves known to us in all their repulsiveness, even though they do have sufficient opportunity to deceive and seduce us. And so the north wind is hostile to the Earth. Its disorder indicates our own inconstancy and willfulness. But there is also another reason for this evil, which helps us to recognize good, just as the left hand has to help the right hand.]

VISION FOUR: 97

God, however, turned the face of the good blossom opened up in Adam toward the west, as the Godhead awakened humanity and elevated it. Our right hand indicates the southern regions of bliss, while our left hand points to the borders of darkness known as the north. God has fitted into this form of ours the power of the elements, as well as the capacities of all the other creatures. By this power, we ought to work against the north, which is the abode of the fallen angels who have separated themselves from the Godhead. Did they not, in their willfulness, deny God and seek to make themselves God? On this account God wants us to reject the north with our left hand and rebuff it. We should not imitate the north at all because, in fact, none of us can see what lies behind us. Like all the forces of nature, we ought to join in Michael's struggle against the serpent. We should keep the north in a state of complete forgetfulness on our left, just as darkness is cut off from the light.

In this way, God has strengthened us with all the power of nature. God buckled upon us the armor of creation so that we can know the whole world through our sight, understand it through our hearing, and distinguish it through our sense of smell. As a result, we will be nourished by the world and dominate it by our sense of touch. And, in this way, we come to know the true God, who is the author of all creation. We should not add our power to the struggle against God, no matter how often we have been deceived by the serpent's counsel. God has not filled us with the above-mentioned power so that any of us might contemplate the folly of the fallen angel. Instead, God has shaped our form according to the bulwark of the cosmic system and the universe, just as potters have forms they use to turn out their pots. And just as God made the mighty instrument of the universe according to careful standards, the Divinity also made humanity with its short, insignificant form in the way we have described above in some detail. God created humanity with one limb fitted to another in such a way that no limb should exceed its proper proportion unless this was what God wished. And every limb was supposed to fit into the many points of our body—the neck, shoulders, elbows, hands, shins, knees, and feet—as well as into the rest of the whole organism. And God arranged the nature of the human species in the same way as the seasons of the year.

VISION FOUR: 99

Therefore, under my inspiration the Psalmist says: "You made the moon to tell the seasons, the sun knows when to set" (Psalm 104:19). This statement is to be understood in the following way: God established the moon to relate to the seasons in such a way that it would give nourishment at all times, as a mother nourishes her child first with milk and later with more substantial food. At its waning the moon becomes weak, and therefore to a certain degree it allows the seasons to be nourished, so to speak, with milk. At its waxing, on the other hand, the moon nourishes the seasons with substantial food. As for the sun, God has disposed that it should both shine over the Earth and hide beneath it. Therefore, by day the sun shines over the Earth, just as we remain awake with open eyes during the daytime. But at night the sun goes under the Earth, just as we sleep at night with closed eyes. For this reason we are earthly according to our fleshly essence, but we are heavenly in our soul in accord with the elevation of heaven. And we know the time of the seasons because we are kept in motion by everything that is alive.

VISION FOUR: 100

When God looked upon the human countenance, God was exceedingly pleased. For had not God created humanity according to the divine image and likeness? Human beings were to announce all God's wondrous works by means of their tongues that were endowed with reason. For humanity is God's complete work. God is known to human beings, and for our sake God created all creatures. God has allowed us to glorify and praise God in the kiss of true love through our spirituality.

But the human species still needed a support that was a match for it. So God gave the first man a helper in the form of woman, who was man's mirror image, and in her the whole human race was present in a latent way. God did this with manifold creative power, just as God had produced in

great power the first man. Man and woman are in this way
so involved with each other that one of them is the work of
the other (opus alterum per alterum). Without woman, man
could not be called man; without man, woman could not be
named woman. Thus woman is the work of man, while
man is a sight full of consolation for woman. Neither of
them could henceforth live without the other. Man is in
this connection an indication of the Godhead while woman
is an indication of the humanity of God's Son. And thus the
human species sits on the judgment seat of the world. It
rules over all creation. Each creature is under our control
and in our service. We human beings are of greater value
than all other creatures.

VISION FOUR: 101

David speaks about this matter under my inspiration:
"Yahweh's oracle to you, my Lord, 'Sit at my right hand and
I will make your enemies a footstool for you'" (Psalm
110:1). This statement is to be understood in the following
way: Human beings should also state that God has spoken
to the divine Son, the Incarnate One to whom God has
given all power in heaven and on Earth. The Son must be
my ruler while I am but a sinful human being: "As a ruler
you will be seated at my right hand" ruling over the human
species, which is my right hand because I have subjected all
creatures to it so that it will abandon its false gods and turn
to its Creator, the true God. You will do so when I subject
the rebels who in their infidelity are your enemies and
make them your footstool. From time immemorial I have
made them subject to you. Thus do I wish them to revere
the trace of your feet. For if they are converted from their infidelity, they will know you as the true God.

In this way God has brought all creation to the light
through God's own Word. That same Word took on human
flesh in his humanity. The Word is the right hand of God
because it is, according to its essence the summing up of
God's entire might. This Word, the Son of God, has erected

its place of dominion over the human species. And this dominion will endure until the number of his brothers has been completed, which will occur at the Last Judgment. Then the Satanic host with its followers will be subjected, so to speak, to the Son as his footstool. This footstool is the image of the situation that will occur at the end of time in the world. Then what and who the Lord is will be made known and revealed. Satan himself will be shattered like a footstool; he will be totally and utterly annihilated.

VISION FOUR: 102

Now God rules heaven in divine power and majesty. The Deity keeps an eye on the heavenly bodies illuminated by this power: God beholds all of creation. [Thus do we humans sit upon our sovereign throne, the Earth, and rule the other creatures because our senses have been marked by the signs of the all-powerful God.]

These signs are our five senses. By means of them, we gain insights into God's power and know that we must worship in true faith the God of the Trinity in unity and the unity of God in the Trinity. This worship is also an adornment of the nine choirs of angels through whom Satan's band was expelled and toppled to its doom. We humans, however, are the tenth choir which God has restored within the divine Self in place of the original condition once held in creation by the fallen angels. For God decided to become a human being! God's humanity is the fortress in which those who belong to the tenth choir have their being. On this account, as stated above, God has marked both the higher and lower creatures within the human species. We stood up, illuminated by the living breath of our soul, and came to a realization of all creation. In our spiritual nature and sincere love, we have enfolded all the world within our arms.

VISION FOUR: 103

Whatever the soul achieves within us has a fiery substance. The soul arouses the entire human organism and gives life to the body. Because the soul has a fiery nature, we are warm-blooded creatures. Its paths are windy in nature. The soul inhales the breath of life into the body and then expels it. By inhaling, we dry out, which is good for us since our flesh remains healthy and flourishes as a result of the dryness. By exhaling, the fire of the organism is diminished and warmth is removed. Thus the whole body is constructed with the greatest sensitivity so that we can be alive, so that we can control all five senses of the body with their cluster of functions. If that warmth were not discharged from the body, the fire of the soul might burn the body, just as a house might be completely destroyed by the heat of a a fire.

The power of the soul clothes us with flesh and blood and completes us as a total unity, just as all the fruits of the Earth are ripened by the blowing of the winds. Through the fiery capacity of the soul, we are also able to realize that we possess God, and through the breath of the spirit we understand that we can act within our body. On this account, we have received the following principle from God: to do correctly whatever we do. We should not pay attention to the empty place in the north, where the first angel decided to establish his dominion and where he fell down to his doom. In his obstinacy, that first angel arrogantly concentrated upon himself. As a result, that haughty creature flew off totally on his own and turned toward the north, where he sought to achieve his obstinate desires. Such arrogance and high-flying pride, however, are like waters over which no ship can sail because they are troublesome to both God and humanity and because they are destructive to everything. Therefore, their work amounts to nothing, and there is no love within it. They can neither love believers nor be loved by them. This arrogance seeks to seize things that do not belong to it and to have a say even about things over which it has no control. And thus arrogance rushes to its own destruction.

The soul is like the mistress of a house. God has formed the whole abode for the soul's sake so that it can take possession of that house. To be sure, no one can see the soul while it is in the body, just as we cannot see God unless faith makes us clairvoyant and gives us knowledge. Through the help of all nature, which has emerged from God, the soul acts within us. Just as a bee forms honey in its comb, we do our work as if it were honey. And we do so through the powerful knowledge in our soul, which is something fluid, so to speak. Sent by God, the soul pours its thoughts into the heart and collects them in the breast. Thence, these thoughts ascend to the head and into all the limbs of the body. They penetrate into the eyes as well; for the eyes are the windows through which the soul knows external nature. Full of spiritual power, the soul is only able to distinguish the power of nature through the spoken word. In these circumstances, we complete our tasks in accord with the aspirations of our thoughts, as necessity may require at a given time. When the spritual wind of knowledge is stirred up within the brain, it descends from the brain into the thoughts of the heart. This is the way in which an intended task reaches completion. In its power of knowledge, the soul is, indeed, like a sower. It sows whatever is to be done as the work of its thoughts; it thoroughly boils this work in its fiery nature; and it gives savor to the work for those who knowingly taste of it.

In addition, the soul brings food and drink to the organism as nourishment so that the body's fabric can be constantly renewed. By this function, we flourish in all the parts of the body and keep ourselves in good condition. The soul distinguishes, orders, and fills with power the different organs. Of itself the soul is in no way flesh and blood, but it is of service to the flesh and blood and causes them to have life through the soul. The soul, which is endowed with reason, has its origin in God, who breathed life into the very first form. Therefore, both body and soul exist as a single reality in spite of their different conditions. We understand this unitary "opus" when we see how the soul brings air to its bodily organism through its thought processes. It brings

warmth through every power of concentration; it brings fire
through the intake of matter; in addition, it brings water by
incorporating watery materials and basic power by the process of procreation. And we humans are put together in this
way at the first moment of our destiny. Up above and down
below, on the outside as well as on the inside, and
everywhere—we exist as corporeal beings. And this is our
essence.

VISION FOUR: 104

If we behave correctly, the elements will keep to their appointed path. But if we succumb to evil deeds, we will draw
down upon ourselves elementary forces with punishing
blows of fate. Of course, the body deals with the soul according to the body's own desires, and God judges us according
to our work—either for praise or for retribution. In this connection, the soul flows through the whole body along with
the power of thought, speech, and breath like a wind blowing
through a house. As long as the body cooperates with the soul,
the body will stay rooted to the spot and be so heavy that it cannot free itself from its close attachment to the Earth. But if the
body is renewed by its living soul—something that will take
place on the Day of Judgment—it will become so light that it
can fly off like a bird on pinions. So long as the soul abides
within the body, it experiences God because it comes from
God; so long as it performs its service within creatures, it cannot see God. But if it is taken outside its bodily abode and appears before God's countenance, it will know its own essence
as well as whatever adhered to the soul while it dwelt within
the body. Since the soul will recognize the splendor of its own
worthiness, it will ask to have back again its bodily abode so
that the body, too, can attain an awareness of its own splendor.
Therefore, the soul will eagerly await in time to come the
Day of Judgment. For then, of course, it will be free of its dear
garment, the body. If the soul should receive the body back
again, it will behold God's splendor in perfection along with
the angels. Afterward, the angels will be enraptured once

their hymns of praise, just as they were on the first day of creation when the victory they won in battle illuminated them. For only after the Day of Judgment will they find fulfillment in their praises of God. They will strike up hymns of glory over the new wonders of God's creation—men and women. Henceforth, they will play upon the zither—a sound full of great joy. They will never cease to do so, and they will never grow weary of this task. And just as they wish to behold constantly and forever God's countenance, they will never cease to wonder over the works God has accomplished through men and women.

Such is the human form, as has been explained previously: We are an essence made up of body and soul, and we exist as God's work together with all of creation (*opus Dei cum omni creatura*). This is what is meant by the words John set down under my inspiration:

IN PRINCIPIO ERAT VERBUM.

GOD'S WORD IN THE WORLD: 105

In the beginning was the Word.

This statement is to be understood in the following way:

I who am without origin and from whom every beginning goes forth, I who am the Ancient of Days, do declare that I am the day by myself alone. I am the day that does not shine by the sun; rather by me the sun is ignited. I am the Reason that is not made perceptible by anyone else; rather, I am the One by whom every reasonable being draws breath. And so to gaze at my countenance I have created mirrors in which I consider all the wonders of my originality, which will never cease. I have prepared for myself these mirror forms so that they may resonate in a song of praise. For I have a voice like the thunderbolt by which I keep in motion the entire universe in the living sounds of all creation. This I have done, I who am the Ancient of Days. By my Word, which was and is without beginning in myself, I caused a mighty light to emerge. And in this light are countless sparks, which are the angels. But when the angels came to

*awareness within their light, they forgot me and wanted to
be as I am. Therefore, the vengeance of my punitive zeal rejected in thunderclaps those beings who had presumed to
contradict me. For there is only one God, and no other can
be God.*

*Afterward, I spoke within myself my small deed, which is
humanity. I formed this deed according to my own image
and likeness so that it would be realized with respect to
myself because my Son intended to adopt the garment of
flesh as a human being. I have established in a spiritual way
this deed of mine through my Reason and indicated my
possibility in it, just as the human spirit comprehends
everything in its artistic ability through names and
numbers. Only by names can humanity grasp the essence of
a thing, and only by numbers can humanity know the
multiplicity of things. I, too, am an angel of might because I
make myself known to the heavenly hosts through wondrous signs and appear to all creatures in faith. In this way
they can know me as their Creator, even though I can be
proclaimed by none of them in a perfect way.*

*Meanwhile, humanity is the guise in which my Son,
clothed in heavenly power, reveals himself as the God of all
creation and as the Life of life. But no one besides God can
number the host of angels who especially surround God's
kingly power. No one can follow up to the very end the
other creatures who acknowledge God as the God of all creation. And finally, no tongue would suffice to designate those
who invoke God as the Life of all life. Blessed, therefore, are
those who abide in God!*

As previously indicated, God has inscribed the entire
divine deed on the human form. This will be shown here by
means of various examples with respect to humanity.

The sphere of the *skull* indicated the dominant power of
humanity. For the brain maintains and rules the whole
human organism. When hair adorns the head, we have in
this way an indication of our artistic abilities. God also

gives a hint of humanity's power in our eyebrows because they protect our eyes by keeping away all harmful influences. In addition, they appear to be an adornment of the face and are like flapping wings of winds that enable the winds to rise up and remain in space, like a bird that sometimes flies upward and sometimes soars in space. For the wind, also, blows out of God's power, and the wind's blowing is the flapping of God's wings.

In addition, God reveals through our *eyes* the knowledge by which God foresees and knows everything in advance. Our eyes clarify many things since the eyes are clear-sighted and watery, just as the shadow of other creatures appears on the surface of water. That is to say, with the help of our sight we can recognize and distinguish all things. If our sight were lacking, we should be like the dead.

In addition, God opens up to us through our *ability to hear* all the sounds of glory about the hidden mysteries and angelic hosts by which God is continuously praised. It would be unfitting if God were not known wholly of God while one human being was able to be known by another person as a result of our ability to hear. Yes, and what is more, by ourselves we are able to come here to an understanding of the whole. We should also be quite vacant if we were unable to hear and perceive.

In addition, by our *nose* God displays the wisdom that lies like a fragrant sense of order in all works of art, just as we ought to know through our ability to smell whatever wisdom has to arrange. For a sweet smell, so to speak, extends over all things and urges wisdom to learn to recognize whatever is here and what manner of thing we have to contend with.

Finally, by our *mouth* God indicates God's Word—the Word by whom God has created everything. In a similar way by the mouth everything is announced with the sound of the spirit. We achieve very many things by this sound, just as God's Word did in the work of creation by the embrace of love so that nothing would be lacking to God's work. And

just as our cheeks and chin are placed about the mouth, the
origin of all creatures was imprinted upon the Word by the
sound of God when everything was created.

And the Word was with God and the Word was God.

This is to be understood in the following way: In the very
beginning of things, God's will opened itself up to the creation of nature. Without such a beginning God would have
remained within God without revealing God. For the Word
had no beginning at all. "And the Word was with God," just
as the Word is found in Reason because Reason has the
Word within itself. This is because Reason is already the
Word and thus neither of them can be separate from the
other. For the Word was without any beginning; it was
before the beginning of creation, just as it was at the origin
of creation. The same Word was with God both before the
beginning as well as at the making of all creatures, and in no
way was the Word separate from God. With the Word, indeed, God wanted the Word to create everything, just as had
been planned from all eternity. And why is he called the
Word? Because he has awakened all creation by the
resonance of God's voice and because he has called creation
to himself! For whatever God expressed in a verbal way was
ordered by the Word with his resonance, and whatever the
Word ordered was spoken by God once again in the Word.
And so the Word was God. The Word was in God and God
expressed in him God's total will in a secret way; and then
the Word resounded and led all creatures to the light. In this
way the Word and God are one. As the Word resounded, he
committed himself to all of creation which had been
predestined and established in eternity. His resonance
awakened everything to life, just as God had indicated
within humanity. God secretly speaks the Word within
God's heart before God emits the Word. This is the Word
that still remains within God, even though sent forth. Thus
whatever is said of the Word remains in the Word. Now
when the Word of God resounded, this Word appeared in

every creature, and this sound was life in every creature. By the same Word the human spirit achieves its deeds. By the same sound Reason does its deeds in such a resounding way, either by calling out or by singing, just as Reason causes musical instruments to resound as a result of the artistic skill and ability of creatures. For is not humanity gifted with reason after God's image through its living soul? And does not the soul in its fervor take on flesh? In humanity appears the first creation of God's finger, which God formed in Adam. The soul fills it with the power of life and fills it with its fullness as it grows. Without such a spiritual soul the flesh has no motion. The soul puts the flesh in motion and brings it to life. For the flesh is as intimate with the spiritual soul as all creatures are with the Word. In this way he created humanity in the will of the Father. Just as we should not be human if we were without blood vessels, we could not live if we had no connection to an outer nature. And since we are mortal, we cannot endow our deeds with life. For we ourselves exist as an original form of life in God. It is God who can give life to deeds because God is life without any beginning whatsoever.

He was with God in the beginning.

This phrase means that beginning about which Moses said under God's inspiration: "In the beginning God created the heavens and the earth." The Word that caused "Let there be . . ." to resound (as in the expression, God said, "Let there be light"), was originally present as creation had its beginning from the Creator with God. Consubstantial with the Godhead was the Word who is with God; he is like God in divinity because the Word exists within God and is inseparable from God since he is consubstantial with God. Thus everything has been made by the Word. All creatures, according to God's will, have been created by the Word of God. For there is no Creator but God alone! All the deeds of the world, all its forms and shapes, all its forms of life—everything has been made by the Word.

By our *arms* and the nearby body parts the Word indicates the power of the structure of the world as well as the heavenly signs that support and maintain this firmament, just as the arms and connections of the joints tell of the dominance and active power of our whole body. In this connection the right side of our body resembles the south wind and the left side the north wind: Both maintain the structure of the world so that — as it was written — none might exceed its prescribed measure: ". . . between us and you a great gulf has been fixed . . ." (Luke 16:26). For the darkness should neither extinguish the light nor should the light totally drive away the darkness.

Not one thing has its being but through him.

Without God's Word no creatures were made. For by God's Word all creation — whether visible or invisible — has been made, each and every creature that exists in that essence, that is to say, in the living spirit — whether in the power of greening or in the power of action. Without God nothing has been made, except for evil, which is of the Devil. This evil has been removed far from God's eye and plunged into nothingness. For there is but one God, and there is no other. Human beings who have a soul and to whom God had given the freedom of decision over their conduct were the ones who committed the sin that will be brought to nothingness. For sin was not created by God. God covered this nothingness with infinite darkness because it had rejected the light and had fled.

All that came to be had life in him.

All creation appeared in the spirit of this Creator. Creation was in God's providence, but not equally eternal with God. Rather, it was known and seen in advance and preordained by God. For God is the only life that does not originate in another form of life with a beginning. Therefore, everything that has been created was life in God, since it was within God's providence. It had its life in God. God has never begun to remember anything since there is no forgetting with God. For that particular creature was in God's providence even though it did not yet exist in time. Just as nothing exists unless God exists, the whole reality of creation also advances through God alone, for it was known in advance in the divine wisdom and preordained. Whatever was formed during the act of creation became life without extinction in God because it had to be created in such a way that natural creation would not lack for anything. For it had to guarantee the fullness of developmental possibilities along with the capacity to grow. In addition, whatever we achieve is for us full of life and moving toward life, since we have our stability in it and find our completion in this way. And because God is life to the fullest, without beginning or end, God's achievement also is alive in and of itself. This is no laughing matter. For God has given an indication of it in the *thorax*. In our wish-projection we gather what is good and what is evil in our thoughts, no matter what may develop or arise. Then we consider what might please or displease us. Afterward, we retain with pleasure whatever pleases us because it is a promise of life. Whatever displeases us is rejected with disgust so that it cannot do harm to anything that is alive. Thus everything God does is life because it is alive in the nature it has from God (*vitale in natura sua*).

And just as the Word has endowed us with our bodily life, he has also shown us the life of the spirit by taking on his own garment. We human beings were supposed to progress and expand in spiritual bands by means of another kind of life—not by means of the flesh. Thus God maintains control over every social group because God is the Son of God, both God and man. God embraces with love the clergy because they are God's children. God maintains the laity under the natural law in accord with the statement in Genesis: "Be fruitful, multiply." For the Word is the Son of man.

And that life was the light of men.

The life that awakened the creatures is also the life of our own life, which becomes alive as a result. Through understanding and knowledge it gave us light. In the light we should look at God in faith and acknowledge our Creator. We are flooded with light itself in the same way as the light of day illuminates the world. For we imagine our conscience's ability to soar to be like the heaven that gives rise to the sun and moon. Moreover, the day indicates a knowledge of good and the night a knowledge of evil, even as the sun indicates the day and the moon the night. And just as we human beings along with the rest of nature would be blind in our vital functions, so to speak, without those lights in the sky, we could also not understand our own essential condition without the wings of our conscience. Therefore, we speak of:

A light that shines in the darkness.

By the moon, the light of day also gives illumination at night, so that we can recognize through our good deeds the evil deeds that are cut off from the light. In the same way our knowledge of the good, on the basis of reason, holds back evil and turns it away.

A light that darkness could not overpower.

Night cannot darken the day because evil does not wish either to know or to understand goodness but flies from it. God informs us of this through the human *heart.* The heart is the life and structure of our entire organism. It contains the whole body. Within it our thoughts are arranged and our will is brought to maturity. Therefore, the will is, so to speak, our light. Just as light penetrates everything, our will overflows into whatever we wish. In willfulness of this kind, which claims to be the light, our will often enters into the darkness of evil deeds in order to carry them out. But the darkness has not grasped our will to such an extent that it is able to abstract our knowledge of the good. We know very well what is good, even when we do not do it.

A man came, sent by God.

This man had no appreciation of earthly dampness. He was not sent by any human being but by the Creator on high. For the fire of God's Word has caused the dry flesh of his parent to turn green again. Therefore, his flesh behaved in most circumstances differently than is usual for those born in sin. His parents, who had been touched by God's grace, brought him in this way into the light of the world. And under God's grace he strode into the world as a witness to the Son of God. Therefore, the angels named him John.

His name was John.

All his deeds were in accord with his name. For God's favor preceeded him and stood helpfully at his side. The favor of the Word, which is God, sent John to disturb our human attitude of vacillation. He was to purify the inconstant nature of sinful men and women. Hence he had a sturdy nature and a proper and spiritual attitude in which no human vacillation or sinful desire could be found.

But God the wonder-worker associated the wondrous deeds he achieved in John with the *stomach.* For the stomach claims the powers of the creatures it absorbs and then expels so that it can derive nourishment from their juices. God has decreed this to be the way of nature. For there are concealed in all of nature—in the animals, reptiles, birds and fishes as well as in the plants and fruit trees—certain hidden mysteries of God which no human being and no other creature can know or feel unless this is especially granted by God. But John was sent out to the elements in a wonderful way, and he was wonderfully maintained by them. As he was free of the usual sins, he was able to live in a wonderful way with the help of the elements, despite his solitude. For he was a wholly pure human being—someone dignified enough and worthy to be received as the messenger of the hidden Son of God, who had established the world in its infinite variety and had created all the creatures. This is obviously done by means of the stomach. Just as the world contains everything, we human beings also absorb all other creatures through a change in the matter of which they are made. And just as all creatures have emerged from God, Adam also bore all human beings in his own form. For Adam's sake the Son of God really became a pasture land [that is, a source of nourishment] when the Son of God on his side bore the human species in his humanity.

He came as a witness, as a witness to speak for the light, so that everyone might believe through him.

Indeed, John became a human being in wonderful circumstances. Even though he was born according to the usual pattern of an earthly birth, his birth took place in an unusual way. And he lived also as a wonderful human being. In accord with God's instruction, he came as a witness to God's mystery. He was to bear witness through the powers active in him — to bear witness to the light, that is to say, to the God from whom all light is enkindled so that all who are inflamed by the Holy Spirit might believe in God. And they did so through the witness John gave in a wonderful way. Thus he came as a witness of the Godhead which had clothed itself in human nature. While he himself was born to a withered nature without the greening of life, he pointed to the Son who was born of the Virgin Mary and without sin. That was my will. People were to believe in the miracles of my Son through the miracle I had accomplished in John. And just as the witness was revealed in John, a true witness was clarified through the man's *thighs*, which are the witness of all who have been born. By this is meant the sex of the whole body. In this corporeality we human beings see and feel; we think and desire things; and we evaluate all our deeds according to our knowledge. For humanity is God's wondrous work (*homo miraculum Dei*). Thus it is only proper that we should bear witness to God's wonderful deeds.

He was not the light, only a witness to speak for the light.

John was not, so to speak, the light that is indivisible and unchanging—the light that is God. Instead, he came as one sent by God to bear witness to the One who is the true Light that gives light to all lights. For God is the pure example of frugality—God is totally within God as well as totally out of God. It is God who has made everything in the whole world. Therefore, God lives in every created thing. In this respect John announced Christ like a convinced witness. Just as a fruit bears witness to the roots and their nature, John himself also arose among the wonders of God. Hence he was able to bear witness to these wonders.

But humanity is both a significant achievement and a light from God (*designatum opus et lumen a Deo*). We begin to live in our flesh and again we perish in our flesh. This characteristic, too, appears as a testimony for God because God, of course, is not of such a nature.

The Word was the true light.

The Word was the light that has never been concealed by a shadow and which has never been given a time to serve or to rule, a time to wane or to wax. Rather, the Word is the principle of all order and the Light of all lights, and it gives light of itself. For God has never arisen at the dawn of day, ascending with the sunrise. Instead, he has always been where he is for all eternity.

The true light that enlightens all men; and he was coming into the world.

With its living breath this light floods through all people of flesh and blood who enter this world of ours with its changing condition of waxing or waning. This occurs as soon as we have our beginning. And just as the sun has adopted us with its light, we ought to look upon all creatures and know them. For God awakened the first human being with the living spark of the soul. Out of clay God so shaped humanity that through this tiny spark of the soul we become flesh and blood out of clay. Therefore, we shall become totally flesh and blood by the fiery spark of the soul in our descendants, provided that the foam of the human seed is mixed in a natural way. If we were not thus awakened by the soul's fire, our flesh and blood could not come into full being. In addition, the substance of the first human being would have remained only clay unless the soul had transformed it. Just as bread is made in an oven with water and fire, our flesh and blood take on humanity because of our soul.

In fact, humanity is, so to speak, the light of all the other creatures abiding on the Earth. Hence, these creatures often rush toward us humans and attach themselves to us with great affection. We, too, have a natural longing for other creatures and we feel a glow of love for them. We often seek out nature in a spirit of delight. But all living creatures that do not love human beings flee from us. They scorn other forms of life that respect us and persecute them. Despite this fear of the human species, such creatures are dangerous to us. They attack us all the more and seek to kill us.

He was in the world.

Out of the Virgin's flesh the holy Godhead put on a royal robe when he descended into her womb. Thus he became in an unusual way a human being who was not like any other. For his flesh had been enkindled by the holy Godhead. Therefore, after the Last Day when every human being will be transformed, the souls of the elect will lift up in faith to heaven the bodies which they once had in this world. God will bring this about in the power no creature can measure. At that time, as previously stated, we shall be clothed in flesh. Our bones will again be filled with marrow even though we shall not experience a lack of food or drink or other kind of nourishment. For then we shall enter into the Godhead's power without undergoing any unstable transformation because we shall become members of Christ in goodness. We shall become members of Christ who, although the Son of God, suffered in this world much sorrow and contradiction. The Devil, the discoverer of all snares, could not be aware of this. For he has after all a beginning. The Devil, to be sure, hastened to deny Christ as did all his followers who do not wish to listen to God. Yet the Devil, in spite of all his efforts, was not able to prevent our elevation into everlasting life.

The world had its being through him.

The world has its being through him, not the Word through the world. For all creatures — both the visible and the invisible — came out of the Word of God. For there are creatures that cannot be seen or touched; others, however, can be both seen and touched. We include within ourselves both kinds, that is to say, in the form of our soul and our body. For we have been formed in the image and likeness of God. Hence, we have dominance through the Word and we accomplish things by our own hand. In this way God has ordained the human species according to God because it was resolved in God's will that the Son should assume human flesh.

And the world did not know him.

For the sons of this world, dominated by worldly change, have not noted, in the blindness of their ignorance, either his coming or his achievement. They are like a child who is not aware of this knowledge or achievement. God has called attention to this fact through our *thighs* and *knees*. By these limbs God indicates the unwittingly childish aspect of the human species.

A child cannot run well because its marrow and bones are not strong enough since it has been nourished on milk and soft foods. Similarly, adults could not walk by themselves if they had no legs and feet but only thighs and knees. On this same analogy, if such persons were knowingly and willfully without faith, they would lack the fire of the Holy Spirit by which to recognize God and they would be unable to walk on the path of justice.

He came to his own domain.

For he had created the world and clothed himself in human nature. Hence, all creatures are an indication of him, just as a coin displays the image of the ruler. God had created the world which God wished to prepare as our home. Because God wished to attract us, God made us in God's own image and likeness. Hence, everything belongs to God.

And his own people did not accept him.

As human beings we were his because he had created us, because he had made us especially in his image. Nevertheless, we denied him by not recognizing him as our Creator. This is because we did not realize that we were created by him alone. Unbelievers did not accept his humanity. In their unbelieving blindness they did not recognize God in his human nature. This situation has the following analysis with respect to our body: Our *legs* indicate our youth—a period that is silly and empty. It is the time when we should like to possess greenness and blossoming and the whole world. It is a time when we think madly that we are cleverer than others because our marrow and our bones have reached their fullest strength. This is how the Jews and pagans behaved. They loved the vanity of the world. They believed they knew things they did not know, and they believed they were what they were not. But they had no regard for the One who had given them flesh and spirit, and they did not believe in him. Just as youth, when deluded by external nature, feels delight, the world wandered about in an empty kind of madness. Hence, it was necessary for God to show God to us in order to draw us to God. In a similar way God ordered donkeys and foals to be released and brought to God while placing God above them through the law of truth.

But to all who did accept him, he gave power to become children of God.

All people, both men and women, who accepted him in faith as God and as a human being (for God is first of all grasped in faith and then God is accepted as a human being) —all obtained from his mighty power the strength to become of their own free will sons and daughters of God in the heavenly kingdom. This means that as heirs of his legacy they were to share with him in his kingdom. And they were to do so in the same power by which a son is heir to his father. Those who recognized him as their God and Creator, those who received him in love and gave him the kiss of faith and who let him zealously and carefully examine what was theirs — all such individuals were infused with the dew of the Holy Spirit. From them the whole Church began at once to send forth shoots and to bear fruits of highest joy. Hence it is given to them to be children of God through the power of true faith.

To all who believe in the name of him.

All who had so much trust in faith that they were healed through baptism in his name were given a share in the kingdom of heaven. We do our deeds in ardent love as if we were gazing at God. We do not revere the name of God in the shadow of faith without good deeds. We also reject the strange gods who could not create us and from whom we could not arise. Instead, such gods are but companions of ours. But the name on which true faith is based is of such a nature that is has no beginning. From that name all creatures arise. It is the life by which all life draws its breath. Hence, it is worshiped by all creatures. In accord with the three basic forces that hold sway in this name, every creature with a name consists also of three principles. But creatures that are withered and rotten have no special name because they are not alive. But these three forces are inherent in the names of living creatures: the first force is seen, the second is known, and the third is invisible. The body of a living creature can be perceived by the eyes. Whatever is engendered can be known. But whence that creature has the power of life is not known and cannot be seen.

In this way God caused great wonders to appear in our *feet.* Just as the feet sustain our whole body and carry it about in accord with our pleasure, faith powerfully sustains and wonderfully displays everywhere God's name with all its visible and invisible wonders. Both our body and our deeds can be seen. But much more lies within our body that no one sees and knows. If mysteries hold sway in us human beings, how could we expect the Being who created us to

appear in the light of day! For none of us, no matter how
long we may live in this world, can know how this could actually come to pass.

*Those who are not born of blood nor of the true urge of the flesh
nor of the will of man but of God himself.*

God's Son states: ". . . what is born of the flesh is flesh;
what is born of the Spirit is spirit" (John 3:6). The flesh is
conceived in sin and born of the flesh. But since God is a
Spirit, all spiritual beings arise from God. The spirit does not
become flesh nor does the flesh become spirit. But by the
flesh and the spirit we are completed. If it were otherwise,
we could not be human beings or be called human beings.
God created Adam to live forever without any change. But he
fell because of his disobedience and as a result of heeding the
serpent's advice. Hence, the serpent believed Adam to be lost
once and forever. But that was not God's wish. He granted
the world as a place of exile for us, and in the world thereafter
we humans conceived and bore our children in sin. Thus we,
as well as our descendants, became subject to death. Indeed,
when we are conceived, the sinful foam of human seed is
transformed into an inferior material. And this situation will
continue until the Last Day. Then God will renew the
human species so that we shall henceforth live in an unchanging form of life, like the one in which Adam was
created. Such a life could not occur for children conceived
and born in sin. Yet it came to pass again in the humanity of
the Son of God by which God intended to redeem the human
species, which had gone astray. Those who become God's
children by the power of good works do not have the power of
their childhood in God as a result of exchange of blood between their parents; this only makes them blood relations.
Neither does it occur out of the desire of our weak flesh,
which stimulates the propagation of the species, nor does it
occur as a result of the strength of our generative functions.
Instead, they are born of God and become heirs of God's
kingdom because of the gift of divine revelation in the
purification of baptism and through the ardent effusion of the
Holy Spirit.

God foresaw all deeds before their formation. As they acquired form and image at their creation, they did not remain empty but were full of life. The flesh could not be flesh without this vital power, just as the flesh fades away as soon as the vital power has fled. The breath of the spirit which God had infused into Adam was fiery in nature, full of understanding, and vital. Hence, through its fire the clay of the earth became red-hot blood. Just as all creation was in God's counsel before the existence of time, the whole history of human generation up to the present was in divine providence.

We are gifted with reason and capable of sensitivity. We are endowed with reason because we understand everything; we are capable of sensitivity because we sense what lies within our area of competence. For God fills our flesh through and through with life when God breathes the spirit of life into the human species. Hence we choose whatever pleases us in the knowledge of good and evil, and we reject whatever displeases us. But God sees what we have in mind. When we busy ourselves with something that is not of God, God turns away from us. At once we fall into the hands of those who fomented the first evil and thus wished to destroy heaven—something that does not even affect God. For it would be inadmissible to think that God would destroy God. If now we send up sighs to the name of God and call upon God with genuine longing, the protection of the angels rushes to our side so that we shall no longer be annoyed by the Enemy. If we ask for the good and long for it, God will send us milk right away—at first quite gently. Then God will flood us with streams of divine grace; in this way we shall rise from virtue to virtue. By divine grace we shall be constantly renewed until the day of our death. Those of us who are able to make relatively little progress will continue our way, full of anxiety to achieve our desire. But those of us who can achieve a great deal in a competent way will display both moderation and stability. Meantime, the devil has but one desire: to bring about the death of souls. He seeks this alone and nothing else, and can scarcely contain himself until he has carried out his purpose.

God, who has absolute power in all things, has a sense of
proportion in all deeds. God behaves moderately and
discreetly in order to strengthen us more and more and
make us more steadfast in what is good. For those of us who
move ahead too violently are often overtaken by perdition.
Thus we are an indication of God's complete honor. Our
good conscience points to the hosts of angels who praise and
serve God. But our evil conscience reveals God's might
since God overcomes the thing that drove the first man and
woman out of Paradise. Such is the human condition in
general. Those of us who decide for and behave according to
a good conscience display God's loving-kindness. But those
of us who seize upon and behave according to an evil conscience display God's power since God is both quick to judge
and quick to pardon.

This is the way and manner in which – as explained – we
are living beings. For God has created us with all our en-
cumbrances under the sun so that we should not live alone
on the Earth, just as God is not alone in heaven but is
glorified by a host of heavenly harmonies. All things that
form our surroundings on Earth will persist on Earth until
that number is completed which God decided in the beginning. But after the resurrection that is to come, we shall not
need anything for our natural development or support. For
we shall dwell in the glory that never fades and that shall
know no change. At that time our blessed humanity will be
clothed in radiant glory by the Holy Trinity. We shall
behold the One who was never limited by a beginning or an
end. No longer shall we be overcome by old age or distress.
We shall constantly strike up new songs of praise.

Thus, as we have stated, the flesh becomes alive through
the vital force. By this vital force alone it lives as the flesh.
Flesh and life, and life with the flesh, are a single form of
life. This was God's plan when God strengthened Adam's
flesh and blood by the spirit God breathed into him. For
God even then had in mind the flesh in which God planned
to seek concealment. And God had a burning love for that
flesh.

The Word was made flesh, he lived among us.

The Word, who dwelt with God eternally before all time and who was God, adopted flesh from the Virgin's womb through the fire of the Holy Spirit. The Word accepted this flesh in the same way as our blood vessels are the support and covering of the body as well as the carriers of our blood circulatory system. This is so even though the blood vessels are not themselves blood. God created us so that all creation should serve us. Hence, it pleased God to adopt the garment of human flesh. The Word is concealed in the flesh in the following way: The Word and the flesh formed a unified life. But they did not do so as if one of them had been transformed into the other; but rather they are one with the unity of a person. Thus it is that our body is the concealing garment of our soul, and the soul offers services to the flesh through its actions. Our body would be nothing without the soul, and our soul could do nothing without the body. And thus they are one within us, and we accept this arrangement. And thus God's work, humanity, has been created in the image and likeness of God. As soon as the spirit is breathed into us by God, this breath and flesh form a single person. But the Word of God adopted flesh from the unfurrowed flesh of the Virgin without any flame of passion. As a result, the Word remained Word and the flesh remained flesh. Yet they became one because the Word, which was within God without time and before all time and which does not change, concealed itself within the flesh.

He lived among us.

Having become human without any stain of sin, the Word lived among us like a human being. He did not in any way despise our humanity. For are we not given the spirit of a living person and formed after God's image and likeness? Therefore, we also live in the Word. For we are God's work. God carries us forever in the divine providence and does not forget us.

And we saw his glory.

We who lived with the Word saw him in an intimate association, just as the Word came into this world without sin and according to his own wonderful nature.

The glory that is his as the only Son of God.

This phrase once again emphasizes that he—the only begotten Son who was born of God in a wonderful way before all time—has revealed his glory—the glory which comes in a wonderful way from God. This occurred when he was conceived by the Virgin through the fire of the Holy Spirit. To that end there was no need of the sex act of a man in the same way as every other human being is begotten in sin by the man who is that person's father. God formed us out of clay and breathed into us the spirit of life. Hence, God's Word also adopted in his humanity a royal garment along with a soul endowed with reason. He took the garment totally and completely to himself, and remained in it. For the spirit in a human being, which is called the soul, penetrates completely and fully the flesh and considers it to be a delightful garment and a beautiful adornment. Hence, we as human beings are fond of the flesh and agree with it, even though we cannot perceive our inner being with our eyes. Thus we require this concealing garment of life, partly through a natural urge and partly through the soul's prompting. Since God had not created anything in nature that is without some special capacity or that has the characteristic of emptiness, we, too, can do wonderful things. And this Word is *full of grace and truth.*

In the fullness of grace, the Word created the cosmos in his divinity and redeemed it through his humanity. The Word exists in the fullness of truth because no lie as well as nothing unworthy or guilty could touch him, nor was the Word ever associated with such things. For the Word is the Lord who through his struggle overcame evil—that evil that is without God and has no stability of being. Thus it is this Word, the true Son of God, who is full of the grace which the Word sends as a gift and proclaims in accord with God's mercy. This Word is not diminished in his divinity as a result, but he has taken on the human condition. His humanity, too, is full of abundance because no defect of human sin has touched him. The Word is the fullness of truth because he gives gifts, he pardons, and he judges in a just way. We cannot do these things because we were conceived and born with the strain of sin. In this way God is as round as a wheel. God creates everything and wills and completes what is good. For God's will prepared in advance everything that God's Word created. Let all those, then, who fear and love God open their hearts to these words in complete salvation of the body and the soul—not by a human voice but by myself, by the One who is.

Second Part
The Kingdom of the Hereafter

Fifth Vision: The Places of Purification

VISION FIVE: 1

Then I saw the globe divided into five areas: One part lay to the east, the second to the west, the third to the south, the fourth to the north, and the fifth lay in the center. The eastern and western parts were the same size, and each of them had the form of a bow under tension. Similarly, the northern and southern parts were also the same size; in length and width they resembled the first two bows, but their inner edges seemed truncated because of the bent shape of the first two bows. Apart from this limitation the northern and southern parts also resembled bows under tension.

The other two parts—that is, the southern and northern parts—were divided into three segments of which the two middle segments had the same shape and size. The remaining four parts that lay at the outer edges had a similar shape and were at a similar distance; in length and width they seemed somewhat like the two segments in the middle. But they seemed shorter at their inner edges while they seemed broader at their outer edges than the two other parts. In accord with the above description of the eastern and western parts, the southern and northern parts were also curved and showed in one place a narrower dimension while in another place they showed a broader dimension. The fifth of these parts—the one in the middle—had the form of a rectangle. On one side it was exposed to heat, on another side to cold, and on still a third side to a moderately warm breeze.

The eastern part shone with great brilliance, the western part was somewhat overshadowed by darkness, while the southern part was. split into three districts. The two districts at the edges were full of punishments while the third part, which was in the middle, was without punishments but seen to be ghastly as a result of other dreadful monsters. The northern part of the Earth had also three districts, the two outer segments of which were seen to be

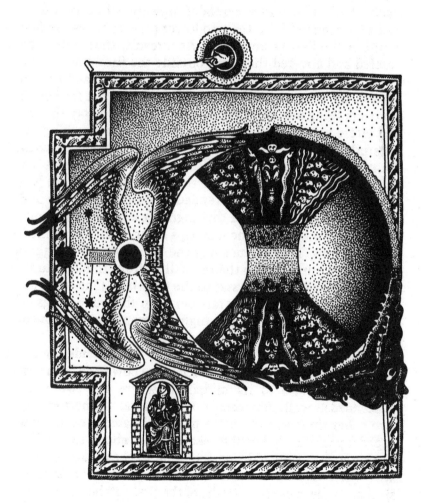

full of the most varied punishments while the middle segment with its countless horrors and punishments was seen to be ghastly. To the east I saw—above the curvature of the Earth and at some distance from it—a red ball surrounded by a sapphire-colored circle. From the right and left sides of this ball two wings emerged. On each side of the circle, each of the two wings extended upward while two other wings descended from the two lower parts as far as the midpoint of the Earth's curvature. As a result, these wings encircled and covered the Earth outside the firmament. From this midpoint a red circle extended like a bow and encompassed the entire outer part of the west, except for certain districts lying beyond this curvature in such a way that the red circle was curved from the end of the eastern wing in a westerly direction as far as the tip of the northern wing. From this curvature there also appeared to the east and within these wings a structure that ascended up to the ball. From this ball a highway extended upward as far as the middle of the wings, and over this highway a bright star shone.

Then I saw between the wingtips a fiery ball that shone in all directions. The distance was the same from the height of the Earth's curvature to the red ball as from this ball to the bright star and from this star to the fiery ball. One could distinguish different rays of stars between the front wings extended on either side of the highway from the ball toward the star as far as the fiery ball described above.

In the west patches of darkness appeared outside the curvature of the Earth. They extended like a bow from both parts of this curvature to its midpoint, where the two wings descended as well. Between the western and northern corners two other thicker, even more powerful patches of darkness gaped open like a horrible set of jaws about to swallow [everything up]. In addition, clinging to these patches were still other extremely thick and evil patches of darkness similar to the jaws and mouths of the first patches. I only surmised these immense patches of darkness but could not see them. And once again I heard a voice from heaven say to me:

VISION FIVE: 2

God has suspended the Earth in the midst of the three elements in such a way that it cannot dissolve or disintegrate. Thus God shows the divine to be wonderful and mighty. For God does not let even our flesh and bones rot in the dust. Instead, on the Day of Judgment God will restore them once again to their wholeness (ad integritatem). God created one part of the Earth in a clear light, the second in darkness, and the third part horrible to behold. The fourth part was created as a place of punishment, and here some of its regions were intended for human beings while others were uninhabitable. In the same way God placed some souls in the divine kingdom, while others were condemned to hell after a just judgment.

See how the sphere of the Earth is split into five parts in such a way that one part lies to the east, the second to the west, the third to the south, and the fourth to the north. The fifth part remains in the middle. This is because the Earth, if it were rectangular instead of round, would have to have a weakness and inequality of weight at its corners. But if the Earth did not have five parts, it could not have a proper distribution with respect to its mass. For the four outer parts give to the Earth sufficient weight for its stability while the middle part maintains the Earth in this place. This means that we human beings who are symbolized by the Earth are strengthened and brought to our soul's salvation by the five senses that stimulate us to everything we need.

VISION FIVE: 3

Hence, the part turned to the east shares its excellent humors and useful greening power with the middle district. In a similar way our sight serves, so to speak, for the origin of our glory as human beings who are in the midst of the elements; it serves for the salvation of both our body and our soul.

The part facing the west brings to this district a dampness that sometimes has a good effect and at other times a bad effect. Thus our sense of hearing, which penetrates and stimulates our bodies from the west, sometimes announces good fortune and at other times misfortune, sometimes salvation for the soul and then again despair.

The third part, which faces the south, brings to the abovementioned district a heat that is moderated by cooling winds. Similarly, the odor that rises like smoke out of the heat and causes the odor from the mixture of warmth and cold indicates to us human beings the scent originating in a higher form of longing.

The fourth part, which faces the north, brings to the above-mentioned middle districts the cold of the north as well as the warmth flowing from the east. Thus our sense of taste admits the cold and, by distinguishing what is cold from what is warm, affects us with a rich taste and a heavenly sweetness.

The fifth part, which lies in the middle, is strengthened in its steadfastness by the other parts and moderated by various influences. Accordingly, our sense of touch, which is to a certain degree in the middle of the other senses, is strengthened by them because all of them share their own powers with this sense and strengthen it for its role. This is also shown by the structure of our fingers since through them all the deeds are carried out that should lead to our eternal reward.

As you can also see, the circumference of the eastern part has the same dimension as the circumference of the western part. Each part has the form of an outstretched bow since the sun in its orbit is just as far from the Earth at its rising as at its setting. This indicates that our ability to see remains the same in our knowledge of both good and evil. Just as our ability to see ascends in its knowledge of good to what is good, it also descends in its knowledge of evil to what is evil. This is because our sense of sight recoils from evil as a result of its knowledge of good, while it turns away from good as a result of its knowledge of evil. . . [*The cycle of the southern and northern areas behaves in the same way.*] Thus our ability to smell turns to the right as a result of the sweet scent of the virtues while our ability to taste turns to the left as a result of the enjoyment of vices. In this respect our senses display the same amount of eagerness, although in different directions. They are like their sources inasmuch as one sense conforms to good while another evil. Similarly, at the very outset neither of these two senses can maintain the impetus of its direction. This is because when we start to do either evil or good, we will deliberately place a limit on such conduct because we do not dare to abandon ourselves totally to either evil or good.

VISION FIVE: 4

The two areas to the south and north are split once again into three districts that are uninhabitable for human beings — partly because of the cold or the heat and partly because of the serpents. This indicates that both the odor with which we ascend into the sweetness of virtue and the gusto with which we sink down into the enjoyment of vice affect our body and soul. Similarly, our deeds affect us but in a different way. These regions reveal that we are, so to speak, uninhabitable. After all, why can we not gain insight into the body and soul? Why can we not see what our works signify? We have not learned how to distinguish a proper standard for ourselves.

The two middle districts have the same shape and dimension. This is because the southern and northern parts are both the same size. In their correct situation, they are in full agreement with this arrangement. This also indicates that the soul exists, as it were, in the sweetness of virtue as well as in the appetite for vice right between the body and its works. In this connection, the soul keeps a firm grip on our guidance and our associations, because it fears evil and sends up sighs to God.

The remaining parts, which are located out at the extremity have yet another similar form; they are also found at a similar interval. They extend both to the south and north on either side of the above-mentioned middle regions.

But they are somewhat contracted at their inner dimension, which extends to the above-mentioned fifth district. At their outer edge, they are able to attain a certain width and thus seem to have another shape than that of the above-mentioned middle parts. But they are similar both in their shape and in their disposition (*et in forma et in dispositione*).

This has the following meaning: The human body as well as its actions—which to some extent occur at the outer edges of the body because of some feelings of self-inadequacy—have a task that is different from that of the soul. This is true, even though both body and soul are to some degree in agreement, because it is the soul which brings the vital power of the body and the senses to us in full measure. If the body shows signs of irresolution, its works also become hesitant. But if the soul sustains the body, the body's achievements are also upheld.

The middle parts have the same length and width, even though they may appear shorter on their inner edge and wider on their outer edge. Similarly, the above-mentioned eastern and western parts are curved so that at times they take up less space at their outer edge and at other times more space. This situation takes place because the parts on each side of the middle are as long as the middle parts but not so wide in the middle parts toward the above-mentioned fifth district. Near their outer edge they are wider, but they are the same size elsewhere since both ends—the one to the east and the one to the west—are contracted because of the size of the bow that is close to the inner edges of the above-mentioned four similar parts.

All this should indicate that the body (together with its works) helps to preserve itself, just as the soul organizes us in a spiritual way. Therefore, the body often causes these works to appear shorter in the absolute repose of the mind but wider in a condition of doubt than the soul can find acceptable. For the soul strives after a proper dimension while the body in its actions often succumbs to a kind of excess.

VISION FIVE: 5

The fifth of these districts, which lies in the midst of all
the others, is shown in the form of a rectangle inasmuch as
it is both maintained and penetrated by them. This part indicates that even our sense of touch ought to possess a
perfection of deeds and not a frivolity of mistakes. Some
areas are penetrated by the heat, others by the cold, and still
others are uniformly moderated by the air since the sun's
fire warms them here as a result of its nearness, thus making such areas uninhabitable for the human species.
Moderate heat and cold, therefore, allow us to make our
homes in an area. In the same way our fingers, despite many
differences, maintain the power of the hand and strengthen
it. Despite differences in their nature, our five senses per-
vade with fire and water, so to speak, our sense of touch,
thus making their helping powers available to the total
functioning of the body.

These inhabitable regions, in addition, are like believers
who have a constant regard for the divine law and address
themselves totally to the heavenly life. This is because such
persons show themselves to be inhabitable by reason of
their good deeds. But the uninhabitable regions symbolize
unbelievers who attempt to resist God's Word and work
against God. They deny the faith and attempt to harm and
destroy both the truth and the firmness of faith. By this contradiction such persons cause themselves to become, so to
speak, uninhabitable since they will not allow within
themselves an abode for the Holy Spirit.

VISION FIVE: 6

The above-described eastern part shines in great clarity.
Therein lies a place of joy and bliss. Here the blissful souls
find refreshment. This place warns our soul to direct its inner countenance toward the true light. But against the vices
and countless sins by which people sin against justice, there
have been placed at the four corners places of punishment

and regions of transition. In them the souls of those who are to be redeemed after their liberation from the body are punished because of the guilt for which they bear responsibility.

Therefore, the western part is covered by a certain dark layer and is obscure. Its darkness indicates the punishments for venial or small sins of those who could not put aside their uncertainty and in whom the sense of hearing showed itself to have varied from the truth.

The area to the south, which is divided into three regions, has two border areas full of torments. In them atonement is made for the grave sins of souls who during their stay in the body neglected to put on the sweet odor of virtue.

In the corner of virtue situated between the east and the south are found the most severe punishments. They consist of the fiery and stormy powers of the air and other tortures by which the evilest deeds of murderers, robbers, thieves, and similar individuals are punished. For God's judgment is always swift against wicked and treacherous deeds as well as against the vicious and fearful views of those who wish to resist God.

In the corner between the south and the west are many of the worst punishments. They take the form of cold in summer and heat in winter as well as other punishments by which are purged (after the dissolution of the body) the souls of those who failed to obtain atonement at the end because of the amount and severity of their sins. Since they did not possess the sweet odor of virtue, they can scarcely be saved.

Meanwhile, the third zone, which appears in the midst of the other two, reveals itself as a dreadful place—not as a result of particular punishments but because of other terrors. For if this place were full of punishments like those we find in the other zones, such punishments would be so excessive that the places where we live on Earth would become uninhabitable. As it is, because of the many terrors in this place, plagues and blights to fruit crops often pose a threat to both human beings and animals. This occurs because we human beings do not convey the sweet odor of virtue to our souls.

The northern part is also divided into three regions and very many forms of punishment take place in the two outer sections of this part. Here are purged the souls of those who have misapplied our enjoyment of living and have followed the lusts of the flesh. In the corner between the east and the north are found the most severe punishments. They consist of the cold, storms, and other torments by which the treachery of certain unbelievers is punished. While in this world, they surrendered to disbelief and scorned the enjoyments brought by the true faith. Since they found the way back to the Catholic faith through atonement at the hour of death, however, they will obtain the enjoyment of justice.

Finally, the corner between the north and the west is filled to the brim with the most foul kinds of punishments: stinking dampness, death-causing odors, and smoke as well as other tortures by which the deeds of adulterers, gluttons, and drunkards are punished. Such people tasted life's enjoyment as if it were some strange treasure.

The middle zone is a dreadful place with countless terrors but without punishments, as has already been stated. For this zone acts as a shelter for many hideous things. Now if it were also full of punishments, the places where we humans live would be infected. But simply as a result of the terrors found there, there is a danger for both human beings and other creatures. This is because we convert the wise and appropriate enjoyment of life into foolishness. And just as worms ooze out of the stench of filth, punishments, too, emerge from the stench of sin in the above-mentioned corners. Hence, fumes extend from these places of punishment over the Earth where we humans dwell, spreading evil infections among humans and beasts.

VISION FIVE: 7

The judgment, which is of the Earth and human beings, emerges from the above-described corners so that a very great amount of evil pours out of them. Yet against the dreadful darkness of these hellish places of punishment are set the highest and sturdiest mountains which no storm can penetrate. They withstand the darkness and defend the Earth, just as a wall holds up a house to keep it from collapsing.

But because we humans with our five senses are sinning all the time, we must go through a process of purgation in the above-mentioned five parts of the Earth. Smaller punishments are meted out in the darkness of the west to those who, while still in the body, found the present world a prison, so to speak, because of their love for heavenly things. But those who surrendered to the lusts of the flesh are purged in other places of judgment to the south and the north. For even though such individuals sinned, they still did not reject God and the true faith. Mortal human beings cannot live in the two main parts of the Earth's sphere to the east and the west, quite apart from the four corners to the south and the north. Because of the everlasting heat and cold and other discomforts we humans cannot live there, just as we do not receive the Holy Spirit into our hearts if we presume too much or give way to despair or if we neglect the right and incline to the left. In this way God often carries out the divine judgment over the four corners of the Earth, as John saw in the Book of Revelation.

VISION FIVE: 8

"Immediately a white horse appeared, and the rider on it was holding a bow; he was given the victor's crown and he went away, to go from victory to victory" (Revelation 6:2). This is to be understood in the following way: The first age, which began with Adam, was like a white horse. We humans sinned then out of ignorance—and this offense God avenged with divine wrath, which also entailed a punishment. God also gave to us the power to conquer and overcome our enemies so that we might fight in the war of wars against the ancient dragon. Thus God associated divine punishment with the command flouted by Adam, just as God also set up the rainbow in the clouds of heaven after the catastrophe of the Flood. This period lasted from Adam's banishment from Paradise to the Flood when God angrily drowned in torrential rains all the human race with the exception of those sheltered by the ark. And just as at the dawn of history God displayed the bow of divine anger like a judgment, after the Flood God placed the bow in the clouds as a sign that the whole world would never again be submerged by the resounding rage of the waters. In this way God indicated that believers would be saved by baptism.

And then it is said: "And out came another horse, bright red, and its rider was given this duty: to take away peace from the Earth and set people killing each other. He was given a huge sword."

This passage has the following meaning: The horse is the period of history after the Flood when peace was taken away—by God's anger and just judgment—from those opposed to God. This took place because they did not seek God's peace and did not pass it on to the other human beings. On this account God's judgment caused them to slaughter one another cruelly. In many battles they went down to destruction because they had abandoned God out of unfaithfulness. In the same way the soul commits suicide when it no longer clings to God.

And it is further written: "Immediately a black horse appeared, and its rider was holding a pair of scales." And we read further: "A ration of corn for a day's wages, but do not tamper with the oil or the wine" (Revelation 6:6).

This passage has the following meaning: The period of history after the Passion of the Son of God when persecutors arose within the church is that black horse. In their disbelief—for in this lack of fidelity they despised faith—they put on the blackness of disbelief. But the wrath of God placed a just restraint on the martyrs' sufferings. For God gave the tormentors a well-merited punishment while giving the martyrs everlasting glory. The victory of the blood witnesses was, in fact, the pregnant root of all the virtues which raised up branches in these witnesses. By these branches the virtues did away with the feasts of willfulness and the fleshly law. In these witnesses the lack of fleshly desire was realized out of love for eternal life, like the faith all believers have within themselves. This took place in the blessed hunger by which believers hunger and thirst after justice. Thus the scales indicate that we humans are nourished in spiritual temperance by the fruits of the Earth, and that we love our heavenly home with a virginal nature.

Therefore, this was the time of the martyrs, which was mingled with the blackness of the north. For in the sight of the godless, the martyrs were killed like lambs by wolves. Hence the scales have been given to the judgment of this period in order to weigh with both measures: that of temperance and that of love for our heavenly home. As previously mentioned, both measures are characteristic of the martyrs. These blood witnesses restrain their bodies through temperance, and they look longingly to heaven as an eagle keeps its eyes fixed on the sun. This signifies the measure of grain that is like a day's wages in this life. But those who refrain from sin in self-control and in accord with the commands of the Law and free themselves from intercourse with a man or a woman, those who abandon wealth and become poor – a hard and bitter course of action – they will go beyond the three dimensions of bitter feelings into a covenant of love by means of a day's wages, which signifies our heavenly home. This is what Wisdom has done; it has weighed and measured everything in compassion because God is compassionate to all. In this way the wine and the oil are not tampered with since human beings are freed of their sins by remorse and compassion.

And we read further: "Immediately another horse appeared, deathly pale, and its rider was called Plague, and Hades followed at his heels. They were given authority over a quarter of the earth, to kill by the sword, famine, by plague and wild beasts" (Revelation 6:8).

This passage has the following meaning: The horse mentioned above signifies the period of history when all lawful things and God's full justice are regarded as nothing, so to speak, in the paleness of death. For humans cry out: "We do not know what we are doing, and those who ordered us to do this themselves knew not what they have said." And thus they alone, without fear and trembling, are to scorn all of this before God's judgment and carry it out by a diabolical piece of advice.

But the wrath of God will punish such deeds and crush them because it will cause death to those without remorse and damn them to hell. At that time bloody battles will break out among humans in all regions of the Earth. The fruits of the Earth will be destroyed and humans will perish by sudden death or the bites of wild beasts.

VISION FIVE: 9

The old serpent rejoices in all punishments of body and soul that we human beings have to suffer. Because the serpent itself has lost the glory of heaven, it does not wish to let us achieve it. If the serpent senses that we are beginning to agree with it, it will think about starting up a struggle against God, saying: "Now I shall achieve all that I want among human beings!"

Right away the serpent in its hatred will plant the seed of an ugly conspiracy among human beings so that they can destroy themselves. And it will say: "I shall cause the death of human beings. Moreover, they have to be destroyed even as I have been. If I cannot exist neither should they." In its arrogance the serpent also had it in mind to destroy our descendants when men become inflamed with desire for other men and engage in perverse sexual relations. The serpent rejoices greatly over this, exclaiming in pleasure: "This is indeed a tremendous insult to the One who formed the human species when its members transgress against their own nature in such a way that they reject natural intercourse with women!" Because of this diabolical suggestion, people of this kind are disloyal and treacherous. They become robbers and thieves, too, in their murderous hatred.

But in unnatural congress with other men lies the filthiest kind of transgression and everything vicious. If such wantonness holds sway among human beings, the establishment based in divine law will be torn to pieces, and the church—like a widow—will be crushed. Princes, nobles, and the rich will be driven from their lands by their subjects and forced to flee from city to city. Nobles will be destroyed and reduced from wealth to poverty. All these things will occur while the old serpent hisses contemptuously to the serfs about the variety of morals and clothing found among the rich. The serfs, in turn, will only imitate the rich, dropping some features here and adding others there. By such actions they will constantly seek to introduce novelties and keep up with the latest styles.

Our old enemy and the other evil spirits have, to be sure, lost their beauty of form, but have not renounced the arrogance of their minds. Therefore, out of fear of their Creator, they do not reveal themselves to mortals in the form of their depravity. Instead, they lie in wait for us all with temptations having to do with our moral conduct. For they always sense something among other creatures that resembles their own wickedness. But against the serpent's ruthlessness God has led a mighty struggle by opposing human reason to that of the Devil, and God has thus destroyed the Devil's craft. But this strife will go on until the Day of Judgment when its chaos will defile everything and when we shall receive the reward of life as victors.

VISION FIVE: 10

On the east, you can see at a certain height in the above-mentioned curvature of the Earth a red ball, which is surrounded by a sapphire-colored circle. This means that the eastern area symbolizes the origin of justice, which exceeds human understanding and exists on the heights of the heavenly mysteries. Here can be seen God's zeal in punishing as a result of the fullness of divine power and the divine justice of love. For although God is powerful enough to execute the divine judgements, the Godhead carries them out only in the equanimity of love (*per aequitatum charitatis complet*).

Two wings emerge from the right and left sides of the ball. Both wings extend upward in such a way that they bend backward up above and come toward one another. This is the way that divine Providence shows itself to be with regard to protecting us in both happy and unhappy situations – it does so either with a gentle kind of illumination or a harsh form of correction. Providence embraces everything striving for higher things, which it preserves on the heights of divine majesty. Another pair of wings extends on both sides of the figure in such a way that the wings touch the middle curvature, embracing it outside the firmament. Just as the topmost fortress [divine Providence] defends everything of a heavenly nature, it also protects everything in the lower regions. But Providence is inclined toward the fullness of our goodness and embraces it out of true love.

VISION FIVE: 11

A reddish circle in the form of a bow extends from the middle of the figure and embraces the whole outer part of the west, except for certain districts located outside this curvature. As a result of the perfection in which God mercifully protects those who honor the Divinity, the fire of divine wrath punishes by a correctly measured judgment all who go beyond the circle of good works, as well as all who live outside the perfection of true faith. And God condemns them to places of atonement extending back from the tip of the southern wing westward as far as the tip of the northern wing. And since those individuals have put guilt upon themselves even in the happy condition of our present life, they will now be tossed into a place of bitter suffering because they have not stayed loyal to justice.

From that curvature eastward between the two wings, a structure appears, rising up as it were toward the ball mentioned previously. This means that a city built of living stones is arising through the ascent of justice under God's protection and far away from matters of an earthly nature. This city turns its face toward the judgment of God in order to praise the Godhead, since the souls of believers are constantly engaged in praising God. For the Godhead governs everything in wisdom.

VISION FIVE: 12

From that ball, a highway extends upward as if to the midst of the wings, and above the highway a bright luminous star is shining. Thus from the judgment of God's power a way is built to perfect protection. Above it, virginity came into bloom, for the only Son of God was born of a virgin. And after him came a great crowd of people who loved virginity and were able in this way to lay hold of perfection. [The ball and the star indicate the gifts of the Holy Spirit and acquire power through virginity, a condition which accompanies the angels like a companion and promises fellowship with them.]

VISION FIVE: 13

To the west and beyond the Earth's curvature, darkness appears, and the darkness extends from both sides of this curvature, which has the form of a bow, up to the midst of the place where the wings turn downward. Outer darkness reigns in this region beyond the world. On one side the outer darkness extends up to the midst of the southern region, and on the other side to the midst of the northern region. And thus darkness rises up in the wickedness of rebellion against the fullness of God's protection. The old warrior who dwells there rules over the forgotten state of the lost souls. And he rejoices at being able to torment those souls.

Between the northern and western corners of the figure appear other areas of darkness — areas which are even harsher and denser and which have the shape of a dreadful set

of open jaws in the act of swallowing. In those regions outside
our world exists an abyss of immense harshness—the slough
of hell—which swallows up the souls of the damned and
punishes them with severe punishments because they have
accomplished the works of damnation rather than those of the
love of God. And in this way those souls became followers of
the Devil. [In the slough of hell, the condemned souls suffer
unspeakable punishments.] And thus you can come to know
about those immeasureable areas of darkness. You cannot see
them, however, because —even though we can become aware
of hell and its harsh punishments through our knowledge and
understanding— we can still never behold them with our mortal eyes so long as we remain in the body. Neither can we
distinguish how great these torments are nor their nature. As
long as we are in this world, we cannot know the soul and its
merits.

VISION FIVE: 14
God who has created all the things described above is the
universal life from which all life receives its breath, just as the
sunbeam derives its origin from the sun. And God is the fire
from which that fire directed toward bliss has been enkindled
like sparks emerging from a fire. How fitting— we may
ask—would it be if nothing alive should cling to that life, and if
that fire should give off neither warmth nor light? What would
it be like if living creatures did not cling to life, or if life did not
give off warmth and illumination? And what if neither life nor
brilliance were to emerge from the Godhead, which was before
time was? And how would it be if the light enkindled by fire
were not to give light to men and women since the fire neither
conceals its light nor the sun its rays? All this is God: the life by
which the immense host of the angels has been enkindled like
sparks emerging from a fire. And thus it would be regrettable if
this light could not give off any illumination. And this splendor is eternal since it can know no death.

How are we to understand these things? The Godhead is unique: It is of itself and within itself. God has not received the

divine Being from an outside source. God is Being itself. And, in fact, all creatures are indebted to God for their existence. It was the Deity who created spirits in great splendor. God set above those spirits a mighty prince to whom everyone looked up as if to a chandelier on which a burning flame shone. For, in that prince, all the jewels of the spirits were lit up like diamonds. But the prince had fixed his eyes upon an empty place, where he wished to set up his own domicile. Therefore, like pieces of straw, he and his followers were swept away into the abyss of hell, so that as they fell, the places of outer darkness were ready for them. There is no way to measure this abyss since the number of fallen angels is measureless. Against this false god who wished to be like God, the region of outer darkness was erected. And because of the envy by which he refused to give praises to God, the abyss of hell was prepared. God, however, protected the blessed spirits by the power of the divine majesty so that those spirits need have no fear in the future for the old deceiver's attacks. God filled their countenances with such brightness that they constantly longed to behold the divine countenance. And God extended the divine dominion over hell so that the old seducer could not destroy either by strife or by cunning the full number of those who are to be saved. Similarly, that seducer will destroy himself in a snakelike way.

VISION FIVE: 15

Then God created us in the light of divine power. God placed us in the unextinguishable day of Paradise which, without decay, was to live in fruitfulness. Meanwhile, we humans attempted insubordination and thus recognized that we were naked. This was a great source of joy to the Devil. The Devil had stripped humanity because he himself had lost the splendor of his beauty. But God appeared in a white cloud like a flame. At the time God remained alien to the human species, so to speak, just as God later appeared with a veiled countenance to Moses and other favored individuals.

God did not want humanity to remain naked because God
intended that the Son would at some time wear a human
garment. Therefore, out of the air God gave to the human
species the garment in which an animal lives because Adam
and Eve were listening to an animal when they abandoned
God's commandment. Driven into a wretched exile, they
became corruptible along with the other fruits of the Earth.
At their fall and banishment all creatures of the Earth were
darkened, just as a sunbeam shines through a thick cloud.
In the same way the entrance to Paradise was darkened for
the old Seducer so that he should never again step across it.

At that time the human species began to interact creatively with the other creatures. Just as fire enkindles an object
and causes it to burst into flame, we humans have a similar
relationship to the rest of creation. Creation itself is hidden
in a fire that penetrates and tests everything. Also belonging
to us is the water that cleanses everything. Fire burns with
such power that nothing would remain unscathed unless
fire were moderated by water. And just as water exists to
moderate fire, we are tied to the Godhead so that it will
spare the human species. For it would not be good for us if
we were to remain in darkness and not give off light. For we
too are united in fire and flooded in water so that we can
take on form. Therefore, we too achieve by fire and water
every artistic work that we make on this Earth.

God is the living light in every respect. From God all
lights shine. Therefore, we remain a light that gives off light
through God. For we are fire according to our essence.
Therefore, God cooks us in fire and floods us with water. As
a result, and because of the warmth of human flesh, this
water within us is red and flows red. Would it be according
to the plan for us to remain dark—for us who shine from
light? Or would it be right if we could not move—we who
live from fire? For if we had creative activity and no stable
abode, we should be but an empty thing.

God, who is fire and light, enlivens us through the soul
and stirs us through reason. Thus in the sound of the Word

God created the whole world, which is our abode. We are thus creatively at work with our essence, just as God formed us perfectly in every respect.

VISION FIVE: 16

But who could raise up our lost humanity, which, having been led astray, had forgotten its Creator? Who could do this but the One who, although untroubled by darkness, felt pity for human perplexity? When the Devil beheld the woman, who had put on clothing, he closely examined the covering God had given to the human species. And the Devil did so in the envious knowledge by which he knew that he had been cast out of heaven.

It is written in the Book of Revelation: "As soon as the Devil found himself thrown down to the earth, he sprang in pursuit of the woman, the mother of the male child, but she was given a huge pair of eagle's wings to fly away from the serpent into the desert, to the place where she was to be looked after for a year and twice a year and half a year" (Revelation 12:13–14).
This is to be understood in the following way:

When the old dragon saw that he had lost the place in which he wished to establish himself, he turned his wrath against the woman. For he recognized that as the child-bearer she was the root of the whole human species. He conceived a mighty hatred against her and said to himself that he would never cease his persecution until he had drowned her in the sea. For he had led her astray in the beginning. But the woman, who suffers during childbirth, grasped the exceedingly powerful help of consolation. With protection from heaven she opposed the Devil in every way. To her were given two bulwarks of bliss: the desire for heaven (coeleste desiderium) and the protection of souls (salvatio animarum). Through them she was to strive for the mysteries of her heart. There she was to grasp the nourishment of salvation. She was to endure through the period

before the Flood, the ages after the Flood, and half of the age
of the circumcision before the Incarnation of my Son. The
woman would endure until the fullness of time mentioned
in the Gospel. At that time the fullness of the true and
lawful order rose up against the old serpent. Before and after
the Flood, and especially in the age of the circumcision,
there were people who honored God and dedicated
themselves to the redemption of their souls through the
blood shed by my Son. When the age of the shining dawn
came — the age of full justice in my Son — the old serpent was
greatly frightened and disturbed. For now the serpent was
completely deceived by a woman — by the Virgin. Hence,
the serpent flared up in rage against the woman, as has been
written in accord with my will: "And thus in its rage the
snake spewed water against the woman, and this water was
like a stream, so the stream might carry the woman off. But
the Earth came to the assistance of the woman." The mean-
ing of this is as follows: In his wicked greed the old
persecutor brought disbelief and treachery to the Jews and
Gentiles in the period after the innocence of the woman
who bore the man. And he did so in order that they might
subdue the woman who had become exhausted by countless
persecutions. She was to be completely engulfed like a ship
sinking in a storm so that her name would be totally
eradicated from the Earth. In the same way an object from
the surface of the Earth that is cast into a river is totally
submerged. But with the help of the Earth the woman was
snatched away because my Son took from her the garment of
his humanity. And he has endured on his own body countless
abuses and sorrows to the shame even of this serpent.

VISION FIVE: 17

In this way God, as described above, adorned the world
with heaven and strengthened it with the Earth. In the
whole world God glorified the Divine and raised up the
human species through all the things of the world. For God
placed all earthly things at our service. This is what my

servant indicated at the behest of my mystery when he stated: "In the beginning God created the heavens and the Earth" (Genesis 1:1).

Third Part
The History of Salvation

Sixth Vision: The Meaning of History

VISION SIX: 1

And once again I had a vision: that of a mighty city. It had the form of a rectangle, partly surrounded by a special kind of brightness and partly surrounded, as if by a wall, by certain patches of darkness. The city was adorned with a number of mountains and figures. In the middle of the eastern region, I saw a mighty, lofty elevation of hard and bright stone in the form of a mountain spouting forth fire. At the same time a mirror shone from the peak of this mountain with such splendor and purity that it seemed to put into the shade the brightness of the sun. Within this mirror a dove with outstretched wings arose, as if it wished to fly away. The mirror concealed countless mysteries. It emitted a brilliance of great width and height in which countless mysteries and the most varied forms appeared.

Within this brilliance there appeared to the south a cloud that was dazzlingly white above and black below. On this cloud a great crowd of angels shone; some of them gleamed like fire, others sparkled brightly, while still others were like the stars. Like burning lights, all of them were moved by a breath of wind. And all of them were full of voices that resounded like the sound of the sea.

And that wind let its voice ring out with the power of anger, thus unleashing a fire against the blackness of the cloud. As a result, that fire blazed up toward the darkness without giving off any sign of a flame. But soon the fire blew off into the cloud, causing it to disappear and to fade away like a patch of thick smoke. In this way the wind chased the dissolving cloud from the south over the mountain in a northerly direction into an immense abyss. From that point the cloud was no longer able to ascend. Instead, it moved above the Earth only as a wisp of fog.

And I heard trumpets resound and thunder from heaven [and say]:

*What, then is this that with all its strength fell victim to
its own power?*

And thus the white part of the cloud shone even more
splendidly than in the past. But no one was able to resist the
wind that with its threefold voice had chased away the
blackness of the cloud. And once again I heard a voice
speaking from heaven:

VISION SIX: 2

*God has known everything in the divine Providence. God
has foreseen all creatures even before they assumed their
forms. Nothing that has existed from the very beginning of
the world until its end is hidden from God. This is the
meaning of the present vision.*

[The city in the right-hand corner signifies the mighty
work of divine determination. The light and darkness of the
walls indicate believers and unbelievers. The fire-spewing
mountain indicates God in the power of divine justice.]

*For God is just, and destroys all that is unjust. Heaven and
Earth are founded on God who holds together the firmament
with all its creatures just as firmly as a cornerstone holds
together a whole building.*

[The dove flying over the mirror is a symbol of God's order
of creation in the divine Providence. For all creatures have
emerged from God's will. This divine order now spreads its
wings. The two wings reveal the very essence of this ordered
creation: angels and human beings.]

*And so, indeed, a man sits there in silence and reflects and
orders everything he wishes to do. Inasmuch as God has provided human beings with the protection of the angels, God
has also endowed us—both in our wishes and our deeds
—with wings so that we can fly. And thus in the Old Testament God became silent and was, so to speak, dumb
because the whole Law only has meaning as a kind of indication [of what is to come]. For God foresaw everything: That*

form in which a living breath of the spirit and knowledge were found did not as yet know what it was to do. And then it learned how to look to the right and to the left as a result of the living breath of wind, which is the soul. If that form should turn to the right, it would receive the reward of life. But if it should turn to the left, it would become subject to well-deserved punishments. God maintained this order of things under the protection of the divine wings. But whoever has fled to God and said—"I shout to you in joy because you have created me, and my soul, therefore, depends on you"—that person will be taken up into God's right hand. And God can endow that person with the loveliest of gifts. But whoever denies God will be allowed by God—as we have already stated—to go down to his or her own doom.

When the Son of God assumed the garment of the flesh, he associated our flesh with the blessed Godhead and also with the task he wished to accomplish in his humanity. For at the time he had not yet accomplished that task. In an instant the Son took flight in great power, taking with him the human species. And this deed was a cause of amazement to the angels. For no human being, except the Word of God, could have achieved what he did in the flesh. And he sanctified human beings through the garment of his human nature so that, by looking up to him, they might deny themselves and might fly up with him—so to speak, on outspread wings—to the final goal of all our longing.

VISION SIX: 3

Some of these angels are seen in their fiery nature, others shine brightly, and a third group gleams like the stars. The fiery angels stand firmly in their great strength and are not disturbed for any reason. Yet God decided to create them for the divine countenance so that they might constantly gaze at it. In contrast, the angels of brightness can be moved by the deeds of human beings, who are also God's work. The deeds of human beings are alive in God's countenance for these angels. For these angels constantly gaze at our good deeds and carry their fragrance up into God's presence. They select whatever is good and throw away whatever is useless. The angels who shine like the stars feel sympathy for our human nature and place it before God's eyes just as if it were a book. They attend us. They speak to us in a reasonable way, just as God inspires them to do. In the sight of God they praise people who do good deeds but turn away from those who are evil.

VISION SIX: 4

All these angels are borne along by that breath of wind like burning lights. For God's spirit, which lives and burns in the truth, moves these angelic spirits against God's enemies in the power of the divine wrath.

[And thus the roar of the sea signifies the fullness of praise of creation offered up by human beings and angels. But the lost spirits refuse to offer up the glory and praise due to the Creator. On this account they are as lost and empty as a piece of paper on which nothing has been written and which does not bear the honor of handwriting. The tumultuous wind of the choirs of the angels will blow against them for all eternity.]

For most of the good angels look up to God. They acknowledge God with all the melodious sound of their hymns of praise, and laud in wonderful harmony the mysteries that have always been with God and are still with God today. The angels can never stop praising God because they are unemcumbered by earthly bodies. They bear witness to the Godhead through the living resonance of their splendid voices, which are more numerous than the sands of the sea and which outnumber all the fruits that the Earth might ever produce. Their voices have a richer harmony than all the sounds living creatures have ever produced, and their voices are brighter than all the splendor of the sun, moon, and stars sparkling in the waters. More wonderful is this sound than the music of the spheres that arises from the blowing of the winds that sustain the four elements and are well adjusted to them. And yet the blessed spirits, despite all their cries of joy, cannot fathom the Godhead and, as a result, they constantly find something new to praise with their voices. . . . [The power of this angelic gale chases down into the abyss the evil spirits of the dark cloud.]

VISION SIX: 5

A great band of angels lives mysteriously with God in heaven. With their light they radiate through the Godhead even as they themselves remain hidden from human beings unless recognized by luminous signs. Because of its spiritual nature this band is more closely associated with God than with human beings. It appears only rarely to men or women. In contrast, other angels, who are in contact with human beings, show themselves to us under certain forms in accord with God's will. Because God has prepared the angels for various offices, God has also decided that they should have the necessary contact with us. However varied may be the tasks they carry out, all of the angels revere the one God in devotion and knowledge.

Let us assume that this knowledge might seek to be something of itself rather than to fly up as a hymn of praise to the One from whom it derives its origin. If this were the case, how could such knowledge exist since it has no basis in and of itself? Reason, in accord with its very essence, relates the sound of its praises to another being and thus finds joy in that other being. If Reason wished to resound within itself, it would have less honor as its harvest. This is what Satan did as soon as he began his existence. His hymn of praise was not concerned with the Creator. Instead, Satan sought to stand by himself. But he fell, cut off and trampled upon by the Godhead, just as we cut off an ear of corn and trample upon it.

Therefore, every living creature should show respect for its Creator and should not seek to find honor of itself alone. Indeed, we humans cannot have complete joy by ourselves alone. This joy, instead, must be given to us by another human being. But if we perceive the joy that we derive from another person, we shall feel in our hearts a great sense of enchantment. For then our soul will recall how it was created by God. It will look up in faith to God, just as we look into the mirror at our own countenance in order to see how well we are looking. For almighty God created the work of creation in such a way that it will look up to God with a hymn of praise. For God has accomplished this work of creation in such a powerful and beautiful way that blessed souls ought to reject everything opposed to their true happiness. And thus they will cry out: "We shall crush anyone who tries to intimidate us!"

VISION SIX: 6

"Yahweh, the rivers raise, the rivers raise their voices, the rivers raise their thunders" (Psalm 93:3). This image should be understood in the following way: O Lord of all the world, the spirits of the angelic world have burst forth on your behalf. Like the waters of a cataract, they poured forth their power in order to drown your enemies. And once again the army of the spirits rose up on high in raging power and let resound up to God the sound of their infinite songs of praise. The angel's battle array is like the rivers of living water. The tempest of God's spirit moves them to eternal hymns of praise because these voices have taken up the struggle against the dragon of blackness.

Michael it was who, in the outcry of the angelic bands according to God's secret decision, pierced the serpent because it sought to deny God's splendor. Through God's power Michael cast that serpent down into the bottomless pit of hell. And along with the serpent its disciples also fell— those who had accepted the Devil as their leader. But the Devil himself was punished more severely than they because he had sought to look up only to himself while they had only heeded his suggestion.

After the downfall of that ancient foe, the heavenly choirs praised God because their opponent had failed. There could no longer be any place for him in heaven. Then the angels perceived God's wondrous deeds in even greater glory than they had previously beheld them. They realized that such a battle would never again rage in heaven, that no one would ever again be cast down from heaven. But in the mirror of the pure Godhead they saw that the number of the fallen spirits was to be replaced by fragile vessels.* In their joy because the number of the fallen angels would be made up in this way, the angels in heaven forgot the fall, just as if it had never taken place.

God has established, in accord with divine honor, various orders of the heavenly host. Different orders were to carry out their own special tasks. Each order, however, was to serve as a mirror to another order. In each of these mirrors divine mysteries exist that those orders cannot fully behold. They cannot fully perceive, understand, or grasp them. And thus those orders ascend in adoration from hymns of praise to hymns of praise, from splendor to even greater splendor. And thus they are forever young because they cannot come to the end of this process. For the angels owe both their spirits and lives to God. For all eternity they will behold God's fiery splendor. Out of this splendor they will glow like flames.

Believers ought to accept in the humility of their hearts these affirmations that have been proclaimed for their benefit by the One who is both the First and the Last.

*Human beings—TRANS.

Seventh Vision: Preparation for Christ

VISION SEVEN: 1

Then I saw in the eastern corner, right at the beginning of the east, a piece of marble that lay there like a mighty mountain—very tall and all of a block. Only one doorway was cut into it, and it was like the doorway of a great city. A radiance as bright as that of the sun overflowed all the marble block, but did not extend beyond it. Figures of human beings, including children, youths, and old people, extended from this rock to the eastern edge and in a southerly direction. These people were like stars behind a cloud. Their voices penetrated far to the west, like a storm raging in a foam-covered sea. From on high a radiance overflowed them, outshining every beauty possible to human imagination. This radiance permeated the whole vision with a radiance that was quickly withdrawn.

Near the eastern border stood two other figures, which were close to each other. The first had the head and torso of a leopard and human eyes, but its hands were like the claws of a bear. I was unable to distinguish any other features of this figure. It was clothed in a stony garment that permitted no motion. It had its head reversed so that the figure faced the north.

The second figure, which was adjacent, had the face and hands of a human being. Its hands were clasped, showing claws like those of a hawk. It was clothed in a wooden gown that was white from its top to the navel. Underneath, the gown was reddish in color as far as the loins. From the loins to the knees the gown was gray while it was colorful in an unruly manner from the knees to the soles of the feet. Across its hips the figure carried a sword. It stood there without any motion, and its face was turned to the west.

Consequently I beheld everywhere in the southern region a crowd of persons fluttering in the breezes like a cloud.

Some had golden crowns, others flourished palm branches in their hands, and still others held flutes, zithers, or brass instruments. And the music of these instruments resounded like a delightful resonance in the clouds.

VISION SEVEN: 3

"My heart is stirred by a noble theme: I address my poem to the king" (Psalm 45:2). This verse is to be understood in the following way: I, the Father of all, reveal openly and in the sight of all creatures that the power of my heart has brought forth the true Word, which is a noble theme: I begot my Son by whom everything has been created exceedingly well. Hence, I the One who does not change, reveal my deeds to the One who will rule over the entire Earth. All the deeds I have created since the very beginning are known to my Son.

In its power Wisdom indicated the true Word by announcing that the true Word by which everything has been created is the Word become flesh and full of wondrous deeds. Wisdom has presented it [the Word] as the king of future kingdoms and the right seed sprung from an intact kingdom of the Earth, unsullied by human generation. By the inspiration of the Holy Spirit old men and women and young people came to know this wisdom – all those who have spoken through many signs of this offspring, the Word of God, through the inspiration of the Holy Spirit.

God created the [first] man from the Earth and changed him into flesh and blood. But God took the woman from the man, and she remained flesh from flesh, which had not been changed into something else. But both knew from this spirit of wisdom that through the inspiration of the Holy Spirit a woman would bear the Son of God, just as a blossom grows out of the gentle air. Aaron's rod also indicates this. Taken from a tree, it indicates the Virgin Mary. The male has been taken out of her in such a way that she could never be disturbed by the lust of sexual union. Instead, by the loving fire of the Holy Spirit she bore that unique man. But God surrounded that man with all creation so that every creature that has come from him might rejoice that all his voices listen to him. The prophets said that a woman should give birth by an act of love and should enter into life, like a branch sprouting from the tree of Jesse. And all attributed this virgin birth to the king, who is the Son of God.

Since this woman protected the Son of God, those who saw and listened to him in his own form loved him more than if they had not seen him. For they could not fully recognize what they saw in the shadow. And thus this task was given to the prophets because they announced like a shadow in the resonance of a shadow. Nevertheless, all these things have been arranged later among humans because the sound of wisdom has explained them out of the hidden mysteries of the Godhead.

VISION SEVEN: 4

The two adjacent figures in the east have the following significance: At the dawn of justice (to which an allusion is made by means of Abel), God introduced two different moral systems for humanity. These systems are closely related to each other in time, despite many variations. The first figure indicates the period before the Flood, which was without any law at all; the second, the period after the Flood, which was under the law.

[The figure of the leopard signifies the strong and primitive nature of the human species in its natural savagery and its diabolical depravity. The iron garment is a symbol of the harshness and the weight of its sins. The figure has turned its gaze to the north because the people of this primitive period did not wish to turn away from evil toward goodness, even though their conscience showed them the infamous aspect of their doings. The figure's human arms and bear claws, however, indicate that those people, in their contradictory behaviour, had not yet subjected themselves to the disciplined order of a human way of life—a *disciplina humana*.]

When God created heaven and earth, God divided the Earth up in such a way that part of it was unchanging while another part was subject to change. Out of the changeable matter God formed humanity. Therefore, when we are awake and when we are asleep, we are subject to changeability (*homo mutabilis*). In the waking state we can see with the light of our eyes, depending on the position of the sun. But if we cannot see with the light of our eyes, we are like one whose soul is darkened as if by the night.

VISION SEVEN: 5

And God placed humanity on an Earth full of life (*terra viventium*). The Earth was not supposed to be lighted by the orbit of the sun's rays. Instead, it was supposed to be flooded by the living light of eternity. Meanwhile, humanity transgressed against God's command and was thrown back into the changeableness of our earthly condition (*terra mutabilitatis*). But the first man had begotten two sons: The first son offered sacrifices to God while the other slew his brother, thus becoming guilty of his death. For the second son murdered the one offering sacrifices to God and heeding God's voice! As a result of this bloody deed a mighty lamentation went up.

During the first stage of creation, humanity had so much power and ability that it could overpower even the strongest animals. People played with the animals and rejoiced in them. The animals respected human beings, tamed their own savagery, and became subject to humanity without altering their animal nature. But human beings changed the fair condition of their reason and mated with the animals. If something was born of this union that resembled more a human being than an animal, they hated and scorned it. But if the creature was more like an animal than a human being, they embraced it in a kiss of love.

In addition, the humans of this period displayed an ambivalent attitude, just as the leopard and the bear can exhibit the habits either of human beings or of animals. Such people did not have the dazzlingly fair wings of reason on which they might soar upward in true faith and hope to God.

Because of the above-mentioned transgression their wings were stunted. This sin had been suggested to them by the old serpent in order to destroy the honor of their reason, which the serpent persecuted with a great hatred. The Devil said, in fact, to himself: "What has the One on high done now! Such a deed is more in accord with my plan than God's. On this account I shall overcome God through the divine creation. . . ."

VISION SEVEN: 6

But after the Earth was filled with such a perverse people, I—the One who am—could no longer endure this criminal wickedness. I resolved to destroy by water all human beings, except for a few men and women who knew Me. . . .

By water and fire God accomplished divine judgment on men and women. Since God had formed them from these elements, humanity is hard pressed by both of them. And just as God penetrates the whole Earth with the moistness of water and shapes and strengthens the Earth with blazing heat, God thoroughly moistens men and women with the humors of the divine body and strengthens them with the blazing heat of the soul. But human beings, who had heeded God after the Flood in order to renew their species, became inflamed with the fear of God because they were afraid of the judgment they had already experienced. And they began to bring gifts as sacrifices to God.

VISION SEVEN: 7

From this time forward we human beings—generation after generation—have declined in power with respect to those who lived before the Flood. And as the Earth changed, our altered powers were weakened because we followed the old deceiver who had exchanged his former splendor for the baseness of the serpent. Yet the serpent seeks to deceive those it wishes to deceive and to flee from those it wishes to flee from. This is how the old enemy behaves: He destroys his victim skillfully with the fatal poison of treachery. But he quickly flees from those who overcome him. This is because the Devil will retreat from such individuals just as he himself was cast out of heaven.

That period resulted in such a flowering of our fear of God that we could withstand the old serpent. It could no longer go about with its treacherous advice to us to forget God, as it had done before the Flood. For after that event God created a new Earth and new people. And God placed the rainbow above the clouds as a sign. Never again should the waters drown the entire Earth and the human race with it. . . .

VISION SEVEN: 8

The second figure, which has the face and clasped hands of a human being, as well as the feet of a hawk, indicates the period after the Flood when the life of human beings was subject to the Law.

[The wooden garment symbolizes the Law of the Old Covenant. The colors point to the time of Moses, Abraham, and the Babylonian capitivity, and finally to the coming of the Son of Man. The figure is here motionless because as yet people feel no inclination toward spiritual insight.]

But the fiery dragon felt a mighty hatred for all who had been spared by the waters. Gnashing its teeth, it said to itself:

> *"I shall dedicate all my skills, I shall stamp and sift them so that I can destroy by other impediments those who were not drowned in the Flood. Thus I shall once again make them subject to myself!"*

VISION SEVEN: 9

And thus the period of history after the Flood extends from Noah until the Incarnation of my Son, who converts to spiritual insight all who believe in him. With him began another era, which did not lead to life according to the flesh but according to the spirit.

*For in Noah I have revealed many signs of wonder. And
just as in Adam I was mindful of the whole human race, I
predicted in Noah the age that was to come. From his tribe
came the strong and active prophets who faithfully announced with a skillful tongue what they saw in the Holy
Spirit. This message was that God would send into the
world the divine Word, which was in God before there was
time. And this Word became flesh so that the whole world
was amazed. Their fluent tongues spread this wonder rapidly across the world by affirming that the fairest child of our
species would come into the world.*

Thus Reason speaks first of all and then accomplishes its
deed according to its statement. For if that statement had not
been made, the deed could not have taken place. For God
expressed the world and humanity by the Word. This Word,
which is without beginning, achieved a specific deed as a
result of which the world put on its garment. Thus if we
should sin and then recognize God, God could draw us
again to the divine with this garment. For if the Word had
not adopted this garment, we human beings could not be
saved, just as a fallen angel could not be rescued. But what
would it mean if God were not able to rescue that angel
from his failure in case the angel would only regretfully
recognize God? Just as it pleased almighty God to create the
human species, God was also pleased to redeem anyone
who has trust in the divine.

For this reason God secretly caused Wisdom to emerge
from the divine Spirit. Wisdom was sent forth under a
shadow until God had completed the divine work. Before
this achievement, however, God announced it with advance signs. For in Noah God displayed the ark; to Abraham
circumcision was given; to Moses the Law was taught so
that the restlessness of passion, which rages like a serpent's
tongue might be confused by Wisdom. And just as the Devil
had betrayed human beings by means of animals, he was to
be crushed by animal sacrifices at rites in honor of God prior

to the coming of the Saint of all saints. . . .

[Three signs came in haste before the Son of God: the sacrifice of animals, the circumcision of the first-born children, and the Law. And just as the plough prepares the Earth, the chosen people have been prepared by Scripture, which they could not fully understand at the time. The Son of God first of all revealed to believers all the mysteries of his coming and his rapture.]

VISION SEVEN: 10

The spirit of believers spreads as swiftly as the clouds. The longing of the soul by which blissful persons seek God's work in order to carry it out—that longing can never be put to rest. Thus streams that originate in the sea never cease to flow. And because that holy longing, which is the source of all good, is rooted to such a degree in those persons, God adorns them with the heavenly host. For such persons cling to God in such a way that they cannot be separated from God.

God's order of creation foresaw from the beginning that we were to be renewed in our spiritual life. And if God permitted animals to be bound, slaughtered, and burnt under the Law so that their blood might flow, this was a sign that those persons who hasten like clouds and look up to the divine would be tortured and killed and then offered up for the love of God. Since such persons nurse in this way at the breast of virtue by avoiding lust and other vices, they already bear in their hands the palm of victory. Indeed, they shed their blood before they might have the misfortune to fall out of the net of justice through the faithless acts.

In this way they are crucified in two ways: by fighting against their body and by shedding their blood in accord with God's command. Hence, they resemble the angels who constantly stand before God. But persons who carry out their tasks in life by teaching others according to the command of almighty God resound, so to speak, on flutes of sanctity. For by the voice of reason they chant justice right

into the hearts of men and women. Thus says the Word, and
that sound resounds once more. The Word is heard by
means of sound, and it is also disseminated so that it can be
heard. Just as a flute can strengthen the human voice, the
teacher's voice can be strengthened among other human beings through the fear and love of God. Thus that voice can
bring believers together and drive off unbelievers.

[Other people persist in the virginity and glorification of
the angels. Like eagles they look up to God. They are like
the dawn and live with the simplicity of a dove. They are
the ones who play upon the zither. Still others make use of
the wind instruments by serving humbly upon the Earth
and thus opening themselves up for heaven. And so they are
joined to the hymns of praise of the angels who overcame
arrogance.]

And we human beings have our existence like a deed carried out by the right side of almighty God—a deed of God's
right hand. We shall complete the choir of the fallen angels.
And thus we serve also to defend the good angels. God has
great joy in these two systems of order: the angels' order of
creation and that of human beings. God has joy in the angels'
hymn of praise and in the holy deeds of human beings. By
them God has accomplished in accord with the divine will
everything foreseen from all eternity. But angels are constant
before God's countenance while human beings are inconstant (homo instabilis). Therefore, our actions so often fail
while nothing is lacking in the angels' hymn of praise.

Heaven and Earth concern God so because they were
created by God for the divine honor. But because we
humans are mortal, the divine revelations, which at times
were made known to the prophets and sages, have often
been veiled as if by a shadow. But if in days to come we will
be relieved of our inconstancy and become unchangeable
(homo immutabilis), we shall behold through our understanding God's splendor and may be permitted to abide
forever with God. This has been declared by my servant
David in accord with my will.

VISION SEVEN: 11

"I sing for joy in the shadow of your wings; my soul clings close to you, your right hand supports me" (Psalm 64:78). This passage should mean and be interpreted in the following way: Under your protection and shield, O God, I shall rejoice if I am freed of the burden of sin. My soul will long to come to you with good deeds. This loud sighing snatches me up to you and calls me to the might of your strength so that I may be unafraid before my enemies. For I am an instrument (*opus*) that you have made because you held me in your plan before the origin of time. For you have created me such that creation is at my disposal.

And since you have created me in this way, you have given me also the gift of acting in accord with you. For it was you who made me. Hence I am yours. You have clad yourself with spotless flesh, as it is fitting for you as the Creator, and thus you have stretched the hem of your garment. With a song of praise you have set the heavens in motion and surrounded them with the fullness of beauty in a band of angels who, even as they surround you in a band of praise, cannot cease to be amazed that you created us humans in such a way. With the same band of praise you have girded us in place of the angels who rejected and renounced the teaching of heaven. You have so strengthened us with your garment that we shall not in the future cease our song of praise. But the angels are astonished that you have taken your garment from the mortal Adam even though you did this so that Adam, despite his offence, might receive again new life, and so that the divine splendor —to which no inquiry can even set a limit—might once again shine forth to the angels in heaven.

For this reason you said: "You are always before my countenance; hence you do not need to be called back like the one [Adam] who was found again through my garment. He did not completely deny me even when he was led astray by another. Because he wished to be like me, he fell victim to mortality. Therefore, he had to be called back through the

suffering of my garment. The brotherly association with
you should not be lost in him. For even though I created you
without a body and him [Adam] with a body, I formed each
of you as an individual being.

The hidden Godhead is totally just and is only seen to the
extent it allows itself to be unveiled. Now in this way the
Godhead reveals itself to the angels who remained in
heaven without undergoing the fall from grace. In the all-
embracing power of its justice, the Godhead possesses com-
pleteness to such an extent that no one who looks at the
Godhead with the eyes of faith can go astray. But those who
do not look at the Godhead with the eyes of faith vanish
before the countenance of the Godhead, just as the fallen
angel went astray and all who agree with him. For God, who
has created everything, has also arranged everything well:
Those who look to God receive the reward of their service.
But those who wish to take no account of God will be
judged. This is what this image means.

VISION SEVEN: 12

All of this has been revealed by the only begotten Son of
God. Whoever believes in him will be saved, and whoever
turns away from him will be damned. For he has not emerged from an earthly root but from the intact Virgin according
to the will of God. Together with God he created everything
before the Incarnation. After the Incarnation he saved the
human species, which he had formed. Sinless he accepted a
human form and as a human being—the very creature he
had made—he achieved the redemption. No one could have
done it but the One who created the human species.

When Adam was a simple-hearted and shining child, he
experienced a stage of growth and another stage of sleep.
Through the mind he was to be conscious of the world
when in the waking stage; when he was asleep, his flesh
was to be refreshed. In this way he was brought to an im-
mutable earth of bliss, so that he could attain through his
mind the perception of immortality and also become aware

of the invisible aspect of life through his external eyesight. Immortal existence has no nebulous kind of light, as is the case with our earthly eye, which can only see for a certain limited time until the darkness again overtakes it. And we have to endure this because our eye is covered by a dark lid. The pupil indicates our inner eyesight, which is unknown to corporeal experience. But the eyelid indicates our corporeal sight, which faces outwardly.

Every deed we do is accomplished through these two forms of perception. The perception of our inner vision teaches us what is divine, the aspect which our flesh, in turn, seeks to block. But our deluded perception accomplishes the deeds of the night, resembling a snake that does not look at the light. Hence, our deluded perception seeks to turn away from the deeds of the light as much as possible. This is what happened to Adam when a deluded perception destroyed for him the light of living perception. Perception was in Adam like a prophecy that has lasted until the Incarnation of the Son of God. The Son was to bring to the light the gift of prophecy through his essence, just as the sun illuminates the whole Earth. Thus all promises were perceived as taking place both before and after the Law. And thus the Son was to complete the Law in a spiritual way in his own essence when he offered himself up totally to God, according to the following written statement:

VISION SEVEN: 13

"Using the clouds as your chariot, you advance on the wings of the wind" (Psalm 104:3). This statement has the following meaning: Lord, you have arranged things in such a way that the just and proper desires of believers are the wings by which you can rule over their hearts. You direct your ways by means of the words and writings of the sages, whom you raise up. For you change without blemish and perceive no sin within yourself. Hence, the clouds are the offspring of the wings which you made for yourself when you, O Son of God, climbed above them in your garment. You adopted it from the unique, intact Virgin whose womb was never opened or touched. Just like the dew of the Earth, you entered her. You are not based on a man's root but on the Godhead, as a sun's ray warms the Earth so that its seed may sprout. From this seed you grew within her without harm or pain, so to speak, in a sleep, just as Eve was taken from the sleeping man. And just as the man, who was uninjured, joyfully beheld that [first] woman, this unique Virgin, who was also full of joy, enclosed her Son within the womb.

Eve, too, was not created from a man's seed but from the flesh of a man. For God created her by the same power through which God sent the Son to the Virgin. Neither Eve, the virgin and mother, nor Mary, the mother and Virgin, has found any woman like herself. In this way God put on a human form. God covered the divine Godhead with the Virgin in the sight of the angels in heaven, where God lives. Hence, humility, which God formed in its height and width and depth, is also God's abode.

VISION SEVEN: 14

The Son of God who became man has fulfilled in himself all the historic wonders that preceded him, as has been described above. . . .

[The deception of the Magi by Herod indicates the Devil's deception. The period from Adam to Noah resembles Jesus' childhood. The youth symbolizes the period from Noah to Abraham. He [Jesus] surrendered to the waters and made them holy with his body. The time of his miracles resembles the Law of Moses; his Passion, the Babylonian captivity; the Resurrection, the liberation of the people of Israel. The infusion of the Spirit and the sending forth of the disciples are an indication of the Old Covenant that is expiring and of the conversion to a spiritual way of life. . . .]

Now God received the Son again into the divine heart whence the Son had gone forth, even though he had remained always present within God's heart, just as we humans receive our breath back into ourselves [when we breathe]. For all the choirs of angels and all the powers of heaven looked upon the Son as both God and man. Therefore, the Son inspired his disciples with the same fire he had received within his mother's womb. He poured out a mighty power through the tongues of fire. And this power was mightier than that of a lion, which has no fear of other wild animals but preys upon them. This was so that the disciples would have no fear of other people but would overcome them. The Holy Spirit changed the disciples' life into another kind of life that they had not previously known. Through the breath of the spirit the Holy Spirit awakened them so that they no longer were sure whether they were still human. The Spirit inflicted on them a bigger and greater lot in life than it had ever inflicted on anyone in the past or than it would ever inflict on anyone in the future. Although the prophets had made many predictions about the Holy Spirit, and although many individuals have worked great wonders since the disciples, no one has ever seen the tongues of fire. Because the disciples did so with their outer eyes, they were strengthened inwardly so that they no longer felt fright or anxiety in the face of danger. For the divine power had impressed on them so much power by the fiery tongues.

But God was pleased to preserve the Twelve associated with the Son. This was so that the disciples, in turn, might teach others what they had learned from the Son. Thus God has ordered the firmament. The divine celebrations are preserved by the blowing of the twelve winds and the twelve signs of the recurring months. Just as the firmament accomplishes all God's tasks by the power of fire, the Twelve were strengthened for all their wondrous deeds by the fire of the Holy Spirit. For their teaching was to stream forth over the Earth like the blowing of a wind. Just as the sun shines, their martyrdom burned, so to speak, with the south wind.

As the months accomplish their cycle by everything that holds the firmament together, God, too, accomplished all the divine signs of the Catholic faith by those steadfast men. Through the Son, God brought back to heaven the tenth part—the human species—indicated by the [lost] drachma and rediscovered by Wisdom. And thus the only begotten Son of God is also the son of the Virgin whose name is "star of the sea" (stella maris) from which all rivers flow and into which they will all return. In the same way this only begotten Son of God abides with God and from the Son comes salvation for all souls. He brought to fulfillment in himself everything announced in advance either under the Law or prior to it. He brought everything to a better situation. And thus he is wafted on the blowing of the winds. This means that by his wondrous deeds mentioned above he goes beyond the deeds of the patriarchs, the words of the prophets, and the testimony and writings of all the scholars. In his humanity he is raised above all creation—and this is a human being! From God he receives all creation as his heritage, just as he himself told his disciples.

VISION SEVEN: 16

In this way God created a superterrestrial abode and a Paradise, just as we do when we build a house for our dependents. To this home the Son of God, at God's command, brought the souls of believers after snatching them out of hell. This is what we ourselves do; after we have founded a city with a few settlers, we then bring to it a great many inhabitants. Almighty God decided all these things before the Incarnation of the divine Son, giving to us humans the advantage of being able to cooperate in the task of creation. Only we humans approach this task with our heads held high and looking up to heaven while the other living creatures are bent toward the Earth and are subject to us.

And thus we are imperishable through the rational breath of the mind (rationalis spiritus), but are given over to the maggots of decay through the flesh. Wisdom is like the words of children who as yet cannot understand the meaning of words. But when they grow up, they understand what they are saying. Thus Wisdom was incomprehensible before the

Incarnation of God's Son, but it was revealed in Christ since his is the root of all good fruit. The root first gives rise to the stem of a plant, the stem to the shoot, the shoot to the branches, the branches to the blossoms, and the blossoms to the fruit. Thus the root indicates Adam, the stem the patriarchs, the seed the prophets, the branches the sages, and the blossoms the Law. But the fruit indicates the incarnate Son of God who gave to true believers the forgiveness of sins by means of water. Just as a fire is put out by water, original sin and other sins are washed away in the cleansing waters of baptism. And because the Holy Spirit entered the water, it purified us from sin by means of circumcision. The Holy Spirit also healed our soul, which has been poisoned by the cunning of the old snake. As a result, our soul will thereafter be a temple of the Holy Spirit in the community of true faith. Therefore, David makes the following statement, under my inspiration, about human beings whose sins are not washed away by baptism.

VISION SEVEN: 17

"You bring darkness on, night falls, all the forest animals come out" (Psalm 104:20). This verse is to be understood in the following way:

[Unbelievers persist in the night and are victims of forgetfulness. But believers convert to life by permitting themselves to be purified in the waters of baptism. Only through water in the Holy Spirit can they share in salvation. . . .]

Believers should accept these words in the humility of their hearts because this statement was revealed for the benefit of believers by One who is the First and the Last.

Eighth Vision: On the Effect of Love

VISION EIGHT 1

I saw three forms in the midst of the above-mentioned southern regions. Two of them stood in a very clear well, which was encircled and crowned by a round, porous stone. They seemed rooted in the well, so to speak, just as trees at times seem to grow in water. One form was encircled by such a purple glimmer and the second by such a dazzlingly white brilliance that I could not bear to look fully at them. The third form stood outside the well and beneath the stone. It was clothed in a dazzlingly white garment, and its countenance radiated such splendor that my own face had to draw back from it. Before and above these three appeared — like clouds — the blessed ranks of the saints, who gazed intently down at them.

VISION EIGHT: 2

The first figure said:

I am Love, the splendor of the living God. Wisdom has influenced me, and the humility rooted in the living fountain is my helper. Peace is associated with humility. Through the splendor that is my essence, the living light of the blissful angels shines. For just as a ray of light shines, this splendor shines for the blissful angels. It could hardly keep from shining, for there can be no light that does not shine. I have designed the human species, which has its roots in me like a shadow, just as one can see the shadow of every object in water. And so I am a living fountain because all creation is like a shadow within myself. As regards this shadow, the human species is formed from fire and water, just as I am both "fire" and "living water." The human species has within its soul the ability to arrange everything according to its own wish.

Every human creature has a shadow, and what is alive within that creature moves now this way and now that way

*—just like a shadow. Only a rational form of life can think. Savage
beasts do not think, for they exist from day to day and have instincts by which they know what to avoid and what to seek out.
Only the human soul that receives life from God is rational.*

*My splendor has always overshadowed the prophets who
in holy inspiration foretold the future, just as everything
that God intended to create was only a shadow until it
became a reality. But Reason speaks by means of sound, and
this sound is, so to speak, a thought and a word and—to a
certain degree—a deed (verbum quasi opus). Out of this
shadow the book Scivias emerged. It was composed by a
woman who was, so to speak, only a shadow of strength and
health because such qualities had no effect in her.*

*But the living well is also the Spirit of God. God has
distributed this Spirit among all divine deeds. From this
source they have their life, just as the shadow of all things
appears in water. And there is nothing that can know totally
and completely whence it derives life. Rather, such a thing
feels only obscurely what moves it. And just as water causes
everything within it to turn liquid, the soul is a living breath
of the spirit (vivens spiraculum). This breath is constantly
at work within us and causes us to flow, so to speak,
through whatever we know, think, say, or do.*

*In this shadow Wisdom distributes everything to the same
degree so that nothing can exceed another thing in weight,
and so that nothing can be moved by another thing to
become what it is not. Wisdom overcomes all evil deeds
caused by the Devil's tricks and places them in chains. For
she was before the origin of every beginning and will continue to be in full force after the end of everything, for
nothing can resist Wisdom. She has invoked no one's help
and needs no help, because she is the First and the Last.
From no one has she had a reply because she who is the First
has arranged the order of all things. Out of her own being
and by herself she has formed all things in love and
tenderness. Nor was it possible any more for anything to be
destroyed by an enemy. For she oversaw completely and fully*

*the beginning and end of her deeds because she formed
everything completely, just as everything was under her
guidance.*

Wisdom considers her own achievement, which she has
arranged in the shadow of the living water in accord with a
just decision. She did so by revealing through the untutored
woman mentioned above certain "natural powers of various
things" (virtutes naturales diversarum rerum) as well as
writings about the "meritorious life" (scripta vitae meritorum) and certain other deep secrets which that woman
beheld in a true vision and which exhausted her.

In addition, Wisdom has created from the living source
especially the words of the prophets and the other sages as
well as those of the evangelists. She has transmitted these
words to the disciples of the Son of God so that they might
pour out streams of living water over the whole world and so
that through these streams we human beings might be
taken like fishes in a net and brought back to salvation.

The bubbling source of the living God is the purity in
which God's splendor is reflected. Within this brilliance
God has enclosed with great love all things whose shadows
have appeared in the bubbling source before God caused
them to emerge in their own shape.

All being is reflected in myself, who am Love. My
brilliance reveals the form of things, just as a shadow indicates a figure. Out of humility, which is my helper, the
created universe arises at God's command. In the same
humility God has lowered the Divine to me in order to lift
up the withered, fallen leaves once again to that bliss by
which God can accomplish whatever the Divine desires. For
God formed the creatures from the Earth by means of which
God redeemed them after the Fall.

For the human species is completely the image of God
(homo pleniter factura Dei). We human beings look up to
the heavens and tread upon the Earth, which we dominate.
We command each and every creature because with our soul
we behold the heights of heaven. Therefore, we are of a

*heavenly nature while through our visible body we exist in
an earthly way. But God has opposed in humility the human
species, which is so low, to the one who was ejected from
heaven because of his wickedness. Because the old serpent
in its arrogance sought to destroy the harmony of the angels,
God's power kept this harmony from being destroyed by the
serpent's anger. Satan was well known on high, and he
thought that he could do what he wanted without giving up
the brilliance of the stars. He wanted everything, and
because he made a grab for it all, he lost all he had.*

VISION EIGHT: 3

And once again I heard a voice from heaven say to me:

*Everything God has made has been made in love, humili-
ty, and peace. Therefore, we too should be fond of love, we
should strive for humility, and we should keep the peace so
that we do not perish with those who have scorned these
virtues from the moment of their birth.*

[The three forms represent the following virtues: Love is
God, who became a human being in humility. From on high
God brought down to us peace, which has to be fought for
with difficulty in a changeable world and which can be
preserved only with difficulty.]

*But the human species, which is God's deed, will praise
God because the souls of human beings will live by praising
God, just as the angels now do. For as long as we humans
live in our earthly time, we act upon the Earth according to
our own wishes and desires, and in this way point to God.
For we bear the divine seal. In the company of these forms,
the hosts of the saints appear, and the saints regard the
forms carefully, as they would a cloud. For through love and
humility we attain the honor of the heavens on high, while
the spirit of believers flies like a cloud from virtue to virtue.
This is because love and humility, which are both severe
and gentle, direct the spirit through careful consideration
and concern toward a longing for higher things.*

For love is the adornment of God's deeds, just as a dia-
mond adorns a ring. But humility has revealed itself in the
Incarnation of the Son of God, which emerged from the in-
tact Star of the Sea. . . .[Love has always been fertile and
was never idle. The Church received these three virtues as
an adornment and dowry.]

VISION EIGHT: 4

. . . And thus humanity is the deed of God's right hand.
God's hand clothed us and called us to the heavenly wedding
feast. This is what humility did because the highest God look-
ed down upon the center of the Earth and established the
divine Church through ordinary people. Those who have
fallen should rise up in repentance and renew themselves by a
holy change of life through the multiplicity of virtues like
fresh-blooming flowers. Yet arrogance is always evil because
it oppresses everything, disperses everything, and deprives
everything. By way of contrast, humility does not rob people
or take anything from them. Rather, it holds together
everything in love. God has condescended to the Earth in love
and brought together all the powers of the virtues. For the vir-
tues strive toward the Son of God, just as a virgin rejects men
and calls Christ her bridegroom. Such virtues are associated
with humility when Christ goes with them to the wedding
feast of the King.

Believers should accept these words in the humility of
their hearts because these words were revealed for the benefit
of believers by One who is both the First and the Last.

Ninth Vision: Completion of the Cosmos

VISION NINE: 1

Thereupon, I saw close to the northern corner a figure facing to the east. Its face and feet shone with such brilliance that they dazzled my eyes. It wore a gown of white silk and over it a green mantle richly adorned with the most varied precious stones. There were pendants on its ears, a collar on its breast, and coils on its arms.

In the middle of the northern region I saw a second figure that stood there in an erect posture—a marvelous appearance. On top, where its head was, it shone with a splendor that blinded my eyes. At the center of its stomach one could see a human head with grey hair and a beard. But its feet were like a lion's claws. The figure had six wings, two of which emerged from its shoulders in such a way that they came together again behind the figure with a flourish and covered up all that splendor. Two other wings extended from the shoulders onto the figure's neck. Finally, the last two wings fell from the figure's hips to the soles of its feet. At times these wings were raised as if they were seeking to take flight. But the rest of the body was completely covered with the scales of a fish and not with the pinions of a bird.

Five mirrors appeared on both the wings that descended from the creature's neck. On one of these mirrors, which was at the tip of the right wing, the following was written: "The Way and the Truth". The second mirror, which was in the middle of the figure, bore the inscription: "I am the doorway to all of God's mysteries." On the mirror at the tip of the wing the following writing appeared: "I point the way to everything that is good." The mirror at the peak of the left wing bore the inscription: "I am the mirror in which are seen the good intentions of the elect." And at the tip of this wing an inscription above the mirror stated: "Tell us if you are the One who is to rule over the people of Israel." The figure stood with its back to the north. Above the entire

western region I saw the dreadful vapors of the night. From the northern corner a blackish mixture of fire and sulfur emerged from the thick patches of darkness; this mixture twisted its way almost to the middle of the northern region.

And I heard a voice from heaven that made the following statement to me:

VISION NINE: 2

Almighty God, who founded the universe, has revealed wondrous deeds under various signs. God, who is wonderful in gifts, has distributed them to each and every creature in accord with the divine will. God, who wished to bring humanity back to the bliss of heaven, places before our eyes, in accord with the divine will, everything existing in the heavenly, earthly, and subterranean spheres.

[The figure in the northern corner indicates the Wisdom of true rapture, a Wisdom whose beginning and end are beyond human reason. The silken garment indicates the virgin birth of the Son of God; the green cloak indicates the world of creation along with the human species associated with it; the adornment, too, is a symbol of the order of creation that is subordinate to humanity. But we humans are responsible for the whole of creation.]

God's deeds are established in such a way that no creature remains so incomplete as to lack anything in its nature. Instead, each creature possesses the fullness of all that is perfect and useful. And thus everything emanating from Wisdom lives in it like a pure and uniquely beautiful jewel and gleams in the purest brilliance of its being. In addition, a human being who has fulfilled God's commandments is like the radiantly white and delightful garment of Wisdom. Such persons display on their green garments their good intentions and the living greenness of their deeds. Indeed, they do so with the countless virtues of their marriage portion: an earring when they close up their ears to evil insinuations; a feeling of invigoration in their breast when they reject immodest desires; an adornment bringing strength to their arms when they defend themselves against sin. For all these things arise out of the purity of faith, which is adorned with the profound gifts of the Holy Spirit and the just writings of the teachers. And by our good deeds we believers bring all these things to their completion.

VISION NINE: 3

The second figure in the northern region—a marvelous spectacle—indicates almighty God, invincible in majesty and marvelous in power. . . . On top, where the head is, the figure gleams with such splendor that its brilliance dazzles your eyes. For no one—so long as he or she is burdened by a mortal body—can gaze upon the transcendent Godhead that illuminates everything. Even the angels who constantly surround God in admiration and look up to God cannot exhaust this vision. For God is the splendor that has never had a beginning and will never have an end.

In the middle of the figure's stomach, the head of a man with grey hair and a beard appears. This indicates that the primeval decision concerning human redemption was located in the very accomplishment of God's deeds. This decision reveals the high dignity of a rectitude (*rectitudo*) that no one can measure or even grasp, just as no human being can distinguish the beginning of a wheel from its end when it is revolving. For none of us can encompass within limits what the angels themselves could not grasp, even as eternity swayed in its perfection before them and had no need of anything. This is because eternity has always been perfect.

This head has a human shape because God has created humanity in the divine image and likeness. God gave us the ability to be truly creative by doing good deeds, by praising our Creator, and by never forgetting God. For no one is like God or can ever be so. Whoever should wish to resemble God will be destroyed, for this cannot be. When God wished to demonstrate the power of divine virtue, God gazed upon the womb of the Virgin. Just as God rested from all divine deeds on the seventh day, and just as we humans were meant to conduct ourselves in accord with the divine ordinances, God caused the Son to rest in the Virgin's womb while the entire divine achievement was entrusted to the Son. And the Son had to suffer and endure so much because of our human guilt.

The Son indicated by his circumcision that we humans had to be purified by baptism. By his suffering and death he showed that he would redeem us from all guilt, and by his Resurrection he showed that he would take us up into the fellowship of the kingdom of heaven. By all these things he will complete the number of the saints up until the dreadful time of the Last Judgment.

The lion's feet of this figure point to the fact that God conceals the Godhead from mortal human beings, even though God has shown us countless benefits both in the commandments of divine law and in nature. God will draw all these things to the Divine through the Son as if by the feet of a lion. And God will test us in such a way that the whole Earth will be shaken and the firmament will revolve. This is the end that we mortals must accept. We must give an accounting for our deeds, and then we will gaze upon God's Son in his splendor.

VISION NINE: 4

The figure has six wings. They indicate the deeds of the six days of creation in which humanity calls out to God, praises God and relies upon God's protection. . . .

[The upper wings indicate the love of God and our neighbor as well as the heavenly host of the spirits on high. The two wings in the middle indicate the Old and New Testaments and thus God's omnipotence. The beating of the wings on high, in breadth, and in the depths is a sign that god has justified and ordered in truth all the heavenly mysteries. The lower pair of wings symbolizes the present and future ages and thus the fate of the world.]

In the present age one generation passes away and another follows, while in the future age the stability of eternal life will draw near. Toward the end of this world this condition will be confirmed, even though horrors and many wonders will precede this time and, so to speak, fly before it. But the voracity of the diabolical gullet inspires our loins with pleasure in sinning and fleshly desires in that very place where what we eat descends and is ejected, and where the desire of the flesh is rampant. Yet God's protection has defended our loins and endowed them with chastity by raising up their actions to what is good. For God has thwarted the lewd deeds that sprang up among the first man and woman as a result of the darting of the serpent's tongue. Later God thwarted these deeds by means of a single human being—the One who frustrated the servile licentiousness of human minds by the potent soaring of virgin nature in opposition to the rights of the flesh.

[The fishlike body indicates the hidden nature of fishes. We do not know whence they have their origin, how they develop, or what paths they follow through the waters. In accord with this figure of speech, the Son of God has come into the world along hidden paths and has concealed himself in the dead of night.]

VISION NINE: 5

. . . In the middle of the night, when the ancient Foe in his arrogance thought that he had humanity within his clutches—for this was his intent—and that he held a great number of people, so to speak, within his very heart, the Son of God came in secrecy and without the Devil's knowledge. By his humanity God's Son smashed the hook on which the Devil had snared the human species. After conquering his enemies the Son of God hung up this hook as a sign of his victory on the cross, displaying it to God and the whole heavenly host. Thereupon, the heavenly host struck up a new hymn of praise; they were overjoyed that so many holy souls had been freed from vile bondage and brought to a place of bliss by the Son of God.

But why did almighty God let his only begotten Son, who was without stain of sin, endure such suffering? This was so that the ancient Betrayer should have no reason to resist God. For the human species had often been in accord with the Devil and followed all his commands. Thus, if a sinful man or woman were killed for the sake of others, the evil spirit might have claimed that he could free no one because that same human being was given over to sins in agreement with the Devil. Therefore, that person could not free himself or herself or others from the noose of captivity. Thus the living God offered up God's only Son, who had Adam's form, so that the Son could redeem the human species through the garment of his humanity.

VISION NINE: 6

[The five mirrors indicate the five great lights of salvation history: Abel, Noah, Abraham, Moses, and the Son of God. Abel symbolizes justice and fear of the Lord; Noah, the great miracle of creation. By the law of circumcision Abraham indicates the birth of Christ. Moses indicates the fear of the Lord, which has to precede love and is also an indication of the Incarnation. The mysterious writings also point to the mystery of the God who became man and has promised an eternal reward to his elect, just as God once promised Moses in these words:]

VISION NINE: 7

"'I will let all my splendour pass in front of you, and I will pronounce before you the name of Yahweh. I have compassion on whom I will, and I will show pity to whom I please.' 'You cannot see my face,' he said, 'for man cannot see me and live.' And Yahweh said, 'Here is a place beside me. You must stand on this rock, and when my glory passes by, I will put you in a cleft of the rock and shield you with my hand while I pass by. Then I will take my hand away and you shall see the back of me; but my face is not to be seen'" (Exodus 33:19-23). This passage is to be understood in the following way:

I, the Lord of the universe, who am from myself alone,
shall show you the bliss of eternal life, which contains every
good thing if you will only revere me with a pure heart. I
who am the Creator of the whole world shall be called your
Lord if you, O Israel, gaze upon the garment of my Son,
whom I called Adam when I called him by name and to
whom I gave the garment of darkness because he himself
was dark. Therefore, no one laden with the burden of sin can
see my face while still in a mortal form because that person,
by the prompting of the Devil, is black with the darkness of
the north. And just as the bright side turns away from the
north, the brightness of the true light recoiled from Adam
when he turned to the north on the serpent's advice. Since
from that time forward no mortal has been able to see my
full glory, I have revealed my wondrous deeds in the words
of the prophets: They announced as a shadow what was
formed in light and was even darker than the light, just as
every shadow is darker than the object by which it is cast. In
addition, the sun, the moon, and the stars were wreathed in
clouds so that human beings could not see such pure
brilliance. For the human species every blowing of the
winds was concealed and no longer visible. In this way the
following announcement was made, so to speak, in a
shadow, to the human species: "Tell us if you should have
dominion over the people of Israel." For the Holy Spirit an-
nounced through the prophets the message that should have
been given when Adam was first called. And this message
was that the Redeemer of humanity was to come.

Then the Son of God came, wearing the garment of
humanity. Human beings could not perceive his divine
glory because he seemed to them a stranger. And the basis
of his way of life differed from that of other human beings
because he was without stain of sin. Yet he was seen to be a
man who ate and drank, who slept and wore clothes, and
who had no kind of blemish. But the Jews and many others
knew him only by doubting that he was God's Son. Thus

they darkened their understanding and did not accept his miracles in faith. They hardened their hearts like a rock and hid like doves in the side of a cliff. Nevertheless, his hand will grasp many Jews and pagans and countless numbers of those who are to be redeemed until all his wondrous deeds have passed by. Then he will point with his hand to his great achievement, showing the future to all his friends. And they will know how he has fought against the Devil. . . .

VISION NINE: 12

"Like the sun and moon he will endure, age after age, welcome as rain that falls on the fleece, and showers to thirsty soil" (Psalm 72:5-6). This passage has the following meaning: Adam became mortal by sinning against God's commandments on the serpent's advice. But the Son of God descended like a dew laden with sweetness into the womb of the Virgin, whose ways were mild, gentle, and humble like a lamb. His aim was to awaken the human species from death, just as the seed is awakened beneath the dampness left when a plough turns up the soil. The plough is the Law which the Son of God in his humanity gave to human beings so that they could be reawakened to life through his concern—so to speak, by a plough—and so that by his example the desires of the flesh could be overturned and become more and more fruitful each day after the model of the Holy Virgin, just as the Son of God himself had outdistanced human beings. And thus he sent down rain upon them and made of them a fruitful soil, full of the powers of virtue. He blessed this soil and filled it with all kinds of good fruit—with chastity, self-control, patience, and all other blessings.

VISION NINE: 13

The darkness indicates a place of punishment. The sulfurous fire, which is traversed by a black vapor cloud, indicates the lake of destruction reserved for lost souls. These people no longer have any hope in the kingdom of darkness.

Those who follow the path of madness and scorn the wisdom by which God created everything are their own condemnation. This is because there is no limit to their evil, and because they have no regard for eternal life. They do not even care to know whether there is another life nor do they wish to examine carefully and conscientiously why their own nature is so changeable. We human beings cannot understand our childhood, our youth, or the time of our maturity. Indeed, we have no understanding at all of what becomes of us when we pass away nor of how we shall be transformed. Out of the wisdom of our soul, we realize that we have a beginning. But why the soul does not die and end when we ourselves come to an end—we human beings cannot understand or grasp such matters.

VISION NINE: 14

God has established the firmament in Wisdom and secured it by the power of the stars as if by a key, just as we human beings secure our houses by a key so that nothing can go wrong. The stars assist the moon, which is lit by the sun and gives light to the stars when the sun is concealed. Through an ancient accord between the sun and the moon by which the moon sends down moisture to the Earth, Wisdom has caused the moon to become fruitful for the human species, which constitutes "all of creation" (omnis creatura). The sun signifies the Godhead while the moon signifies the infinite sequences of human generations; both sun and moon are an adornment of Wisdom.

The firmament is the throne of all beauty, just as we humans have the Earth, which is our home. God furnished all this beauty for the divine glory as it was preordained by Wisdom. Therefore, creation was, so to speak, Wisdom's garment because Wisdom clothes her own achievement in the same way as we human beings are aware that we are wearing clothes. For if we were created so that we could do without clothing, we would have no need of any technical skill (opus) nor would we need to be honored by any kind of service. We would only need the body as a garment for the soul, and we would be kept in motion by the soul.

God cannot be seen but is known through the divine creation, just as our body cannot be seen because of our clothing. And just as the inner brilliance of the sun cannot be seen, God cannot be perceived by mortals. Yet God is known through faith, just as the circumference of the sun can be detected by an attentive eye. Everything achieved by Wisdom is opposed to the wickedness of the Devil, who has always hated God's work of salvation and will continue to hate it until the end of time. Then the Devil will be struck down and overwhelmed by such power that he will no longer seek to struggle against God.

All of Wisdom's decrees are gentle and mild since she washes her garments, whenever they become sullied, in the blood of the merciful Lamb. Therefore, Wisdom should be loved more than all the beauty of creation. She is known to be worthy of love by all the saints because they can never become weary of gazing at her dear form. The human spirit experiences whatever Wisdom has ordained. The spirit verifies this experience and is constantly engaged in doing so. But as long as we are in our body, our thoughts increase beyond measure, just as the angels' hymns of praise have no limit. Even when we are quite young, our thoughts are vivid. Then we express such thoughts in words of reason in order to carry out in this way our achievements, which of course could never have life by themselves since each of us has a beginning. Only eternity lives by itself and will never suffer diminishment because it existed before the time of eternal life. But if a soul is transformed to immortality, it will no longer be called a soul because it will no longer act in us through what we think. Henceforth, it will live through hymns of praise among the angels, who are spirits. Then the soul will also be called a spirit because it will no longer act through our fleshly body.

A human being is rightly called a "life" because we humans live only as long as we exist through the breath of the spirit. But if we put on immortality at the death of the flesh, we shall become totally alive. After the Last Judgment we shall continue to live for all eternity. When we were formed, God concealed within us mysteries because we were made in the divine image with respect to our knowledge, thoughts, and deeds. The Godhead had determined the entire work of salvation as well as its method of achievement, and had formed the human species in such a way that we could reflect and make plans. We were meant to consider all our deeds within our heart before carrying them out. And thus the human species is a place of security for God's wondrous deeds (clausura mirabilium Dei). Thus God ordains, we think, that the angels should have the knowledge by which they constantly sing reverent hymns of praise and love for God. They have no other desire than to see God and sing God's praises.

But before there was time, God had within the ground of the divine Being everything that was to be accomplished— and God had all of this without any hesitation. Thus we humans, who are a place of security for God's wondrous deeds, know God with the eyes of faith. We embrace in a kiss of knowledge the One we cannot see with the eyes of the flesh. And we imitate God's example. But the angels carry our finest deeds in an aroma of goodness into the divine presence, calling them to the attention of the Highest God. At the same time, our evil deeds, which follow a path different from that of God, are consigned to their lawful Judge.

Believers should accept these statements with a humble heart because these announcements are made for their benefit by One who is both the First and the Last.

Tenth Vision: On the End of Time

VISION TEN: 1

Then I saw, near the mountain and in the midst of the eastern region, a wheel of wonderful size that resembled a dazzling white cloud. To the east I saw a dark line on the left that extended obliquely to the right, looking like human breath. On the middle of the wheel and above this line another line appeared, as bright as the dawn. From the top of the wheel this line descended to the middle of the first line. The upper part of this half-wheel emitted a green glow from its left side to its midpoint while from its rightside to its midpoint there was a reddish sheen. And this took place in such a way that both colors shared the same space. But the half of the wheel that lay obliquely under the line displayed a whitish color mixed with black.

And behold! In the midst of this wheel I saw again on top of the aforementioned line the figure that at the outset was named to me as "Love." But now I saw her adorned differently from the way in which she had earlier appeared to me. Her countenance shone like the sun, her clothing was a flaming kind of scarlet, and about her neck she had a golden ribbon adorned with costly gems. She wore shoes as radiant as the lightning.

Before the figure's face appeared a tablet that gleamed like crystal. And on it was the following inscription: "I shall display myself in beauty, shining like silver. For the Divinity, who is without any beginning, shines forth in great splendor." But everything that has a beginning is contradictory in its fearful existence; it cannot completely grasp God's mysteries.

The figure gazed at the tablet. And at once the line on which she was sitting sprang into motion. And at the point where the left side of this wheel was attached, the outer side of the wheel at once became somewhat watery for a narrow

space and then—above the half of the divided wheel that lay
obliquely under the line—it became reddish and finally pure
and luminous. But the outer side of the wheel turned again
cloudy and stormy near the end of that half of the wheel
where the line was fastened.

And I heard a voice from heaven say to me:

VISION TEN: 2

*O human being, listen to and understand the words of the
One who was and is here, and who is not subject to the inconstancy of the ages. Enclosed in God was that most ancient plan—the will to carry out each and every one of the
divine works. Before even the days had their origin, God
gazed upon these works like a sun ray because they were
things that were to come. For God is One alone, and nothing
can be added to the divine unity. Yet God foresaw that a certain future work would seek to usurp a resemblance to this
unity. Therefore, God reacted negatively to that creature.
For God is the unity that knows nothing similar to it. If this
were not so, then God could scarcely be called "the One."
On this account God thrust down the creature who improperly sought this unity. And thus every human soul endowed with reason exists as a soul that emerges from the
true God. That soul should choose what is pleasing to it and
reject whatever is displeasing. For the soul knows what is
good and what is harmful.*

*Although God is One, God foresaw within the might of
the divine heart a particular work that would be multiplied
in a wondrous manner. This same God is that living fire by
which souls live and breathe. God was before anything had
its beginning and is both the origin and the age of ages. The
present vision seeks to represent all these ideas. . . .*

[The wheel indicates God who is without beginning and
end. The dark line announces God's intent to separate the
temporal from the eternal. The reddish line indicates the
cosmic order, which has prepared everything in justice. The

green line signifies the creative conduct of all living creatures — a conduct that emerges from the green vitality of
human volition. The reddish glow is an indication of the
end of the world and the fate of the souls of believers in a
burdenless life. The gray area symbolizes distress over the
decline of earthly things.]

Just as eternity had no origin before the beginning of the
world, it will have no end after the end of the world; the
world's beginning and end will be enclosed, so to speak, in a
unique cycle of understanding.

[The entire cycle can also be interpreted in a different way
with respect to the salvation of human souls. In this case
the cycle signifies the fate of the soul prepared in advance
for its eternal rapture.]

In these arrangements the eternity of God's perfect power
indicates what should occur in the total fullness of creation. It
is, so to speak, the greening power of generation in a shoot as it
sprouts forth. For heaven and Earth were not yet in existence
when the gifts of the Holy Spirit poured out this green
freshness of life into the hearts of men and women so that they
might bear good fruit. The reddish glow indicates that things
are to be stable and unchangeable after the end of the world.
This is because everything will be accomplished and nothing
will be lacking when the souls of the saints are taken up into
heaven. And just as God's eternity had no beginning before the
origin of the world, it will suffer no limitation after the end of
the world when the blessed will know an endless joy in
heaven. God's perfect power, which includes in its eternity all
temporary things and their changeable ways, indicates that
everything is subject to God. Whoever denies God will be
brought forward and cast down into hell by this power. For
everything that contradicts God will be scrutinized.

VISION TEN: 3

But there is significance to the fact that you now see the
figure previously known to you as Love sitting on the
above-mentioned line at the middle of the wheel and adorned

differently from in the past. This is what it means: Love is quietly attached, so to speak, to God's will in that perfection by which God's power overcomes everything. For love fulfills every wish of God. Love is now adorned with this gown and at another time with another gown. For the powers of virtue at work in human beings display Love as if she were embellished with jewels. This is because everything good takes place out of Love. Her countenance shines like the sun and tells us in this way that we should turn every aim of our hearts toward the true sun. Her gown is colored a radiant scarlet so that we, by making a garment of our heart of mercy, should cooperate as much as possible with everyone who approaches us as a supplicant. About her neck Love wears a golden ribbon set with gems — an indication of the fact that we impose upon ourselves a yoke of submission by adorning this yoke with the blissful powers of virtue. Thus we who are humble in every way can show ourselves to be truly submissive to God, just as the Son of God was submissive to the Father up to the death of the flesh [i.e., up to his death on the cross]. Love wears shoes that radiate beauty like the lightning, so that all our human ways may be situated in the light of truth. In this way we can follow in Christ's footsteps and offer to others an example of honesty through our fidelity.

VISION TEN: 4

Before the face of this figure a tablet appears, shining like a block of crystal. Its inscription states that no one can fully grasp the Godhead, which is without beginning and is not subject to origin. For God's farsightedness is shown in the view of Love because Love and God's providence are in total and utter agreement with each other. . . .

[The figure now looks at the tablet while the line comes into motion; out of pregnant restfulness the creation of the world arises.]

After the angels were created, some of them denied their Creator and fell irretrievably. But other angels persevered in serving and loving God. After all the other creatures were created, God created humanity so that we human beings would find waiting for us all the things we might need. And God illuminated humanity with the living breath of the spirit. God established this wondrous image in a twofold manner as both fire and flame: The fire was in the human soul, and the flame flaring up out of the soul was in our reason. The flame of reason, however, knew that it was to act through the kiss of choice. This in fact, is the knowledge of good and evil: This flame does not burn in anything it does not select as the area of its activity. Instead the flame flees in horror from anything it does not wish to do. Perhaps an artist may urge the flame to burn to some extent in a spot of his choice. That same artist may then place the flame in the spot chosen for it and where it is now burning.

God placed these two powers in a fragile vessel so that humanity might do what was useful for itself. And just as fire has a flame within it, we rational human beings have within us the ability to act. The two powers mentioned above are found in this fragile vessel, and humanity exists with them as a fragile vessel. If fire and flame did not burn in an object, how could we see their glow? Therefore, it is absolutely necessary for these two powers to express themselves in action, namely, within the fragile vessel where soul and reason are active.

And thus the wind is charged with air and fills the other creatures through which we humans are productive. For we could not be human beings if there were no other creatures here. And God is fire and the living spirit. God has created the great work from which the Son of God assumed the garment in which he concealed his divinity and achieved his countless wondrous deeds. In this activity God's Son passed through the world until he had drawn once again to himself the tenth part that had been lost. God established this work in opposition to the one who lusted after the North, and in this way God totally and utterly overcame him. The Divinity so bruised his jawbone that he could never again lift up his head, as he had done in the past. For the Godhead clothed the good angels in splendor and arranged them in such a way that any self-centered activity that refused to obey the Creator would be punished and smitten. And reason that acts according to the wishes of the flesh will also draw God's vengeance down upon itself. But those who look up to their Creator and say, "You are my God," will light up a hymn of praise to God through the fire of the Holy Spirit in order to increase this hymn of praise, just as the sparks of a fire are increased.

Thus reason has two possible choices. Whatever it selects it will obtain and it will reject the alternative. For in an act of selection, reason cannot obtain two mutually contradictory things. Those who serve someone else have regard in this way for themselves. By contrast, those who work only for themselves cannot serve anyone else in what they do. And thus these two forms of conduct are not in accord. Human beings endowed with reason first seek and long for something, and then achieve their goal in one way or another. But animals devoid of reason live the way they must. They cannot achieve any goal, because they do not possess the eye of conscience as a result of reason and are constantly turned toward their materialistic nature. But human beings dwell with God in faith.

VISION TEN: 5

Since my will was tied to my power to produce creatures and since the world came about in this way, it was the judgment of my power to pour out the waters of the Flood. For human beings fell from evil to even greater evil because of their children. Adam and his sons, to be sure, generated children out of fear of God and according to human nature in a proper way. But their descendants inflicted shameful wounds on nature. Because I could no longer endure such things, I drowned them in the Flood. As a result, the Devil trembled because he understood that my power—the power by which humanity was scattered—was invincible.

One section in the middle of the wheel and beneath the line is red, but later it becomes sonorous and luminous. This is the period from the Flood until the incarnation of my Son whom I sent forth mightily, in the silence of my will, when the strong ages were at an end. Then the judgments of my power were changed into the redness of justice because after the Flood human beings at various times in history usurped by their actions the glory of the awe we should feel for God. Then the bulwark of this feeling of awe for God arose with Noah, circumcision arose with Abraham, the Law arose with Moses, and wisdom arose with the prophets. All of them put an end to the worship of idols, just as day puts night to flight. In them, all periods of history wound down, just as the deeds of human beings could be seen when human beings appeared. Since all these things decline the way the sun sets, and since people increase by breeding, I looked upon the large number of human beings about whom the following statement was written through my inspiration:

VISION TEN: 6

"But when the appointed time came, God sent his Son, born of a woman, born subject to the Law, to redeem the subjects of the Law" (Galatians 4:4-5). This statement is to be understood in the following way: God the Father, who is without beginning and end, sent the Son in the fullness of time—as predetermined for all eternity—for the redemption of lost human beings on the Earth, and the Son was predicted by countless signs and wonders. . . .

[Noah's ark is a symbol of the Church, just as all the other figures in the Old Testament point to the fullness of time and are an indication of the various groups of people in the future Church. But these groups are associated with the orders in which the angels offer their praise. Thus Abraham's obedience erected a tower of great beauty in the heavenly city. Moses produced the Law from this obedience and thus created the pillars of God's house. Obedience was the fire, while the Law was only its brilliance. But in the Son of God, Law and obedience were married: what was past and what was to come, justice and peace. He turned everything upside down and produced out of mere images the true God and out of mere wisdom the life of the spirit.]

And thus the teaching of God's Son produced much fruit and continued in purity, climbing from virtue to virtue. Many people submitted to this teaching and shone in the light of faith so that many others who were in darkness because of sinful Adam's neglect and faithlessness could be illuminated by true faith and holy deeds. It was necessary for the Son of God to come at the end of time because the old serpent had so totally and utterly wounded humanity through its cunning, deceit, and blasphemy. And it was also necessary for the present age of humanity to achieve in the body of the only begotten Son of God the work he has begun to carry out through the highest officials of the Church and other Church leaders—through the priests under their direction, through the hermits who have chosen celibacy, through the battalions of churchmen who are drawn up in the battle order of the angels and who honor God with triumphal hymns of praise, through the confessors who follow and look up to God as well as through married couples who observe their teachers, and through self-disciplined men and women who deny themselves and abandon the world.

In this way the Son of God has been active on his royal throne. And when the Son returned in the flesh to the Father, he presented himself to the Father. After the Son had assembled the just deeds of all human beings, he showed them to the Father. But the social groups mentioned above, which were established by the teaching of God's Son, were inflamed with zeal as they strode from virtue to virtue, just as the day burns more brightly from the first hour until the glow of the sun at the ninth hour.

VISION TEN: 7

Then the greening power of the virtues faded away, and all justice entered upon a period of decline. As a result, the greening power of life on Earth was reduced in every seed because the upper region of the air was altered in a way contrary to its first destiny. Summer now became subject to a contradictory chill while winter often experienced a paradoxical warmth. There occured on Earth times of drought and dampness, along with all the other prophetic signs the Son of God had warned his disciples to expect prior to the Last Day. As a result, many people asserted that the Last Day was near at hand.

VISION TEN: 8

And this is what the Son says to the Father: "In the beginning all created things turned green. In the middle period flowers bloomed, but afterward the greening power of life lessened." Seeing this, the manly warrior said: "I know this period well. But the golden number is not yet complete. Look up, however, to the Divine's mirror. My body is exhausted, and my small children have become weak. Think now that the fullness created in the beginning cannot fade away. For it was then my intent that your eye should not flinch until you should glance at my body adorned with precious stones. I am exhausted because all my limbs are a prey to mockery. Look at me! I shall show you my wounds. Therefore, all you men and women, genuflect before your God so that God can reach out a divine hand to you."

The intent of these words is as follows: In the beginning before the Flood, the Earth had such a greening power of life that it produced fruits without human effort. But later human beings neither observed discipline in worldly matters nor did they revere God properly; they wallowed in their earthly lusts. Yet after the Flood, in the middle period of history—between the Flood and the coming of the Son of God—flowers bloomed from the fresh sap and through every other generative power in quite a new and different way. This was because the Earth was saturated with the dampness of water and the sun's warmth. And just as flowers bloomed more profusely than in the past, the knowledge of men and women grew in the Wisdom enkindled in them by the Holy Spirit until a new star appeared. And this star indicated the King of kings.

Wisdom was aflame with the fire of the Holy Spirit through which the Word of God became flesh in the Virgin's womb. The star mentioned above was an indication of this event, and by this star the Holy Spirit revealed to the nations the deed it had accomplished in the Virgin's womb. The splendor of the Holy Spirit is the sound of the Word that has created everything. The Holy Spirit fructified the Virgin's womb and descended as fiery tongues on the disciples of the Son of God. Through the disciples and their followers the Spirit accomplished many wonders.

Therefore, this period of history, which rose from virtue to virtue, is known as the manly age. It lasted for many years in powerful dedication. Afterward, the greening power of life lost strength and was changed into a womanish weakness. People had no concern for justice and subjected themselves to insane practices of human nature. In those days people did as they pleased. Because of these individuals, the Church became as lonely as a widow deprived of her husband's thoughtful consolation and lacking proper guidance on which people can rely.

Evil moneychangers came, scattering my children in their greed and preventing them from climbing up to the hills and mountains. The moneychangers deprived my children of their nobility, their heritage, their possessions, and their wealth. They acted like hungry wolves, lying in wait along the path of the sheep, snatching them away and devouring them. And such moneychangers chased away the sheep they could not eat. Through sad subterfuges they have devoured my small children like evil tyrants who employ the law of the stronger. Therefore, these days are a prison full of the Devil's wiles.

[But God has promised these days of chastening as well as all the weaknesses and illnesses of the body. Creation itself becomes an instrument of the chastening until finally on

the Last Day justice will rise up in the midst of feminine
weakness and display its rent garment, which justice had
received from the apostles. For justice was the garment and
the adornment of all the apostles.]

VISION TEN: 9

It was *Matthew* who taught people lightly and sweetly
through the mildness of his thought and without any abra-
siveness of mind. In every way he strengthened the teaching
of the apostles and acknowledged it, so to speak, as the
model for his own method of instruction. And thus he converted young people in true faith to God by his preaching,
which trickled down to them as deliciously as honey.
Because of the gentleness of his way of life, people accepted
his teaching just the way an infant sucks milk. Indeed, the
Holy Spirit influenced him in such a way that he gave an accurate account of the incarnation of God's Son. Matthew
himself prepared a garment made from the silk of good intentions, that is, from a righteous contrition. And just as
daylight prepares the way for brightness, he applied all
these things to justice, and for the sake of justice he did not
avoid martyrdom.

By way of contrast, *Thomas* upheld for people a strict and
difficult morality through his own conduct. He did not
undertake anything frivolously and did not come to
agreements easily, but he believed what he had seen.
Anything that was not visible, however, he grasped only
through the evidence of outer signs. And thus signs are
known through deeds because bodily things are seen in a
bodily way, while spiritual things are grasped in a spiritual
way. Men and women, as well, are known as spiritual beings by the holiness of their deeds. In this way Thomas converted many people to God. He gave to justice a long gown
of green silk, which was worn over a white vestment, and
this gown shone with the brilliance of the sun. By the rectitude of his good intentions he adorned justice and caused
it to outshine every other source of light. He converted the

hearts of unbelievers from idolatry to God, and offered himself up in martyrdom for the sake of the Ruler of the universe.

Peter, on the other hand, wove a cloak out of scarlet linen, for he expressed rectitude, mildness, and severity. In this way he adored justice for all classes of Church members and subjected himself to all types of sorrow—both of body and soul.

Matthias was kind and humble—just like a dove. He kept aloof from the changeableness of human affairs as well as from envy and hate. He was a vessel of the Holy Spirit, which dwells in those who do not let their spirit roam about the streets and gaze idly at everything in sight. In addition, he performed many signs and wonders in the sight of believers and unbelievers—and he performed these works in humility—just as if he did not know what he was doing. He longed for martyrdom as if for a banquet. In this way he prepared for justice a royal throne from which it might rule in all dignity. The heads of eagles and the feet of lions supported the throne on four pillars, while Matthias flew about the four corners of the world in humility; no kind of injustice could overcome him. Far and wide he preached and for this reason suffered patiently much hardship. Yet he completed manfully all that he did. Therefore, people listened to him with pleasure and loved him exceedingly. By his humility he caused justice to take its seat upon the throne he had prepared for it. In this way God chose the twelve apostles with all their different characteristics, just as he had chosen the twelve prophets. For God is marvelous.

Afterward, God discovered a tiny spark and stirred it up with the divine fire. This fire is *Paul* in whom God achieved many wondrous deeds. God completes the divine signs both in stormy, active individuals as well as in gentle individuals so that people will not turn away and say that God carries out the divine wonders only in mild individuals. The Holy Spirit crowned all of the teaching of the apostles through Paul. He was a mountain of high intent; he was as brave as a

leopard; he gnashed his teeth against everything he wished
to overcome. For he believed that he could accomplish
everything he set out to do. In him the Holy Spirit
discovered a spark of faith. For Paul did not become a
persecutor out of envy or hate but rather out of love for the
old Law.

Thus God first created the animals and later human beings,
who were created in the divine likeness, only after the animal
world had been made. So God produced first the old
Law—which can be compared to the creation of the animals—and later overturned this old Law through the incarnation of the Son. God gave the Son a spiritual symbolism that
corresponds to the hymns of praise of the angelic army. For
just as God first formed the human species and then breathed
spiritual life into it, God first proclaimed the Law of the Old
Testament and later changed it into a new and better Law.

Thus God came upon Paul, who was filled with a powerful zeal, and God cast him down upon the ground under the
old Law. God showed Paul in this way how the name of the
Son of God was to be worn under the new Law. By snatching Paul up into the heights, God showed him the wondrous
deeds by which the Godhead was fighting against him. Yet
Paul's soul remained so hidden within his body that he
scarcely knew that he was still alive, just as the soul,
though dwelling in the body, does not display its thoughts.
For if God had revealed the divine wonders to Paul more
gently, Paul would have fallen into a fit of rage because of
his stormy temperament. Therefore, God took him in hand
most severely and submerged his entire body in pain. His
was a twofold illness: All the vessels of his body were bathed
in suffering while a series of fiery blows troubled him with a
lust of the flesh. But since he had seen with his spirit the
wondrous deeds of God, Paul's spirit had an extraordinary
strength. And because he had been permitted to behold
countless secrets and hidden mysteries—far more than a
mere mortal can express—Paul's words and preaching were
like nails which, when hammered in, could uphold a house.

For the Son of God, the one born of the Virgin Mary, had selected this man of the tribe of Benjamin. Therefore, Paul accomplished more by his preaching than did all those among whom he lived.

A woman should adorn herself in such a way as to give honor and a good name to her spouse and to appear more beautiful to him. In this way we human beings should know how to adorn our soul to please the highest king. For if we wish to know love, we will put on a golden garment. If we love chastity, we will adorn ourselves with costly jewels. If we deprive ourselves of food, we will wear garments of scarlet linen. Therefore, those of us who wish to keep from sinning, should avoid meat because meat often causes the fleshly part of our nature to fall into sin.

Paul, however, had not yet received the precept of virginity under the Law. Therefore, he did not impose it on us as a precept but rather gave it to us as a "counsel." For the law needs fear, but counsel requires love. On this account the law of fear, which is accepted only in an external way, will often be disregarded while the counsel of love, which we yearn to accept with all our heart, will be kept. Counsel was destroyed by the serpent at the beginning, and as a result of the eternal decision God became a human being. In God love burned so brightly that it illuminated the whole world. Therefore, Paul, in accord with the eternal decision, gave virginity as a counsel and not as a precept. For no one may impose virginity as a precept because God brings virginity to perfection within the Godhead. Therefore, chastity has no legal authority by way of service or of fear. It is alone and free within God and without any kind of fear.

And thus Paul is the wheel of the carriage of justice. Just as the wheel bears a carriage and the carriage bears a burden, Paul's teaching bears the Law of Christ. The new Law has been woven out of the old Law in which Moses ordained circumcision and sacrifice, which the Holy Spirit totally renewed with a new holiness and which Paul fused with a new fire to the necklace of justice described above. He sanctified every activity in great dignity so that marriage might be conducted in the fear of God, and that all who live justly might be chaste. Human beings should not discipline themselves in self-denial more than they can bear, while virginity should adorn itself with the crown of the highest king since virginity comes from God. For God formed the first human beings without any fleshly desire. Just as all these things are true, God accepts from virginity the garment without any trace of sin. In these three human conditions—marriage, continence, and virginity—Paul brought together all the virtues and all the lives of the saints, and adorned the teaching of the apostles with a dazzling beauty. He formed the shoes of justice out of scarlet silk and totally and completely abandoned all that was worldly. He accomplished more than all the disciples as he hastened down the ways that the Church would follow. He adorned these shoes with the purest gold as if they were shining stars. For by his good deeds he held out to believers the bright example of holiness while eagerly surrendering his body to suffering. . . .

James, John, Philip, Bartholomew, Andrew, and Thadeus also contributed to the adornment of justice.

VISION TEN: 10-11
Sections 10 and 11 continue the theme of the relationship between justice and the Church.

VISION TEN: 12
[God sees the extent of injustice over the course of the ages and waits until the completion of the golden number of the elect will be reached at the end of time. . . .]
The golden number—which means the martyrs who gleam like gold in the redness of their blood and who were killed for their faith in the early days of the Church—is not yet complete. For these martyrs await others who quite recently—to the shame of a false teaching that has now been destroyed—surrendered their bodies to suffering as martyrs. My beloved disciple John has testified to this event in the following words:

VISION TEN: 13

"They were told to be patient a little longer, until the roll was complete and their fellow servants and brothers had been killed just as they had been" (Revelation 6:11).

This statement is to be understood in the following way: By divine inspiration it was shown to the martyrs that those who submit to an earthly death out of love of God so that their bodies might rest in the dust of dissolution . . . are God's servants, just as they and their brothers are. . . . The outcry of the blood of the martyrs who knew no sin and did not know why they were being killed rises up to God. God's glory radiates again in them so that we can foresee in it countless future martyrs. For the splendor of eternal life will be given them inasmuch as they will find an answer to the things revealed to them. Their outcry has not been overshadowed by the filthy deeds of sinners, for the martyrs remained innocent and their blood was shed for the incarnation of the Son of God as a witness to the Lamb, which would later shed its own blood. They are comrades of those killed for faith and justice and brothers of those who will be snatched up on the last day by the Antichrist. In just the same way were the children killed by Herod who denied the Son of God, just as the Antichrist will deny him. For the outcry of a martyr's blood will mount high above that person's soul. It will cry out in accusation because that outcry has been driven out of the body in which God placed it. But then the soul will receive for its deeds either glory or punishment. The first outcry of blood began with Abel to raise an accusation up to God, for Cain had overturned and then impudently destroyed God's stronghold.

VISION TEN: 14

"Father, you are the mirror of divine justice in which the heavenly host of the angels shines just as figures are seen in a mirror. For this mirror shines again without interruption in the angels. Behold and reveal how much wrong I suffer from those who despise me! My body and my limbs are exhausted because those who should cling to me in an upright way of life lash out against me in wickedness. I find no repose where I should expect to find it in the vitality of good deeds.

"My little ones, who should walk in humility and reject all the pomp of the world, are enfeebled by things of little value. For they embrace vanity in their arrogance; they foolishly believe themselves to be holy; and they boast of their deeds so as to be praised and honored by others. And because they cease to give praise to God in their virginity they do not heed the angelic hymn of praise. For the angels constantly praise the Holy Godhead; they constantly discover new praises for God; and they will never cease to do so."

God is the brightest of lights which can never be extinguished, and the choirs of angels radiate light from the Divinity. Angels are pure praise without any trace of a bodily deed. But humanity is a form of praise based on a fleshly deed, and its deeds extol the angels. In the praise by which the angels extol God, they know also of the holy deeds of human beings and regard them as a mirror of the divine glory. For God formed humanity wondrously of soul and body. We humans do not lack the splendor of the angels because we are in their fellowship. For God has ordained that both divinity and humanity should be praised gloriously in the one God.

This was viewed with contempt by Satan who, although an angel, wished to be God. But God deceived him, so to speak, by creating humanity out of the clay of the earth. We humans, who are a union of soul and body, do not exist either as a soul without a body nor as a body without a soul. Rather the soul is active in the body and the body in the soul. Our body is, in fact, a closed chamber (clausura) in which the soul is concealed. The body often urges the soul to surrender to the body and not to prevent whatever the body longs for. After all, the soul is possessed by the body. The desire of the flesh is displeasing to the soul, of course, even though such a desire is often achieved despite the soul's wish and by means of the vessels in which the soul has to act. But if we long for the next life, which is opposed to fleshly desires, the soul will quickly carry out this longing. For such an attitude is quite in accord with the desire of the soul's core.

VISION TEN: 15
[The age of injustice was described in the book *Scivias* under the sign of the fiery dog. Men and women will have to suffer as if they were among hungry wolves; where there should be physicians, none will be found. And yet justice will triumph.]

VISION TEN: 16
After justice brought its complaint before the highest Judge, God received its accusation. According to the divine decree, God will allow punishment to strike all who have exceeded what is right, just as punishment will strike the tyranny of those who are God's foes. And people will say to each other, "How long must we suffer and endure these predatory wolves? They should be physicians but are not." But because they have the power to bind and to loose, they bind us as if we were the most savage of wolves. Their wantonness attacks us, and the whole Church is diminished as a result. For they no longer announce what is just, and they undermine the Law just as wolves devour sheep. They are voracious in their carousing and often commit adultery. And because of their sins, they condemn us without mercy. They are thieves attacking Church property, and in their voracity they eat up whatever they can. Thanks to their high office, they impoverish us and leave us destitute, besmirching themselves and us. On this account we should like to judge them in a proper way and isolate them because they are seducers rather than teachers. We must take this action so as not to be destroyed. For if they were to stay as they are, they would subdue the whole society and reduce it to confusion. But now we must tell them that they should

wear their spiritual robes in awe of God and take their positions seriously, just as the early Fathers did. Otherwise, they should depart from us and leave us all their possessions. Shaken by the divine judgment, we should face them with this statement and similar statements. We should fall upon them and cry out, "We do not want such people to rule over us with their estates and their farms and their other affairs over which we have been established as princes." How can it be suitable for those who wear the tonsure as well as stoles and cassocks to have more soldiers than we do? Is it fitting that a clergyman should be a soldier, and that a soldier should be a clergyman? For this reason we wish to deprive them of what they do not possess properly but improperly. Still we wish to look respectfully on whatever has been offered for the souls of the dead and to leave such offerings with the clergy because there is no connection between these offerings and robbery.

The almighty Father has divided up everything properly: heaven for heavenly concerns, Earth for earthly concerns. Thus everything should be properly divided among human beings: Churchmen should have their proper share, and the laity should have what is right for it. Neither group should oppress the other by robbery. In no way has God ordered that a cloak and a mantle should be given to one son while another goes naked. Instead, God gives to the first son a mantle and to the other a cloak. Lay people should wear a mantle because of the significance of their worldly concerns and because of the rapid increase in the number of their children. The cloak, however, was lent to churchmen so that they might not suffer a lack of food and clothing but not possess more than is needed.

[Thus order in the world and order in the Church should be separate, and each order should take care of its own interests.] All of this should be undertaken—both by churchmen and members of the laity—in the first hour of the day and be brought into full swing in the third hour of the day. It should be totally and utterly concluded in the sixth hour so that all classes of society can consider what they do after the sixth hour and take control of it in a different way than is now the case. Each social class should have its own integrity: Freemen should glory in their freedom and serfs should respect the obligations of their servitude.

VISION TEN: 17

[In the meantime occurs the age of the lion, which has been described in *Scivias:* terrible and cruel wars that cause the death of countless men and women and raze many cities to the ground.]

Just as a man conquers by his strength the weakness of a woman and a lion overawes other wild beasts, the cruelty of certain individuals will destroy the peace of others in these days, according to God's decree. Then God will permit dreadful punishments for enemies as a purification of their sins, just as the Divinity has constantly done since the beginning of the world. When human beings are purged by these challenges, they will be disgusted at their quarrelsomeness. Out of the awe for God they will seek justice in all Church institutions that are pleasing to God, and will do much good. They will do this in the days of freedom as well as in days of war and in every kind of difficulty. And then justice will be properly called a bride. . . . [God, the true "Soloman," will adorn the bride and let this adornment shine openly in the Church.]

Then so many new and unknown arrangements with respect to order and peace will occur that people will be a-mazed and talk about them. For such things have not in the past been heard of or known. And since peace is given to them before the Day of Judgment, just as a period of peace came quickly before the coming of the Son of God, they will not be able to rejoice fully because of their fear of the judgment that is to come. Instead, they will petition almighty God to grant the fullness of justice in the Catholic faith. Jews, too, will rejoice and say that he whose coming they have denied is already here. That period of peace that preceded the coming of the incarnate Son of God will be totally and utterly realized in those days. Then brave men full of the gift of prophecy will arise so that in this time every seed of justice will come to flower among the sons and daughters of the human species, just as was announced by my servant the prophet, in accord with my will: "That day, the branch of Yahweh shall be beauty and glory, and the fruit of the earth shall be the price and adornment of Israel's survivors" (Isaiah 4:2). This should be understood and interpreted according to the following statement:

VISION TEN: 18
On that day when the angels sang, "peace to men of good will," the One given to them was my Son, who was born of the Virgin. He was glorified by the angels and praised by the shepherds who sought him out in awe. And the fruits of the Earth—the Earth to which peace was restored and which the air served in gentleness—were most generous, and joy ruled among the sons of Jacob who, although previously most downcast by countless difficulties, were now free from all their past oppression. When the light of true faith illuminates the hearts of believers, my Son will be glorified by them: For they will believe that he has arisen from me, and they will acknowledge in hymns of praise that he has returned to me in splendor. And thus the fruits of good works will spring up among them and their bliss will increase. Snatched away from the power of the Devil and free of the punishments of hell, they will be numbered among the children of God. . . .

[The Old Testament and its offspring will wither away like the winter which has hidden within it all the green freshness of life when the New Testament, which is like the summer, causes every kind of seed and bud to reach maturity.]

VISION TEN: 19
Therefore, he said to the people who were lamenting and weeping over him: "For if men use the green wood like this,

what will happen when it is dry?" (Luke 23:31). This is to be understood in the following way: Jesus himself was the green wood because he caused all the greening power of the virtues. Yet he was rejected by unbelievers. The Antichrist, however, is the dry wood because he destroys all the living freshness of justice and causes things that should be green in their integrity to wither away, and for this reason they will be brought to nothingness. In addition, the green wood consists of the days when human beings were aware that they were healed from their suffering; on those days they no longer were afraid of the horrors of the future judgment. At the time of the separation about which Paul, my chosen vessel, has spoken, the dry wood will appear before the son of corruption when great suffering will befall you and heaven and Earth will be shaken. For heaven and Earth will be stirred up in the judgment that is to come, as was foretold by the green wood. The wheel of the firmament, along with all its signs, has collapsed and taken back the gleam of light, just as all these events were predicted in the aforesaid words of the prophets.

VISION TEN: 20

In these days sweet clouds will touch the Earth with a gentle breath and cause the Earth to overflow with the power of greenness and fertility. Then people will prepare themselves completely for justice, which was lacking in the above-mentioned period of womanish weakness, for the elements, harmed by the sins of men and women, had fallen totally into the service of disorder. The princes and everyone else will put God's decrees into proper practice. They will forbid all weapons used to kill people and only tolerate such iron tools as are needed in farming and for the benefit of humanity. Those who disobey this command will be killed by their own swords and cast away in some remote place.

And just as clouds let down a mild rain suitable for the germination of seeds, the Holy Spirit will pour forth the dew of grace, along with wisdom, prophecy, and holiness, upon people so that, just as if turned around, they will lead different and good lives. The old Law was a shadow of spiritual life, for it was completely distinguished by its creativity. Thus in winter all the Earth's fruits are hidden and invisible because they have not had time to ripen. And thus this old Law had no summer because the Son of God had not yet appeared in the flesh. But at his coming the whole world was changed into a spiritual meaning, and everything displayed the fruit of eternal life through the commandments of the gospel, just as summer produces blossoms and fruits. In these days a true summer will reign through God's power because everyone will be steady in the truth: priests and monks, virgins and those who practice celibacy, as well as other classes of society will have their dignity by living well and honorably and by rejecting every kind of arrogance and excessive wealth.

Then, just as through the balance of clouds and air the necessary conditions of life for fertility are created, the seed of spiritual life will sprout through God's grace. There will be prophecy; wisdom will be gentle and strong, and all believers will see themselves in it as in a mirror. The true angels will then cling to human beings in trust, for they will see in them a new and holy transformation so that human beings will shudder over their own rotten vices. Then there will be joy among the just, who will strive for the promised land and look for eternal life. And yet they will not be completely merry because they will see that the judgment is still to come. They will do all of this like pilgrims hastening toward their father's house but who, even though full of joy, cannot be happy so long as they are on the pilgrim's path.

The Jews and heretics will be full of joy and will cry out: "Our glory is approaching, and those who have broken our spirits and scattered us will be ground down." Nevertheless, countless heathens will cling to the Christians, for the fullness of their honor and inner wealth will become apparent. The heathens will be baptized; united with Christians, they will announce how all this happened at the time of the apostles. They will cry out to the Jews and heretics, "What you call honor will be eternal death, and the one you call your prince will end his life before your very eyes under the most awful perils. Then you will be converted to us and look to the day that the offspring of the dawn—of Mary, the star of the sea—has shown to us."

These days will be strong and glorious, full of peace and stability, like armed soldiers lying on a cliff to waylay their enemies and accomplish their destruction. These days will announce the coming of the Day of Judgment. For whatever good and glorious event the prophets announced will be fulfilled in these days. Wisdom, piety, and holiness will be strengthened. For if the Son of God had not been predicted and if he had not come in a moment (*in ictu oculi*), we should have quickly forgotten him. Similarly, the depraved person who comes in secret, so to speak, will very quickly be destroyed.

VISION TEN: 21

Although in these days justice and piety will grow increasingly weary and disappear, they will soon regroup their forces. Now evil will rise up, only to decline again. Often wars, famines, pestilence, and mortality will achieve power and then fade away. None of these things will be able to maintain itself for long in power. Each of these developments will waver to and fro, achieving prominence at one time and then moving into the background.

[This will be the period that in *Scivias* is described as under the sign of the horse.]

It is a time of decadence and clerical ostentation, of bold pleasures and vanities that always spring up when we humans doze away in a kind of lazy peace and are smothered by too many possessions. This is because we are no longer disturbed by conflicts or restrained by a lack of food. In view of our enjoyment of such luxuries, we do not wish to show God the honor we owe to the Deity for all these things. Therefore, such dangers as we have never known will follow

this time of rest and comfort. For if people cling to the kind
of indolence described above and have no fear of danger,
other days will come that are full of suffering, days in which
the complaints of the prophets and the voice of the Son of
God will be fulfilled. In anguish, then, as a result of these
continuous trials, people will long for death and cry out:
"Why were we born?" And they will long for the mountains
to fall upon them. For the days of yore, despite all the suffering and havoc, offered at times the possibility of refreshing
and renewing themselves. But these days, which will be full
of suffering and injustice, will not renounce evil. Instead,
torment upon torment and injustice upon injustice will ac-
cumulate. At any moment murder and death will be planned
for no reason at all. Just as animals are slaughtered so that we
can eat, in those days we humans will be killed by the cruelty of our foes.

[Foreigners will invade Christendom and destroy Church
institutions by taking advantage of the Christians' lack of
weapons. All this is an indication of the coming of the Antichrist. These days will be saturated with filth, yet all the
same they will suck up even more filth. And so it will go
with the garment of Christ and the vestment of his
Church.]

VISION TEN: 22

[Yet the Church, like the bride of Christ, will pray for its
members who are members of the Son of God. Christ
himself at this time will remind his Father of the eternal
plan of salvation and will plead for his body, the Church:]

VISION TEN: 23

"Father, I am always with you, and you were the One who
sent me off to put on the garment of flesh. Thus I walked
about the Earth and did all that you bade me do. For I am
your truth. Therefore, you have placed all my enemies
beneath my feet and I stand above them. They lie to the left
and cannot come to you because your true work is at your

right hand. This I achieved with you, just as you ordained before the origin of days. I judge my enemies, just as the Lord treads upon his footstool. Therefore, send me your help and save me from my enemies. For I, your Son, march upon vipers and adders. Behold my concern for my members! I have, after all, brought to a successful conclusion the whole work you desired and gave me as my task. And thus I am in you and you are in me: We are One."

And once again the Son says to the Father: "Now be mindful lest the full number created in the beginning should fade away. When the world began, did you not see its end? And did you not refuse to forget the world, as you forgot those who had fallen into corruption? The full number of human generations foreseen and created in the beginning along with the first men and women should not fade away and disappear. For it was not your plan for human beings to fade away completely in their generations prior to the appointed time. When you created humanity, it was your eternal decree that your eye, that is, your power of perception, should foresee everything, should arrange things in a proper way, and should never depart from your decision. Humanity should not be destroyed because of its lack of self-control, and the world should not disappear until you can behold my body with all its members—my members who are loyal to your decree. And the members will be adorned with precious jewels and completed by all those who trust and revere you because of me. They will be like precious jewels sparkling in the power of virtue."

VISION TEN: 24

A time will come when unbelievers and dreadful people— people like those described above—will break everywhere into the property and possessions of the Church and strive to destroy them, just as vultures and hawks slaughter whatever lies beneath their pinions and talons. At this time Christians especially will be oppressed in many ways as a punishment for their sins, and they will attempt armed

resistance, feeling no concern for the death of their bodies.
Then a mighty storm will descend from the north, bringing
a heavy fog and a very thick cloud of dust. This storm will
blind the eyes of the foes with fog and dust, and it will rage
against them in accord with the divine judgment so that
their eyes will be full of dust and their throats full of fog.
Then the foes will reduce their savagery and they will be
full of amazement.

Then the holy Godhead will accomplish signs and
wonders within the Christian people, as it did at the time of
Moses with the pillar of cloud and as the archangel Michael
did when he fought the heathen for the sake of the Christians. Thanks to Michael's help, the faithful children of
God will march under his protection. They will crush their
foes and achieve victory through God's power. Some of
these foes will be put to death, and the rest will be driven
into exile. As a result, a great number of heathens at this
time will join the Christians in true faith and say, "The God
of the Christians is the true God because such wonders have
been achieved among the Christians." The victors, too, who
will have God as their defender will praise the Deity and cry
out, "Let us praise the Lord our God. God has truly been
glorified among us because we are victorious in God's
name. Therefore, God's glory is our power because we have
humbled our foes and God's foes with the divine aid and
because we have believed in the Deity." And again they will
say, "We wish to heed the words of the Lord in the gospel.
The heathen will rise up against the Christians, as they
have done against us. Let us therefore rebuild the cities
nearby and raise up the people who have been ravaged today." And with all their power and all their might they will
accomplish this aim courageously and generously.

VISION TEN: 25

In those days the emperors, despite their Roman solemni-
ty, will experience a decline in the power by which they
once held the Roman Empire. They will lose their glory and

the empire in their hands will little by little crumble away and fall into pieces. And since they will become dissolute, lukewarm, servile, and immoral in their way of life, they will be unsuccessful in all their undertakings. Although unwilling to carry out their subject's wishes, the emperors will still expect to be honored. But in the end they will be neither honored nor revered. And so kings and leaders of countless peoples once subject to the Roman Empire will grow independent and no longer submissive. Thus the Roman Empire will be doomed and broken up. Every tribe and nation will select a new ruler and obey that person, claiming that the expansion of the Roman Empire has been more of a burden than an honor. Once the imperial rule has been shattered so that it can never be reestablished, the bishop's office will also be shattered.

Since princes and other secular or spiritual leaders will find it hard to find anything religious in the apostolic name, they will form a low opinion of both that office and that name. They will prefer teachers and bishops with other names and from different regions. As a result, the Apostolic See will find that the territory over which it has authority will be diminished. Only Rome and a few nearby regions will remain under papal control. This will come about partly as a result of warlike invasions and partly as a result of agreements and decisions made by spiritual and secular leaders. Such leaders will then propose that every secular leader should protect and guide his own kingdom and people. Similarly, every bishop or spiritual leader should rule his own subjects so that they will not be afflicted by the evils inflicted upon them in the past at God's suggestion.

VISION TEN: 26

Error will again be diminished, but afterward it will try to rise up once more. In the meantime, justice will remain steadfast so that people in those days will turn honorably to their original morality and to the discipline of the ancients. People will observe and esteem morality and discipline just as the ancients were wont to observe and esteem them. Each king or prince or Church official will accept correction from another king or prince or Church official. Each ethnic group will let itself be corrected by another group when it hears how that group is making progress in virtue and is being elevated to justice. The atmosphere will once again grow mild, the fruits of the Earth will prove beneficial, and people will be healthy and strong.

In those days there will be many wise sayings and many sages: The riddles of the prophets and the writings of the sages will be completely explained in this way. Their sons and daughters will prophesy, as it was foretold long ago. And all these things will take place in such purity and truthfulness that the spirits of the air will no longer be able to ridicule the sons and daughters. They will prophesy, as the prophets of old announced God's mysteries and as the apostles proclaimed their teaching, which exceeded all human understanding. At this same time, however, so many false teachings and false deeds will arise along with other misdeeds—as a sign of the imminent arrival of the Antichrist—that the people in these days will claim that never before have there been such crimes or such iniquities as then.

[The pig in the book *Scivias* indicates this time: an epoch full of disturbance and constant upheavals. For the world can never remain fixed in a single situation.]

VISION TEN: 27

Moreover, O human being, you can now see how the outside of the wheel described above looks at last like a mighty and violent storm; this occurs at the end of that half of the wheel where the line referred to above fits into the wheel. This means that the judgment of God's power will resound in those days like a mighty tempest. . . . [The time of crisis has arrived, for purity and tranquility of faith will disappear and believers will fall away on a massive scale.]

VISION TEN: 28

At that time an impure woman will bear an impure son. And the old serpent that deceived Adam will infect that son in such a way that nothing good can go into him or remain with him. He will be lifted up to remote and changeable places so that people cannot know him. Trained in all the diabolical arts, he will remain hidden until he reaches a man's estate. He will not openly display the vices hidden within him until he sees that he is mature and copious in every kind of evil. From the moment of his birth many conflicts and enmities against the legal system will swagger about. Fiery justice will be darkened in its purity, and love will be extinguished among human beings. In place of justice and love, bitterness and brutality will come to the fore, and such heresies will develop that the teachers of heresy will even preach their false beliefs openly and without hesitation. And among Christians so much doubt and uncertainty will arise about the Catholic faith that people will not know whom to invoke as God. Countless signs will appear in the sun, moon, and stars, in the waters and the other elements as well as in all creation, so that people will be able to predict the disaster that is to come through these signs as if in a painting. Such melancholy will then take hold of men and women that they will regard dying as if it were nothing.

Those who remain steadfast in the Catholic faith, however, will await in deep contrition whatever God decides. And these tribulations will progress to such an extent that the son of corruption will at last openly expound the teaching of contradiction. And when he offers his words of falseness and deceit, heaven and Earth will tremble.

Then the necklace of justice, which, as previously stated, Paul extended as far as the feet of this virtue, will be seized by a kind of roaring windstorm and it will begin to stir for the first time. Up to then this necklace had been tranquil and intact. Indeed, Paul established his teaching with so many miracles and adorned it honorably with so many profound

affirmations that it could last until the end of the world,
just as this necklace shows. In the elevation of his spirit,
Paul has spoken the following words to believers about the
Second Coming of the Son of God and about the deadly attack of the son of corruption:

VISION TEN: 29

"Please do not get excited too soon or alarmed by any
prediction or rumors or any letter claiming to come from
us, implying that the Day of the Lord has already arrived.
Never let anyone deceive you in this way. It cannot happen
until the Great Revolt has taken place and the Rebel, the
Lost One, has appeared. This is the Enemy, the one who
claims to be much *greater than all* that men call 'God,' so
much greater than anything that is worshipped, that *he en-
thrones himself* in *God's* sanctuary and claims that he is
God" (2 Thessalonians 2:2-4).

The meaning of this statement is as follows: You who are
of God and believe God's words, take care lest you be
shaken in your hearts by fear or spiritual deceit or worldly
charms or writings that are truly directed at you as if that
day were already here when the Creator of all things will
reveal the abyss of hearts.

[Human beings should keep themselves free from every
threatening temptation of the end of the world and they
should seek in faith help and means now that the mystery
of evil (*mysterium iniquitatis*) is so openly at work. . . .]
But human beings are in the midst of God's power. For
before humanity was formed, God was, and when humanity
will have come to the end of its bodily existence, God will
continue in all the divine power.

VISION TEN: 30

The power of the Godhead has cast the old enemy down
into the lake of an abyss, just as a lump of lead falls with a
thud into stormy waters. This is because God wished to an-
chor wickedness securely while the Divinity alone is just

and truthful, and no one can be like God. For God, who has always existed, has created everything out of nothing. But now this old enemy believes that, because he overcame humanity at its very beginning, he will be able to complete through another human being, that is to say, through the Antichrist, the task he began when he tried to fight against God. From the Devil the Antichrist has received the inspiration to open his mouth in order to preach a perverted teaching (*doctrina perversa*) and to destroy everything God has established under the old Law and the new Law.

He will teach that incest and similar vices are no sins. He will also maintain that there is no sin when flesh warms itself on flesh, just as we human beings quite naturally are comforted by the warmth of a fire. He will explain to us that all the precepts of chastity are without any scientific basis. For we humans, according to our natural disposition, are sometimes cold and at other times warm; thus we have to reach a natural balance between heat and cold. And he will further tell believers, "Your moral principal of chastity has been established contrary to the natural law. Why should a man not be warm when we consider that there is a fire in his breath that causes his whole body to burn? Is it possible for him to remain cold when this would be contrary to his own nature? And why should human beings be forbidden to warm their flesh on the flesh of others? The One you call your 'Teacher' gave you a principle that goes beyond your natural capacity when he taught you to look at natural things in this way. But I tell you: You live only once in this dual situation as a cold pole and as a warm pole. Therefore, warm yourselves without any qualms and have no doubt that this individual has given you instructions that are unreasonable. Indeed, you can see for yourselves that, no matter how much he has preached that human beings should not warm each other, people constantly indulge in the pleasures of the flesh. Then, see to it that henceforth you do not let yourselves be led astray by this impossible teaching. For within me is to be found what you can do and what you cannot do. Your Teacher has not given you the proper precepts. He wants you to live like a spirit, which is not clothed in the flesh and which does not act as if the human body were not a natural creature. And still human beings have been infused by fire and formed by fire. If people did not bring children into the world in the natural way, they could not amount to anything. Just on this basis alone you can see what you should be. The One who first instructed you has betrayed you and been of no help to you. But I impress upon you the fact that you first need to know yourselves and to understand what you are by reason of your own nature. For I have created you, and I am completely within the things of this world. But that One has ascribed all his works to Another and says nothing at all about himself because he could do nothing by himself. But I speak for myself alone, and I can do everything by myself."

With such words and similar statements, the accursed son of corruption will lead human beings astray by teaching them to live according to the burning impulses of the flesh and to accede to every desire of the flesh. And this he will do even though both the old Law and the new Law invite us to a life of chastity, provided chastity does not exceed its natural limitation. In this way Lucifer will deny the justice of God by means of the Antichrist, and Lucifer will think that he can now carry out all his diabolical schemes through the Antichrist. He will fancy that the Jordan is flowing into his own mouth and that, as a result, baptism will henceforth no longer be even mentioned. Instead, he will imagine that he can cast baptism aside, just as he himself has been cast aside by baptism. When he appears, he will think that he can conquer so many individuals that, by comparison, the Son of God will retain only a small group of believers.

VISION TEN: 31

This individual will be called the "man of sin," because he carries out everything that is evil and because all vices will be showered upon him. He is also known as the son of corruption because death and corruption dominate him and because he seduces and wins over many, many people in every way. He does so by obtaining the homage due to God, just as John described the savagery of the Antichrist by comparing him to a beast. For John gave witness to the truth when he said: "And all people of the world will worship it, that is, everybody whose name has not been written down since the foundation of the world in the book of life of the sacrificial Lamb" (Revelation 13:8). The meaning of this statement is to be understood in connection with future events: With bowed bodies and spirits those who have erected the tent of their hearts upon earthly things will worship the monster of iniquity. And their names will not be marked with the sign of holiness in the eternal life of the One whose mouth was not known to harbor any deception. Therefore, all who revere the inscriptions of this vile man will dwell in corruption because they have paid homage to him. Such individuals will have within their hearts the inscription by which Satan was cast out by God for seeking to become God. Thus his name is "death" because he flies from the life that is immortal and that gives life to everything.

But all who cling to this son of corruption and carry out his deeds will not be entered into the book of life of the Lamb. And this Lamb is the *Word* of God through whose word "Let it be made," all creation emerged. Yet in both the Old and the New Testaments the Devil was constantly surrounded by disciples. Under the old covenant they were the followers of Baal, while under the new covenant they were Sadducees, who were the main sources of schism. The followers of Baal were the first to wound the law of God— the roots of justice that nourished the patriarchs and the prophets—through the baseness of Baal. But the Devil also took possession of those who under the New Testament denied, along with the Sadducees, the resurrection [of the body] and thus debased the concept of justice. For the boughs springing

from the roots mentioned above are the gospel. And the
fruit of the boughs is Christ's witness that destroyed in
power the false god Baal and the Sadducees.

Afterward, these people will give rise to heretical leaders
who will contradict the creation of the original powers of
nature. Their false teachings will be worse than earlier errors because they will completely deny God in the order of
creation and in living beings. But all these people will worship the accursed beast, the "lost human being." They will
abandon faith in almighty God and claim that no harm will
befall them for disregarding the divine commandments.

VISION TEN: 32

And thus human disbelief will descend to the golden head
of the leopard seen on the necklace. This is the Antichrist
who calls himself "God" or "golden head." He will cause
dreadful monstrosities and mighty tempests by diabolical
tricks and by stirring up the elements. God will tolerate
these things until the whole human race knows of the fall of
the Antichrist.

Thus the Antichrist will feign death for the redemption of
his people and resurrection. He will have inscriptions marked
on the foreheads of his followers. In this way he will in-
scribe all evil upon them, just as the old serpent did for
human beings by deceiving them and arousing their passion
in order to keep them in its power. By means of this inscription and in opposition to baptism and Christ's name, the
Antichrist will so capture human beings through magical
spells that they will no longer wish to be free of him. They
will name themselves after him, just as Christians take on
the name of Christ.

For a long time Lucifer has had this inscription, which he
has never shown to a member of the human species. The
only exception was to the one Lucifer wished to possess
completely within his mother's womb. Thus Lucifer planned
to accomplish all his desires through that individual. Yet
this vile person will owe his very soul and life to God and

not to the Devil. This is because even this accursed ringleader of the old temptation, who will hate all goodness, will receive life from God. For God alone is life. Every breath and all that lives is moved by God because the Divinity alone is the original origin. And just as Lucifer fought against God in heaven, he will seek to fight again on Earth by means of this vile person and against the humanity of the Son of God. And Lucifer will do this by means of the inscription denying God, the creator of the universe. The Antichrist will promise to those who acknowledge him even more luminous gifts of the spirit than those Christ, the son of God, has bestowed on those who believe in him.

Previously this inscription was neither seen nor imagined in any language. Lucifer has devised it himself and offered it as a scheme to seduce humanity so that it will no longer respect its creator. He has deluded unbelievers to such a degree that they will no longer seek to honor anything except what at the moment is pleasing to the Antichrist. Indeed, the son of corruption will claim that just as a piece of wood cut from a tree must be aged until an artist can assemble it and carve it into an object of admiration, people born according to nature remain without honor until they have been glorified by this same inscription. In the essence of this inscription, according to the Antichrist, more salvation and power lie than in the creation of humanity. But God will destroy all the efforts made by this inscription along with the one who devised it. But the inscription of the Holy Spirit will not fade away. When the Antichrist begins to gather around himself people of all generations through this false sign, the saints and the just will be shaken by a powerful feeling of revulsion.

VISION TEN: 33

I who am shall be mindful, however, of how I formed the first human being and of how I foresaw all the deeds by which Lucifer would struggle against me with the help of human beings. And I am mindful of how I proceeded with

Enoch and Elijah, whom I chose out of the tribe of those who adhered to me in total devotion. Around the end of the world I shall show people how to accept the testimony of these two men who have my complete confidence. In my mystery I shall instruct Enoch and Elijah, revealing to them the deeds of men and women. Enoch and Elijah will know those deeds just as if they saw them with their own eyes. For are they not wiser than the writings and words of the sages? Because they have been removed bodily from the midst of humanity, fear and trembling have also been removed from them. And thus they endure everything about them in indifference. I shall keep them in a hidden place and no harm will come to their bodies. When the son of corruption spews out his perverted teaching, the same power that removed Enoch and Elijah from our midst will restore them, so to speak, on the wind. So long as they remain on Earth among human beings, they will accept nourishment at intervals of forty days, just as my Son felt hunger after forty days.

These strong and wise men are signified by the ibex on the necklace of justice mentioned previously. Just as the ibex is strong and climbs up to high places, they also will be raised up through my power to be strong and swift upon the heights of my wonders. They will possess such power in my wounds that they will be able to accomplish even greater signs in the firmament, the elements, and other creatures than the son of corruption. And so his deceptive deeds of magic will become objects of ridicule as a result of the true miracles of those men. Because of their great and wonderful power, men and women from all ethnic groups will hasten to them, believing their words and rushing toward the martyrdom that the son of corruption will prepare for them. They will do so in ardent faith as if rushing to a banquet. And their murderers will no longer be able to count the victims because of the gigantic numbers of those who will be slaughtered. For the stream of their blood will flow like running water. Since the son of corruption could neither win over these two truly holy men by flattery or threats nor darken their signs and wonders, he will cruelly order their martyrdom and will seek to extirpate their memory from the Earth. Thus there would no longer be anyone in the whole world who would dare resist him. Then the golden number of the blessed martyrs who died for the true faith at the time of the early Church will be completed by the martyrs who will be handed over to death in the heresy of the end days. For this period will trample everything under foot and swallow up everything. This is the age described in my book *Scivias* as under the sign of the wolf. For just as a wolf devours because of its rapacity, believers who put their trust in the Son of God will be devoured at this time. Therefore, the Son of God once again turns to his Father:

VISION TEN: 34

"Now I am overwhelmed that in accord with your instruction I assumed the garment of flesh and have to endure the fact that my own members, who are bound to me by the sacrament of baptism, should turn away from me and fall victim to the contempt of diabolical laughter as they listen to the son of corruption and revere him. Yet I bring home again those among them who have fallen. But I reject those who remain rebellious and cling to evil.

"O Father, since I am your Son, look at me with the love in which you sent me into the world. Gaze at the wounds by which, according to your instructions, I redeemed humanity. I am showing them to you so that you may have mercy on those I have redeemed. Do not permit them to be expunged from the book of life. By the blood flowing from my wounds, bring them back in repentance to you so that the one who has ridiculed my incarnation and my suffering should not rule over them in damnation.

"And now, all you men and women who long to abandon the old serpent and return to your creator, take note of the fact that I, the Son of God and of humanity, am showing to my Father the wounds I suffered for you. And therefore, bend

your knees, which you have so often bent to the vanity of
unjust obstinacy. Bend down before your Father who has
created you and given you the breath of life. Genuflect in
the purity of faith and acknowledge freely your guilt so that
he may extend to you in your distress of body and spirit his
strong and invincible hand and snatch you away from the
Devil and all of his wickedness."

Thus the Son speaks to the Father and recommends his
members to him. He takes them in hand so that they will
cling to his leadership, and so that the corruption of the first
and last corrupter will never devour them. For just as often
as the almighty Father is disturbed by the evil deeds of men
and women, the Son shows his wounds to the Father so that
the Father will spare those people. The Son did not spare his
own body so that the sheep who have gone astray might be
redeemed by his blood. Therefore, his wounds will remain
unhealed as long as we humans in this world continue to
sin. And so the Son of God urges us to bend our knees before
the almighty Father whenever we have merited the divine
judgment. On this account God will free us from all evil
because of the wounds the Son has suffered in the flesh—
the same wounds on which the Father constantly gazes.

VISION TEN: 35

After Enoch and Elijah suffer bodily death because of the
son of corruption, the followers of that man will greatly rejoice because the two prophets are apparently destroyed.
But the spirit of life will awaken them and raise them up
again into the clouds and change the rejoicing of that man's
followers into fear, sorrow, and dismay. For by the reawak-
ening of those two men and their elevation, I, the almighty
One, shall prove that the resurrection and the life of the
dead are not incompatible, despite all the statements to the
contrary by unbelievers. If on those days even the elements
by which we human beings have sinned are cleansed, then
we will be awakened from death and restored to even
greater glory than at our original creation—indeed,

this will happen through our remorse, which is most pleasing to God. For just as every bodily connection in the human organism is shaken by remorse, we can move heaven by the sorrowful voice of our remorse. Together with the Cherubim we shall praise God with all our heart.

Then the old serpent, which will fall into a furious rage because of the awakening of those two men, will try to help that accursed person occupy once again the throne from which it was driven, so that the resurrection of those two men and the memory of the Son of God might be completely destroyed among human beings. And the serpent will say to itself, "By means of this son of mine I shall now fight an even greater battle than I once fought in heaven. All that I desire I will achieve now through him. Neither God nor humanity will be able to resist my wishes. And I know and am certain that no one will be able to overcome me. And thus I shall gain a total victory."

Thereupon, the son of corruption will assemble a large group of people so that his glory will be openly displayed. He will attempt to stride through the heavens so that any remnant of the Catholic faith that might still survive in the world would completely disappear as a result of his ascension into heaven. In the sight of the crowds standing and listening there he will order the higher elements of the sky to bear him up during his ascension into heaven, and the words of my loyal servant, Paul, will be fulfilled. And these are the words that Paul, who is full of the spirit of the truth, utters:

VISION TEN: 36

"The Lord will kill him with the breath of his mouth and will annihilate him with his glorious appearance at his coming" (2 Thessalonians 2:8). This statement is to be understood as follows: At this time the son of evil will be revealed; and it will become obvious to people everywhere that he is a liar. For he dared to ascend into heaven, and the Lord and Savior of the nations, the Son of God, will kill

him. The Son will accomplish this with the power by which
he, who is the Word of the Father, will judge the whole
globe in a just judgment. When the son of corruption
ascends on high through diabolical tricks, he will be thrust
down again by the divine power. And the fumes of sulfur
and pitch will devour him in such a way that the crowds
standing about will flee for protection into the mountains.
Such terror will take hold of all who see and hear these
things that they will reject the Devil and his son and be converted to the true faith through baptism. Quite beside itself,
the old serpent will again gnash its teeth and admit, "Now,
we have had a total failure. We shall no longer be able to
overcome men and women as we could in the past."

VISION TEN: 37

But all who remained loyal in faith to the Son of God will
praise God fervently and exultantly, as my beloved and true
witness has pointed out: "Victory and power and empire forever have been won by our God, and all authority for his
Christ, now that the persecutor, who accused our brothers
day and night before our God, has been brought down. They
have triumphed over him by the blood of the Lamb and by
the witness of their martyrdom, because even in the face of
death they would not cling to life" (Revelation 12:10-11).
This statement is to be understood in the following way:
After the Devil has been overcome and his son, the Antichrist, has been cast down, salvation will be at hand as a
result of God's decision. No longer need we fear the Devil's
power, which has been completely ground down. The
kingdom rules over all who accept God's dominion. God has
established the power of the invincible Christ, the Son
chosen as our true priest by the Divinity for the salvation of
our souls. For the stubborn accuser and persecutor has been
cast out into eternal damnation. He is the one who stirred up
a spirit of unrest among people who are children of God like
us, and who are destined to possess the inheritance of heaven
like us. Because such individuals agreed to his contradictory

temptations, the Antichrist accused them before the highest Creator and Judge. And this is what he has always done with respect to both spiritual and worldly transgressions. For we human beings are constant sinners.

In the first battle fought by the lost angel—the battle he fought against God out of a desire to become God—God was the victor. God then foresaw the final battle that would be fought between the Godhead and the fallen angel in which God would cast down that angel's son, the Antichrist, and bring about his complete doom. People who professed their loyalty to God have also conquered the son of the fallen angel by refusing to agree with him. They remained loyal because of the blood of the Lamb by which they had been redeemed and by whose power they had resisted all their bodily tribulations. They were able to emerge as victors and to conquer through the Word, that is, through the teaching proved in the Catholic faith. And this faith has been spread by that same Word by which the whole world was created. Those people did not love their souls so much that they retained them in their bodies. Instead, they let their souls march forward by submitting their souls to death in this earthly life through countless sufferings. In this way they gave their souls back to almighty God. For as martyrs they hastened toward death. Rather than deny the Son of God, they submitted to these sufferings. Thus, Abel, the prophets, and the other martyrs killed for God up to the time of the Last Judgment have testified that the Son of God shed his blood for them in accord with the Father's will. In this way will the battle of the son of corruption come to an end. And never again will he be seen among human beings.

Therefore rejoice, O you who have your dwelling place in heaven as well as on Earth. After the fall of the Antichrist the glory of the Son of God will be seen to its full extent.

EPILOGUE: 38

And once again I heard a voice from heaven that gave me the following instructions:

Now praise be unto God in his work of humankind! For our redemption the Divinity has fought the mightiest battles on Earth. God deigned to lift us up above the heavens. Together with the angels we should praise the divine countenance in the unity by which God is both truly divine and truly human.

And thus may almighty God deign to anoint with the oil of divine mercy the wretched woman through whom God has made known the preceding writings. For she has no stability in life and does not possess the knowledge to interpret the writings produced by the Holy Spirit for the instruction of the Church. And this knowledge is like a wall surrounding a mighty city. From the very day of her birth this woman has lived with painful illnesses as if caught in a net, so that she is constantly tormented by pain in her veins, marrow, and flesh. Yet up to now it has not pleased the Lord to deliver her. For she was meant to behold certain mysteries in a spiritual way and through the core of a soul endowed with reason.

This vision (visio) has penetrated the veins of the woman in such a way that she has often collapsed out of exhaustion and has suffered fits of prostration that were at times slight and at other times most serious. Therefore, her way of life differs from that of others. She is like a child who is too immature to know how people live.

For she is under the inspiration of the Holy Spirit in a life of service. She derives her bodily makeup from the air. And thus illness is stamped on her from this airy sphere by rain, wind, and every change in the weather to such a degree that she has no stability of body. If things were otherwise, the inspiration of the Holy Spirit could not dwell in her. At times the spirit of God awakens her from this mortal illness with the great power of its kindness as if with a refreshing dew, so that she can continue her life of service to the inspiration of the Holy Spirit. May almighty God—the one who knows well every fit of prostration suffered by this woman—be kind enough to accomplish divine grace within her in such a way as to glorify the divine kindness! May her soul—when it makes its pilgrimage out of this world to eternal glory—be gently raised up and crowned by God!

The book of life is a "book about the Word of God" by whom the whole world came into existence and by whom all life was inspired, according to the will of our eternal God and the divine providence. Now this book of life has not made these things known out of human experience. Instead, all these things have been made known by a simple and uneducated woman. This was the divine pleasure.

Therefore, let no one be so rash as to alter in any way the content of this book—either by adding to it or by diminishing it by omissions—lest such a person be blotted out of the book of life and out of all good fortune under the sun! There is but one exception to this rule—the editing of words or sentences that have been put down too simply under the inspiration of the Holy Spirit. But anyone who presumes to make changes for other reasons will sin against the Holy Spirit and will not be forgiven in this world or the next.

Now once again let there be praise of almighty God in all divine works—both before time was and since the beginning of time! For God is the First and the Last.

Believers should accept these statements in the humility of their hearts, for they have been made known by the One who is the First and the Last.

Letters

Translated by
Ronald Miller

TRANSLATOR'S NOTE

I have studied Hildegard's letters in both the original Latin and the German translation. The first is found as volume 197 of Abbe Jacques-Paul De Migne's *Patrologiae Cursus Completus: Series Latina*, 221 vols. (Paris: 1844-1864). The second source is Adelgundis Fuhrkotter's translation of the Latin into German, entitled, *Hildegard von Bingen, Brief-wechsel* (Salzburg: 1965). The page numbers listed in the appendix of this present volume are from the German critical edition, since this is readily available in most college libraries.

I also must confess that I hear Hildegard's voice best in her native tongue. Much as translating Matthew's gospel from Greek into Aramaic communicates some of the flavor of Jesus' Galilean homeland, so too, do we find the native patterns of Hildegard's thought when we study the German versions of her letters. Never seeing herself as philosopher or theologian, Hildegard speaks in the sensuous language of the mystic. It is this direct and vigorous language that I have tried to communicate in my English translation. Wherever meaning or power falter, the fault is mine. Wherever the reader encounters mystic vistas, saintly wisdom, and profound humanity, the source is Hildegard's magnificent spirit and the even greater Spirit that moved in her.

Hildegard of Bingen spent her entire life in the lovely Rhineland area of Germany. I once spent an evening at a wine festival in Bingen, but that was before I ever heard of the great mystic who bears that name. She was born in 1098 and in 1106 was sent to the convent of Disibodenberg to study under Jutta von Spanheim. She became a Benedictine abbess in 1136 and founded convents for women and monasteries for men; wrote books and letters; passed on the healing arts; wrote music; painted pictures; and administered a small kingdom (or queendom) until her death in 1179.

R.M

LETTER ONE
Hildegard to Bernard of Clairvaux

The oldest extant letter of Hildegard was sent in 1147 to no less a person than Bernard of Clairvaux. She writes this letter out of deep concern. Since 1141 she was convinced that God wanted her to write down her visions and religious experiences. She spent five years on her work, *Scivias*. But she wonders who will take her seriously, and she turns to the great abbot of Clairvaux for advice, this man who is stirring Europe in preaching a great crusade.

Most praiseworthy Father Bernard, through God's power you stand wonderfully in highest honor. You are formidable against the indecent foolishness of this world. Full of lofty zeal and in ardent love for God's Son, you capture men with the banner of the holy cross so that they will wage war in the Christian army against the wrath of the pagans. I beseech you, father, by the living God, hear me in what I ask you.

I am very concerned about this vision which opens before me in spirit as a mystery. I have never seen it with the outer eyes of the flesh. I am wretched and more than wretched in my existence as a woman. And yet, already as a child, I saw great things of wonder which my tongue could never have given expression to, if God's spirit hadn't taught me to believe.

Gentle father, you are so secure, answer me in your goodness, me, your unworthy servant girl, whom from childhood has never, not even for one single hour, lived in security. In your fatherly love and wisdom search in your soul, since you are taught by the Holy Spirit, and from your heart give some comfort to your servant girl.

I know in Latin text the meaning of the interpretation of the psalms, the gospels, and the other books which are shown to me through this vision. It stirs my heart and soul like a burning flame and teaches me the depth of interpretation. And yet this vision doesn't teach me writings in the German language; these I don't know. I can simply read them but have no ability to analyze them. Please answer me: what do you make of all of this? I am a person who received no schooling about external matters. It is only within, in my soul, that I have been trained. And that is why I speak in such doubt. But I take consolation from all that I have heard of your wisdom and fatherly love. I have not talked about this to anyone else, because, as I hear it said, there is so much divisiveness among people. There is just one person with whom I have shared this, a monk [Volmar] whom I have tested and whom I have found reliable in his cloistered way of life. I have revealed all of my secrets to him and he has consoled me with the assurance that they are sublime and awe-inspiring.

I beg you, father, for God's sake, that you comfort me. Then I will be secure. More than two years ago, I saw you in my vision as a person who can look at the sun and not be afraid, a very bold man. And I cried because I blushed at my faintheartedness.

Gentle father, mildest of men, I rest in your soul so that through your word you can show me, if you wish, whether I should say these things openly or guard them in silence. For this vision causes me a lot of concern about the extent to which I should talk about what I have seen and heard. For a time, when I was silent about these things, I was confined to my bed with serious illnesses, so intense that I was unable to sit up. This is why I complain to you in such sadness: I will be so easily crushed by the falling wooden beams in the winepress of my nature, that heavy wood growing from the root which sprang up in Adam through Satan's influence and cast him out into a world where there was no fatherland.

But now I lift myself up and hasten to you. I say to you: you will not be crushed. On the contrary, you constantly straighten the wooden beam and hold it upright; in your soul you are a conqueror. But it's not only yourself that you hold upright; you raise the world up towards its salvation. You are the eagle who gazes at the sun.

I ask you by the radiant clarity of the Divine and by the marvelous Word and by sweet tear-gifted repentance, the Spirit of truth, and by the holy sound which echoes through the whole creation: by him, the Word, from whom the world has come to be. By the majesty of the Divine, who in sweet greening power sent the Word into the womb of the Virgin, from whom he took flesh, as the honey is built up around the honeycomb.

And may this sound, the power of the Divine, strike your heart and elevate your soul, so that you do not grow stiffly indifferent through the words of this woman [Hildegard], since you yourself seek out everything with God or with human beings or with any mystery until you press so far forward through the opening of your soul that you discern all of these things in God. Farewell, live well in your soul and be a strong warrior for God. Amen.

LETTER TWO
Hildegard to Pope Anastasius IV

The eighty-year-old Anastasius IV was pope from July 12, 1153 until his death on December 3, 1154. He was a decent and moral person, but weak and all too easily manipulated by ecclesiastical politicians. Neither his age nor his office protected him from Hildegard's challenging words. Near the end of this letter of 1153, Hildegard makes reference to herself in the image of the little tent; she also seems to be referring to her secretary Volmar as the file that can smooth her works.

O shining bulwark, peak of guiding power in the lovely city prepared as Christ's bride, hear him, whose life is without beginning and never dissipates into fatigue.

O man, the eye of your discernment weakens; you are becoming weary, too tired to restrain the arrogant boastfulness of people to whom you have trusted your heart. Why do you not call these shipwrecked people back? They can be rescued from serious danger only through your help. And why do you not cut out the roots of the evil which chokes out the good, useful, fine-tasting, sweet-smelling plants? You are neglecting justice, the King's daughter, the heavenly bride, the woman who was entrusted to you. And you are even tolerant that this princess be hurled to the ground. Her crown and jewelled raiments are torn to pieces through the moral crudeness of men who bark like dogs and make stupid sounds like chickens which sometimes begin to cackle in the middle of the night. They are hypocrites. With their words they make a show of illusory peace; but within, in their hearts, they grind their teeth, like a dog who wags its tail at a recognized friend but bites with his sharp teeth an experienced warrior who fights for the King's house. Why do you tolerate the evil ways of people who in the darkness of foolishness draw everything harmful to themselves? They are like hens who make noise during the night and terrify themselves. People who act like this aren't rooted in goodness.

Listen then, O man, to him who loves exceedingly sharp discrimination. For he has put in place a strong instrument of uprightness, one that should do battle with evil. But that is precisely what you aren't doing when you don't dig out by the root that evil which suffocates the good. And you tolerate even more than that, allowing the evil to raise itself up proudly. And why? Because of your fear of the evil men who lay snares in nocturnal ambush and love the gold of death more than the beautiful King's daughter, justice.

But all the works made by God radiate the brightest light. Listen, O man. Before the world came to be, God spoke in divine inwardness the Word: "O my Son!" And the world came to be because it picked up the sound that went forth from God. The various kinds of creatures still lay hidden in darkness. As it is written, when God said: "Let it be!" the various types of creatures came forth. So it was through the Word of the Father and for the sake of the Word that all creatures were fashioned through God's will.

God sees and knows everything beforehand. But evil, on the other hand, through itself can neither by its rising or

falling do anything or create anything or cause anything —
for it is nothing. Evil should be valued only as the deceptive
product of wishes and rebellious fantasies. For human beings do evil when they deal deceptively and rebelliously.

God sent the divine Son into the world so that through
him the Devil, who had produced evil in its entirety and
seduced humanity, might be conquered and thereby the
human race, given over to corruption through that evil,
might be saved. Therefore God abhors the perverted works
of indecency, murder, theft, rebellion, tyranny, and
hypocrisy of the godless. For God has crushed all of these
under foot through the divine Son, who has totally scattered
the plunder of the hellish tyrants.

Therefore, O man, you who sit on the papal throne, you
despise God when you don't hurl from yourself the evil but,
even worse, embrace it and kiss it by silently tolerating cor-
rupt men. The whole Earth is in confusion on account of
the ever recurring false teaching whereby human beings
love what God has brought to nothing. And you, O Rome,
are like one in the throes of death. You will be so shaken
that the strength of your feet, the feet on which you now
stand, will disappear. For you don't love the King's
daughter, justice, with glowing love but as in a delirium of
sleep so that you push her away from you. And that is why
she also will flee from you, unless you call her back. Nevertheless, the high mountains will still offer the strength of
their help to you; they will raise you up and support you
with the strong branches of their high trees, so that you don't
completely collapse in your dignity, namely in the dignity of
your marriage to Christ. So there still remain for you a few
blades of your beauty, until the snow of manifold sarcasm
comes and blows out much foolishness. Protect yourself that
you don't fall, since you open the doors to the ways of the
pagans.

Therefore, hear him who lives and who cannot be pushed
out of the way. Already the world is full of aberration; later it
will be in sadness, and then in such a horrible state that it

will not matter to people if they are killed. But from the heart comes healing, when the red sky of morning becomes visible, like the light of the first sunrise. Words cannot express the new longings and enthusiasm that follow.

But he who is great without limit has in our time touched a small tent so that it might behold wonders, fashion unknown letters, and let an unknown language be heard. And it was said to this little tent: "What you express in the language announced to you from above will not be in the ordinary human forces of expression, for that was not given to you. But let him who has the file eagerly smooth this speech so that it receives the right sound for human ears."

And you, O man, who have been placed as the visible shepherd, rise up and hasten quickly to justice, so that you will not be criticized by the great Doctor for not having cleansed your flock from dirt and for not having anointed them with oil. But if the will knows nothing about these things that have passed and the man does not cling to these cravings, he will not incur heavy judgment. But the guilt of this ignorance will be washed away through acts of penance.

And so, O man, stand upon the right way and God will rescue you. God will lead you back to the fold of blessing and election and you will live forever.

LETTER THREE
Hildegard to Bishop Eberhard II of Bamberg

Eberhard was consecrated bishop by Pope Eugene III in 1146. He played an important role in mediating conflicts between pope and emperor. He was a capable theologian and true pastor. He writes to Hildegard and asks her to explain a theological thesis: eternity lives in the Father; equality in the Son; and in the Holy Spirit the union of eternity and equality. Hildegard's letter contains her response to this theological assignment.

He who is and from whom nothing is hidden says: O
shepherd, may you never desire to wither when you are so
close to the streaming of sweet balsam fragrance. It is the
strength one must offer foolish spirits, those who lack
motherly compassion. For it is at her breasts alone that they
can be nourished. Whoever lacks this dies of thirst. Hold
out for your people the lamp of the king so that they will
not be scattered through a wounding hardness. Raise
yourself up as one who lives in the light.

O father, I am a poor soul but one who now has directed
my gaze to the true light. So because of the request you have
made of me, I will respond to you, according to what I saw
and heard in a true vision and what was explained to me.
My response isn't in my words but in the words of the true
light that never refuses.

"Eternity lives in the Father." This means that no one can
increase or decrease eternity. For it is like a wheel that has
neither beginning nor end. So eternity is in the Father before
any creature, for it was always and forever eternity. And
what is eternity? God. But eternity is eternity only because
it is unending life. No tree blossoms without greening
power; no stone is without moisture; no creature is without
its own power. In what way?

The Word of God placed every creature in his charge. So
God isn't idle in mighty power. The reason we call God
"Father" is that all things take their origin from Him. And
that is why eternity too lives in God, for God already existed prior to the beginning and eternally before the incep-
tion of His shining works; all of those works appeared out of
the foreknowledge of eternity. What lives in the Divine
isn't like human existence: full of doubt, past or future, new
or old. What lives in the Divine is changelessly constant.

The Father is brightness and this brightness has a flashing
forth and in this flashing forth is fire and these three are
one. Whoever doesn't hold fast to this in faith doesn't gaze

on God, because he or she wants to separate from God that which is. For no one should divide God. Even the works God has made disappear when someone conceptually divides them up, splitting up the full content of these names. The brightness is therefore the fatherhood from which all things come and which surrounds everything. For all things live from its power.

The same power also formed the first human being and communicated to him the breath of life. It is thus from this power that human beings have the ability to be active in the world. In what way? Flesh proceeds from flesh; goodness—whatever is of good reputation—proceeds from what is good and it is increased through the good example of other people. This takes place bodily and spiritually in human beings, for the one proceeds from the other as the other. Human beings love the things they make because from their recognition they see that they gain reality. God wants the same thing. God wants the divine power to be manifested in all created forms because they are divine works.

The "flashing forth" gives eyes. And this "flashing forth" is the Son who gave eyes when he said: "Let it be." Thus in the living eye everything appeared in physical form and the "fire" that God is as Holy Spirit penetrates both of these names. For it would not be possible that the brightness could forego its flashing forth. And if the fire were lacking, then the brightness would not shine, nor would the flashing forth radiate. For flame and light are in the fire; otherwise, it would not be fire.

"Equality lives in the Son." In what way? Before time, all creatures were in the Father. He organized them in Himself and afterwards the Son created them in fact. How is that to be understood? It is similar to the situation among human beings when one carries the knowledge of a great work in herself and then later through her word brings it to the light of day, so that it comes into the world with great acclaim.

The Father puts things in order; the Son causes them to be. For the Father organized everything within and the Son brought everything to fullness in deed. He is the light from the light, the light that was in the beginning, before all time, in eternity. This light is the Son who flashes forth from the Father and is He through whom all creatures come to be. And the Son, who had never before appeared physically, put on the garment of human nature, that nature that He had made from clay. In just the same way, God had all of the divine works in view as "light" [likeness of the Son], and when God said: "Let it be!" each creature put on the garment appropriate to its kind.

Then God bent down to work. And so from this viewpoint, too, the "equality" holds good precisely in regard to the man [Christ] in the Son of God. For God put on humanity, just as the works of God put on their bodies. Thus it is that in the humility of being human, God bent down to humanity. For the Godhead is so perfect that if God hadn't taken on human nature, the Godhead would have spared nothing in a human being that was contrary to the good.

For "everything was made through the Son and nothing was made without God." All things able to be seen or touched or perceived through taste were made through the Son. And the Son saw ahead of time how each of these things was somehow necessary for human beings: for full love, for fear, for the cultivation of or the precaution against every occasion.

"And without the Son nothing was made." This nothing is pride. It is the attitude that looks only at oneself and trusts no one else. But pride wants what God doesn't want and constantly believes in what it puts down itself. It is dark because it despises the light of truth and has begun a course it can't complete. That is why it is nothing, because it was neither made nor created by God. It took its beginning from the first angel. When this angel beheld its own radiance it fell into darkness in its failure to see the source of that radiance. But that angel spoke by himself: "I want to be the Lord and have no one else above me." And so, radiance disappeared from that angel; he lost it and became the Prince of hell.

Then God gave this radiance to the second son [the human being]. God equipped him with such robust strength that all creatures serve him. And God established him with such strong power that he might never lose the radiance. With the same blasphemous intent with which Satan denied God, the foolishness in human beings craved equality with God in honor—in other words, they wanted to be God. Nevertheless, the human beings didn't lose this love, because they acknowledged God's existence. This is why the nature of the Devil is completely darkened, because he rejected the splendor of God. Adam, however, affirmed the grandeur of God. What he desired was only to have a share in the glory. That is why in his nature he remains perfect, because something of the light still remains within him. This isn't to deny that he is also full of many miseries.

"There lives in the Holy Spirit the union of eternity and equality." The Holy Spirit is like a fire, not one that can be extinguished, which suddenly bursts out in flames, and just as suddenly darkens. For the Holy Spirit streams through and ties together "eternity" and "equality" so that they are one. This is like when someone ties a bundle together—for there would be no bundle if it weren't tied together; everything would fall apart. Or it is like when a smith welds two pieces of metal together in a fire as one. It is like a circling sword swung in every direction. The Holy Spirit bears witness to eternity, sets fire to equality, and so they are one. The Holy Spirit is in this eternity and equality; there God lives, the fire and life. The sun is brightly shining; its light flashes; and the fire in it burns. It illuminates the whole world and appears as a unity. Everything in which there is no kind of power is dead, just as a branch cut off from a tree is dry because it has no greening power.

The Holy Spirit is the firmness and the aliveness. Without the Holy Spirit eternity would not be eternity. Without the

Holy Spirit equality would not be equality. The Holy Spirit is in both, and one with both of them in the Godhead. The one God.

The intellect, too, as it expresses itself in speech, has three powers: the sound, the word, and the breath. The Son exists in the Father like the word in the sound. The Holy Spirit is in both, like the breath in the sound and in the word. And these three persons are, as stated, one God. Eternity lives in the Father because no one existed before Him and because eternity has no beginning, just as the works of God have no beginning. Equality lives in the Son, because the Son never separates himself from the Divine, nor did the Divine exist without the Son. The union of these two lives in the Holy Spirit, because the Son always remained with the Father and the Father with the Son. For the Holy Spirit is a fiery life in them and they are one.

And it is written: "The Spirit of the Lord fills the Earth." This means that no creature, whether visible or invisible, lacks a spiritual life. And those creatures that human beings do not perceive seek their understanding until humans do perceive them. For it is from the power of the seed that the buds sprout. And it is from the buds that the fruit of the tree springs forth. The clouds too have their course to run. The moon and the stars flame in fire. The trees shoot forth buds because of the power in their seeds. Water has a delicacy and a lightness of motion like the wind. This is why it springs up from the Earth and pours itself into running brooks. Even the Earth has moisture and mist.

All creatures have something visible and invisible. The visible is weak; the invisible is strong and alive. This [the invisible] seeks to get through to human understanding because human beings do not see it. And yet these invisible realities are forces in the workings of the Holy Spirit.

"And there is something that ties everything together." What does that mean? The human person ties everything together. In what way? Through ruling, using, commanding. God has loaned human beings these powers because they are made in God's likeness. "God has the knowledge of the voice." This refers to the understanding heard in the voice. The voice is the body; the understanding is the soul; the warmth of the air is the fire—and they are one. When, therefore, the understanding, taking on form in the world, is heard through the voice, all of its works come to realization. And it is from there that its creative effectiveness comes. For when it commands something, that will come to be. For none of the works of God are empty.

If anyone had a container filled with gold, such a person would experience great joy in that possession. But if there were nothing in the container, the same person would regard it as of very little worth. In evil deeds there is only emptiness, for they run from the fire of the Holy Spirit. It is through the promptings of the Devil that sinful desires immediately appear. But as soon as someone realizes that his evil should be regarded as nothing and turns himself away from them, he is like the prodigal son far away from his father's house who in his hunger remembers the bread he ate at home and says: "Father, I have sinned against heaven and before you" (Luke: 15:18, RSV). "Against heaven"—because in my understanding I am heavenly. "And before you" —because I know that you are God. Thus this person pushes the Devil back and renews his choice of his true Lord. All the ranks of Satan are put to shame and all the angelic choirs fall into awe. For the human creature whom they had up to this time regarded as powerless clay is now someone whom they see as princely, a powerful pillar of cloud. What they had regarded as lowly, they now see as beautiful. All the slanders of Satan are to be regarded as worthless. No value lies in evil deeds. It is only in good works that a human being can fashion true value. And those are the works of the Holy Spirit.

And now may God grant you, O shepherd and father of the people, that you come to that light where you will receive knowledge of true happiness.

LETTER FOUR
Hildegard to Archbishop Eberhard of Salzburg

Eberhard was consecrated bishop of Salzburg in 1149. Caught in
the endless struggles between emperor and pope, Eberhard
became one of the staunch supporters of Pope Alexander III.
Eberhard and Hildegard met personally at least once, and her letter here is in response to Eberhard's request for prayer and advice.

O you, you who in your office represent the Son of the living God, I see now that your situation resembles two walls
joined together through one cornerstone. The one appears
like a shining cloud; the other is somewhat shaded. And yet
their situation is such that the brightness of the one doesn't
affect the shadows; nor does the shadiness of the other mix
with the light. The walls stand for your concerns, and these
concerns meet in your spirit [the cornerstone]. For, on the
one hand, your desires and feelings sigh for the narrow path
that leads to God. But, on the other hand, you have a whole
realm of worries about the people entrusted to you. The
former is in light; the latter in shadow. Your own desires are
in the brightest light and you regard them as house guests,
but this worldly concern lies in shadows and you look on it
as an intruder. You don't allow yourself to see that they
belong together and this is why you so frequently experience depression in your spirit. For you fail to see your
striving for God and your concern for your people as a unity.
And yet they both can be bound together as one gain—whether you are sighing for heavenly things with great yearning,
or whether you concern yourself in a godly way for the people. After all, Christ too adhered to heavenly things and yet
at the same time he drew close to the people. It stands written in Scripture: "I say, 'You are gods, sons of the Most
High, all of you.'" (Psalms 82:6) I interpret this text to
mean that we are "gods" in relation to the Divine and "sons
of the Most High" in our concern for the people.

My counsel, therefore, father, is that you let your toil be saturated at the fountain of wisdom, there where the two daughters clothed with royal robes draw their water. And the names of these two royal daughters are "Love" and "Obedience." For Wisdom, like Love, has ordered all things and she has allowed countless little brooks to arise from her waters. For it is personified Wisdom who says, "Alone have I made the circuit of the vault of heaven." (Ecclesiasticus 24:5) And it is through Obedience that God gave human beings the commandment. And what is the robe of the King's daughter, "Love"? It is the fact that Love, like the angels, looks at the face of God. But the role of the King's daughter, "Obedience," on the other hand, is God's exchange of clothes with humankind.

These maidens knock on your door. Love says to you: "My desire is to abide with you and I would like you to bring me to your bed and be devoted to me in loving friendship. For when you compassionately touch and cleanse the wounds of others, then I am reclining on your bed. And when you meet simple, honest people with goodwill and in a godly way, then I am united to you in loving friendship."

And the other maiden, Obedience, speaks to you also: "I remain with you because of the bond of the law and the instructions of God. And so you should embrace me resolutely and with strong force. Do not embrace me as though I were an administrator or custodian, but embrace me as an intimate woman friend. For you began to draw me to yourself, in baptism and with increasing maturity you held me fast, for in the discipline of your submission in your episcopal office you obey the directions of God. For the primordial source from which I come forth is Love."

O father, Wisdom tells you what is true: "Be like the father of the house who isn't glad to hear about the foolishness of his sons, but nevertheless doesn't give up his own intelligence. In a similar way, I bind together heavenly and earthly things as a unity for the good of the people. And so you should handle and cleanse the wounds of those who are

sick; and you should maintain the innocent and the just.
And, with God's help, let your heart rejoice with the one as
much as the other."

Now, O father, I, poor thing that I am, see how your will
longs for the door to these godly powers. This door will be
open to you so that with these powers you can bring to
fulfillment the difficult work assigned to you by Love. God
who is and who fathoms all will support you both in your
body and in your soul.

LETTER FIVE
Hildegard to Archbishop Philip of Cologne

Philip became archbishop of Cologne in 1167, although this office
was not recognized by Pope Alexander until 1176. In 1169 he
crowned Henry VI as the German King. He accompanied him to
Italy in 1190 and died there the following year. He visited
Hildegard frequently and became a good friend of hers. This letter
from Hildegard is in response to a letter in which he speaks of the
prospect of visiting her.

In the mysterious breath of a true vision I saw and heard
the following words:

> The fiery love that is God speaks to you: what name can
> that star claim in its uniqueness, that star which shines
> under the sun? It is called "the bright one" because it is more
> strongly shone upon by the sun than the other stars. How
> should it be fitting for this star to hide its light so much that
> it shone less than the others, the lesser stars? If it were to do
> that, it would not deserve its praiseworthy title. It would be
> called "the blind one" because people weren't seeing its
> light, even though it had been called "the bright one." The
> fighter, too, who would come to the encounter without
> weapons would certainly be mowed down by the enemy,
> because he hadn't protected his body with armor, nor
> covered his head with the helmet, nor protected himself
> with the shield. He would be taken captive with great
> scandal.

But you have been called "the bright star" shining in the name of the most-high Priest because of your episcopal office. Do not bury your light from those entrusted to you—that means, don't bury the words of justice. For you often say in your heart, "If those who are entrusted to me were brought to dismay through my words, I would be burdensome to them. Perhaps it is possible for me to keep their friendship through my silence!" But it isn't fitting for you to talk and act like this. But what now? Because of your episcopal title and noble lineage you should not be frightening those entrusted to you with fear-inspiring words, like some thieving hawk. Nor should you be attacking them with threatening words as though you had a cudgel. What you should be doing instead is mixing the words of justice with mercy and anointing people with the fear of God. Show them how damaging evil is for their souls and for their happiness. Without fail, certainly, without fail! Then they will give you obedience.

You shouldn't make common cause with these people through filthy and vagrant morals, nor should you even consider what pleases or doesn't please them. When you act in this way, you appear both before God and people as less than the others. Something like that isn't fitting for you in your office. Notice—even clean, cud-chewing animals would befoul their feed if someone mixed with it the garbage pigs eat that makes them fat. So would you soil yourself if you wanted to go along with filthy morals and be in the company of sinners. Evil people would be delighted about this, but the spiritually advanced would be outraged and would say: "Alas, alas, what kind of a man is our bishop! He doesn't light up the paths of justice for us through decent conduct."

Rescue your people from the lack of faith that is their enemy. Make it your own concern not to stand there without the armor of faith, and show your people the path of justice from the holy scriptures. Place the helmet of hope on your head. Cover your neck with the shield of honorable defense, so that, as well as you can, in every need and danger

you can be a defender of the Church. Cling so tightly to the
light of truth that you can be in battle service for me. For I
am the true love that is manifested as a trustworthy warrior.
Be strong and brave in this shipwrecked world in all of your
heavy battles against injustice. Then you will shine as the
"bright star" in eternal bliss.

Now, O father, since you bear the name of shepherd, do
not despise the miserable condition of the person who
writes this to you. For it was neither from my own will nor
from that of any other human being that I have written this
and produced it. But what is written here is from a true vision that I saw and heard while I was awake both spiritually
and physically. It is you who has bidden me to write you
something.

LETTER SIX
Hildegard to King Konrad III

The Second Crusade, which Konrad III participated in through
the urging both of Pope Eugene and of St. Bernard of Clairvaux,
was a failure. His older son Henry died in 1150, and now he turns
to Hildegard for prayers and help. Hildegard responds to his plea
in a letter containing prophecies of future times.

The One who gives everything life says:

Happy are they who in worthy fashion submit themselves
to the beacon — the office of the highest King. God in his far-
seeing providence had borne sorrows for such people and
will not let them leave the divine bosom. O king, remain i.1
that bosom and cast out all filth from your spirit. For God
preserves everyone who seeks the Divine dedication and in-
tegrity. In a similar way, you should lead your kingdom and
carefully show your people every justice so that you will not
depart from the divine Kingdom.
Listen: there are certain ways in which you are turning
from God. The times in which you live are as frivolous as a
gossiping woman. These times, too, tend towards a hostile

injustice which strives to destroy the justice in the vineyard of the Lord. And yet, after these times even worse times will come, in which the true Israelites will be scourged and the Catholic chair of Peter will be shaken through erroneous teaching. And, therefore, the last times will be filled with blasphemies against God, much like a decomposing corpse. The vineyard of the Lord smolders with sorrow. Times are coming that are stronger than those which have gone before. The justice of God will raise itself up somewhat and the injustice of the clergy and religious will be recognized as thoroughly despicable. And yet no one will dare to raise a sharp and insistant call for repentance. Nevertheless, other times then stand before us: the kingdom of the Church will be dissipated; people in clerical and religious life will be torn to pieces as though by a wolf and driven from home and homeland. Very many of them will then move into a kind of solitude, and in deep and heartfelt contrition they will lead a life of poverty and humbly serve God.

In relation to the justice of God, the first times are filthy; the next times are downright loathsome. The times that follow them will move a little bit towards justice, but they will in turn be followed by times that will tear everything to pieces like a bear, and these times will pile up treasures of injustice. But the further times will show the mark of manly strength: all who wear the episcopal colors will hasten the first dawning of justice with godly fear, modesty, and wisdom. The princes, too, will be of one mind and, like warriors, they will hoist the banner of peace against the times that have run astray into the greatest errors. God will destroy and wipe them out according to divine wisdom and pleasure.

And again God who knows all things speaks to you, O king: When you hear this, O man, pull yourself together against your self-will and improve yourself so that you may come purified to the times in which you need no more to be ashamed of your days.

LETTER SEVEN
Hildegard to Frederick

On his deathbed, King Konrad designated Frederick as his heir. He was crowned emperor in Aachen on March 9, 1152 and is known to history as Barbarossa. There are four extant letters from Hildegard to this famous ruler and one letter of Barbarossa to the saintly abbess of Bingen. Translated here are two of the letters from Hildegard to Frederick.

It is wonderful that a man should acquire such an attractive personality as you, O king. Listen: a man stood on a high mountain, looked down into all the surrounding valleys and observed what everything in the valley was doing. He held a staff in his hand and administered everything justly, so that whatever was dry began to grow green and whatever slept was awakened. But the staff also took the burden of apathy from those who found themselves in great dullness. When the man failed, however, to open his eyes, a dark haze came that covered the valleys; and ravens and other birds tore everything all around to pieces.

Now, O king, pay careful attention! All lands are clouded by the plots of the many people who through the blackness of their souls put out the light of justice. Robbers and vagrants destroy the way of the Lord. O king, control with the sceptre of compassion the slothful, changeable, and wild habits of men. For you have a name of renown, since you are king in Israel. For your name is of high repute. Make sure, then, when the highest Judge looks at you, you will not be charged with not having rightly grasped your office, for then you must indeed blush with shame. May this be far from you! It is a well-known truth that it is right that the ruler imitate his predecessors in all that is good. For the idle morals of the princes are black indeed, since they run about in negligence and filth. Flee from this, O king! Be rather an armed fighter who bravely withstands the Devil, so that God doesn't strike you down and thereby scandal come over your earthly kingdom. God protect you from eternal destruction. May your times not be dry. God guard you and may you live in eternity! So cast off all greed and choose moderation. For that is what the highest King loves.

LETTER EIGHT
Hildegard to Frederick

O servant of God, you who have been established by God under the honorable name "judge" and "ruler" to direct and protect God's flock, listen: God gave the first human beings a law. Because Adam violated this law through disobedience—not keeping in mind that he agreed to obey the law through the covenant established with God—the death penalty fell upon him. And so he was driven from this bright land of happiness into a dismal earth, an earth overcast with clouds of sorrow. The evil spirits immediately began to lay snares for him. They were unremitting in their efforts to set traps of betrayal on every one of his paths, so that they could throw this unhappy creature into the jaws of death to wallow in hell with them: for they knew that through God's just judgment Adam had been banished from paradise into exile.

O servant of God, created by God and redeemed through the blood of God's Son, be most careful that you are not thrown into these same jaws of death because of your sins and the snares set by these evil spirits. Imitate the highest Judge and Ruler in compassion. Whoever totally despises God will be buried in death through God's judgment. But God's parental mercy never condemns a person who is truly repentent of her sins and longs for God's presence with a heart full of trust.

Indeed, you must both fear and love this highest Judge and Ruler, under whose divine power all things have been placed, for it is written: "Praise the Lord, kings of the Earth and all peoples, princes and all rulers of the Earth!" (Psalms 148:11) For God governs, embraces and nourishes the whole world. God is like a parent who takes such good care of a son that the child needs nothing else than what it receives from the parent. For it is with just such parental love that God is concerned with all the needs of those who dwell on this Earth. Just as God created the world in the beginning, so does God let the Earth blossom with fruit for all time.

This God who rules all things also directs the ways of justice and the prescriptions of this law. God is the way of truth without any injustice. No one can err on this way or come to shame. For all power and lordship proceed from God alone, who apportions everything in right order, and it is from God that all power and lordship receive their names. It is according to this that all who hold power should rule, instruct, and judge the people. They should point out the ways of truth and justice. Whoever disdains action in this way will be taken to judgment before the highest Judge. For God is the just Judge of all who are called to the wedding of the divine Son. God receives all of them with joy as members of the wedding party. Nevertheless, God decrees through just judgment that those who do the works of death be devoured by avenging death, because they fail to do the works of life.

O servant of God, after whom you are named, may the Holy Spirit instruct you so that you live and judge according to its justice. When you have done that, you will never be overcome by your enemies, just as David could never be overcome by his enemies, because he executed all his judgments in the fear of God. So trust in God and be like Jacob who was gentle and just and offered to God a tenth of all the goods he possessed. Then your enemies will not overpower you. Seek God's justice; observe God's commandments in all of your ways and in all of your words of judgment. Make God well-disposed to you through alms and fervent prayers.

And know that I will pray with my whole heart that God console you through an heir pleasing to God and that God show mercy to you in marvelous ways, so that through a good and just life in this realm of time you may merit after your death to be led by God into eternal joy.

LETTER NINE
Hildegard to Bertha, Queen of Greece and Empress of Byzantium

Bertha was from a noble German family from Sulzbach. She married the emperor of Byzantium and became both queen of Greece and empress of Byzantium. Hildegard writes her a personal letter, filled with images of growth and peace.

God's Spirit breathes and speaks: in wintertime, God takes care of the branch that is love. In summer, God causes that same branch to be green and to sprout with blossoms. God removes diseased outgrowths that could do harm to the branch.

It is through the little brook springing from stones in the east that other bubbling waters are washed clean, for it flows more swiftly. Besides, it is more useful than the other waters because there is no dirt in it.

These lessons also apply to every human being to whom God grants one day of the happiness and the glowing sunrise of glory. Such a person will not be oppressed by the strong north wind with its hateful foes of discord.

So look to the One who has moved you and who desires from your heart a burnt offering, the gift of keeping all of God's commandments. Sigh for the Divine. And may God grant you what you desire and what you pray for in your need, the joy of a son. The living eye of God looks on you: it wants to have you and you will live for eternity.

LETTER TEN
Hildegard to King Henry II of England

Henry was crowned king of England in 1154. He looked to Barbarossa as an ideal ruler and a marriage was planned between their two families. But religious strife ended this alliance and divided England itself when Henry sided with the anti-pope while the English bishops, under the leadership of Thomas Becket, kept their allegiance to Pope Alexander. This conflict eventually led to the murder of Becket in his cathedral at Canterbury in 1170. Henry lived to do penance at the grave of his former enemy for his involvement in Becket's death, a holy shrine and goal of numerous pilgrimages after Becket's canonization in 1173. Hildegard wrote to him before his repentance.

The Lord speaks to a man who holds high office: gifts and more gifts are special to you. Through reigning, guarding, protecting, and providing you should have your heaven. But a bird black as pitch flies to you out of midnight and says: "You have the possibility of doing whatever you want. So do this and that; open the door to such and such a matter. It doesn't do you any good to pay attention to justice. If you always keep your eye on justice, you will be a slave, not a master." But you should give no hearing to the thief who gives you this counsel. For in the primordial past, after you were fashioned from dust to such a beautiful image and likeness and had received the breath of life, that same thief stripped you of great glory. Look then with fervent zeal at the God who created you. For your heart is full of goodwill to do gladly what is good, except when the filthy habits of humankind rush at you and for a time you become entangled in them. Be resolute and flee those entanglements, beloved son of God, and call out to God! God will gladly stretch out a hand to help you. Now live forever and remain in eternal blessedness.

LETTER ELEVEN
Hildegard to her spiritual daughters

The next two letters Hildegard sent to the nuns in her community. The first letter is written in prophetic style as an oracle from God. The second letter reflects the controversy surrounding the convent Hildegard founded at Rupertsberg in 1150. The monastic community at Disibodenberg wanted her to remain with them. The monks also wanted all the dowries and other gifts to remain

with them. After much prayer and deliberation, Hildegard moved
with her sisters to Rupertsberg and the rights to the gifts went
with the women.

> *I am an exceedingly strong fire and I prepare for Myself
> already formed countenances in gentle and humble hearts
> and they hang on Me and hug Me like children. They are a
> "mountain of myrrh and incense" for Me, for they don't pur-
> sue the plague-breath of mortality. And that is what I seek
> and desire in my little children. When they are indeed gentle
> and humble, they receive the brightness of My fiery splendor.
> For goodness kisses the lowliness in which I have formed the
> shape of the first human being. And so all the good works
> which live from My breath present themselves to Me as a
> countenance. For they don't have the plague-breath of an ar-
> rogant spirit. And they are a "myrrh-mountain" because
> they continually kill in themselves all self-willfulness. A
> countenance, however, hardly ever shines forth from ar-
> rogant spirits. They appear before Me as though covered
> with clouds, like the moon when it can hardly shine
> through thick clouds. And yet these faces don't flee from Me
> forever. Although they credit themselves for all their works,
> nevertheless they serve Me. But they do mix things up, as
> though they were their own source. Those persons,
> however, who are humble and of contrite heart are present
> before Me like the burning light of the sun. Such persons are
> found in My flock. I want to purify My daughters from the
> thick clouds, because I would like to have them free of
> them.*

LETTER TWELVE
Hildegard to her spiritual daughters

O daughters, who out of your love for charity are following
the footsteps of Christ and who for the sake of spiritual im-
provement have chosen me, poor creature that I am, in humble submissiveness to be your mother, I have something to
say to you from my maternal heart, something that doesn't

originate with me but comes from godly vision: this spot, the resting place for the earthly remains of the holy confessor Rupert, to whose patronage you have taken refuge, is the site I have recognized according to God's will and with the evidence of miracles as a place for the sacrifice of praise. I came here with the approval of my superiors and with God's aid I have freely taken possession of it for myself and all of those who follow me. After that I went back by God's direction to Disibodenberg, the community I had left with permission, and I presented before all who lived there this proposal—namely, that not only our place of residence, but all the real estate added to it as gifts, should not be attached to them but should be released. But in all of this practical business I had nothing else in mind but the salvation of souls alone and concern for the discipline commanded in our rule.

I then shared with the Abbot [Kuno], the superior at this site, what I had received in a true vision: "The bright streaming light speaks, 'You should be the father over the provost [Volmar] and over the spiritual care of this mystical plant-nursery for my daughters. The gifts made to them belong neither to you nor to your brothers. On the contrary, your monastery should be their shelter.' But if you want to grow stubborn in your opposition and gnash your teeth against us, you will be like the hated Amalekites in the Bible and like Antiochus, of whom it is written that he robbed the temple of the Lord. (I Maccabees 1:21) Some of you have said in your unworthiness, 'We want to diminish your possession.' Here is the response of the Divine: 'You are the worst thieves! But if you should try to take away the shepherd of the sisters' spiritual healing [Provost Volmar], then I further say to you: You are like the sons of Belial and you don't have the justice of God before your eyes. Therefore, God's judgment will destroy you!'"

When in these words, I, poor creature that I am, demanded from the abbot named above the freedom of the place and the possessions of my daughters (as I explained above), all these things were granted to me through a written contract in a legal codex. All who saw, heard, and perceived these things, great and lowly alike, took a favorable view of them, so that it was surely God's will that this was all pinned down in writing. And all who depend on God, experience God, and listen to God's word, should favorably certify, enforce, and defend this legal transaction, so that they might receive that blessing which God gave to Jacob and Israel.

Alas, what a great lament my daughters will raise after the death of their mother, when they will drink no more at their mother's breast and when they will speak with sighs and sorrow and often with tears: "Oh, how gladly we would drink at the breast of our mother, if only we now had her in our midst."

And therefore, daughters of God, I advise you and I have advised you from my youth that you love one another, so that because of your goodwill towards others you might be like the angels as a bright shining light strong in your powers, as your father Benedict taught.

May the Holy Spirit grant you its gifts, for after my death you will no longer hear my voice. But may my voice never fall into forgetfulness among you; may it rather be heard often in your midst in love. Now my daughters blush in their hearts because of the sorrow that they feel because of their mother. They sigh and long for heaven. But later through God's grace they will be radiant in bright, shining light and they will be staunch champions in the House of God.

But if any in the flock of my daughters should want to sow discord or bring about the abandonment of this convent and its spiritual discipline, then I pray that the gift of the Holy Spirit may drive such thoughts out of their hearts. But if someone, God forbid, should nevertheless go ahead and act in this way, then may the hand of the Lord strike such a one down before all the people, for such a person would merit being put to shame.

And so, my daughters, live in this place you have chosen for yourselves, so that you may fight for God with total dedication and constancy and thus gain for yourselves here a heavenly reward.

LETTER THIRTEEN
Hildegard to Abbot Kuno

Hildegard directed communities of monks and of nuns. One of the monks mentioned in an earlier letter was Abbot Kuno of Disibodenberg. This was the location of the community where Hildegard had lived for forty-four years, from the time her parents had entrusted her to the direction of Jutta von Spanheim when she was only eight years old. When Jutta died in 1136, Hildegard was elected abbess (she was thirty-eight years old). In view of her long residence at Disibodenberg, we can understand the resistance of the monks there to her decision to found and move to a daughter house at Rupertsberg. Nonetheless, Hildegard in no way broke off her connections with Disibodenberg and we see her letter here to Abbot Kuno, her former spiritual director. He had written her earlier, asking her if she had received any revelations concerning Disibod, the patron of the mother community. She grants his request but adds some unasked for admonitions.

How great is the foolishness in a human being who doesn't improve but seeks what is in the heart of another. And the evil deeds he finds there are like mighty waters overflowing and out of control, that he cannot hold. Whoever acts this way should take to heart the response of the Lord:

> *O human being, why do you sleep? Why do you have no taste for the good works that sound in God's ears like a symphony? Why do you not search out the house of your heart and renounce your brazen unruliness? You strike Me in the face when you push away My members in their woundedness without looking at me, even though I am the One who draws back to the fold those who wander. You will have to answer for these things in My presence—for the house of your heart and for the city which I created and washed in the blood of the Lamb. Why do you not shrink*

from destroying a person, since it wasn't you who created him! You don't anoint him with oil and you neither protect nor care for him. You want to improve him, but you are violent in doing this. But now the time for your ebbing away has come. Nevertheless, God, who created you, will not let you be lost. So recognize the truth of these things!

Now, father, I come back to your request that I write to you if I have seen or know anything about your guardian patron, the holy Disibod. The following things are what I heard and saw in a vision of the Spirit.

O amazing wonder, that a hidden countenance rises high above others in shining, honor-filled greatness, when the living Majesty brings secrets to light. Thus, O Disibod, you will raise yourself up at the end with the support of the blossoming branches of the world, when you in the days to come are resurrected.

O greening power from the divine hand in which God has planted a little seedling that shines in the heights like a towering pillar. You are glorious because of God's activity. O towering mountain, you will never be shaken by God's testing. You stand in the distance like a solitary person. And yet it doesn't lie in the power of the armed to lay hold of you.

You are the leader of the true city and for the sake of God you have been thrown down to the Earth and you are the cornerstone of the temple as you climb to heaven. You who alienated the seed of the world have out of love for Christ sighed to be an exile. O sublime silence of the heart, you have constantly held your beautiful countenance open in the mirror of the Dove. You held yourself in hiddenness, intoxicated with the fragrance of the flowers in the enclosure of the saints, shining in the presence of God.

O pinnacle of those who open heaven, mild confessor of God's name, for the sake of the living light you surrendered the world and constantly waged battle in the Lord. From your heart the living source of brightest light has channeled the purest waters on the way of salvation. You are a mighty

*tower before the altar of the most high God; you have
engulfed in clouds the pinnacle of the tower with the smoke
of spices.*

*O Disibod, in your light you have through examples of
purest sound composed songs of wonderful praise resounding on all sides through the Son of Man. You stand in the
heights, not blushing before the living God but covered with
refreshing dew and praising God with this voice: O sweet
life, O blessed perseverance, in holy Disibod you let a
glorious light for all time go up to the heavenly Jerusalem.
Now let God be praised who has done divine work so powerfully in the beautiful form of a monk. The heavenly citizens
can rejoice over all who follow him in this manner.*

But you, father, who have requested me, as a miserable
creature, to communicate this vision, so live in the
presence of God that when your days in this world have all
disappeared, your time in eternity might happily run on and
you might stand among the just as one of the redeemed.

LETTER FOURTEEN
Hildegard to Prior Albert

Prior Albert of Disibodenberg wrote to Hildegard explaining his
disappointment at her decision to move to Rupertsberg. He and
his monks console themselves in the loss of her physical presence
with the hope of receiving instruction and consolation through
her gift of mystical vision. She answers him with more vision
than he might have wanted.

In a true vision I heard a voice speaking against the crimes
that members of religious communities as well as lay people commit against Justice:

*O Justice, you are without a homeland; you are a foreigner
in the city of those who make up fables and choose these
over the tasks assigned to them for their own wills. They
neither sigh for your mysteries nor for your friendship and
yet you are Justice, the purple-clad beloved of the king. This*

*is why you complain about this way of life, one on which no
sort of justice is based, and you speak full of sadness: I am
deeply embarrassed and so I hid My face behind My cloak so
that My persecutors do not see Me. You are greatly wrought
by this, O Justice, so that whoever withstands you is guilty
of judgment.*

*And again you speak full of sadness: "Whence do I come? I
come from the heart of the Divine. And all lands are
gathered around Me. I was also there when the form of
peoples and generations was established. And thus it was in
Me that even the pillars of the clouds were grounded.*

*But now I am a source of loathing to those who sprang
forth from Me in the first planting. But instead of giving way
to sorrow, I sigh at the ignorance of the people. My wailing
is like raging waters and the strong roaring of many waves,
because of the great number of fools in the talkativeness of
their scandalous behavior. Alas, alas, O eagles, you who
through the fire of the Holy Spirit and the restorative waters
of baptism merged into Me as into a sparkling sunrise and a
gleaming jewel—now you sleep and are like slow-witted
animals who run forward for awhile, then backwards for
awhile, and then collide with each other in your confused
running about.*

And yet from this mountain of the sons of God I saw the
following things in the gentle breeze of a mystical vision: I
saw a mountain of immense height. A huge man sat on its
peak. He held the law of God with two hands; the law was
written on a tablet, just as one reads in the account of
Moses. And all around the feet of this giant was a crowd of
people who were set apart by a spiritual circumcision. All of
them received the commandments of the Law with joy and
they said with sighs: "O God, when will you come to us?
We will gladly obey you!" And then for a time it seemed as
though they were mixed together as in a whirlpool and
sometimes evil-doers appeared in their midst, and they
washed them nevertheless with many tears and sprinkled

them with the blood of Jesus Christ. For as a person lay there in such heavy sins that he was devoid of all power and unable to raise himself up, God spoke: "I want to raise up this person Myself and I will plant him anew with tender mercy, so that in the mirror of a good confession he can come to rest, for on his own power he will never escape the snare of Satan."

I, poor wretch that I am, observed two burdens on them. Pride, however, I didn't see on them, that stiff-necked pride which throws stones at sinners and despises them.

In the midst of these crowds of people I saw another group, surrounded by a bright cloud. They had beautiful countenances and gazed towards heaven. But, with their hankering after useless things, they were like fat steers and their actions sometimes resulted in impudence because, with their glance directed to heaven, they aimed their bows and shot their arrows at it. They even struck at heaven with leaden clubs. And thus, "They set their mouths against the heavens, and their tongue struts through the Earth" (Psalm 73:9). And so thunder rolled over them and hail rained down on them and thick fog enveloped them. And they complained about the reason for such bad weather surrounding them.

Then God's grace gave them the following answer: "I have led you together for great blessedness. But in your audacity you have repulsed Me and asked who could reach to your level, what speech could defeat you, what heights or trees could throw you down." In the same way did the children of Israel also neglect God, because through the blessing of Abraham, God raised over them the horn of blessings and through a delight-giving they were drawn to the divine bosom. Only they murmured in self-deception and offered God bold resistance and they rejected the healing that comes through the pouring out of Christ's blood. So the blessing given to them withdrew and disappeared, for they gave themselves to the downfall of death. But God built from sacrifices and burnt offerings a new order of justice for

the Church, till all the spring water was channeled into the
valley of the black fog. Then all the eagles, because they
stood under the blessing in the beginning, were united in
the circling wheel of divinity to the one flock.

I saw yet another flock at the feet of these men. In front of
their eyes a ram hung in gold-colored thorns, and with shining eyes they looked at him in a haze of myrrh and incense.
And now little brooks flowed down to their breasts from the
hands of the large man who sat on the peak of the mountain. So they cried with a loud voice to the heart of wisdom
on high: "Once God brought us together for many offerings.
Yet we have all sinned against God's many commandments. Therefore we were placed in the winepress. And we
say with the prophet: "'I have trodden the winepress alone,
and from the peoples no one was with me.'" (Isaiah 63:3a)

And there was more: When the net was thrown into the
sea and caught all sorts of fish, the fisherman sought out the
good fish and put them in containers. So has God's grace
chosen certain person to glory who are people of humble
heart, given over to the fear of the Lord, people who don't
reach out for robbery.

Now may the first call, which brought you together for
the praise of God, make you good in your roots like the first
monks who were consecrated in the walls of this temple.
But you, O mountain, listen to God's warning: God has
established you like Mount Sinai, so that you might offer
the Divine the sacrifice of praise. Now be converted to your
God and be a light of the Divine, so that you don't need to
be ashamed of your original root, for that is how the right
hand of God planted you.

LETTER FIFTEEN
Hildegard to Abbot Helenger

Abbot Helanger wrote a letter to Hildegard, asking for her help. He
speaks of his lukewarmness and lack of enthusiasm for work in the
vineyard. He complains: "But now, my mother, the spiritual wine

at the Lord's wedding feast is all gone because zeal for the monastic-religious life is almost extinguished. For neither the mother of Jesus is there anymore nor is Jesus himself." This is a poignant image of his spiritual aridity – not only is the wine of consolation gone, but neither Jesus nor Mary seem present to his life and prayer. In his desolation he asks for a comforting word from his spiritual mother.

In a spiritual vision that comes from God I heard the following words:

> *It is extremely necessary for one who is longing to find his life to kill the evil works of the flesh and make his own the knowledge of how he should live – namely, so that the soul is the mistress and the flesh is the serving girl, as the Psalmist says: "Blessed is the man whom thou dost chasten, O Lord, and whom thou dost teach out of thy law." (Psalms 94:12) And who is the person? One who considered his body to be a serving girl and his soul to be a beloved mistress. And even someone who in his godlessness is as wild as a bear but who rejects this wildness and sighs for the sun of justice, which is gentle and mild, such a one is pleasing to God. God places him as guardian over his commandments and gives him the iron staff in his hand so that he might lead his sheep to the mountain of myrrh.*

Now listen and learn so that you blush with shame when you taste in your soul what I now say: Sometimes you have the style of a bear who often grumbles to itself in secret; sometimes you have the style of an ass, for you aren't solicitous in your duties but are glum and in many things bungling as well. That's why there are times when you don't bring the evil of the bear in its godlessness to execution. In a similar way, you also have the style of certain birds who belong neither to those who fly high nor to those who fly low, with the result that the higher-flying birds swoop past them overhead and the lower-flying birds cannot harm them.

To such behavior the heavenly Father gives an answer:

> *Alas, alas, this inconsistancy of your behavior isn't according to My will. For your heart grumbles over my Justice. You don't*

seek the right answer in her but you harbor in yourself a certain grumbling like that of the bear. When you have good insight into yourself, then you might pray for a little while but you soon succumb again to weariness so that you don't finish your prayer. But the way that agrees with your body is one that you walk with pleasure and you refuse completely to cut yourself off from it. But sometimes, too, your desires climb to me in a way that isn't thoroughly holy in deed but only rests on a certain faith in wishes. Nevertheless, I have here and again helped such people to become aware of the inconsistency of their behavior, so that they can hear from the tones of their intellects what they think by themselves. Yet they thus showed themselves to be unfit and perished. But now may your heart not mock the work God does because you don't know when God's sword touches you.

But I, miserable creature, see in you a plague-black fire ignited against us. And that's something you should consign to forgetfulness in good conscience, so that during the time of your office the grace and the blessing of God do not leave you. So love the justice of God in which you are loved by God and believe confidently in God's marvelous deeds so that you may receive an eternal reward.

LETTER SIXTEEN
Hildegard to the monks of Zwiefalten

There were Benedictine monks and nuns at Zwiefalten, a monastery founded by Wilhelm von Hirsan in 1085. Abbot Bertold was a recipient of several letters from Hildegard but the present letter is directed to the entire community of monks.

The clear-shining brightness speaks:

The strong light of the Godhead knows and recognizes all things even to their last details. Who rests on this insight and who grasps it, if not that person who sees with sapphire-blue eyes that God who is over all is so changeless in divine

*justice that God lets no injustice stand, for injustice can find
no rest in God!*

*God the Father had such delight in himself that he called forth
the whole creation through the divine Word. And then the
divine creation pleased God, too, and every creature that God
lovingly touched, God took in divine arms. O what great delight
you have in your work!*

*God the Father is changeless in justice and spares the unjust
only because they pray to the divine Son for forgiveness. For God
looks at the divine Word made flesh and is reminded that it is
through the Word that all creatures were made. God's saints,
too, in a similar way touch God through their pleas with their
clear voices, like shining clouds on a gentle mist over the water.*

Listen, therefore, you who break out in your evil deeds!
You were called "Mountain of the Lord" because you should
imitate the Son of God through your cloistered behavior. So
why do you transgress the motherly inner realm of love and
modesty, like those who on Horeb disciplined their bodies
according to the Law but then went astray on another path?
Or like sentinels at the gate, who call up the guard with
loud voice and thereby insidiously clear a way into the city.
Your spirits are like storm-pregnant clouds—first they give
themselves over to slothful anger, but then they turn about
and give themselves in high spirits to bestial filth. And thus
you neglect the sacrifice you are called to make and say:
"We don't have the will to oppose our own natures, for we
cannot gird the loins of our bodies since we're born from
Adam." For even though your life in the cloister puts you in
the palace of the Divine, you don't want to tame the fire in
your loins. You were rescued from the stall of the ass and
placed by the highest Lord in the exalted service of honor in
the festivals of the holy Church. Why then are you not
ashamed to run back again like dummies to the stall of the
ass? Alas, in this you are like Balaam who, rabid with
wounds and burning scars, took his repose in the land of the

shadow of death. (cf. Numbers 31:8 & 16; II Peter 2:16; Revelation 2:14) Don't, therefore, abandon the holy mountain in scandalous adultery. Woe to the disgrace of the prostitute who is cast forth abroad! For those who fail against the holy institution go to ruin.

So take hold of the discipline [of the Lord] so that you don't wander from the ways of justice, as though you had no law and as though the sun didn't shine over the blessed censer, so that the Lord isn't angered and that you don't go to ruin far from the right way. For ruin is what lies under your feet because of your transgressions. O awesome offering deserving of every honor, to which neither the unbelief of idols nor the burden of mortal wounds clings.

Alas, what pain over this misery! For God will throw you down with all your grumbling just like the Ninevites, unless you hasten quickly to the olive tree of salvation in Christ. A sweet fragrance streams forth from this tree and it allows the blossoms of the just fulfillment of the law to sprout. Why are you so twisted in your lies that you don't realize your blindness? For you are blind, because you have not kept earnestly in mind the guilt in which you were born through Adam's fall. But you have embraced that guilt with laughter and jokes, as though it didn't exist for you. Avoid this so that your salvation may quickly come. Use your eyes and walk on the paths of justice.

LETTER SEVENTEEN
Hildegard to Abbot Helmrich

The abbot of a Benedictine cloister, St. Michael in Bamberg, wrote Hildegard for advice and help. This is the second part of her letter to the abbot.

. . . Dear troubled Father, understand the statements directed to you. Be resolute in showing to your sons, with mercy and reverence, these lofty pronouncements and oracles from God. If you have begun the war on evil works and if you want to carry it out on the street of your own self-will, then screen the eyes of your desire with the sun of justice and the cloud of punishing discipline. For according to your spirit you are divine, and according to your body you belong to Christ. Don't allow it to happen that you put out the light of your soul which has so much merit in heaven above. Extend to your monks a shield of defense from the sun of justice. Give them the armbands and weapons of obedience to protect them from the cloud of discipline, although you can hardly be grieved by them, since you yourself are so weighed down with sin. You also should spread out before them in their defense the net of instruction and urge them to walk the right path. For God has made heaven and earth in great glory. And he has mixed soft realities with hard ones, so that life is bearable. So, too, should you imitate the divine mercy that makes everything balanced, so that mere mortals are able to succeed. You also must be able to separate the times for discipline from the times for mercy and pay attention to the bodily weakness of your sons according to that word of God which says, "I desire mercy and not sacrifice." (Hosea 6:6) The apostle Paul also speaks to this point, "They need milk, not solid food." (cf. I Corinthians 3:2) Anoint them, too, in oil so that they don't pine away through bitterness of heart or go astray through ignorance.

And so, true son of God, pay attention that your temple is illuminated with good will and that your spirit does not wander about with every cloud-change as in a time of unrest or war. Set your heart secure in God, the purest spring, and embrace God with the most tender love.

LETTER EIGHTEEN
Hildegard to Abbot Adam of Ebrach

The Cistercian abbey of Ebrach was founded in 1127 and Adam, a close friend of Bernard of Clairvaux, was its first abbot. In a letter to Hildegard, Adam praises the gifts of the Holy Spirit in her, especially her "spirit of prophecy." He asks for her prayers and a consoling and strengthening message from her. This letter is her response.

In a true vision of the spirit, with my body awake, I saw
something like an extraordinarily beautiful young woman. I
wasn't able to look her fully in the face because of the
lightning-like brilliance radiating from her countenance.
She wore a robe whiter than snow and more shining than
the stars. She also was wearing shoes that seemed to be of
purest gold. She held the sun and moon in her right hand
and she embraced them tenderly. There was an ivory plaque
on her breast and on it one could see the shape of a human
person and the color of this image was sapphire-blue. And
the whole creation called this young woman "Lady." And
she spoke to the image which appeared on her breast:
"Dominion is yours on the day of your power in the radiance of the saints. I have brought you forth from my own
womb before the morning star."
And I heard a voice speaking to me:

*The young woman whom you see is Love. She has her
tent in eternity. For when God wanted to create the world,
God bent down with the most tender love. God provided for
everything that was necessary, just like a parent who
prepares an inheritance for a son and with the zeal of love
makes all of her possessions available. For in all its varieties
and forms, creation recognized its Creator. For it was love
which was the source of this creation in the beginning when
God said: "Let it be!" And it was. As though in the blinking
of an eye, the whole creation was formed through love.*

*The young woman is radiant in such a clear, lightning-
like brilliance of countenance that you can't fully look at
her. That is because the fear of the Lord is represented there
in such clear judgment that mortal beings don't have the
power to advance towards her without inhibition. She wears
a robe whiter than snow and more shining than the stars.
For without deception and in the white radiance of innocence, Love embraces everything in the saints with
bright-shining works. She also wears shoes of purest gold.
For Love walks on ways that for the best part belong to the*

*choice of God. She holds the sun and moon in her right hand
and embraces them tenderly. For the right hand of God embraces all creatures and is especially extended over peoples,
kingdoms, and all goods. And that is why it stands written
in the Scripture: "The Lord says to my lord: 'Sit at my right
hand.'" (Psalms 110:1) On the young woman's breast is an
ivory plaque. For in God's knowledge there always blossoms
an unspoiled land, the virgin Mary. And so there appears on
the plaque a human shape of sapphire-blue color. For it is in
love that God's Son streams out from the "Ancient of Days."*

*The whole creation calls this maiden "Lady." For it was
from her that all of creation proceeded, since Love was the
first. She made everything. This is indicated by the image
on her breast. It is out of love that God, for the sake of
human beings, clothed the Divine in human nature. For as
the whole creation was completed at God's command, when
God said: "Be fruitful and multiply and fill the Earth!"
(Genesis 1:28) so did the glow of the true sun rise like dew
in the womb of the Virgin and form from her flesh the new
Adam, just as it had also formed the first Adam in flesh and
blood from the clay of the Earth. But the Virgin bore this
new man in innocence.*

*But it wasn't fitting that love lacked wings. For as the
creature in the beginning circled the universe, with the
result that in its urge to fly it fell, it was the rush of love that
raised it aloft. That was holy humility. For when monstrous
schemes threw Adam to the Earth, God paid very careful attention that he should not be completely destroyed in his
fall. What God had much more in mind was that the Divine
might redeem him through the holy incarnation of the Son.
These wings were most powerful, for humility raised up a
humanity gone astray. This happened through the human-
ness of the Redeemer. If love created humankind, it was
humility that redeemed it. Hope is like the eye of love; the
love for heavenly things is its bond. Faith is at the same
time the eye of humility, obedience is its heart; the contempt of evil is its bond. Love was in eternity and brought*

*forth, in the beginning of all holiness, all creatures without
any admixture of evil. Adam and Eve, as well, were produced by love from the pure nature of the Earth. And just as
Adam and Eve produced all the children of humankind, so
did these two divine powers of love and humility bring forth
all the other virtues.*

But now, O man, these divine powers knock on your
door, yes, you, the man to whom I speak; and these divine
powers say to you: "Oh, the tent of this man who earlier
dwelled with us is already hanging slack." And Love says to
you: "True friend, it isn't our will that you evade the commitment of your office. For when God in circling the
heavens wanted to sow the seeds of the whole of creation,
we embraced all God's works and labored with God.
Nevertheless, the human being fell and we cried with him
and didn't forget him, even though he struck us in the face."
And, on her side, Humility said: "Alas, I have embraced
humanity with such great sorrows. But you say, 'I want to
run away.' And yet you have a burden that you carry to the
vineyard. But you stand there and don't want to move. You
have all the more passed your time away in weariness and
looked away for another path. But whoever is attached to us
will surely not act in this way. For when the howling of the
storm breaks loose with the threat of war and the whirlwind
of human misconduct, then look to me, and in the circling
power of my wings, I will help you."
Samson lost his uncommonly strong power through the
foolishness of a woman. Therefore, you have to protect
yourself so that it doesn't happen in the same way to you
when you respond agreeably out of your weariness.
Solomon's fame, too, was ruined through the foolishness of
a woman. You must be very diligently on your guard so that
the greening power you have from God will not dry up in
you because of the fickleness of your thoughts. You must
protect the jewels of gold and precious stone with which
Love and Humility have endowed you. Also, give God the

glory because of the ornament of poverty which Wisdom has given you, and for the sake of which the people come to you. Concern yourself for these people. It is in this way that you will endure like the sun.

LETTER NINETEEN
Hildegard to Abbot Withelo

The Benedictine monastery of St. George in the Black Forest was a center of reform in the twelfth century. Withelo was abbot there in 1152 and it is to him that Hildegard sends this brief missive.

In the mirror of a true vision I saw you very agitated, much like when a dangerous air forms into a whirlwind by mixing with the current of a heavy rain-filled wind. This is how your thoughts are because your spirit is restless due to a circumstance you bear deep in your heart.

And I heard a voice and it was speaking about you:

A man is working on dry land with plow and oxen and he says to himself, "I cannot bear this work; it is too hard for me." And so he goes into an area without water and finds nonetheless that delicate flowers are growing there without any human effort. And yet these flowers are being stifled by weeds. And again the man says to himself: "I'll let the plow stand here for awhile and I'll pull out these weeds." What use is there in that? Now I want you to consider this: whether this man proves more of a success when he works the land with the plow or when he works on pulling up the weeds that stifle the flowers.

But I saw that the matter you aspire to is useless for you. Pull yourself together for the office that has been given to you. And take hold of the plow. May God come to your aid in all your needs, and never let it happen that you sweat and strain for nothing.

LETTER TWENTY
Hildegard to the five Burgundian abbots

It is interesting that several Burgundian abbeys were in correspondence with Hildegard. This connection probably was made through Barbarossa's wife Beatrix, whose homeland was Burgundy. Barbarossa took these cloisters under his official protection in 1156. The abbots write to Hildegard, praise her for her virtue and visionary power, and make a request. They are writing on behalf of a noblewoman who bore a child who subsequently died. She and her husband are saddened by the fact that they seem unable to conceive more children. They ask Hildegard for her prayers in this matter.

You are men who have been placed by God's grace in a vocation of pastoral concern; you have grasped the first address spoken to Adam when God said to him: "Where are you?" This was after Adam became a transgressor through his disobedience. At that time, God's name was like a land covered with fog for Adam. But God gave him a garment, knowing that the Divine would one day take on the garment of humanity for the sake of this man. With the same clear voice of compassion, God called back the son who had gone into a distant land, when he came to himself and said, "How many hired hands have an abundance of food in the house of my father while I am here dying of hunger?" And his father received him with joy.

It is fitting that you masters see with the original eye of clarity that God called Adam back in another way, namely by joining himself in love with human nature. That's what he said with the fatted calf at the time of the celebration of the lost soul's homecoming. "The first humans went astray through disobedience: I will call them home again through repentance."

Climb the high mountain; build tents in the valley and dwell forever therein! Look to the heights and thus, in following God, you will scale the mountain. And then look, too, into the depths of humanity, because the Son of God carried all of humankind in his own humanity. Pay attention to this humility in all that you do, all your own good works and all that you do for others, and always remain steadfast in that humility.

Be careful then that your hearts aren't like the dark mountains where metal is molded on glowing coals through the skill of the smith. This signifies customary unclean behavior. Soon

one is thinking, then wishing, then doing things that are
useless, that don't lead to holiness but which strike wounds
of dissipation and excess. Flee all of this, you champions of
God! Look to the light, that has cost you so little, and raise
yourselves up to holy deeds, for you don't know when the end
to all your doings has been set.

God gave humans reason. For it is through the Word of God
that humanity is gifted with reason. The poor, reasonless
creature is like an empty noise. Thus it is in the human person that God has brought all creatures together. But God gave
reason two wings. The right wing signifies the knowledge of
good, while the left wing stands for the knowledge of evil.
Human beings are similarly equipped with these two wings.
A person is like day and night as well. When the day overcomes the night in a person, that same person will be called a
brave warrior because he overcomes evil with combative pro-
wess. And so, O sons of God, fight for Christ through the day
and flee in peaceful spirit that fog which darkens the day. Defend yourselves against the nighttime snares that willfully
want to vent the feeling of the heart through excessive chat-
tering. Be like the day which is touched by the falling dew in
the early morning and afterwards grows mild with a gentle
coolness. So should you be as you discern all things and prove
all things and concern yourselves in the right way, that is
good for yourselves and for others.

Live with clear simplicity in the clefts of the walls, so that
you can sing songs of praise and salvation in the tents of the
just. For God has sunk deep in our reason the lively, bursting
sound of the breath of life—namely, the sound of rejoicing,
that through the knowledge of the good sees and recognizes
God in faith. This sound reverberates in all the works of good
will like the full-toned notes of a trumpet. It carries in itself
an all-embracing love, so that it is also able through humility
to gather around itself the gentle and thorough compassion to
be a balm to every wound.

Love streams down with the outpouring water of the Holy
Spirit, and in this love is the peace of God's goodness. And

humility prepares a garden with all the fruit-bearing trees of God's grace, containing all the green of God's gifts. Compassion, on the other hand, drips balsam for all the needs that adhere to the human condition. This sound of love rings in harmony with every hymn of thanks for salvation. Through humility it sounds in the heights where love beholds God and victoriously battles against pride. This love calls out in compassion with a pleading yet lovely voice. It gathers the poor and the lame around itself and begs so intensely for the help of the Holy Spirit that this same love is able to bring everything to fulfillment through good works. Love sounds in the tents where the saints shine on the thrones they have built for themselves in this world.

LETTER TWENTY-ONE
Hildegard to the monks of St. Eucharius

The abbey of St. Eucharius in Trier was the oldest Benedictine cloister on German soil. Hildegard maintained close relations with the cloister from her own convent at Rupertsberg. She wrote personal letters to Abbot Bertulf II (1136–1162) and his successors, Ludwig and Gerwin. The following letter, which is the longest directed to St. Eucharius, is addressed to all the monks there.

All of you who have put on the garment of Christ and want to follow him, listen to the words of the Psalmist: ". . . who makest the clouds thy chariot, who ridest on the wings of the wind. . . ." (Psalms 104:3) What does that mean? At the very foundation of the world, God made the clouds to carry aloft those winged, living beings who are high above us in the air. This also can be understood in another way: God saw ahead of time that a spiritual people would be established in the Divine, as we read in the prophet: "Who are these that fly like a cloud, and like doves to their windows?" (Isaiah 60:8) Spiritually minded hearts are like the clouds beneath the lights of heaven: the sun, the moon, and the stars. In the same way, obedience lies under

and provides the basis for humility, love and the other
divine powers on which the faithful fly like doves. This
happens when they bind their own self-love and cut off their
base desires, so that they come out of the window of the
dovecot of innocence and gaze into the sun as though they
were not mere human beings with fleshly wills.

And so was it, too, that the Creator of all things rode on
the wings of the wind to come to the place where God's Son
sprang up like a beautiful flower in the humility of chastity,
and there this same God came to rest on gentle stillness.
That is why it is written: "Which is the place of my rest?
. . . he that is humble and contrite in spirit and trembles at
my word." (Isaiah 66: 1 and 2) It is clear, then, what the
wings of a spiritual people are. Whoever lacks them will
surely fall, just as birds who have no wings to fly. It is with
them, too, that, as the Scripture says, ". . . the abundance
of the sea shall be turned to you, the wealth of the nations
shall come to you." (Isaiah 60:5) For a crowd of people past
all counting hurries to these wings. And yet some of them
glance to the north, stirred up through vainglory and pride.
Living in worldly affluence, they trust in themselves and do
not follow the words of the Psalmist who said, "It is better
to take refuge in the Lord than to put confidence in princes."
(Psalms 118:9) What does that mean? It is far better and
more useful to gaze upwards in the garment of Christ and to
fly into the clouds than to trust in oneself, as was the case
with the guilt of the fallen angel of light. In his pride he
wanted to elevate himself above God before Whom he could
not stand, and yet he fell like lead into the abyss.

In the same pride, life fled from Adam, too, and he ended
up in a foreign land. In his alienated state God appeared to
him as a stranger, although when he was still in a state of
humility and innocence he had known this same God very
well. So it is that all human beings place their trust in
themselves. They deceive themselves because they place
their hope in princes. But when God called out, "Adam,
where are you?" God knew already that the creature of the

divine hands should by no means be lost but would be
redeemed in days to come, as it is written: "Remember thy
congregation, which thou hast gotten of old, which thou
hast redeemed to be the tribe of thy heritage! Remember
Mount Zion, where thou hast dwelt." (Psalms 74:2) What
does that mean? God remembered the man when God trod
on the head of the snake through the woman when the
Word became flesh. That was Mount Zion, where God
dwells in lowliness, and where God remains as Son in the
heart of the Divine.

Listen to me now, O assembled community, so that you
may be Mount Zion. God has foreknowledge from the very
beginning that the Divine would fashion every creature.
The Word of God took form in the virginal bough as a
human person. And this bough was the basis for all the
divine powers of holiness; and thus it is from the same
bough that you, O spiritual people, take your origin. It is
true that Eve brought forth the whole human race. And yet
this bough has in truth, because of its life-power, brought
forth the whole human race afresh, since it is from this
womb that the Son of God came forth. And so are you, O
spiritual men, Mount Zion, for God has planted you in the
Word. The Son of the exalted Divine has lived in the tent of
the Virgin Mary and he came forth from her like a strong
lion so that the whole world has seen him.

That same Son of God has joined you all together in
himself as a spiritual people so that you fly to him like
clouds, not carrying your sins as deliberately committed
acts. He was certainly without sin. And you imitate him
when you walk as he did, when you reject your own self-
will so as not to sin, when you are not like dust that the
wind sweeps away off the face of the earth, when you are
not like viper's poison nor like lead in raging waves. But
when you run around in vain luxury, you are like dust
strewn here and there. But this empty activity doesn't sow
the fruitful seed of justice, nor does it plant a select
vineyard but it produces arrogant rumors and harms your

souls. For when you fall into malicious pride, you pick up
unhealthy, deadly viper's poison. And when an unrest of
spirit raises itself up in your midst, then you are like lead
that falls heavily into a spring of water. For vainglory and
malice are the kernel of pride, and when you are ensnared in
unrest of spirit among yourselves, then envy and hate will
hasten to offer their services. And at that point, peace and
security disappear. And the love of Christ withdraws. And
those who are stuck in these evils will "sink like lead in the
mighty waters" (Exodus 15:10) because they don't have any
wings with which they can raise themselves up. For the zeal
of the Lord complains loudly of you in wrath, as the Divine
once rang out when hurling the proud fiend into the abyss.
So the Psalmist says: "Raise your hands against their pride
forever. How much evil has the enemy perpetuated in your
sanctuary!" [Hildegard obviously has a different version of
what we find in Psalms 74:3 in the RSV: "Direct thy steps to
the perpetual ruins; the enemy has destroyed everything in
the sanctuary."]

But now the living light speaks to the sons of your community: you are the temple walls because the early Church
has established you. So flee the vain search of praise and
pride and the storm of frequent unrest. Look now with living eyes and hear the following words with the ears of inwardness: I don't see that your abode will revert to ruin,
although it will suffer many lashes of the scourge. So live
and be watchful in the Divine!

For, in a true vision I saw some in your community shine
like the morning light, and some gleamed like sapphire and
others again shone like the light of the stars. Those who
shine like the morning light are God-fearing. They observe
the prescriptions of the rules joyfully, out of love for God,
although they sometimes swerve from the path according to
the flesh, like the sacrificial animal that is led to slaughter.
Those who gleam like sapphire love God and do not,
therefore, commit any great sins, although they sometimes
fail. And they also are happy to discipline themselves on

account of their offences and they make all of this customary. Those who shine like the light of the stars are filled with goodwill, and therefore don't engage in strife with men. They keep the light-heartedness of childlike conduct and carefully preserve themselves from the serious sins that are so hateful to them. But, on the other hand, I have seen those who because of the habits of their unclean conduct are in the blackness of a bitter smoke. Some among them are bitter because of their self-will. They love worldly goods and have no attraction, therefore, to spiritual conduct. They often afflict those who live in the three ways described above.

And I hear a voice which calls from heaven: "As long as this community holds fast to these ways of living, it will not be abandoned by God." But also for those who, as we said, found themselves in the blackness, I heard the voice say: "Raise yourself up, O north wind, and come, south wind, blow through my garden, and its fragrance will stream forth." Fall back, evil of injustice, and moisten with divine power the gardens of holiness so that works may shine forth that never fade. The north wind symbolizes those quarrelsome people, who with bickering speech, avaricious excuses, and greedy provocation want to trample on the beneficial plants of divine power. This is just like the north wind that levels everything in its path. But those who are afflicted by it in this way will learn patience thereby. With sighs and tears they plead to God for their own sins and for the sins of others. At the same time, contempt for their sinfulness lays hold of them. Thus a sweet-smelling smoke of incense rises from their hearts and it is taken up to God by the angels. And so it is that even the north wind blows the power of life to the good.

Those who delight themselves in earthly possessions remonstrate with the three groups who strive in the way described above, so that they might fall into confusion. They try to throw these people down, even in relationship to the necessary acts of obedience. They get themselves entangled in the filth of the flesh, like pigs wallowing in the mire, and by this habitual depravity they even sometimes break down the resistance of others with all this winking of their serpent eyes.

But any of you who love injustice must keep this admonition firmly in your memory, so that you may realize that the selfish strivings of your wills constitute a worship of false gods; and there is no way that this is able to be united to the orders of the angels, in other words, the level of religious life, just as the false gods of deceit cannot be brought into union with the true God. And you should avoid all other sins as well and flee to the spring of bubbling waters where you can wash yourselves. You should remember also that second baptism of your religious profession, for it was through that profession that you left the world so that you could retreat from sins. So concern yourself that the offering you have made to God be pleasing, so that you can persevere in the good which you have begun. For as often as a man breaks his selfish will on the torturing rack of the flesh, this is an offering for God. It will be accepted like the sacrifice of Abraham when this man in obedience bound up his son in order to sacrifice him. Those who abandon evil works must rule their own hands; those who put limits to the paths of their own selfish will must bind their own feet; they must bow their heads and obey, as Isaac bowed his head under the sacrificial sword; and those who get rid of fleshly desires must be in charge of their own bodies.

It is here that the victory lies for whoever bears the banner that waves in the winds of good reputation and streams in the gentle fragrance of virtue. Whoever wins this victory walks along secure in the presence of all enemies. And so the offering will be like the fatted calf, without blemish of any sort and fat for sacrifice; and in the soul, too, the shortcoming of gauntness will disappear. For the fully worthy sacrificial offering is fat. Even though he was persecuted by the unjust, Christ remained without sin and he thereby sanctified the patience of the saints.

And so, O men of faith, prepare your hearts to do battle for him who has given you the example. Throw off your concern for matters which are unimportant and be zealous that you stand with the Divine, who is the Alpha and Omega. It is true that you are darkened through the inclination of your senses to sin. But you have raised yourself up from your sins and so the virtues will gloriously take on form in you. And may God's hand protect you.

LETTER TWENTY-TWO
Hildegard to Abbot Philip

Two letters of Hildegard to Abbot Philip of the Premonstratention Cloister of Park in the Netherlands are extant and can be read today in the original twelfth-century handwriting of this Rhineland seer. When Hildegard wrote the first letter, she was very ill. There were three times of special physical suffering in her long life-span. The first was immediately before her move to Disibodenberg. The second time fell between the years 1158–1162. It was in this period that she wrote this first letter to Abbot Philip. Her third period of illness was from 1170–1173. Hildegard's attitude toward and use of these times of sickness are an integral part of her spirituality. Her second letter includes a discreet plea for a woman she judges ready to receive the sacrament of penance.

The belief in God that one carries in a heart on fire through the inspiration of the Holy Spirit is truly lovely, when that person in true love embraces things not seen just as much as the things that are seen and are so delightful. It is also praiseworthy of you that out of your love for God you have deigned to see and hear a weak and uneducated woman like myself.

A wind blew from a high mountain and, as it passed over ornamented castles and towers, it put into motion a small feather which had no ability of its own to fly but received its movement entirely from the wind. Undoubtedly almighty God arranged for this to show what the Divine could accomplish through a creature that didn't have the least hope of accomplishing anything of itself.

You are a man who resolutely stands in the prophetic office, to which the concern of the apostolic office is bound. I ask that you send me the help of your prayers, so that I can persevere in the grace of God. For, as you yourself have seen, I am still lying on my sickbed. And since I retain no form of security in myself, I have placed all my hope and my total trust on the mercy of God alone.

But now, O father, you who stand in the place of Christ, show concern for the sheep of your flock with the staff of God's commandments. It is by these commandments that you should lead and guide them, so that they don't raise themselves up in pride. For this vice is like a city not built on rock that is thereby destroyed and falls into ruin because it is without a firm foundation. You also must frequently anoint sinners with the oil of compassion, sinners who are wounded with all kinds of vices. Do this so that they, through their evil tendency to sin, do not begin to smell, as Lazarus did who lay in the tomb for four days.

In all your concerns hold aloft the horn of salvation, which is the power of true humility. This virtue is like a sapphire-blue cloud through which the sun powerfully shines. And in this it is like the true son, the Son of the Virgin, who came down to Earth in deepest humility and in that same humility went up to sit at the Divine's right hand. You also must cut away from them the evil habit of sin and be zealous to decorate them with jewels like a fine necklace, so that along with them you may attain to eternal joy, you with them and they with you.

And now may the grace of the Holy Spirit make you a light of true love in the presence of almighty God. And may that same God give you an eternal reward for the help which you render me, both for my soul and for my body.

LETTER TWENTY-THREE
Hildegard to Abbot Philip

(see introduction to Letter 22)

O father, with all your inadvertence you fear God and you love the Divine, so much that you sigh deeply for all your deficiencies. Hurry now to the spring of living waters, so that you may wash not only yourself but other sick people as well, whom you see covered with wounds. Pour out on them, too, the wine of contrition and do not cease to anoint them with the oil of compassion. In this you should imitate the Divine, the living spring and the unbroken circle, embracing sinners who take refuge in God's saving mercy and judging with sharp sentence all godless opponents. No mountain can touch the circumference of this circle because its shadow looms high above everything. And this circle itself cannot be thrown into the shadow by anything higher because it towers above all things. For God lives only and alone through the Divine and therefore without beginning or end. And so whoever takes flight to God's saving grace will never lose the happiness of eternal life. For the spark of salvation will be kindled anew by the living God, for the Divine does not want the death of sinners but that they begin to live for God.

But now, O gentle father, you stand in the place of Christ, and I ask you to accept this woman, Ida, who has not yet fully recognized her hidden wounds. Take care of her and all of those who flee to you for help; minister to her very gently with the medicine of penance, so that you may live forever in the company of the true Trinity!

LETTER TWENTY-FOUR
Hildegard to Philip, the dean of the cathedral, and to the whole clergy at Cologne

A heretical group called the Cathars tried to gain a foothold in Cologne. While stopping over there on a trip through the Rhineland in 1160, Hildegard scolded the clergy for their lukewarmness and urged them to good example in the face of threatening heresy. After her visit, the dean of the cathedral and the clergy of Cologne wrote a letter to her asking for her further advice. This is her response:

The Divine Who was and Who is and Who is to come speaks to the shepherds of the Church: "Beloved sons, you

pasture my flocks according to the explicit direction of
God's words. Why are you not ashamed, then, when you see
how all the other creatures on the face of the Earth don't
neglect, but rather fulfill, the directions they have from
their Master? I have put you in place like the sun and the
other heavenly lights, so that you might illuminate people
through the fire of your teaching, that you might glow
through your good reputation and make the hearts of all
people burn within them. This is the way I made things in
the first age of the world. I chose Abel; I loved Noah; I showed myself to Abraham; I poured myself out on Moses for the
establishment of the Torah; and I put the prophets in place
as my dearest friends. Thus it is that in Abel there is the
model of obedience; in Noah the model of highest leadership; in Moses the office of kingly messenger; and in the
prophets the manifold of all the other offices. Abel poured
out his light like the moon, for in his sacrificial gift he announced the time of obedience. Noah was like the sun,
because he perfected the house of obedience. Abraham was
like the great planets, because he introduced circumcision.
Moses shone like the other stars, because he received the
Torah through obedience. And the prophets are like the four
corners of the world that determine the Earth's boundaries.
For they persevered courageously and therefore rebuked the
whole world because of prevalent sacrilege and thereby at
the same time revealed God. But your tongues are dumb
despite the loud-calling trumpet blasts of the voice of the
Divine. You don't love the holy knowledge that, like the
stars, has its own course.

The trumpet of the Lord is the justice of God that you
should deeply consider with great zeal in holiness. It also is
your duty in obedience, at appropriate times and with holy
discretion, again and again to present this divine justice in
the sight of the people and to pound it into their heads excessively. But it's because of the stubbornness of your own
self-will that you fail to do this. That's why in your sermons
there are no lights in the firmament of God's justice, just as
when the stars aren't shining in the sky. You are night, a

night which exhales darkness. And you are like a people
that does no work and out of inertia fails to walk in the
light. You are like a naked snake that creeps into its hole. It
is in much the same way that you give yourselves over to
the stench of the lowest beasts.

Alas, alas, you should be, as it is called, "Mount Zion on
which God dwells." For you are blessed and signed as
heavenly men. You should be a dwelling place where there
is a fragrance of incense and myrrh and where God dwells.
But this is not what you are. Whatever your flesh desires,
that's what you do. That's why the word of Scripture applies
to you. "Raise your hands finally against their proud deeds.
How much evil has the enemy done in the sanctuary!" [This
is how Hildegard translates Psalm 74:3 which in the RSV is
translated: "Direct thy steps to the perpetual ruins; the
enemy has destroyed everything in the sanctuary."] Your
necks are held high in wickedness, but the power of God
will bend them low; in the same way God will destroy what
is puffed up, as though with gusts of wind. For you neither
acknowledge God nor respect human beings. Nor do you
despise injustice to the extent that you actually crave to
destroy whatever justice is in yourself. You neither look to
God nor do you desire to see God. What you are concerned
about are your own activities and you judge things according to your tastes. You're guided by nothing more than your
own pleasure in doing and allowing to happen whatever you
desire.

What a great evil this is and what a malevolent attitude,
when people do not want to stand in the direction of what is
good, either for God's sake or for that of their fellow human
beings! But what they want is honor without effort, and
eternal reward without ever having to deny themselves.
And they desire to sound as though they're holy; but such a
sound is empty noise. It is as though the Devil says, "I am
good and holy." This is not to be tolerated!

So, now, what do you have to say for yourselves? You
have no eyes if your works do not illuminate in the fire of

the Holy Spirit, and if you do not again and again provide a good example for them. Thus the firmament of God's justice in you lacks the light of the sun, and the air lacks the sweet fragrance that comes from the cultivation of virtue. This is why it is written, "They have ears, but do not hear; noses, but do not smell." (Psalms 115:6) For just as the winds blow and circle the globe, so should you be like swift winds going out to all people with your teaching. For it is written, "Your sound goes out over the whole world." [The reference is to Psalm 19:4, ". . . their voice goes out through all the Earth, and their words to the end of the world."] But for the sake of this transitory, worldly reputation you let yourselves be crippled. Soon you'll all be soldiers, then slaves, then buffoons. With your empty and silly behavior, you might well be good for nothing more than to scare away some flies in the summer!

Through the teaching of those writings composed in the fire of the Holy Spirit, you should be strong corner pillars, supporting the Church just like those pillars that hold up the ends of the Earth. But, instead of that, you are thrown to the ground and are no support for the Church; rather do you flee into the hell of your desires. And because of your disgusting riches and greed as well as other vanities, you don't allow the people to seek teaching from you, since you say: "It's impossible for us to do everything!" You should be pillars of fire to draw people out and call them to do good works in your presence and to say to them: "Serve God with fear; with trembling kiss God's feet, lest God be angry, and you perish in the way; for God's wrath is quickly kindled." (Psalm 2:11-12)

The Devil himself is able to look at you and say: "With you I can find everything I need: food to devour and whatever else I want in the way of banquet delicacies. My eyes, too, and my ears, my belly, and my veins are filled with your venom, and my breast is full from your depravities."

But I, the One Who is, say to those who listen to Me: In the time that these things come to pass, a heretical people worse than the heretics among you now, will fall upon you and seek to destroy you, for you have abandoned your duty and despised the law. This persecution will come upon you from all sides and will not conceal your works. No, this group will uncover you and say of you: "Scorpions are in their morals and snakes in all their works."

Why do you tolerate people like this around you? Why do you put up with people under you who soil the whole Earth with their filthy scandals? They are given over to drunkenness and debauchery. If you don't banish them, the whole Church will be destroyed. For the Devil is with these people and he says to himself: "God loves chastity and modesty. So that is what you will mimic with these people." And so the old enemy blows through the spirits of the air so that they might refrain from sins of lewdness. Thus they don't love women but flee them. So from the outside they will present themselves before men in all holiness and sarcastically say: "The others who were before us and wanted to keep chastity dried out like baked fish. But no stain of the flesh and lustful desire dares to touch us, for we are holy and permeated by the Holy Spirit." In this way they lure women and catch them in their own error. In the pride of their puffed up spirits they boast, "We surpass all others," and yet behind all of this they secretly pursue their lust with these same women. Thus their corruption and their heretical nature often come to light.

But I, the One Who is, says: Therefore the depravity that will cleanse the evil will come upon you, as it is written: "God made darkness a covering and thick clouds dark with water a canopy." (Psalms 18:11) For God has appointed punishment for your dark and evil works. Law and learning originate in heaven, and it is through these that God desires to live in your midst. But this only could be possible if you were an ornament of virtues and a fragrant garden of delight.

But you are a bad example in the hearts of people, for the stream of a good reputation does not flow out from you. You lack a correct and spiritual appreciation regarding what you eat and wear. You do evil works because you lack the benefit *of discernment. This is why your honor will disappear from you and the crowns will fall from your heads. Thus injustice drives out justice. You search out and examine all temptations, as it is written: "Woe to the world for temptations to sin! For it is necessary the temptation comes!" (Matthew 18:7) It is true that the evil deeds of people must be cleansed through persecutions and afflictions. And yet people bring much misery on their own heads by plunging other people into distress through their own wickedness.*

These unbelievers, these Devil-deceived people, will be like a whip for your punishment, because you don't pray to God in sincerity. And they will plague you until all your evil deeds and crimes are washed away.

And yet these evil-doers are not those traitors who will come before judgment day when the Devil flies into the heights, as when he began to fight against God in the beginning. But they are their sprouting seed. But after they are discovered with their perverse idols and in their other wicked acts, the princes and the other powers will fall on them and kill them like mad wolves wherever they find them. And then the morning sun of justice will rise and your last condition will be better than the first.

Placed in holy fear from all of these things past, you will shine like purest gold and will persevere, therefore, for a long time. And many people will wonder, then, that such a mighty storm came forth from such mildness. The people who lived before these times had to stand up against their will, and at the risk of their lives to much fiercer struggles than the ones from which you are not able to rescue yourselves. But in your times, because of your selfish willfulness and your undisciplined conduct, you will experience much of the disturbance of war, a time when you will be destroyed.

So, those who want to flee these dangers should protect themselves lest their eyes are darkened and they become ensnared in a nest of misery. They should do everything in their power through good works and clinging to the good so

*that they might flee this nest. Then God will come to their
help.*

I am but an anxious and poor woman, who for two years
was driven to represent this matter personally to teachers,
professors, and other learned people in the prestigious
places where they live. But because the Church was in a
schism, I have given up this preaching.

LETTER TWENTY-FIVE
Hildegard to Werner of Kirchheim

Hildegard made various apostolic tours, denouncing heresies and
calling for a reform of the Church from within. Her last trip of
this sort led her to Kirchheim. She spoke to an assembly of priests
there in 1170 or 1171 and then returned to her convent. Werner
was the leader of this group of priests who heard her, and he wrote
to her and asked her to send them a copy of what she had said, so
that "it will not slip from our memory and we might more atten-
tively keep it before our eyes." She responds with the following
letter:

When, in the year 1170 after the incarnation of the
Divine, I lay in my sickbed for a long time, I saw, while I
was awake both in body and spirit, the form of a very
beautiful lady. She was a woman of exquisite charm, so attractive in her loveliness and possessed of such beauty that
the human spirit was unable to comprehend it. Her form
towered above the Earth all the way up into the heavens.
Her face sparkled with the most incredible brightness. Her
eyes looked up to heaven. She was clothed in a brightly radiant robe of white silk and in a cloak decorated with costly
jewels: emeralds, sapphires, and pearls both large and
small. On her feet she wore shoes made of onyx. But her
face was smudged with dust and her dress was torn on the
right side. Her cloak, too, had lost its exquisite beauty and
the tops of her shoes were soiled. She cried to high heaven
with a loud, plaintive voice and said: "Hear me, O heaven,

for my countenance is sullied. Mourn, O Earth, for my robe
is torn. Tremble, O abyss, for my shoes are soiled. The
foxes have their holes and the birds of the sky have their
nests, but I have no helper, no consoler, not even a staff to
lean on that might give me some support."

And she went on to say: "I was hidden in the heart of the
Divine until the Son of Man, conceived and born in virginity, poured out his blood. It was this blood that was his
dowry when he married me, so that I might bring forth
anew, in the pure and simple rebirth in the Spirit and in
water, those who were stunted and sullied by the venom of
the serpent. Priests are supposed to be those who nourish
me, who see to it that my face sparkles like the morning
light, that my robe shines like lightning, that my cloak
radiates like costly jewels and that my shoes brightly
gleam. But instead they cover my face with dust, tear my
robe, and make my cloak dark, and my shoes black. Those
who should be beautifying me in every way have been
faithless and have totally abandoned me. They soil my face
when they celebrate the sacraments, and they receive the
Body and Blood of my Son while they are covered with the
great impurity of their debauched morals, with the wicked
filth of prostitution and adultery, with the rapacious greed
of their evil practice of buying and selling all sorts of
unseemly things. And they envelope themselves in their
own filth, just as though someone were to put a child down
in the mire in front of pigs.

"The wounds of my Bridegroom (Christ) remain fresh and
open, so long as the wounds of the human race's sins are
open. Even this fact, that the wounds of Christ remain open,
is the fault of priests. For they are the ones who are supposed
to make me radiantly pure and serve me in purity; but instead
in their limitless greed they move from church to church (in
their practice of simony). And even my robe is torn thereby,
for they are violators of the law, of the gospel, and of their
priestly duty. They also take the radiance from my cloak, for
they totally neglect the commandments prescribed for them.

They do not fulfill them in moderation—neither in the goodness of their intentions nor in the performance of their duties. Yet this moderation is like emeralds and other good and righteous works are like various jewels with which God is honored. They soil the tops of my shoes because they do not adhere to the straight ways, that is, to the hard and rough ways of justice, and furthermore fail to give good example to those who are placed under them. And yet with some of them I find on the bottom of my shoes something which is like my own essence, the light of truth."

And I heard a voice from heaven which said:

> This image represents the Church. Therefore you who see this and hear this must get the message to the priests, who have been appointed for the direction and education of God's people. What was said to them was like what was said to the apostles: "Go into all the world and preach the gospel to the whole creation." (Mark 16:15) For when creating human beings, God inscribed in them the whole creation, just as when someone writes the time and date of a whole year on a small piece of parchment. That is why God named humankind the "the whole creation."

And another time I, poor woman that I am, saw a sword drawn out of its scabbard that waved in the air. One side was turned against heaven and the other against the Earth. This sword was stretched out over the clergy whom the prophet had foreseen when he cried out, full of wonder: "Who are these that fly like a cloud and doves to their windows?" (Isaiah 60:8) For these men are raised above the Earth and separated from ordinary people. They should live in a holy manner and walk and work with the simplicity of doves. But now they are evil in their ways and works. And I saw that the sword destroyed some of the dwelling places of these clergy, just as once Jerusalem was destroyed after the sufferings of the Lord. But I also saw that God in the divine visitation preserved many God-fearing, pure, and sincere priests for the Divine, just as when God answered Elijah and said to him that seven thousand men would be left in Israel who had not bowed their knee to Baal.

But now may the unquenchable fire of the Holy Spirit pour itself out in your midst, since you have chosen for yourselves the better part!

LETTER TWENTY-SIX
Hildegard to a religious superior

The name of the recipient of this letter is unknown to us. The letter itself contains some powerful creation images. The recipient of the letter is apparently the spiritual director of a community of religious women.

O master, you are thoroughly permeated by the teachings of the Holy Scripture. May God, the Creator of the world, kindle in you a thirst for the works of justice. And may the living Source intoxicate you out of the stream of divine delights with good and holy convictions, and may the Source so enlighten you that in the light of the Divine you may see the light (cf. Psalms 36:9). And may God endlessly satisfy you in a vision such as the angels long to see.

I am but a poor woman who listens to the instruction of the masters. I barely know the letters of the alphabet and I'm very much afraid to say or to write to the masters, i.e. to men, those things I have seen in my soul and in a true light without any perceptions of my external senses. Nevertheless, I say to you: I saw in a true vision that these women are like the people who were placed under the old Law. The root of the "Just One" (i.e. the promised Redeemer) did indeed lay with them but it remained almost dry. For this people did not accept the teaching of the Son of God that the prophets had announced with loudcrying voices. This is also the case with these women who profess the faith but do not follow through with the works of faith because they live in the luxurious desires of the flesh. They should rather be continually crying to God with contrite hearts. They must be told that they should guard themselves from striving after the dead letter of the Law rather than the lifegiving Spirit. And how should they do this? The only way is through faith, a faith that is dead without works, just as it was for those who stood under the old Law. These women should also be admonished to give up their wicked, sinful behavior; through their culpable lukewarmness this has become their habitual condition. But they must hasten in the opposite direction towards the fullness of justice, just as the deer of which the Psalmist sings thirsts for springs of fresh water (Psalm 42:1). For they delight in sinful desires just as people enjoy the taste of food. But they should take refuge in the right conduct of their lives. Like the man who sold everything he had to obtain the pearl of great price, they should give up the ways they are presently pursuing and in which they can find no salvation and prepare themselves for spiritual warfare so that they might win the priceless pearl of eternal life. O master, may the Divine make you a mirror of holiness, so that you might be happy with God forever.

LETTER TWENTY-SEVEN
Hildegard to an abbot

We see Hildegard concerned again here about a popular heresy, the Cathars. We also see her larger vision of times of spiritual corruption within the Church followed by times of reformation and Spirit-filled activity.

Listen, you who bear Christ's name in your office as his representative. Our age stands before us full of pain, with wounds both old and new. And why is that? Because of a way of life that resembles a snake playing with people one minute and biting them the next. For the Church has lost her condition of justice. The north wind blows fiercely over the Church and shakes her crown and tears at her garments, so that the leading clergy of God's sovereign name become unsettled. This condition will continue until that reformation is accomplished that the sins of the whole people demand. For there are many who

run along with the Sadducees (i.e. the Cathars) in their ab-
surdity. Through these and other sins people will tear the
garment of the Church — namely, justice — and veil her sovereign name with sadness. Nevertheless, the Church keeps
the trust of her Bridegroom so that through him she can
again receive the brilliance of her crown and garment. And
she will see the glorious day when evil and faithlessness
have been destroyed and she is adorned with the light of
faith as though with precious earrings.

Now may the Holy Spirit so enflame you that through
God's grace you cleanse yourself from every sin and contribute as much as possible to the glory of the Church, so
that, because of your faithful perserverance, you may one
day hear these words from the highest Judge: "You are my
servant; my soul is well pleased with you." Thus will you
live happy for all eternity.

LETTER TWENTY-EIGHT
Hildegard to a priest

This brief letter gives us considerable insight into Hildegard's
holistic view of human nature and, consequently, of personal and
spiritual growth. We also see her strong theology of the Word of
God as this is applied with gentle, pastoral concern.

O servant of God in the adornment of Christ's office, do
not be afraid of the burden that frightens you in your sleep.
This arises in you through the blood-rich juices that are in a
state of unrest because of your black bile system. This is the
reason your sleep is troubled and why the images in your
sleep so often fail to correspond with reality. For the old
deceiver will use this illusion to bring you to a confused
state, even when he does not harm your senses. But it is by
the power of God's decree that you will be disciplined
through such affliction. For it is through this fear that the
bodily desires in you will be tamed. Read every night in a
prayerful state of soul, with your hand laid on your heart,
the opening words of John's Gospel: "In the beginning was

the Word." And then say these words: Lord, almighty God, in the abundance of your goodness you have awakened me through the breath of life. By the most holy garment of our tender human nature with which your Son was clothed on my account, I entreat you: Do not let it happen that I am plagued any further through the bitterness of this unrest. But for the sake of the love of your only begotten Son, free me from this affliction through your merciful help, and defend me against all the snares of the spirits of the air!

May the Holy Spirit make you a tent of holiness, so that you may always live with God in the joys of the highest blessedness.

LETTER TWENTY-NINE
Hildegard to an abbot

This letter is significant in that it shows how Hildegard avoids extremes of mortification and bodily asceticism and counsels that discretion, discernment, and balance that St. Benedict considered to be the mother of the virtues.

Honorable father, from your love for God you have received me in your most inward compassion. I ask you for God's sake to listen to me, an unworthy serving-girl of the Divine. In regard to this monk, who because of his sins is longing to be taken in to your fatherly mercy, I ask you to receive him. And give him counsel so that he doesn't destroy his body through unreasonable abstinence and end up fading away with weakness. Give him a moderate penance through which he can overcome the Devil who is seeking to outwit him. He can do this with the help of your discretion, for discretion is a powerful mother who directs and orders all the virtues so that they are pleasing to God. For the old serpent hides itself in immoderate mortifications so that it can outwit and catch all those who strive after virtue without wise discernment. So you should bring this sheep as an offering to the almighty God, out of love for him who left the ninety-nine behind and placed on the divine shoulder the one who had gone astray. Hope in God, so that your striving may be like the burning sun and you might be a true servant of God and live in God's presence for eternity.

LETTER THIRTY
Hildegard to a priest

This letter shows the kind of pastoral questions Hildegard was called upon to address. The question which elicits this letter is: "How should I respond to someone who wants to receive communion but suffers from frequent bouts of vomiting?" Hildegard's answer not only shows pastoral sense but her holistic approach to Christian life and the sacraments.

When someone suffers from attacks of vomiting because of bodily weakness, and yet out of great devotion longs to receive the Body of Christ, the priest should not presume to offer the sacrament to such a person. This clearly follows from the respect the priest should have for the Body of Christ which is hidden under the appearance of the bread. But what the priest can do is to hold the Body of Christ over the head of such a person and beseech God, who has sent the soul into the body of this person, to heal the soul of this person through the divine Body and Blood. Then the priest should also hold the sacrament over the heart of this sick person and say: "Almighty God, whose Son was conceived in faith by Mary, grant, we beseech you, that the soul and the body of this person may be healed in true faith through the holiness of this Body and Blood." For the divine sacrament is hidden under the form of the bread, just as the soul of a person is also invisible. Thus it is that the invisible soul can draw invisible healing into itself from this place. For the spirit of a person directly perceives the One who has sent it. And God will never hold back from someone who receives the Divine in faith. But every holiness will be taken away from the unworthy person, just as it was from Judas. So the person who suffers from vomiting should refrain from receiving the Body of

Christ, both out of caution and out of respect. The faith in this sacrament, which is solemnly made holy in the form of the bread, must most firmly be preserved.

LETTERS THIRTY-ONE & THIRTY-TWO
Hildegard to Gertrude, a former countess

Here are two letters written by Hildegard to Gertrude. Gertrude had been the wife of a count, the sister of a king, and the aunt of an emperor. She and her husband remained childless throughout their married life. While the count was alive, the couple gave generously to various cloisters. The count died on September 20, 1156 and his widow decided to enter the Cistercian convent of Wechterswinkel in the diocese of Wurzburg. Hildegard had known Gertrude while her husband was still alive and the letters reflect her sensitivity to the countess' understandable problems in adjusting to life in a convent. The second letter is obviously Hildegard's answer to a letter from Gertrude (which is not extant) about the possibility of changing communities.

THIRTY-ONE

Those days which stood at your disposal through noble birth and the riches of this world have been allowed by God to decline, so that the originality of your spirit will not be a seduction for you through Adam's Fall. And yet, your heart will not be confused. So may God allow this decline to continue ever further so that the mountain of pride will not oppress your spirit. For God chastises the person God loves very much so that she cannot run on the broad paths of self-will. Therefore, rejoice, O daughter of Sion, for God has you so securely in the divine hand that you do not need in any way to rely on your own security. And God does this work in you so that you can be a true cornerstone (of God's temple). God sees and knows you and God will never abandon you.

THIRTY-TWO

O daughter of God, deep inside you bear a troubled soul. O Gertrude, beloved child of God, you are continually restless

of spirit. Regarding your question about a place where you
can stay and find pasture for soul and body, that is
something about which God has given me no sign. Nevertheless, I have heard the following words with great clarity:

> Through consulting your own intuition and with the wise
> counsel of others as well, inquire into and choose for
> yourself a place to live that meets your needs, but not such
> as offers an incompatible mixture of religious and secular
> society. For God has set you the task of finding those things
> you need for your life, while at the same time avoiding emp-
> ty luxury. For that person can find God everywhere who
> seeks the Divine with a sincere cry for help.

Therefore, O daughter of God, that wisdom which is won
in holy knowledge does not despise God, for God created
humankind in the divine image. Yet I see your living place
glowing, wherever the dwelling is which God provides for
you. So now be happy again and hold fast to your purpose in
God.

LETTER THIRTY-THREE
Hildegard to Bishop Eberhard of Bamberg

We now bring Gertrude's story to its conclusion. Hildegard wrote
to Bishop Eberhard, urging him to offer Gertrude a place at
Bamberg. He listened to Hildegard, and the result was that Gertrude found a place there and spent the rest of her days in fruitful
monastic life. Here is the text of Hildegard's letter.

A man rose at daybreak and planted a vineyard. Afterwards, he turned his attention in other directions for a
variety of reasons. Thus his zeal for the vineyard passed.
Now, father, look at this homeless daughter, Gertrude, who
like Abraham was called from her native soil and left her
fatherland. For she gave up everything to buy the pearl of
great price of which the gospel speaks (Matthew 13:44). But
her heart now is greatly distressed, pressed like a grape in

the wine press. Help her, then, as much as you can, for the love of the One who existed before all beginnings and who has filled all things in divine compassion, so that the vineyard in this daughter will not go to ruin.

LETTER THIRTY-FOUR
Hildegard to Elisabeth of Schöngau

Hildegard's correspondence with the young Benedictine nun, Elisabeth, has a special character, because Elisabeth was a visionary, too. Elisabeth had been taken by her parents to a convent when she was 12; in 1147, when she was 18, she received the veil. She wrote several visionary treatises which were distributed through her brother, Egbert, a monk in Schöngau. We have three letters of Elisabeth to Hildegard and two from Hildegard to Elisabeth. It is these latter which are translated here, with summaries of the letters of Elisabeth.

Elisabeth had written to Hildegard of her inner doubts and conflicts, especially because of the people (both lay and religious) who mock her visions and deny their authenticity. She shares with Hildegard her inner life and the nature and content of her visionary experiences. Hildegard consoles her and helps her to focus on the purpose of visionary gifts as charisms of service. This counsel is especially valuable, of course, for giving us insight into Hildegard's understanding of her own visionary gifts.

I am but a poor creature and fragile vessel; yet what I speak to you comes not from me but from the clear light. Human beings are vessels God has made and filled with the Spirit so that the divine work might come to perfection in them. For God does not do things the way we humans do. It was through the divine Word of command alone that everything came into existence perfect. The grasses, the woods, the trees came forth. The sun too and the moon and the stars went to their appointed places to perform their service. The waters sent out fish and birds. [Note that Hildegard's order of creation has birds coming from the water; this is connected to the Genesis text: "Let the waters bring forth swarms of living creatures, and let birds fly above the Earth

across the firmament of the heavens." Genesis 1:20] Cattle
too and wild beasts arose. All of these creatures—each according to the assignment given it by God—came into being
to serve human beings with all of creation.

It was only humans themselves who did not know their
Creator. For although God bestowed great knowledge on
humans, they raised themselves up in their hearts and turned away from God. It had been God's intention that all of
the divine works should be brought to completion in
humankind. And yet the old trickster deceived those first
human beings and in a flattering whisper infected them with
the virus of disobedience, so that they strove for more than
they were supposed to. Alas, all the elements got entangled
in the confusion of light and darkness, just as humankind did
through its transgression of God's command.

But God endowed certain persons with insight so that
humankind should not completely fall into derision. Abel
was good; Cain a murderer. And many saw God in a
mysterious light, while others committed very serious sins
until that time came in which the Word of God shone forth,
as it is written: "You are the fairest of the sons of men."
(Psalm 45:2) Then the sun of justice arose and it made
humans shine with good works in faith and deed, just as it is
when the redness of morning first appears in the sky and then
the other hours of the day follow till the night breaks in.

How the world changes, O daughter Elisabeth: The world
no longer has the driving force from which the green of virtues blossoms, neither in the early morning nor in the first,
the third, nor especially in the sixth hour of the day. It is
truly necessary in our time that God choose certain people
so that the divine instruments are not idle.

Listen, then, my troubled daughter: The whispering of
the ambitious serpent sometimes seeks to wear down
precisely those people our God instructed through divine
inspiration. For when the old snake spots a gem of special
worth, he hisses, raising himself up, and says: "What is
that?" And then he torments with many afflictions the heart

that longs to fly above the clouds (as the old serpent himself once did), as though human beings were gods.

And now I want you to listen further to me. Those who long to bring God's words to completion must always remember that, because they are human, they are vessels of clay and so should continually focus on what they are and what they will be. They should leave heavenly things to the One who is heavenly, for they are themselves exiles who do not recognize what is heavenly. They only announce the mysteries like a trumpet which indeed allows the sound but is not itself the source that produces the note. For someone else is blowing into the trumpet and causing the note to be produced.

They should put on the armor of faith, being mild, gentle, poor, and despised. This was the condition of that Lamb whose trumpet notes sound in them from the childlike intuition of their behavior. But God always disciplines those who blow God's trumpets and God sees to it that the earthen vessel does not break but pleases the Divine.

O daughter, may God make you a mirror of life! But even I who suffer from a heart of little courage and am again and again disturbed and crippled by fear, even I sometimes sound with a weak note from the trumpet of the living light. And may God help me to persevere in divine service!

LETTER THIRTY-FIVE
Hildegard to Elisabeth

Elisabeth was severely ill, partly through her own excessive asceticism, when Hildegard wrote her this last letter. Elisabeth died on July 18, 1165.

In a true vision I saw and heard the following words:

> O daughter of God, out of your love for God you call a poor creature like myself, "Mother." Listen, then, to your mother and learn moderation! For moderation is the mother of all the virtues for everything heavenly and earthly. For it

is through moderation that the body is nourished with the proper discipline. Any human being who thinks about her sins with sighs of regret—all those sins which she has committed in thought, word, and deed through the Devil's inspiration—must embrace this mother, discretion, and with the counsel of her religious superiors repent of her sins in true humility and sincere obedience. When there are unseasonable downpours, the fruit and vegetables growing on Earth are damaged; when a field has not been plowed, you do not find good grain springing up; instead, there are only useless weeds. It's the same with a person who lays on herself more strain than her body can endure. This is a sign that the effects of holy discretion are weak in such a person. And all of this immoderate straining and abstinence bring nothing useful to such a soul.

And so it is that when that pitch-black bird, the Devil, finds out that someone wants to get away from all her inadmissible desires and sins through fasting, praying, and bodily asceticism, then that same Devil coils himself up like a serpent in its lair and whispers to such a person: "Your sins will be destroyed only when you trample your body underfoot through sorrows, tears, and strivings without moderation, to the point where your body is completely withered." Such a person lives then without hope and without joy. It's not unusual for her zest for life to disappear and she will be seized by a heavy illness. [It is interesting that Hildegard notes the connection between depression and a susceptibility to certain illness.] Through this devilish stratagem the person is robbed of the merits of holiness, and she lets that very task lie unfinished which she had begun without moderation. And so it is that the last state of affairs is worse than the first.

That person who, through the example of Christ, stands in the commitment of obedience, protects herself with great care from choosing something according to her own will, thereby relying more on herself than on the good counsel of others. The practice of this kind of obedience insures that *one is not overcome by that pride that casts one down from heaven, a pride of people who want to be better than other good people and who want to count themselves as good and holy, which is always the way they explain it to themselves. But people can be instructed by their own natures to learn the lesson that they should not concur with their own self-will. For human beings consist of body and spirit, which, in their very nature, contradict each other. What pleases the one displeases the other. How can human beings, then, if this is their condition, escape harm by going along with their own self-will for the salvation of their souls? For the self-will belongs to the body, not to the spirit. But people who out of fear and love for God despise their self-will and submit themselves to the prescriptions and teaching of the rule and of their superiors—such people in true humility give others an example of good works and they make themselves into living tents in the heavenly Jerusalem. It is on such people that the Holy Spirit rests.*

O happy soul, you hasten quickly to the living God with great courage, like the deer longing for springs of living water. Pay attention then to these words I have written to you so that our mighty King will help you to persevere in this courage and happily will lead you to eternal blessedness.

LETTER THIRTY-SIX
Hildegard's letter to Christian lay people

Since so many of the letters Hildegard wrote were to clergy and members of religious communities, it is important to realize that she was concerned with lay people as well, and not only those highly placed. Here is a general letter directed to the laity.

All of you people who were born and cleansed through God's wisdom, hear what I, the radiant light and Creator of all of you, have to say to you. You were planted in My heart at daybreak on the first day of creation. When I created the first human being, I made him a touchstone of what the Devil mocked. In other words, I gave him the commandment the Devil through his evil nature had disregarded. but evil does not correspond to My nature, for I am the good in all its fullness, power, and penetrating clarity.

But you, O people, do not know what you say. The crafty traitor has sneaked up behind you so that he can teach you the opposite of what I command. When I gave you the commandment, I did not prescribe that you carry on indecently with adultery, murder, theft, and imprisonment. It was also not My intention that you throw someone in prison whom you did not create. Rather I commanded that you should increase through having offspring in the lawful institution of marriage and not in mere lust. I also specified that you should possess the Earth by building it up* through your work, with fruit and wine and everything needful for life. And this is why you must adhere to my commandment and not discard it. For I specified that you love your children in an environment of lawful love and not in the poisonous atmosphere of adultery. But you act as though you are at liberty to do whatever you want and to carry out whatever evil purpose you can complete. But why do you cast off the cohesive structure of law by saying: "The regulation that we restrain ourselves and exercise discipline—as though we were angels—does not apply to us. For life in the world does not allow us to be heavenly. Then, too, our children and our farmlands, our sheep and our cattle and all the rest of our livestock and all our possessions make this kind of attitude impossible." It is God who has given us all of these things. Why do you forget the One who has created you and given you everything! When God gives you what is necessary, God does it in such a way that sometimes allows you certain things and sometimes does not.

---

*The word *bebauen* can also mean *cultivate* but I think the phrase "building up" catches more the spirit of Genesis. —TRANS.

But you say: "It is not our job to live a good, disciplined life. That is the business of priests and those who are in religious communities." Since you are not concerned about these things, there is something which is important for you to hear: More than all these clergy, you are bound as God has commanded, to live in that way which was declared to you. For those who live in the religious state do not carry those legal responsibilities incumbent on you. And thus they are free, because the binding character of the commandment, that was established in a special way for you, is not applicable to them. But they embrace Me with the kiss of love when for My sake they leave the world and by climbing the mountain of holiness become My beloved children. But through the binding character of the Law which is especially placed on you, you are like My servants. Thus you must understand Me and obey your law, so that when the Lord comes your conscience cannot accuse you of having thrown off God's commands. For the guiltless Lamb of God embraced you with great love when because of your sins God allowed the Divine Son to be placed in the winepress of the Cross.

O beloved sons and daughters, remember your loving Creator who redeemed you from all the wounds of your burdens and cleansed you in the blood of the beloved Son from the worst of all sins, murder. Woe to this evil that Cain committed through his shameful rage, the companion of death. For that same end adheres to you as well, that the disintegration of your bodies is accompanied by great pain. That was Abel's experience in his sufferings when his bodily life ended in pain through that first murder, because his brother Cain in that sinful fratricide forced Abel's soul, before its time, to forsake the tent of its body.

Now may there be salvation and redemption in the blood of My beloved Son for all those who because of their sins have decided to run on the path of true repentance.

LETTER THIRTY-SEVEN
Hildegard to an excommunicated Christian

In the following letter, Hildegard writes to someone who is physically ill and caught up in the teachings of the Cathars (who she calls Sadducees in this letter).

O man, you are the image of God, for God formed you in the very first human being. But it is now this same God who has also picked you out through the judgment of sickness. Listen! It is the will of God almighty that every sin of ours — whether of the body or of the soul — be cleansed. So, too, must you bear up under this illness of your body and not understand it as an unmerited burden you bear with heavy heart. For we are blessed when we are chastised by God for the salvation of our soul. On the other hand, those who are without the fear of God and sinfully pursue their own self-will without being chastised, such souls very often run all the faster to their damnation.

The Church under the afflicted apostolic see has already long suffered heavy humiliation through God's judgment. The reason for this lies in the sin of the whole people, for scorning the commandments of God. They follow only their own self-will. And it is the same with the meaningless unbelief of those Sadducees who contradict the commands of the law with their teaching and through their unrighteous ways in the sight of God are like people already buried in the Earth. And you can add to that the folly of those who agree with the teachings of these men insofar as they offer them no resistance.

As a result of this and many other sins, the Church — already so long divided in its leadership — threatens to shatter on this division, because she does not want to recognize either of the two rival popes unanimously as the rightful heir of Peter's chair. This is why all the faithful out of concern for their souls should find refuge in their spiritual directors to find out what they ought to do according to the true faith. For the souls of subordinates must always be directed through the teachings of their spiritual superiors. For people should have great respect for the binding power given to the priests, first among the princely apostles. But the priest himself, who has the power of binding and loosing, should be zealously careful that he will not be called to account by the highest Judge for having killed his brother through an unjust excommunication. But you, servant of God, exert yourself most zealously under the rod of God's discipline, with the help of your secular and religious friends, that you might be freed from the ban of excommunication and its condemnation to punishment. Guard yourself that you are not called to court by the highest Judge on the charge that you are lazy in your fear of the Lord. People must show the greatest care in avoiding the consummation of marriage with blood relatives for this is against God's command-ment. Order all of these situations according to the counsel of the priests, so that you can be healthy and whole in your soul.

I see in the true vision of my soul that your sickness has not come upon you through that woman but through God's permission. Regarding a marriage with this woman, handle the situation according to what the priests advise from the sacred books. Seek the healing of your wounds with God. Hasten to God like the prodigal son to his father, who received him in fatherly love and with a joyous feast. Then you too will live forever in the heavenly homeland.

LETTER THIRTY-EIGHT
Hildegard to an unknown lay person

O son of God, your life is like the Earth which brings forth both useful plants and useless weeds. For through the heavenly nature of your soul you take joy in doing good. But the useless things you draw to yourself block and inhibit you from pursuing the good. And so it often happens that you follow the cravings of your flesh through your neglect of the commandments of your Creator and the yearnings of your divinely tuned soul.

But now you must heed the warning of the Holy Spirit. Be a strong warrior, nobly clothed with the magnificent armor of a true Solomon. You must be manly in your power and

strength and untiring in your battle against the lust of the
flesh and all your sinful cravings and against the enemy of
your soul. For it is through that same soul that you have
your life and your whole longing for God. Therefore, with
fear and love for the God who made and redeemed you, cast
out of your heart the various drives which burden your
spirit.

   When the pride of the vain pursuit of fame attacks you, so
that you consider yourself wiser and more trustworthy than
others and all their dealings thereby displease you, then
remember that you are ashes and that you will return to
ashes and that you are capable of nothing without the grace
of God. But when your fleshly nature attacks you, cast your
eyes on the sufferings of Christ that he bore on the cross in
great patience. And wear out your body through prayer,
vigils, and spiritual practices in that measure to which you
are conscious of having freely sinned. When you do that,
then the enemy, conquered by you, will howl in his shame
and God will rejoice in you and will make you God's chosen
and beloved dwelling place. [literally, a *tent*]

LETTER THIRTY-NINE
Hildegard to Wibert of Gembloux

Wibert is one of Hildegard's most interesting correspondents.
Born c. 1125 in Gembloux, he received an outstanding education
at the renowned Benedictine abbey there. Not only did he learn
the Bible but he could readily quote Ovid, Virgil, and Horace. He
entered the abbey there and lived his life as a model monk. When
he heard about Hildegard and her unique charisms, he wrote to
her and asked her with all humility and respect some forthright
questions—e.g. "After your visions have been written down, is it
true that you no longer remember them?" "Do these visions speak
to you in Latin or German?" "Does your knowledge of the Bible
come through study or only through the action of the Holy
Spirit?" He remarks ingenuously that since he is a cloistered
monk he cannot visit her in person, so he is very grateful for her
response. This first letter was taken to Hildegard at Rupertsberg

in the summer of 1175. When he receives no answer, he writes a second time at the end of the same summer and gives his letter to a knight who is on his way to Rupertsberg. This time, Hildegard, who is now 77 years old, answers him. Wibert was naturally very excited and read the response to the whole community. Here, in slightly abbreviated form, is the letter he received from Hildegard.

The words which I speak are not my own nor those of any human being, but what I say comes from the vision which I received from above.

O true servant of God, if it had pleased God to raise not only my soul but my body as well to a prophetic vision, still that could not cause the fear to diminish from my spirit and my heart. For I know that I am a human being, even though I have been cloistered from my childhood. There have been many who were wise and whose lives were so filled with wonders that they proclaimed a great number of mysteries. And yet, from a vain pursuit of glory, they ascribed these things to themselves, and thus came to their downfall. But those, on the other hand, who in their spiritual advancement derived their wisdom from God and regarded themselves as nothing — they became pillars of heaven. This is what happened in the case of St. Paul who, although he excelled the other apostles in preaching, regarded himself as nothing. The same is true of the evangelist John who was filled with tender humility, and because of this was able to obtain so much from the divine spring.

How would it be understood if a poor creature like myself were not to recognize this gift? God works where God wills, for the honor of the divine name and not for the honor of earth-bound mortals. But I am continuously filled with fear and trembling. For I do not recognize in myself security through any kind of personal ability. And yet I raise my hands aloft to God, that I might be held by God, just like a feather which has no weight from its own strength and lets itself be carried by the wind.

I cannot fully understand the things I see, not as long as I remain in bondage to the body and the invisible soul. For in both cases we human beings suffer from want.

I also saw in my vision that the first book of my visions should be called *Scivias*, because it would proclaim the way of the living light [she describes this term "living light" later in this letter and distinguished it from the ordinary light by which she is illumined] and not derive from any other teaching.

From my childhood days, when my limbs, nerves, and veins were not yet strong, the gift of this vision brought joy to my soul; and this has remained true up to this very time when I am a woman of more than 70 years. And as God wants, my soul climbs in this vision high above, even to the height of the firmament. But I do not see these things with my external eyes nor do I hear them with my external ears. I do not perceive them through the thoughts of my heart or through the mediation of my five senses. I see them much more in my soul alone, with my physical eyes open, in such a way that I never experience the unconsciousness of ecstasy, but I see all of this awake, whether by day or night.

The light which I see is not bound by space. It is much, much more light-filled than a cloud that carries the sun in itself. There is nothing in it to recognize of height, length, or breadth. It was described to me as the "shadow of the living light." And just as the sun, the moon, and the stars are reflected in water, so writings, talks, powers, and certain actions of people are illuminated for me in this light.

I was often severely hindered by sickness and involved with heavy sufferings that threatened to bring me to death's door. And yet God has always made me alive again, even to this day.

I keep for a long time in memory all the things I see and learn in the vision, because as soon as I see or hear it, it enters my memory. I simultaneously see, hear, and understand. In an instant I learn what I know through the vision. But whatever I do not see in the vision, I have no knowledge of, for I am without formal education and was only instructed to read simple letters. And I write what I see and hear in the vision and I don't add any other words. I communicate the plain Latin words just as I hear them in the vision. For I do not become educated in my vision so that I can write like the philosophers. The words in the vision do not sound like words from a human mouth, but they are like flaming lightning and like a cloud moving in the pure ether. I am not able to perceive the shape of this light, just as I cannot look with unprotected eyes at the disk of the sun.

It is in this light that I sometimes see, though not often, another light that I call "the living light." When and how I see this, I cannot say. But as long as I see this "living light" all sadness and anxiety are taken away from me. The result is that I feel like a simple young girl and not like an old lady.

[During these experiences] I do not know myself, either in body or soul. And I consider myself as nothing. I reach out to the living God and turn everything over to the Divine that God, who has neither beginning nor end, can preserve me from evil in every situation. And that is why I ask you to pray for me too, since you have requested this reply from me. And ask all of those to pray for me, too, who, like you, desire to hear these words in good faith. Pray that I may persevere in God's service.

But I want to say something to you, too, O son of God, for you seek God in faith and are filled with desire for the Divine. God wants to save you. Pay attention to the eagle who with his two wings flies towards the clouds. If he lost his wings, he would fall down to the Earth and not be able to raise himself up again, no matter how eagerly he sought to lift himself up in flight. Human beings also fly with two wings; the right wing is the knowledge of good and the left wing is the knowledge of evil. The knowledge of evil serves the good, insofar as the good is sharpened and highlighted through the knowledge of evil; and so through this knowledge human beings become wise in all things.

O true son of God, may God raise the wings of your knowledge so that you can fly the right paths. Thus when sin hankers after you and touches you—for you are born such that you cannot exist without sin—you will be able not to satisfy it through action. Then you will have a good flight. The heavenly choir sings the praises of God for people who conduct themselves in this way and they praise such people. For though they are created out of ashes, they love God so much that, for God's sake, they are able completely to despise themselves. So persevere in this battle, strong warrior, so that you may enter into the heavenly harmony where God will say to you: you belong to the children of Israel. For in the zeal of your desire for heaven, you have kept your eyes on the mountain peak, past all the craggy clefts. And may all of those names you included in your letter to me be so guided by the Holy Spirit that they will be inscribed in the book of life.

LETTER FORTY
Hildegard to Wibert and the monks of Villers

Wibert's story does not end with the famous letter of 1175. In the autumn of that year, Wibert had the chance to accompany a priest who was travelling to Bingen. In a letter to his friend, Radulf, a monk at the Cistercian Abbey of Villers in Brabant, Wibert talks about this trip and how he and his priest companion were hospitably received and spent four days visiting Hildegard. On his return trip, Wibert stopped to visit Radulf. He and the other monks of Villers had prepared a catalog of thirty-eight questions which they wanted Wibert to ask of Hildegard. But Wibert went back to Geinbloux and left the questions behind.

In 1176 we meet Wibert back at Villers, this time as a travelling companion of his abbot. The monks again want Wibert to write to Hildegard about their questions and this time he agrees. Hildegard sends the monks her *Liber vitae meritorum* but pleads age and sickness as an excuse for not answering all the questions. In 1177 the persistent Wibert again urges Hildegard to respond. She does.

In the Spirit-filled vision of my soul, I saw and heard the following words: O sons of light! You have drunk from that unquenchable spring which overflows into eternity and you have been enflamed by the Word of God that can never be extinguished. Tirelessly you seek the things of God in pure faith and you long to know them. Hear then with grateful receptivity the following words:

"The king led me into his wine cellar and put in order all the love that was in me. He revived me with flowers and refreshed me with fruit, for I was sick with love." [This seems to be based on *Song of Solomon* 2: 4 & 5: "He brought me to the banqueting house, and his banner over me was love. Sustain me with raisins, refresh me with apples, for I am sick with love."] The meaning of this is that God set up the law of the Old Testament much like the hollow shapes or forms that artisans skillfully prepare out of clay according to their design. They do this so that later they can use them as the forms in which to cast their work in metal. The Old Testament was the shadow of that noble bud which God in the eternal plan had decided to bring forth from the Virgin Mary. This bud is the Son of God. He is the radiant sun that brightens the whole world. He is the true vine who provides us with the best wine, when, as a result of his generous grace, we recognize the glorious shape of his divinity through the garment of his humanity, and when we have learned in wisdom the true teaching of a pure faith.

Thus, "he has put in order all the love that is in us." Love is an unquenchable fire. It is from love that the sparks of true faith that burn in the hearts of the faithful have their fire. It is through love for God that these sparks are ignited to faith. For we could never have this fire of faith if we did not first love God in our hearts. This is the "ordering of love" in us.

It was through these sparks springing from true faith that martyrs for Christ were borne aloft by the pouring out of their blood in their longing for heaven. Glowing with the unquenchable fire of love and strengthened through the blood of martyrdom, they attained eternal bliss. Even today this same love, through the sparks of true faith, fills the hearts of many of the faithful who hunger for the justice of

God. Just as the angels can never be satiated with their vision of God's face, a vision they always enjoy, so too can
such souls have enough of God's justice. For God is that
love which has neither beginning nor end.

Happy are those people who, like ripe fruit, are filled with
reliable hope in the countless goods of eternal happiness
and sigh after God. For they despise the desires of the flesh
that came to the human race when Adam tasted the apple.
And through the martyrdom (of the religious vows) they
conquered these fleshly desires. For the living spring pours
itself out in them so abundantly in grace that fleshly desire
is killed by their insatiable hunger and thirst for God's
justice. They are "sick with love" for the Divine until they
are happily satisfied in God's glory in eternal life.

O sons of God, you too are sealed with this love, for in your
flesh you have disdained the world out of love for the true sun,
the Son of God, who blossomed as a true human being from
Mary's flesh. He, too, it is who "has put in order all the love
that is in us." And now may the pure light of the true sun so
shine in you and teach you so to persevere in your holy journey
that you might reach a happy end and live in true blessedness!

But I am an unworthy and unlearned woman, one subordinate to your direction in your deeply grounded wisdom,
and I have looked to the true light for the fulfillment of the
faithful request of your love. And I have worked at the solu-
tion of your questions as far as I have been able to do so with
God's grace. There have been hindrances, for I am busy with
some writing I have begun but have not yet finished, and I
have been held back by a serious illness that has been with
me for a long time. Nonetheless, I have finished fourteen
solutions to these questions. And I am happy to work further on them, as well as I can with God's help.

The correspondence between Wibert and Hildegard ends with
this letter. In 1177 Wibert went to Rupertsberg again. Wibert
meets Hildegard's brother, Hugo, and another priest. When these
two die, Wibert decides to remain awhile at Rupertsberg, and he
writes to his friends about the marvelous spiritual environment

there and the even more marvelous woman who is its founder and guiding spirit. He was at Rupertsberg when Hildegard died on September 17, 1179, and he lived to edit some of her most important works.

LETTER FORTY-ONE
Hildegard to the prelates of Mainz

The last years of Hildegard's life were not free from conflict. In fact, one of the heaviest burdens fell on her when her community was placed under an interdict. This meant, of course, that the Eucharist could not be celebrated, nor communion received, nor the divine office sung. The reason for the interdict was the allegation that she allowed a young excommunicated nobleman to be buried in the Church cemetery. The prelates of Mainz wanted the body removed from the Rupertsberg cemetery. Hildegard declined, arguing that the man in question had indeed been reconciled with the Church (albeit privately), and girded herself for what was to be her last great combat, which left her a victorious but worn veteran of 81 years.

In the vision which was impressed upon my soul before its birth from the Creator, I see myself compelled to write something relating to the ban placed on us by our spiritual superiors. It deals with a dead man, whose transferral and burial in our cemetery through his priest took place without opposition. When our superiors ordered us a few days after the burial to remove him from our cemetery, I was overcome with no insignificant alarm and, as I usually do, I looked to the true light and with open eyes I saw the following words in my soul: If we were to follow your instruction and dig up the body of this dead man, then through that removal a great danger would threaten our locale and would beset us like the black cloud which serves to point out coming storms and bad weather. Therefore, we do not presume to dig up the body of the deceased, since he went to confession, received anointing and communion, and was buried without opposition. Also, we agree neither with the counsel nor the instruction of those who told and ordered us to do this. It is not as though we do not lay proper store on the counsel of proven men or the instruction of our prelates. But we only want to avoid the appearance that the sacrament of Christ, with which the man was strengthened in his body, should be brought to disgrace through distraught women. But lest we appear to be disobedient, we have followed the ban and have suspended the singing of the divine office and our reception of the Lord's Body, which we were accustomed to receive monthly. All my sisters and myself have experienced great sorrow because of this. Finally, almost overwhelmed from such a heavy burden, I received the following words in my vision: *It is not good for you, because of the words of human beings, to forego the mysteries of my Word clothed in human nature and born as your salvation in the spotless womb of the Virgin Mary. And so you must ask your prelates to release you from this ban they have placed on you.*

For from the time that Adam was driven from the bright land of Paradise into the exile of this world, the conception of all human beings is burdened with the guilt of this first transgression. Thus it was necessary that according to the unfathomable decision of God, one man would be born from our human nature but without any stain of that injury. It is through him that all of those who are called to life are cleansed from every stain. In order that he might remain in them and they in him for their strengthening, in the reception of his Body they can become one with him and thereby be sanctified. But whoever is like Adam in being disobedient to God's commandments and totally forgetting him, such a person must be excluded from receiving the Lord's Body. For he has already turned from that same Lord through his disobedience. And this excommunication should continue until he is cleansed through penance and again receives permission from his superiors to unite himself once more with the Body of the Lord in Communion. But whoever is not aware of being under such a ban, either in conscience or volition, such a one proceeds with confidence to the reception of this lifegiving sacrament to be purified through the blood of the spotless Lamb, that same Lamb who offered himself on the altar of the Cross out of obedience to the Divine, to re-establish salvation for all.

In the same vision, I heard that I was guilty because I had not gone with all humility and submission to my spiritual superiors to personally ask for the removal of the excommunication of this man. And this was especially important because we were not involved in any guilt in receiving the dead man. For he was equipped with everything belonging to a Christian, and he was buried by a priest with all of Bingen in attendance, and no one raised any objection. To communicate this to you, my lords, was something placed upon me by God.

But I was also given some vision about the fact that up until now we have, in obedience to you, neglected singing the divine office. And I received a word from the living light regarding the diverse kinds of musical instruments that praise God. For it was of these that David speaks: "Praise him with trumpet sound; praise him with lute and harp." etc. to "Let everything that breathes praise the Lord!" (Psalm 150)

In these words we are taught about inner matters through external ones, namely, how we, according to the material and character of our instruments, should do our best to bring our inner devotion to the praise of the Creator and give it full expression. When we lovingly engage ourselves in this way, we are doing it with rememberance of the way humankind went in search of the voice of the li ing Spirit. Adam had lost it through his disobedience. Because he lost his innocence, his voice in no way harmonized with the voices of the angels who sing God's praise. These angels, because they are continuously inspired by the Spirit which is God, persevere in this choir through their spiritual nature. But Adam had lost that harmony with the angels' voices, a harmony he had possessed in Paradise. And so he became like a person who wakes up from sleep and knows nothing or only vaguely what transpired in his dream. For Adam was like this when he lost that knowledge which he had before his sin. When he was deceived by the Devil's temptations and acted against the will of his Creator, he ended up in the darkness of inner ignorance. That was his punishment.

But God permeates the souls of the elect with the light of divine truth, and thereby rescues them for the bliss which human beings had once enjoyed in Paradise. God carried in the divine heart the plan in days to come to renew the hearts of many through the outpouring of the prophetic spirit. Through this inner enlightenment they could win back something of that light that had been lost, that light which Adam had before he suffered punishment for his sin.

The holy prophets, taught by the same Spirit they too had received, composed not only psalms and hymns to increase the devotion of their hearers, but also invented various musical instruments as sonorous accompaniments. And why did they do this? So that human beings would not live from the memory of exile, but with thoughts of heavenly bliss and the song of praise that Adam enjoyed with the angels in God's presence before his fall, and furthermore so that human beings would be enticed to praise God. All this was done so that through the form and character of these instruments, and especially through the meaning of the words, the listeners, as we said, might be so excited by these external things and brought into their rhythm that inwardly they might delight in their meaning.

Zealous and wise people have imitated these prophets, and they too, through their human ingenuity, have developed a variety of musical instruments in order to be able to sing in joyfulness of heart. And through the appropriate movement of their fingers they brought the melodies to expression. And in this way they imitated Adam, too, for he was educated by God's finger, the Holy Spirit, and before the Fall his voice carried in itself, in full, harmonious sound the loveliness of every musical art. If

he had remained in his original condition, then the
weakness of our mortal nature could not have endured the
power and melodic fullness of his voice.

But when Adam's traitor, the Devil, heard that humans
through God's inspiration had begun to sing and saw
themselves thereby invited to think about the lovely songs
of their heavenly homeland, then that same evil spirit
suspected that his scheming machinations might be
thwarted. This scared him so much that he was uncommonly tortured. With his never-stopping, evil, lying chatter
he thinks and seeks unceasingly to bring to disharmony,
and even to ban, God's praise and the beauty of spiritual
songs. He works at this not only through evil temptations,
impure thoughts, and a variety of diversions springing from
human hearts, but also, wherever he can, through discord,
arguments, or unjust persecution.

This is why both you and all spiritual leaders should proceed with the greatest caution. Before you close the mouth
of the Church — in other words, the choir which sings God's
praise — through your judgments, and before you forbid the
celebrations and reception of the sacraments, you must prove
and examine the grounds for these measures with the greatest
care. And in all of this you must keep in mind that you are
acting solely out of zeal for God's justice and not letting
yourself be led by anger, revenge, or any other base emo-
tion. And when you make judgment of this sort, you must
constantly be careful that Satan, who deprived humankind
of heavenly harmony and the pleasure of Paradise, will not
encircle you.

So remember: just as the body of Jesus Christ was born by
the Holy Spirit from the spotless Virgin Mary, so too the
singing in the Church of God's praise, which is an echo of
the harmony of heaven, has its roots in that same Holy
Spirit. But the body is the garment of the soul and it is the
soul which gives life to the voice. That's why the body must
raise its voice in harmony with the soul for the praise of
God. This is also the command, symbolically, of the spirit

of the prophets: God should be praised with crashing cymbals, with cymbals of clear praise and with all the other musical instruments that clever and industrious people have produced. For all the arts serving human desires and needs are derived from the breath that God sent into the human body. And that is why it is fitting that God be praised in all.

Sometimes when we hear a song we breathe deeply and sigh. This reminds the prophet that the soul arises from heavenly harmony. In thinking about this, he was aware that the soul itself has something in itself of this music and expressed this in a psalm: "Praise the Lord with the lyre, make melody to him with the harp of ten strings!" (Psalm 33:2) The lyre with its deep tones points to the discipline of the body; the harp with its higher tones indicates the coordination of the spirit. The ten strings cause the prophet to reflect on the ten commandments of God's law.

What about those in the Church who through an interdict impose silence on the singing of God's praise? If on Earth they have committed the wrong of robbing God of the honor of the praise which is God's due, then they can have no fellowship with the praise of the angels in heaven, unless they make the situation right again through true penance and humble reparation. Those, therefore, who possess the keys of heaven should resolutely guard themselves from opening what should be closed and closing what should be open. For the harshest judgment will be pronounced on prelates who fail, in the words of the apostle, to carry out their office with caution. (cf. e.g. Romans 12:8)

And I heard a voice that said: Who has created heaven? God. Who opens heaven to the faithful? God. Who is like God? No one. Therefore, no one of you, O faithful, should offer resistance or opposition to God. Otherwise God will fall upon you with great strength and you will have no helper who can protect you through God's judgment. This is a "womanish time," for the justice of God dwindles away. And yet the strength of God's justice is at work and shows itself as a warrior against injustice until that injustice lies conquered on the ground.

LETTER FORTY-TWO
Hildegard to Archbishop Christian of Mainz

Despite Hildegard's impressive efforts, the prelates did not get the situation resolved. Hildegard describes what transpired next in this letter to Archbishop Christian who was in Rome at the time, taking part in the Third Lateran Council from March 3 to March 19, 1179. This is the last letter of hers that has been preserved, for she died on September 17th of this same year. But before her death, the archbishop recanted and set in motion the process to remove the interdict. It had clearly been one of the most difficult struggles in her long career, a struggle revealing the never-ending dialectic between official structure and charism. This stalwart warrior was 81 years old when she passed on to her reward.

Gracious lord and father, you have been set in the place of Christ as shepherd for the flock of your Church. In all humility we thank almighty God and your fatherly kindness that you have received our letter, written out of desperate need, and that you have agreed for our sakes—and we are all very depressed and anxious about this—to write something to our prelates in Mainz. We thank you, too, for the lovely message, so typical of your gentle nature, which we received through Herman, the lord deacon of the holy Church of the Apostles in Cologne. That message brought us much consolation and joy and we are grateful that, in all of our sadness and anxiety, we can turn to you and be filled with trust, like children running to their beloved father. Gracious lord, we throw ourselves humbly at your feet. We who are your servants, sitting in sadness and desolation, share with you our tears, in fullest truth the ground of our unbearable pain. And we trust that the fiery love which is God will grant you to hear mercifully and with fatherly love the voice of our complaint, the voice with which we are crying to you in our need.

Gentle father, our prelates in Mainz had ordered us to remove from our cemetery the body of the young man who before his death was freed from excommunication, strengthened with all the sacraments of Christian faith, and buried with us (the details of which we have already communicated to you in a letter). Otherwise, we had to stop the celebration of the sacraments. As always, this led me to turn to the true light. In that light God ordered me: the corpse must never be removed with my willing permission, for God has taken this man from the bosom of the Church as someone for whom the joy of the redeemed has been prepared. To do anything contrary to this would bring upon us the shadow of a great danger, because it would be contrary to the will of the truth. If the fear of almighty God had not hindered me, I would have immediately obeyed my superiors in all humility. In fact, if he had still been excommunicated, I would have agreed, for the good of the Church, with all of those who ordered the removal of the dead man in your name—for you are our lord and protector.

And so we suspended the divine service for a time, and not without great pain and deep sorrow. And then I turned to our prelates in Mainz. I did this because I was thus instructed by a true vision of my soul and by the highest Judge (whose command I did not dare to disobey), who laid on me the weight of severe illness. I put in a letter for them the very words I had seen in the true light, just as God had commanded me, so that they could see from that what God's will was in this legal matter. With bitter tears I asked their pardon and pleaded humbly for mercy. But when I saw that their eyes were so darkened that they did not have one glance of mercy for me, I went away from them with many tears. And yet there were many other people who were moved by pity on our behalf but, although they wanted to, they couldn't help us in any way.

Then my true friend, Archbishop Philip of Cologne, went to Mainz. A free knight accompanied him, one who had all the witnesses and proofs to make it clear that he himself and the deceased (while that young man was still alive) had found themselves in the same desperate situation. And they had gone together to the same place, at the same time, and had the ban of excommunication lifted by the same priest. The priest he was talking about who had absolved them appeared on their behalf, too. When the prelate heard the true state of the affair from these witnesses, he gave us the permission—taking for granted your concurrence with this decision—to celebrate the sacraments in security and freedom until your return. We put the greatest trust, gracious lord, in your mercy, but we received from this same prelate, after your return from Rome, your letter from the synod with the interdict of the divine service. Yet we have such confident hope in your fatherly love that we know you would never have allowed this to happen if you had known the truth of the situation. And so, now, gentle father, because of your own command, we find ourselves in greater pain and sorrow than under the earlier decree.

You have never said a word to lead me to have any doubt about my visions. And I received in a vision of my soul the commission to speak from my heart and from my mouth: "It is better for me to fall into the hands of human beings than to forsake the law of my God." Therefore, gentle father, I beseech you by the love of the Holy Spirit, for the sake of the goodness of the eternal One, who for our salvation sent the Word in tender awakening-power into the womb of the Virgin—do not despise the tears of your sad and weeping daughters. Because of our fear of God we bear the misery and distress of this unjust interdict. May the Holy Spirit grant that you be moved with pity for us, for you too will long for mercy after the course of your earthly life is run.

Songs

Translated by
Reverend Jerry Dybdal and Matthew Fox

Introduced by
Brendan Doyle

INTRODUCTION

Why sing the music of a twelfth-century composer? Why struggle to learn an old form of notation? Why befriend the modal intervals so foreign to those of us raised on hymns sung in specific keys with single and double bars? And, yes, repeats. My answer to these questions is: "Because all music is a revelation." Music throughout the ages has been revealing, i.e. waking up new feelings and emotions that words can only hint at. Hildegard of Bingen knew this. She once said that *singing* words reveals their true meaning directly to the soul through bodily vibrations. I think we can conclude from this statement that her world view centers around an intimate relationship between body (the mouth, throat, vocal chords, diaphragm, and lungs) and the spirit (breath). Even the angels eternally sing the praises of their Creator. The goal of creation for Hildegard is that all creatures sing with one voice the same praises. We wake up to an awareness of eternity, a revelation of the inexhaustibility of feeling, through song.

Hildegard's compositions are incredibly physical. This makes wonderful sense if we realize that she was a physical scientist as well as a musician. Singing her music comes close to hyperventilation at times. When she writes about the Spirit, you know she understands the Spirit as wind, as breath, because you become the wind. When she writes about Divine Mysteries, you sing out of the deepest space of your physical being from the comfort of normal range to the extremes of your vocal potential. Here music reveals that we, too, are divine mysteries. And living is profoundly erotic.

During the Middle Ages, musical composition was based upon the modes: Dorian (d to D), Phrygian (e to E), Lydian (f to F), Mixolydian (g to G), Aeolian (a to A), Locrian (b to B) and Ionian (c to C). In modern times, five of these have been neglected in favor of the Aeolian and Ionian, our minor and major keys respectively. A medieval composition was written in *one* of these modes. Hildegard's cosmos could not be limited to *one* mode. So, in the course of one of her songs, she is likely to jump ahead 500 years and move into another mode. She does this in her *To The Holy Spirit*, where she begins in the Dorian mode to express the life-giving movement of the Spirit, and then switches to the Phrygian to sing of her cleansing and healing power. We find ourself in a whole new world of feeling. In this way, we give praise to the Creator of feeling through co-creation.

Another vast leap we experience in her music is thematic development. Her hymns *Praising Virgins* and *In Praise of Mary* both illustrate this very classical trait à la Haydn and Mozart. She makes connections through musical themes. They are so filled with life that they enter, disappear, and reenter, and then are transformed through their relationship with other themes. A concrete example of this is where in *Praising Virgins* the theme for "viriditas" (greening power) reenters to express the word "divinorum" (of the divine). As you sing her works, you will find that many themes return like old friends making connections with new expressions of faith.

I have been singing and sharing Hildegard's songs for almost four years now. She is still revealing whole new worlds of feeling to me and hopefully to those who come to her for the first time. She is not limited to an historical period. Her melodies are as memorable to me as a melody of Mozart or Mahler—romantic in their wholeness and vast in their expansiveness. Her music is unique for its time and, I am tempted to say, *for any time.*

BRENDAN DOYLE
INSTITUTE IN CULTURE AND CREATION SPIRITUALITY
OAKLAND, CALIFORNIA

1. Kyrie

1. KYRIE

Creator God, draw compassion from us.
Christ, draw compassion from us.
Spirit God, draw compassion from us.

2. O Virtus Sapientiae

O vir-tus* Sa-pi-en-ti-æ, quæ cir-cu-i-ens cir-cu-i-sti com-pre-hen-den-do o-mni-a in u-na vi-a, quæ ha-bet vi-tam, tres a-las ha-bens, qua-rum u-na in al-tum vo-lat, et al-tera de terra su-dat, et terti-a undi-que vo-lat. Laus ti-bi sit, sicut te de-cet, o Sa-pi-enti-a.

2.   O VIRTUS SAPIENTIAE
O Moving Force of Wisdom

O moving force of Wisdom, encircling the wheel of the cosmos,
Encompassing all that is, all that has life,
in one vast circle.
You have three wings: The first unfurls aloft
in the highest heights.
The second dips its way dripping sweat on the Earth.
Over, under, and through all things whirls the third.
Praise to you, O Wisdom, worthy of praise!

3. De Sancta Maria

a- ve, * Ma - ri -
a, o au - ctrix
vi ____ tæ, re -
æ ____ di - fi - can - do sa - lu -
tem, quæ mor ____ tem con -
tur ____ ba - sti et ser - pen -
tem con ____ tri -
vi - sti, ad quem se E - va
e - re - xit e - re ____ cta

cer - vi - ce cum suf-fla - tu

su-per - bi-æ. Hunc con -

cul - ca-sti, dum de cæ - lo Fi -

li - um De - i ge-nu-i-sti,* quem

in - spi - ra - vit Spi - ri -

tus

De -i. ℣. O dul-cis-si-ma atque

a-man-tis-si-ma Ma - ter, sal - ve,

quæ Na - tum tu-um de cæ-

lo mis - sum mun-do e-di-di —
sti. * Quem in — spi — ra –vit.
Glo — ri – a pa — tri et Fi – li –
o et Spi — ri – tu - i San —
cto. *Quem in — spi - ra — vit.

3. DE SANCTA MARIA
In Praise of Mary

O Mary, artist of life, hail!
By recreating wholeness, you have convulsed death itself.
You have destroyed the serpent which, blown up with pride,
raised its outstretched neck to Eve.
You have trampled on it by giving birth out of heaven
to God's Son,
breathed into you by the Spirit of God.
O loveliest and most loving Mother, hail!
You have given forth into this world your Son,
sent from heaven and breathed into you by the Spirit of God.
Praised be the Father, the Son, and Holy Spirit.
Breathed into you by the Holy Spirit.

4. De Spiritu Sancto

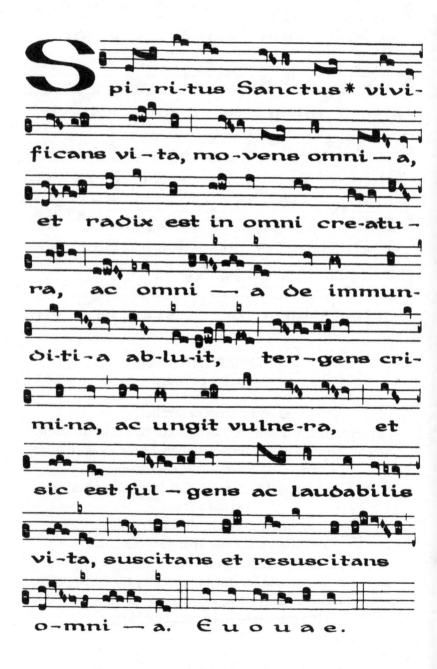

Spiritus Sanctus * vivificans vita, movens omnia, et radix est in omni creatura, ac omnia de immunditia abluit, tergens crimina, ac ungit vulnera, et sic est fulgens ac laudabilis vita, suscitans et resuscitans omnia. Euouae.

4. DE SPIRITU SANCTO
To the Holy Spirit

Holy Spirit, making life alive,
moving in all things, root of all created being,
cleansing the cosmos of every impurity, effacing guilt,
annointing wounds.
You are lustrous and praiseworthy life,
You waken and re-awaken everything that is.

5. Item De Virginibus

* no-bi ‑‑

lissi ‑‑ ‑‑ ma viridi ‑‑ ‑

tas, quæ ra·di ‑‑ cas in so ‑‑ ‑

le, et quæ in candi ‑‑‑‑‑ ‑

da se·re·ni ‑ ta‑

te luces in ro‑ta, quam

nulla terre ‑ na excellen‑ti ‑‑

a compre‑hen‑

dit, tu circumda‑ta es am‑

plexi — bus ði-vi — .

norum my-steri -o - rum.

𝒱.Tu ru-bes ut auro-ra et ar-

ðes ut so-lis flam - ma.

5. ITEM DE VIRGINIBUS
Praising Virgins

O most noble Greenness, rooted in the sun,
shining forth in streaming splendor upon the wheel of Earth.
No earthly sense or being can comprehend you.
You are encircled by the very arms of Divine mysteries.
You are radiant like the red of dawn!
You glow like the incandescence of the sun!

6. De Sancta Maria

O viridissi-ma virga, a – ve,

quæ in ventoso flabro sciscitati-o-

nis sanctorum pro-disti. Cum venit

tempus, quod tu floru – isti in ra-

mis tu-is, ave, ave sit ti-bi, quia ca-

lor solis in te su-da-vit sicut o-dor

balsami.   Nam in te floru-it pul-

cher flos, qui odorem dedit omnibus

aroma-tibus, quæ a – rida e-rant.

Et illa apparu-erunt omni - a in

viriditate ple —na. Unde cæli de-

derunt rorem super gra-men, et

omnis terra læta facta est, quo-

ni-am viscera ipsi-us frumen-tum

protulerunt, et quoni-am volucres

cæli nidos in ipsa habu-e —runt.

De-inde facta est esca homi-nibus

et gaudi-um magnum epu-lan-ti-

um. Unde, o sua-vis Virgo, in te

non defi-cit ullum gau — di-um.

Hæc omni-a Eva contempsit. Nunc

autem laus sit Al — tissi-mo.

6.   DE SANCTA MARIA
To Mary

Hail to you, O greenest, most fertile branch!
You budded forth amidst breezes and winds
in search of the knowledge of all that is holy.
When the time was ripe
your own branch brought forth blossoms.
Hail, greetings to you!
The heat of the sun exudes sweat from you
like the balsam's perfume.
In you, the most stunning flower has blossomed
and gives off its sweet odor to all the herbs and roots,
which were dry and thirsting before your arrival.
Now they spring forth in fullest green!
Because of you,the heavens give dew to the grass,
the whole Earth rejoices;
Abundance of grain comes from Earth's womb
and on its stalks and branches the birds nest.
And, because of you, nourishment is given to the human family
and great rejoicing to those gathered round the table.
And so, in you O gentle Virgin,
is every fullness of joy, everything that Eve rejected.
Now let endless praise resound to the Most High!

7. O Felix Anima

fe — lix a —ni — ma,*

cu - ius corpus de ter ——

ra or –tum est, quod tu

cum peregri — nati-o-ne

hu – ius mundi con – cul — ca –

sti. * Unde de di-vi-na rati-o-na-

li-ta-te, quæ te spe — cu-lum

suum fe – cit, co -ro-na — ta es.

℣. Spiritus San –ctus et –i–am

te ut   ha-bita — cu-lum su —

um in-tu — eba ——— tur.*Un —

de. Glori-a pa — tri et Fi — li – o

et   Spiritu — i San —— cto.

7. O FELIX ANIMA
O Happy Soul

O happy soul,
whose body has risen from the Earth which you wander
and tread on during your sojourn in this world.
Made to be the very mirror of Divinity,
you have been crowned with
divine imagination and intelligence.
The Holy Spirit looks upon you
and discovers its very own dwelling place.
Made to be the very mirror of Divinity,
you have been crowned with divine imagination and intelligence.
So—glory to the Father, to the Son, and to the very same
Holy Spirit.

8. O Vis Aeternitatis

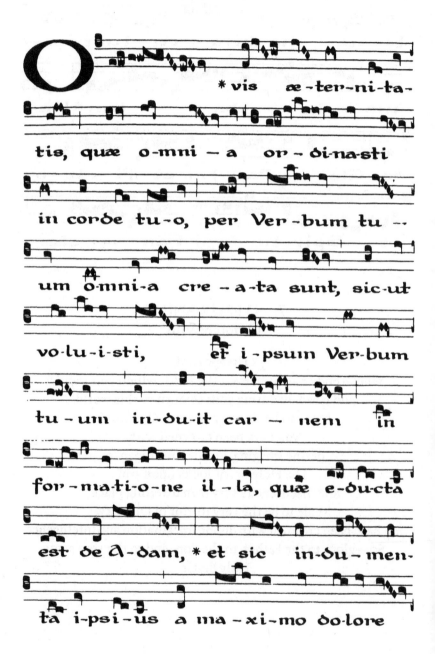

O * vis æ-ter-ni-ta-tis, quæ o-mni - a or - di-na-sti in corde tu-o, per Ver-bum tu -- um o-mni-a cre - a-ta sunt, sic-ut vo-lu-i-sti, et i-psum Ver-bum tu - um in-du-it car - nem in for - ma-ti-o-ne il - la, quæ e-du-cta est de A-dam, * et sic in-du - men-ta i-psi-us a ma - xi-mo do-lore

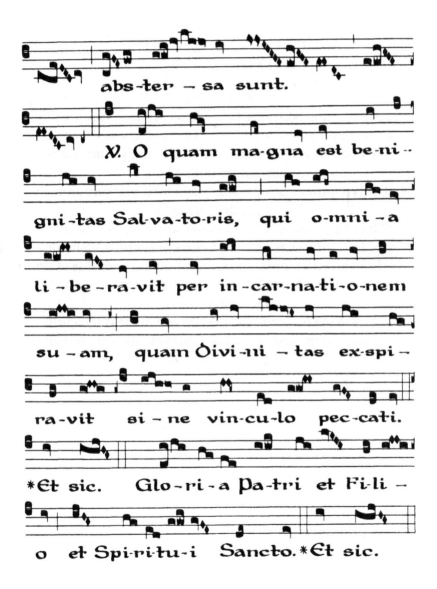

abs-ter – sa sunt.

℣. O quam ma-gna est be-ni --

gni-tas Sal-va-to-ris,   qui   o-mni – a

li – be – ra-vit   per   in -car-na-ti-o-nem

su – am,   quam Ôivi -ni – tas   ex-spi –

ra-vit   si – ne   vin-cu-lo   pec-cati.

*Et sic.   Glo – ri – a Pa-tri   et Fi-li –

o   et Spi-ri-tu-i   Sancto. *Et sic.

8.   O VIS AETERNITATIS
O Eternal Vigor

O Eternal Vigor,
all of creation is arranged and in order in your very heart.
Through your Word, all things are created just as you wish.
Your very own word even took on flesh in the same form
that derived from Adam,
and thus removes heart-breaking pain from that very garment
humanity wears.
O how magnificent is the compassion of the Saving One,
who frees all things by his becoming one with human life.
Divinity breathes into compassion without the chains of sin,
And so removes heart-breaking pain from that very garment
humanity wears.
Glory to the Father and to the Son and to the Holy Spirit.
And so removes heart-breaking pain from that very garment
humanity wears.

9. De Martyribus

* vi-cto-ri-o-

sissimi triumphato-res, qui in

effusi-one sanguinis ve-stri

salu-tantes æ-dificati-onem Ec-

cle-si — æ, intra — stis san-

gui-nem a — gni, e-pu-lan-tes

cum vi-tu — lo occi — so.

O quam magnam mercedem habe —

tis, qui-a corpora vestra vi-ven-

tes despexi-stis, i-mi-tan-tes a-

gnum De - i, ornantes poenam e-

ius, in qua vos introduxit in

re-staura-ti-o — nem hæ-re-di --

ta — tis. Euouae.

9. DE MARTYRIBUS
In Praise of Martyrs

O, most victorious conquerors,
In shedding your blood,
you have entered into the blood of the Lamb.
You bring wholeness to the body of the Church,
celebrating the banquet with the offering who was slain.
How magnificent is your reward!
This earthly life seemed slight to you.
So, imitating the Lamb of God,
and embellished with a punishment similiar to his,
you have been brought to your newly restored inheritance.

10. De Innocentibus

Rex no-ster*promptus est sus-ci-pere sangui-nem In-no-cen-tum. Un-de An-ge-li con-ci-nunt et in lau-di-bus so-nant, *sed nu-bes su-per e — un-dem san-gui-nem plan — gunt. ℣. Ty — ran-nus au-tem in gra-vi som-no mor-tis pro-pter ma-li-ti-am su-am suf-fo-ca-tus est. *Sed nu-

bes.   Glo – ri-a Pa-tri   et Fi-li-o

et Spi-ri-tu-i   San – cto. *Seð.

10.   DE INNOCENTIBUS
To the Innocents

Our King is eagerly ready
to welcome the blood-witness of the Innocents.
Angels gather in chorus singing highest praise,
yet the clouds cry out in pain over the Innocents' blood.
Because of his malice, the Tyrant has suffocated
in the heavy sleep of death.
And the clouds cry out in pain over the Innocents' blood.
Glory be to the Father, the Son, and Holy Spirit.
And the clouds cry out in pain over the Innocents' blood.

11. De Sancto Disibodo

O vi-ri-di-tas * di -
gi-ti De-i, in qua De-us con-sti-tu-it
plan-tati-o — nem, quæ in excel-so
resplendet ut sta-tu-ta co-lumna
*tu glo-ri-o-sa in præ-para-ti-o ——
ne De – i. V. Et o alti-tu ——
do mon-tis, quæ numquam dis-
si-pa-beris in diffe – ren-ti-a De –

i, tu tamen stas a longe

ut ex-ul, sed non est in po-te -

sta-te ar - - ma — ti, qui

te ra-pi-at.*Tu glori-o-sa. Glo--

ri - - a Pa-tri et Fi-li — o

et Spi —ri — tu-i Sancto.

*Tu glori-o-sa.

11.   DE SANCTO DISIBODO
In Honor of St. Disibode

O life-giving greenness of God's hand!
Through you, God has planted an orchard.
You rise resplendent into the highest heavens
like a towering pillar.
You are glorious in God's work.
And you, O mountain heights, will never waiver
when God tests you.
Although you stand far off as if in exile,
still no armed power is strong enough to attack you.
You are glorious in God's work.

12.   O Coruscans Lux

O co-ru-scans * lux stel-la -

rum, o splen-di-dis-si-ma spe -

ci-a-lis for — ma re-gali-um

nu-pti-a-rum, o ful-gens gem —

ma, tu es orna-ta in al-ta per-so-

na, quæ non ha-bet macula-tam

ru-gam. Tu es et-i-am soci — a

An-ge-lo - rum et ci -vis sancto —

rum. Fu-ge, fu-ge spe-lun-cam an-

ti-qui perdi-toris, et ve-ni-ens

ve-ni in pa-la-ti-um Re

(♮)

gis.

12. O CORUSCANS LUX
O Burning Light

O burning light of the stars,
O most splendid model of the regal nuptials,
O glowing jewel!
You are arrayed as a high-ranking woman
with neither stain nor fault.
And you are the playmate of the angels,
a companion to the holy ones.
Run, O run from the cave of the tempter of old.
Come, come to the palace of the King.

APPENDIX: THE BOOK OF DIVINE WORKS

The following are the titles of the sections for each vision. The titles of sections that have been omitted are in brackets.

FOREWORD

PART I: THE WORLD OF HUMANITY

FIRST VISION: ON THE ORIGIN OF LIFE

1. No title.
2. The figure made the following statement.
3. Humanity as God's image in the midst of creation.
4. In love, humanity recognizes the hand of God.
5. On the unity of the love of God and our neighbor.
6. On the angels as beings of light and figures in a mirror.
7. On the creation of the world in God's providence.
8. On the decision and fall of the angels.
9. How we humans ought to be in the light of our rational nature.
10. God endowed human nature with the light of reason.
11. God makes weak human beings citizens of the heavenly community.
12. Turning from humanity, our attention is again directed to the superhuman figure of this vision's beginning.
13. Love destroys all evil and frees us from all fear.
14. On the bright splendor of the human species and the temptation of the woman.
15. On the loss of Paradise and the fateful loyalty between man and woman.
16. On the fecundity of spiritual people.
17. On the origin and goal of spiritual life.

SECOND VISION: ON THE CONSTRUCTION OF THE WORLD

1. No title.
2. The Godhead is round and fully developed like a wheel.
3. On the shape of the world.
4. On the two fiery circles.
5. On the circle of pure ether.
6. On the fourth circle of watery air.
7. On the zone of the sheer white clear air.

8. On the sixth circle of the thin stratum of air.

9. On the inner solidarity of the structure of the cosmos.

10. On the meaning of different views of the world.

11. On the mysterious region in the north.

12. In the Book of Revelation it is written:

13. The world in its balanced construction resembles the moral world of humanity.

14. Paul thus summons human beings to their worldwide moral responsibility when he says:

15. What the human figure in the midst of the heart of the world means.

16. On the area of decision of human beings in their cosmic existence.

17. No title.

18. Why animal heads in the cosmic wheel have a relationship to human beings.

19. And as the Song of Songs says:

20. On the power of the winds in the universe.

21. On the fatal link between human beings and the things of the world and on the sphere of our moral freedom.

22. No title.

23. On the winds as a system of direction in the cosmos and their significance for humanity.

24-26. No titles.

27. On God's action in the soul.

28. What the image of the bear signifies.

29. These powers of the world have an effect on body and soul.

30-31. No titles.

32. What the sun and moon signify to humankind.

33. On the spiritual meaning of the planetary system.

34. No title.

35. On the radiation of the sun.

36-41. No titles.

42. On the inner meaning of the starry systems.

43-44. No titles.

45. Believers follow the traces of the Son of God.

46. On love as the vital power of the universe.

47. No title.

THIRD VISION: ON HUMAN NATURE

1. No title.
2. All creation is at the service of humanity.
3. No title.
4. Our salvation comes from God's might.
5. God is the source of human power.
6. Just as the winds in the universe vary, so also do the different humors of human beings vary.
7. No title.
8. How the cosmic powers override human beings.
9. On the play of humors in the human organism.
10. On the metabolism of the liver.
11. Isaiah has emphasized this thought in words of warning:
12. On the metabolism of the inner organs.
13. On the function of the kidneys.
14. On weariness.
15. How human beings become ill.
16. No title.
17. On kidney infections.
18. The effect on our spiritual life of a disturbance in the humors within the chest cavity.
19. How human beings remain healthy.

FOURTH VISION: ON THE ARTICULATION OF THE BODY

1. No title.
2. And once again I heard a voice from heaven make the following statement to me:
3. On the firmament and its powers.
4. On the influence of the upper spheres on the human world.
5-6. On the influence of the layers of ether.
7. On the gentle layer of air.
8. On the power of the clouds and its significance.
9. On the formation of the clouds.
10. No title.
11. Humanity resembles the structure of the world and praises God in its reason.

12. On the beauty of the angels and their bright world.

13. On the fall of the first angel.

14. On the battle among the spirits and on God's plan for humanity.

15. All of this refers to spiritual relationships.

16. The world resembles humanity and is reflected in the human soul.

17. On the significance of the head.

18. What the various measurements of the head signify.

19. On the twofold capacity of the soul.

20. Omitted in German text.

21. The head as the firmament of the body.

22. How the starry heaven is depicted in the human head, and how it becomes an image of the gifts of the Holy Spirit.

23. On the brain and its functions.

24. On the effect of the soul and the body.

25. On the brain as a nodal point for the exchange of fluids.

26. The brain resembles the natural rhythm of the world.

27. [How a wind is like reason for the soul and like light for fire.]

28. [On the contradiction in the world and the human body.]

29. The brain as the sun of a small world.

30. [Thus every human action resembles the fixed orbit of the sun and is subject to a severe law of nature.]

31. [On the ability of the eyes, which are like luminous stars, to look about themselves, and what this means for our moral life.]

32. On the gift of tears and its relation to rain in the world and to repentance in the soul.

33. Everything in the world has its name and its own definite dimension. And thus sighted persons have their own knowledge and their own standard.

34. In their contradictions, the people of the Earth are like day and night.

35. In their sensory world, people resemble the starry heavens.

36. On the balance of heat and cold in the cosmos, the human organism, and spiritual life.

37. [On the value of the senses, their image in the cosmos, and their function in our moral life.]

38. [The eyebrows as the bastion of our eyes and as a mirror of the moon's path.]

39. [What our nose, mouth, and ears do for us; their significance for our moral life; and how they mirror the control that is exercised over the world.]

40. [The human tongue is an indication of the irrigating power of the waters.]

41. [The power and strength achieved by the teeth.]

42. [On the growth and decay of the teeth.]

43. [How our teeth develop, and what a toothache should tell us.]

44. [Our set of teeth is like a mill, and the soul grinds in the same way in our spiritual life.]

45. [The chin lifts up our face so that we can recognize the essence of things.]

46. [The adornment of our hair resembles the fruitful dew as well as childish innocence.]

47. [The hair of our head produces bodily and moral strength.]

48. [The human figure stands mysteriously with outstretched arms at the crossing point of the world.]

49. [The shoulder strap resembles the cosmic wind system and indicates the basic spiritual powers of the human species.]

50. [In its bodily firmament, the soul resembles the fiery power of the wind in the universe.]

51. [Like the system of the winds, our arms and legs maintain our balance.]

52. [The joints of our body indicate the binding force of the upper and lower worlds, as well as the responsibility for moral action.]

53. [On the torso as a mirror of the relationships in the world and as a model for the length of human life.]

54. [The power of our soul resembles the wide world.]

55. [On the proportions of our arms and legs and on the proportion of human deeds.]

56. [This is also valid for the proportions among the navel, thigh, and the backside.]

57. [Our chest is like the layer of air that makes the Earth fruitful, just as the human soul makes our earthly actions fruitful.]

58. The flight of the soul resembles that of a bird in the air.

59. The sea and the rivers resemble the blood system in the human body.

60. Like the Earth, humanity has also its seasons of the year.

61. [On the organs within the chest and what they tell us about human thought and actions.]

62. [On the heart as the vital center of a human being.]
63. [Just as the stomach takes everything we eat into the body, the soul retains everything we do and think.]
64. [Our breast is a center of power and fullness and indicates the exhuberance of the layer of air as well as the longing innate to the human heart.]
65. [On the subservient position of woman.]
66. [On the nature and power of repentance.]
67. [On the heart and its power of maturity.]
68. [On this account, David speaks of the purification of the human species.]
69. [The stomach resembles the Earth.]
70. [On bodily hunger and the hunger of the soul.]
71. [On the stomach and its extensive power of comprehension.]
72. [On the creative capacity of the soul.]
73. [On the seasons of the year and the stages of the soul's existence.]
74. [On the vessels of the digestive system and their symbolism.]
75. [On the power of the stomach to take in what we eat.]
76. [Just as the navel is the center of our inner organs, our soul is the source of power in our life of grace.]
77. [On the body's digestive process and on the excrement of the soul.]
78. In our stages of life, we human beings resemble the seasons of the Earth.
79. On the power of sexuality and its symbolism in nature and the life of the soul.
80. Just as the Earth lies in the middle of the atmosphere, the soul is in the midst of a struggle for life.
81. The Earth has the same relationship to the sun as the soul has to God.
82. Like the Earth, people are created as spiritual beings.
83. [The soul is in the midst of the body like the Earth in the midst of space.]
84. [Our bladder indicates the flow of the rivers and displays the purifying role of the soul.]
85. [On the place and significance of the process of elimination.]
86. [The hind quarters indicate the central position of the Earth as well as the supporting powers of the soul.]
87. [On this account, St. John in the Book of Revelation addresses the soul as a bride with her adornment.]
88. [A comparison between the desolate portion of the Earth and the difficult work of salvation of the soul.]

89. [David laments the precarious situation of a person without a dwelling place.]

90. [Humanity with its inconstant way of life resembles the uneven surface of the Earth.]

91. [Just as the Earth is solid at its core, the soul is as hard as steel, and it intensifies the creative work of human beings in the world.]

92. [Our knees symbolize the circulation of the waters of the world and human passion.]

93. [Our twelve joints indicate the twelve powers of the winds and the balance between the cosmic and bodily powers.]

94. [On the dangerous north wind.]

95. All these things—both with respect to the construction of the world and the end of time—have a relationship to the soul.

96. On the significance of the north.

97. On humanity and its dimension in the universe.

The Yearly Cycle

98. [On the order of time in the cycle of the universe and in the cycle of our bodily humors as well as in our spiritual life.]

[The first month.]

[The second month.]

[The third month.]

[The fourth month.]

[The fifth month.]

[The sixth month.]

[The seventh month.]

[The eighth month.]

[The ninth month.]

[The tenth month.]

[The eleventh month.]

[The twelfth month.]

99. In this way, the nature and basic powers of the months are adapted to the human essence.

100. Humanity as God's image is sovereign over the entire world and as a work of God is made in the likeness of the Godhead.

101. Concerning God's Incarnation and divine power over the world.

102. On the mysterious designation of the human species.

103. On the nature of the soul and its threefold function with respect to God, itself, and the body.

104. On the final destiny of the soul and the body.

God's Word in the World

105. In the beginning was the Word.

And the Word was with God and the Word was God.

He was God in the beginning.

Not one thing has its being but through him.

All that came to be had life in him.

And that life was the light of men.

A light that shines in the darkness.

A light that darkness could not overpower.

A man came, sent by God.

His name was John.

He came as a witness, as a witness to speak for the light, so that everyone might believe through him.

He was not the light, only a witness to speak for the light.

The Word was the true light.

The true light that enlightens all men; and he was coming into the world.

He was in the world.

The world had its being through him.

And the world did not know him.

He came to his own domain.

And his own people did not accept him.

But to all who did accept him, he gave power to become children of God.

To all who believe in the name of him.

Those who are not born of blood nor of the urge of the flesh nor of the will of man but of God himself.

The Word was made flesh, he lived among us.

He lived among us.

And we saw his glory.

The glory that is his as the only Son of God.

PART II: THE KINGDOM OF THE HEREAFTER

FIFTH VISION: THE PLACES OF PURIFICATION

1.   No title.
2.   What the Earth means to humanity.
3.   The five regions of the Earth resemble our five senses.
4.   The poles of the Earth make humanity into a being of limitations.
5.   On the central portion of the Earth and its significance for the human species.
6.   On the place of various punishments and purifications.
7.   On God's judgment of the Earth.
8.   On the four horses as images of this period of history.
9.   On the wickedness of the old serpent.
10.   The red ball indicates God's punishing zeal, which is just and which punishes with love.
11.   The reddish circle in the form of a bow indicates human guilt and its punishment.
12.   On the star above the ball.
13.   On the place of outer darkness.
14.   God remains the fullness of life.
15.   On humanity's creative essence and its achievement in the world.
16.   On the persecution of the woman by the serpent.
17.   God created the world for God's own honor, thus glorifying humanity as well through the work of creation.

[*Creation*]

[The first day of creation]

18.   [In a symbolic way, the work of creation proclaims the foundation of the church and its work of salvation for humanity.]
19.   [On the fruitfulness of the God who has become a human being.]
20.   [The emptiness of the Earth and God's spirit moving over the waters are a symbol of the life of grace.]
21.   [The Psalmist indicates the uniform function of the prophets, apostles, and doctors.]
22.   [On the coming of light within the sphere of the Church.]
23.   [And once again we can understand the story of creation in another way—namely, in a moral way.]
24.   [The second day of creation.]

25. [In an allegorical way, Christ is the foundation of the life of faith.]
26. [Within the heart of believers, the inner firmament ought to be founded that has stability in and with Christ.]
27. [In a moral way, the firmament is understood as discretion.]
28. [No title.]
29. [Discretion is not active by itself but rather serves as an auxiliary force.]
30. [The third day of creation.]
31. [On the silence and creativity of the Creator.]
32. [In an allegorical way this day of creation proclaims the early life within the Church.]
33. [The womb of the Church resembles the fertile Earth that becomes pregnant.]
34. [This day of creation, too, can have a moral significance.]
35. [The fourth day of creation.]
36. [The firmament signifies also the stability of Christian faith at whose disposition there are two lights that are like eyes: the priesthood and worldly power.]
37. [All of this is interpreted once again with respect to our bodily and spiritual life.]
38. [The fifth day of creation.]
39. [In an allegorical way, the fifth day of creation indicates the spiritual conversion of human beings and their communion with the world of the angels.]
40. [Christ speaks of the two possible ways of life within the Church: life in the spirit and life in the world.]
41. [And on the fifth day God blessed the creatures of the waters and the birds as well as life in the spirit.]
42. [What the fifth day of creation signifies for the transformation of the moral life of every human being.]
43. [The sixth day of creation.]
44. [The last day of creation, too, is interpreted with respect to the life of the Church.]
45. [All of this can also be interpreted in another way:]
46. [The work of creation of the sixth day is interpreted with respect to the moral life of human beings.]
47. [The seventh day of creation.]
48. [By the Incarnation of the Son of God and the working of the Holy Spirit, the seventh day also is completed in the Church.]

49. [The seventh day is also completed in the life of every believing human being.]

PART III: THE HISTORY OF SALVATION

SIXTH VISION: THE MEANING OF HISTORY
1. No title.
2. How God has ordained everything, and how humanity will be tested throughout history.
3. How God's deeds shine forth from the mirror, and how a flood of light from the angels radiates out over the cloud.
4. On the world of the angels and on the creation of the human species.
5. On the nature and office of the angels.
6. What the Psalmist says about the angels who are like the reflecting waters in which God's word bubbles up.

SEVENTH VISION: PREPARATION FOR CHRIST
1. No title.
2. [How God prepared for the story of salvation.]
3. God gives the Son power over the Earth.
4. The first form represents the time before the flood.
5. On the savagery of human beings before the flood.
6. On the destruction of the human species by the flood and on its renewal.
7. On the change in the matter of the world and on the meaning of the rainbow.
8. The second figure represents the period of history until the coming of the Lord.
9. On references to the Incarnation of the Word by the patriarchs and prophets.
10. The crowd in the south stands for all believers who follow the Son of God and climb from virtue to virtue.
11. The whole world strives for God.
12. Everything has been created and redeemed through God's Word.
13. God adopted a human form.
14. God has fulfilled all promises in the divine humanity.
15. [On the task of the Son of God.]
16. On the maturing of God's work in history.
17. On the conversion of believers to life.

EIGHTH VISION: ON THE EFFECT OF LOVE

1. No title.
2. The first figure is Love, which radiates throughout the angelic world and the human world.
3. God has completed the world in love, humility, and peace.
4. Love leads the human species to a royal wedding.

NINTH VISION: COMPLETION OF THE COSMOS

1. No title.
2. The first figure signifies Wisdom. Its beautiful garment indicates the multiplicity and wealth of the order of creation.
3. The second figure indicates God's omnipotence.
4. What the six wings of the second figure indicate.
5. On the coming of the Son of God.
6. What the five mirrors indicate.
7. On the mystery of the Incarnation.
8. [What God promised through David will be fulfilled.]
9. [How God has made the world firm and unshakeable.]
10. [The figure tells of God's decision to become a human being.]
11. [On the kingdom of God in this world.]
12. On the mystery of the Incarnation.
13. What the darkness in the west signifies.
14. God ordains all things in wisdom and power.

TENTH VISION: ON THE END OF TIME.

1. No title.
2. The wheel signifies the one eternal God.
3. Why the figure of "Love" is adorned.
4. What the inscription on this tablet says.
5. The lines indicate the inner commitment of creation, which burst forth at only one place and led to the flood.
6. Paul writes about the fullness of time.
7. In the fullness, of time the apostles accepted the new teaching and intensified it until this manly age, under diabolical influences, turned into a womanish period.
8. What the Son has to say to God about his passion and salvation.
9. A mysterious description of how the apostles adorn and dress up justice.

10-11. No titles.

12. God keeps an eye upon this period of history.

13. On waiting until the number of martyrs should be complete.

14. Therefore the Son of God says once again:

15. On the age of the fiery dog.

16. And yet justice will have its victory.

17. On the age of the lion.

18. The prophet Isaiah testifies to the coming of the Lord.

19. On the green wood and the dry wood.

20. On the age of peace that is to come and on its justice.

21. On the end of the age of peace and its decline into the age of the horse.

22-23. No titles.

24. In the battle at the end of time, God will not abandon those who are faithful.

25. On the decline of the ancient West and the fall of the Roman Empire.

26. Once again people will find their way to justice and discipline while the Antichrist is approaching.

27. During the age of the pig, the moment of crisis draws near.

28. On the coming of the Antichrist.

29. That the day of the Lord is close at hand.

30. On the enticements of the Antichrist.

31. On the Antichrist and his corruption.

32. On the tricks and magical deeds of the Antichrist.

33. On the return of Enoch and Elijah.

34. During the age of the wolf, the Son of God entreats his Father.

35. On the bodily resurrection of the returning prophets, Enoch and Elijah.

36. The Antichrist will have a collapse during his ascension into heaven, and Christ will destroy the Antichrist by the brilliance of his coming.

37. How, after the fall of the Antichrist, the honor of the Son of God will be glorified.

Epilogue

38. Afterword to this book, in which praise and honor are returned to God with a heavenly voice for the divine achievement—the redemption of humanity. This small work, together with its author, is recommended to God as well as to all believers.

APPENDIX: LETTERS

For readers who wish to study Hildegard's letters further, the translator
cites the following pages in Adelgundis Fuhrkotter's *Hildegard von
Bingen, Brief-wechsel* (Salzburg: 1965), where the letters can be read in
German.

Letter One:	pp. 25-27
Letter Two:	pp. 38-41
Letter Three:	pp. 66-71
Letter Four:	pp. 73-74
Letter Five:	pp. 76-77
Letter Six:	p. 80
Letter Seven:	p. 82
Letter Eight:	pp. 84-85
Letter Nine:	pp. 86-87
Letter Ten:	pp. 90-91
Letter Eleven:	pp. 103-106
Letter Twelve:	pp. 104-106
Letter Thirteen:	pp. 108-110
Letter Fourteen:	pp. 111-113
Letter Fifteen:	pp. 115-116
Letter Sixteen:	pp. 126-127
Letter Seventeen:	p. 136
Letter Eighteen:	pp. 140-142
Letter Nineteen:	pp. 144-145
Letter Twenty:	pp. 147-148
Letter Twenty-One:	pp. 158-162
Letter Twenty-Two:	pp. 150-152
Letter Twenty-Three:	pp. 150-152
Letter Twenty-Four:	pp. 169-172
Letter Twenty-Five:	pp. 175-177
Letter Twenty-Six:	p. 182
Letter Twenty-Seven:	pp. 182-183
Letter Twenty-Eight:	pp. 183-184
Letter Twenty-Nine:	p. 185

Letter Thirty: p. 186
Letter Thirty-One / Thirty-Two: pp. 187-189
Letter Thirty-Three: p. 189
Letter Thirty-Four / Thirty-Five: pp. 190-200
Letter Thirty-Six: p. 217
Letter Thirty-Seven: pp. 218-220
Letter Thirty-Eight: p. 220
Letter Thirty-Nine: pp. 226-228
Letter Forty: pp. 230-231
Letter Forty-One: pp. 236-241
Letter Forty-Two: pp. 241-243

APPENDIX: SONGS

For readers and musicians who wish to consult the source for this
translation, the following list cites appropriate page numbers in
Pudentiana Barth's *Hildegard von Bingen: Lieder* (Salzburg: 1969), where
the Latin songs are reproduced. Note that the numbers given to the songs
in this text do not correspond with the numbers in the German edition.

1. Kyrie   p. 144
2. O Virtus Sapientiae   p. 131
3. De Sancta Maria   p. 24
4. De Spiritu Sancto   p. 46
5. Item De Virginibus   p. 99
6. De Sancta Maria   p. 44
7. O Felix Anima   p. 139
8. O Vis Aeternitatis   p. 129
9. De Martyribus   p. 82
10. De Innocentibus   p. 108
11. De Sancto Disibodo   p. 76
12. O Coruscans Lux   p. 143

BOOKS OF RELATED INTEREST

Hildegard of Bingen's Medicine
by Dr. Wighard Strehlow and Gottfried Hertzka, M.D.

Illuminations of Hildegard of Bingen
by Matthew Fox

Hildegard von Bingen's Physica
The Complete English Translation of
Her Classic Work on Health and Healing
Translated by Priscilla Throop

Hildegard von Bingen's Mystical Visions
Translated from *Scivias*
by Bruce Hozseki

Hildegard of Bingen's Spiritual Remedies
by Dr. Wighard Strehlow

Meditations with Meister Eckhart
Edited by Matthew Fox

Christian Mythology
Revelations of Pagan Origins
by Philippe Walter

The Book of Grimoires
The Secret Grammar of Magic
by Claude Lecouteux

Inner Traditions • Bear & Company
P.O. Box 388
Rochester, VT 05767
1-800-246-8648
www.InnerTraditions.com

Or contact your local bookseller